The Regions of Pyrenees Roussillon

See the maps below and opposite.

THEGREENGUIDE
Pyrenees
Roussillon

Carcassonne / © Javier Gil / Fotolia.com

THEGREENGUIDE **PYRENEES ROUSSILLON**

Editorial Director	Cynthia Clayton Ochterbeck
Edited & Produced by	Jonathan P. Gilbert, Azalay Media
Contributing Writers	Terry Marsh, Anne McDowall
Production Manager	Natasha G. George
Cartography	Anne McDowall
Photo Researcher	Sean Sachon
Interior Design	Chris Bell
Layout	Jonathan P. Gilbert, Natasha G. George
Cover Design	Chris Bell, Christelle Le Déan
Cover Layout	Natasha G. George

Contact Us
Michelin Travel and Lifestyle North America
One Parkway South
Greenville, SC 29615
USA
travel.lifestyle@us.michelin.com
www.michelintravel.com

Michelin Travel Partner
Hannay House
39 Clarendon Road
Watford, Herts WD17 1JA
UK
✆01923 205240
travelpubsales@uk.michelin.com
www.ViaMichelin.com

Special Sales
For information regarding bulk sales,
customized editions and premium sales,
please contact us at:
travel.lifestyle@us.michelin.com
www.michelintravel.com

HOW TO USE THIS GUIDE

PLANNING YOUR TRIP

The blue-tabbed PLANNING YOUR TRIP section at the front of the guide gives you **ideas for your trip** and **practical information** to help you organize it. You'll find tours, practical information, a host of outdoor activities, a calendar of events, information on shopping, sightseeing, kids' activities and more.

INTRODUCTION

The orange-tabbed INTRODUCTION section explores Pyrénées Roussillon's **Nature** and geology. The **History** section spans from the Palaeolithic to the Cathars. The **Art and Culture** section covers architecture, art, literature and music, while the **Region Today** delves into modern Pyrénées Roussillon.

DISCOVERING

The green-tabbed DISCOVERING section features Principal Sights by region, featuring the most interesting local **Sights**, **Walking Tours**, nearby **Excursions**, and detailed **Driving Tours**. Admission prices shown are normally for a single adult.

ADDRESSES

We've selected the best hotels, restaurants, cafés, shops, nightlife and entertainment to fit all budgets. See the Legend on the cover flap for an explanation of the price categories. See the back of the guide for an index of where to find hotels and restaurants.

Sidebars

Throughout the guide you will find blue, orange and green-coloured text boxes with lively anecdotes, detailed history and background information.

😊 A Bit of Advice 😊

Green advice boxes found in this guide contain practical tips and handy information relevant to your visit or to a sight in the Discovering section.

STAR RATINGS★★★

Michelin has given star ratings for more than 100 years. If you're pressed for time, we recommend you visit the ★★★, or ★★ sights first:

★★★   **Highly recommended**
★★   **Recommended**
★   **Interesting**

MAPS

- 🅐 Region maps
- 🅐 Maps for major cities and villages
- 🅐 Local tour maps

All maps in this guide are oriented north, unless otherwise indicated by a directional arrow. The term "Local Map" refers to a map within the chapter or region. A complete list of the maps found in this guide appears at the back of this book.

© B. Rieger / hemis.fr

PLANNING YOUR TRIP

© Franz Waldhäusl / age fotostock

INTRODUCTION TO PYRENEES ROUSSILLON

CONTENTS

© René Mattes / hemis.fr

DISCOVERING PYRENEES ROUSSILLON

Pyrenees Roussillon

Behind the sandy beaches, lagoons and secluded coves of the Mediterranean coast, the landscape of the far south of France progresses through vineyards and wild garrigue countryside to reach high and lonely crags topped with ancient medieval fortresses and finally the snow-capped peaks of the Pyrénées. This area is officially divided into two departments that sometimes go by other names: the Aude (dubbed the Pays Cathare or Cathar Country) and Pyrénées-Orientales (also known as Roussillon or French Catalonia).

1. NARBONNE, CARCASSONNE AND CANAL DU MIDI *(pp70–111)*

Two thousand years of history has left plenty of sights to see in the lower Aude valley and on the Languedoc coast. The medieval walled city of Carcassonne, with its impressive ramparts, towers and gateways is one of the great sights of France and deserves a leisurely visit. It is connected to the sea by an extraordinary feat of engineering, the Canal du Midi, built in the 17C to link the Atlantic and Mediterranean. Today the waterway is used for cruising and its towpath for walking and cycling. Set back from the coast is Narbonne, the capital of an important Roman province that was strategically sited on the Via Domitia; it still has many historic buildings. Culture aside, the beaches here are popular and wherever you go there is good wine and food. On the coast there is an excellent choice of fish and seafood while Castelnaudary claims to be the home of authentic cassoulet.

2. LES CORBIÈRES AND THE PAYS CATHARE *(pp112–133)*

In the 12C the beautiful but often forbidding landscapes between Limoux and the Pyrénées became the last refuge of the persecuted followers of the Cathar religion. They sought safety in dramatically-sited castles such as Quéribus and Montségur, which today stand in ruins. Other splendidly crumbling castles testify to the fact that for a long time this was frontier country between Spain and France. In between these fortresses is austere garrigue countryside and the vineyards of the Corbières, producing distinctly robust red wines.

Houses along the Canal du Midi, Castelnaudary

3. PERPIGNAN, CÔTE VERMEILLE AND THE ROUSSILLON PLAIN *(pp134–161)*

Roussillon, the French part of Catalonia, centres on the capital city of Perpignan, which was once the hub of a trans-Mediterranean kingdom, testified by its grandest monument, the Palace of the Kings of Mallorca. The plain of Roussillon is a famous centre of production for fruit and vegetables. Its prime sights for visitors include the geometrically conceived Fort de Salses — built by the Spanish, a reminder that these lands have not always been French and the Romanesque cathedral of Elne standing among apricot and peach orchards.

The extensive beaches near Perpignan get crowed in summer but south of the resort of Argelès, the coast transforms into the rocky Côte Vermeille, a series of cliffs, coves, headlands and pretty harbours. Most attractive by far, and long an inspiration to artists for its colours and clear light, is Collioure. Another coastal town, Banyuls-sur-Mer is renowned for its fortified wine.

4. PYRÉNÉES ORIENTALES AND ANDORRA *(pp162–195)*

Head inland from Perpignan and the coast and you quickly get into the mountains. The most spectacular of them all being Mont Canigou, held to be sacred by the Catalans. Below it are two great medieval abbeys – St Michel de Cuxa and St Martin de Canigou – and not far away the equally beautiful priory of Serrabone. Tucked into the Pyrénéan foothills further south is the town of Ceret, known for its cherries and modern art: Picasso came here to experiment with Cubism.
Deeper into the mountains, and straddling the border with Spain, is the independent state of Andorra, which draws visitors for its mountain scenery, skiing and shopping.

5. EXCURSIONS IN SPANISH CATALONIA *(pp196–223)*

Across the border, Catalonia continues as the Spanish region of the same name. It is easily explored on day trips or a short tour. The dramatic cliff and cove scenery of the Costa Brava is a must. There is also a wealth of art from Romanesque to Surrealism; the painter Salvador Dalí established an extraordinary "theatre-museum" here, in his home town of Figueres.

Vineyard above Port Vendres, Côte Vermeille

© Richard Manin / age fotostock

Château de Puilaurens, Les Corbières
© B. Rieger / hemis.fr

When to Go

WHEN TO GO
CLIMATE
Although much of this region is predominantly Mediterranean in climate, it is open to oceanic influences from the Atlantic.

As for the Pyrénées mountain range, its valleys are under the influence of several weather systems determined by the altitude and the direction the slopes are facing.

Late **winter** and **early spring** offer plenty of snow for Alpine skiing in the Pyrénées.

Eus in the Pyrénnées Orientales

© Michael Busselle / age fotostock

Spring is the ideal season for hiking and riding tours and for discovering the region in general.

Summer is dry and hot with luminous skies, particularly along the Mediterranean. Sudden, violent storms bring relief from the scorching heat from time to time but the sun rarely admits defeat for more than a few hours.

In **autumn**, rainfall is often abundant, while warm southwest winds blowing over the whole region bring alternating periods of dry and wet weather.

WEATHER FORECAST
Météo-France offers recorded information at national, departmental and local levels. This information is updated three times a day and is valid for up to seven days.

- **National and departmental forecast:** ☏ 3250 followed by
  1 – for all the information about the département for the next 7 days, or
  2 – for information about towns.
- **Local forecast:** ☏ 08 99 71 02 followed by the number of the *département.*

Weather forecasting is also available on www.meteo.fr.

*Parc Naturel Régional des Pyrénées
near Angoustrine in the Cerdagne*
© R. Soberka / hemis.fr

What to See and Do

SEA BATHING

Much of the northern section of coast, between Saint-Pierre-sur-Mer and Argelès, consists of one long sandy beach, which is often sandwiched between the sea and a lagoon (étang) and is extremely popular for swimming. To the south, the cliffs of the Côte Vermeille are indented with coves. There are **naturist beaches** at La Franqui and Port-la-Nouvelle. Resorts strive to maintain a high level of water quality and European **blue flag** awards for environmental standards. **Water conditions**: *www. baignades.sante.gouv.fr.*
Bathing conditions are indicated by flags on beaches which are surveyed by lifeguards (no flags means no lifeguards): green indicates it is safe to bathe and lifeguards are on duty; yellow warns that conditions are not that good, but lifeguards are still in attendance; red means bathing is forbidden as conditions are too dangerous.

IN LAKES AND RIVERS

Swimming in **lakes and reservoirs** is not always permitted: ask at the local tourist information office. Bathing is normally possible in the **Étang de Leucate** (Aude) and in the **Lac de Matemale** (Pyrénées-Orientales).

BOATING
ON LAKES AND RESERVOIRS

Lakes and reservoirs suitable for sailing and windsurfing :
Aude – Étang de Bages, Étang de Sigean, Étang de Leucate, Lac de la Ganguise, Lac de Jouarre.
Pyrénées-Orientales –
Lac de Matemale.

ON THE SEA

Ligue de voile du Languedoc-Roussillon (regional sailing association) Espace Voile, Bât. C, Le Patio Santa Monica 1815 av. Marcel-Pagnol 34470 Pérols. &04 67 50 48 30. www.ffvoilelr.net.
France Stations Nautiques (marinas and sailing resorts). 17 r. Henri-Bocquillon 75015 Paris. &01 44 05 96 55. www.station-nautique.com.

Marinas

The numerous marinas dotted along the coast offer pleasure craft in the Languedoc Roussillon over 100,000 moorings. Information is available from the various harbour master's offices:
- Le Canet-Plage - &04 68 86 72 73
- Narbonne-Plage - &04 68 49 91 43
- Port-Barcarès-Port-St-André - &04 68 86 07 35

- ◆ Port-Leucate - ✆04 68 40 91 24
- ◆ Port-Vendres - ✆04 68 82 08 84
- ◆ St-Cyprien - ✆04 68 21 07 98

…or from:
- ◆ **Association des ports de plaisance du Languedoc-Roussillon**, Mairie, 34132 Mauguio-Carnon. ✆04 67 29 05 36. www.upvir.com.

Useful addresses
- ◆ **Fédération française de Voile** 17 Rue Henri-Bocquillon, 75015 Paris Cedex 16. ✆01 40 60 37 00; www.ffvoile.org.
- ◆ **Ligue de voile du Languedoc-Roussillon** Espace Voile, Bât. C, Le Patio Santa Monica, 1815 Ave Marcel Pagnol, 34470 Perols. ✆04 67 50 48 30. www.ffvoilelr.net.
- ◆ **France Station Voile – Nautisme et Tourisme** 17 Rue Henri-Bocquillon, 75015 Paris. ✆01 44 05 96 55. www.france-nautisme. com.
- ◆ **Fédération française de ski nautique** 9 rue du Borrego, 75020 Paris. ✆01 53 20 19 19. www.ffsnw.fr

CANAL CRUISING
There are various ways of enjoying a boat trip on the **Canal du Midi** (♨see *p84*).

NAUTICAL MAPS AND GUIDES
Éditions Navicarte – 125 r. Jean-Jacques-Rousseau 92132 Issy-les-Moulineaux Cedex 20. ✆01 41 54 38 97. www.navicarte.fr.
Éditions du Plaisancier – 43 porte du Grand-Lyon 01700, Neyron. ✆04 72 01 58 68.

CANOEING, KAYAKING AND RAFTING
The white-waters of the middle and upper courses of the Tech, Têt, Aude, and many other rivers are suitable for canoeing and kayaking.
Canoeing is a popular family pastime on the peaceful waters of the

Languedoc Roussillon. **Kayaking** is practised on the lakes and, for more experienced paddlers, rapid sections of the rivers.
Various canoeing guides and a map, *France canoe-kayak et sports d'eau,* are on sale from the **Fédération française de canoë-kayak**, 87 quai de la Marne, BP 58, 94344 Joinville-le-Pont, ✆01 45 11 08 50; www.ffck.org.
Rafting is the easiest of these freshwater sports, since it involves going down rivers in inflatable craft steered by an instructor; special equipment should be provided.

- ◆ **L'Échappée Verte** organises trips throughout the region. ✆06 13 07 04 03. www.echappeeverte.com.

CANYONING & HYDROSPEED
These sports can be practised in mountain rivers, particularly around Axat (Aude). One of the most scenic canyoning routes is the descent of the Gorges du Llech (Pyrénées-Orientales). **Canyoning** is a technique for body-surfing down narrow gorges and over falls, as though on a giant water slide, whereas **hydrospeed** involves swimming down rapids with a kickboard and flippers. These sports require protection: wear a wet suit and a helmet.
Information: **Fédération Française de la Montagne et de l'Escalade**, 8–10 Quai de la Marne, 75019 Paris. ✆01 40 18 75 50; www.ffme.fr.

CAVING
Cavers have plenty of opportunity to indulge their passion in this region, which is pockmarked with caves and potholes. In certain places – the Grotte de Fontrabiouse in the Capcir, the Grotte de l'Aguzou near Quillan and the Gouffre de Cabrespine north of Carcassonne – subterranean "safaris" are organised. These trips don't require any special skill and are a good compromise between a classic visit and more serious caving. With a snack

packed in your bag, you set off for an expedition lasting several hours, led by a guide.

Exploring caves can be a dangerous pastime; it is therefore essential to have the right equipment and be accompanied by a qualified guide – many local clubs can provide both. For more information contact:

- **Fédération Française de Spéléologie**
  28 rue Delandine, 69002 Lyon
  ℘04 72 56 09 63. www.ffspeleo.fr
- **École Française de Spéléologie**
  As above.
- **Comité Régional de Spéléologie Midi-Pyrénées**
  7 rue André-Citroën, 31130 Balma.
  ℘05 34 30 77 45.

CYCLING AND MOUNTAIN BIKING

Many GR and GRP footpaths are accessible to mountain bikers. However, in areas particularly suitable for cycling, there are special trails waymarked by the **Fédération Française de Cyclisme** (5 rue de Rome, 93561 Rosny-sous-Bois Cedex; ℘01 49 35 69 00; www.ffc.fr); these are graded in difficulty *(green is easy; blue is fairly easy; red is difficult; black is very difficult)*; ask for the *'Guide officel des sites VTT'*, which supply itineraries and brochures as well as information on where to stay and where to call for urgent repairs.

The **Office National des Forêts'** website, www.onf.fr, publishes cycling maps and guides for adults and children, focusing on ways to actively discover forests.

For additional information about cycling clubs, rental etc, contact the **Fédération Française de Cyclotourisme** (12 rue Louis-Bertrand, 94200 Ivry-sur-Seine; ℘01 56 20 88 88; www.ffct.org), the **Ligue Languedoc-Roussillon de Cyclotourisme** (28 chemin de l'Ancien Relais, 34600 Herepian; ℘04 67 95 29 80; www.languedoc-roussillon.ffct.org) as well as local tourist offices.

Compagnie des guides des Pyrénées catalanes (mountain guides service) 2 av. de l'Aude 66210 Les Angles. ℘04 68 04 39 22. www.guide-montagne-pyrenees.com. Guided trips : climbing, mountain-biking, horseriding, white water sports, via ferrata.

DIVING

The list of **diving** clubs in the region is available from the **Fédération Française d'Études et de Sports Sous-marins**, 24 quai de Rive-Neuve, 13284 Marseille Cedex 07; ℘04 91 33 99 31; www.ffessm.fr.

FISHING
FRESHWATER FISHING

Anglers are drawn to this region for its lakes and many fast-running rivers. In particular, the **plateau des Bouillouses** is sprinkled with natural lakes and has preserved its unspoilt character (access from Font-Romeu and Mont-Louis).

Information about fishing is available from the **Conseil Supérieur de la Pêche**, Delegation du Sud-Ouest; ℘05 62 73 76 80; www.csp.ecologie.gouv.fr, or from the **Fédération Nationale de la Pêche en France**, 17 rue Bergére, 75009 Paris; ℘01 48 24 96 00; www.federationpeche.fr (which has branch offices at Carcassonne and Perpignan).

Mountain lakes and streams of the Pyrénées region are ideal for trout fishing. Two-week holiday fishing permits are available in some areas – contact the local federation for details (or try local fishing tackle shops or tourist offices). For information on fishing regulations in the 20 or so lakes in the Bouillouses area, contact the tourist office in Font-Romeu.

SEA FISHING

- **Fédération Française des Pêcheurs en Mer** can provide information about marinas, and fishing clubs and schools along the coast. Résidence Alliance, Centre Jorlis, 64600 Anglet;

☏05 59 31 00 73;
www.ffpm-national.com.

FLIGHT

For an aerial view of the region either as passenger or pilot, apply to flying clubs usually located within the perimeter of airports:

♦ **Fédération Française de Planeur Ultra-léger Motorisé**, 96 bis rue Marc-Sangnier, 94709 Maisons-Alfort. ☏01 49 81 74 43. www.ffplum.com.

GOLF

The Michelin map *Golf, les parcours français* (French golf courses) will help you locate golf courses in the region covered by this guide.

For further information, contact the **Fédération Française de Golf**, 68 rue Anatole-France, 92309 Levallois-Perret Cedex; ☏01 41 49 77 00; www.ffg.org. The **Ligue de Golf Languedoc-Roussillon** (ch du Golf, Vacquerolles, 30900 Nîmes; ☏04 66 68 22 62; www. guidedesgolfs.fr) publishes a guide of golf courses in the region.

HANG-GLIDING, PARAGLIDING AND KITE-FLYING

On **hang-gliders** *(deltaplanes)*, fliers skilfully suspend themselves from what is little more than a rudimentary, kite-like wing.

Almost anyone with the willpower to jump off a cliff can give **paragliding** *(parapente)* a try (with the assistance of trained professionals, of course). A number of centres offer instruction in the Pyrénées (Barèges, Campan, Peyragudes, Superbagnères, Moulis near St-Girons, Prat d'Albi near Foix). **Kite-flying** is a popular activity in the region, particularly on the beaches. General information (hang-gliding, paragliding and kite-flying) is available from: **Fédération Française de Vol Libre**, 4 rue de Suisse, 06000 Nice; ☏04 97 03 82 82; www.ffvl.fr.

HIKING AND WALKING

There is an extensive network of well-marked footpaths in France which make walking *(la randonnée)* easy. Several **Grande Randonnée** (GR) trails – recognisable by the red and white horizontal marks on trees, rocks and in town on walls, signposts etc – go through the region.

LES CHEMINS DE GRANDE RANDONNÉE (GR)

The **GR 7** (from the Vosges to the Pyrénées) crosses the region, passing near Castelnaudary on its way to Andorra. The **GR 10**, one of the legendary GRs, runs from one end of the Pyrénées to the other. The **Haute Route des Pyrénées (HRP)** also follows the Pyrénées east to west but at a much higher level. The **GR 36** passes near the Cathar chateaux and skirts around Canigou before reaching the Spanish border. The **GR 107** is known as the Chemin des Bonshommes, as the Cathars once used it as a route to Spain.

NATIONAL PARKS

For information on the **Parc national des Pyrénées**, apply to 2 rue IV Septembre, 65000 Tarbes; ☏05 62 54 41 40; www.parc-pyrenees.com. Several Maisons du Parc throughout the park provide information on the park's flora and fauna and on rambling opportunities in this mountainous area.

MAPS AND GUIDES

To use these trails, obtain the *'Topo-Guide'* for the area published by the **Fédération Française de la Randonnée Pédestre**, 64 rue du Dessous des Berges, 75013 Paris; ☏01 44 89 93 90; www.ffrandonnee. fr. Some English-language editions are available, as well as the magazine *'Passion Rando'* which includes ideas for overnight itineraries and places to stay, together with information on the difficulty and accessibility of trails. Topo-Guides for this region include: *Aude, pays cathare à pied;*

Leave only footprints; take only memories

Choosing the right equipment for a walking expedition is essential: flexible walking shoes with non-slip soles, a waterproof jacket or poncho, an extra sweater, sun protection (hat, glasses, lotion), drinking water (1–2l per person), high energy snacks (chocolate, cereal bars, bananas), and a first aid kit. Of course, you'll need a good map (and a compass if you plan to leave the main trails). Plan your itinerary well, keeping in mind that while the average walking speed for an adult is 4kph/2.5mph, you will need time to eat and rest, and children will not keep up the same pace. Leave details of your itinerary with someone before setting out (innkeeper or fellow camper).

Respect for nature is a cardinal rule and includes the following precautions: don't smoke or light fires in forests, which are particularly susceptible in the dry summer months; always carry your rubbish out; leave wild flowers as they are; walk around, not through, farmers' fields; close gates behind you.

In the dry, rocky scrubland of the *garrigues* and the *causses*, walkers may come across snakes, so it is important to wear stout footwear, preferably with some protection around the ankle. Most of the time the snakes will make themselves scarce as soon as they hear someone coming, so make plenty of noise, and avoid lifting up rocks so as not to disturb any snakes resting beneath them.

Le Languedoc-Roussillon… à pied; *Les Pyrénées-Orientales… à pied*. Tourist information offices at regional, departmental and local level publish their own walking guides, which recommend routes to explore the best landscapes and monuments.

Along with the GR trails are the **Petite Randonnée (PR)** paths, which are usually blazed with blue (2hr walk), yellow (2hr 15min–3hr 45min) or green (4–6hr) marks. Of course, with appropriate maps, you can combine walks to suit your desires.

Another source of maps and guides for excursions on foot is the **Institut Géographique National (IGN)**, which has a boutique at 50 rue de la Verrerie, 75004 Paris; ✆01 43 98 85 10. To order from abroad, visit www.ign. fr, for addresses of wholesalers in your country. Among their publications, there is a series '*Carte à la Carte, Randonnée et Découverte*' which you can personalise with your own route, photographs and maps, at a scale of 1:25 000 (1cm=250m). In the region, you can find many of the publications cited above in bookstores, at sports centres or equipment shops, and in some of the country inns and hotels which cater to the sporting crowd.

In the UK, **Stanfords** (12–14 Long Acre, London, WC2E 9LP; ✆020 7836 1321); www.stanfords.co.uk) has a wide selection of books and maps for travellers.

TOUR OPERATORS

♦ **Compagnie des guides des Pyrénées catalanes**,
2 av. de l'Aude, 66210 Les Angles, ✆04 68 04 39 22, www.guide-montagne-pyrenees.com.

♦ **La Balaguère**
route du Val d'Azun, 65403 Arrens-Marsous. ✆05 62 97 46 46. www.labalaguere.com. Organises walking trips in the Pyrénées, sometimes round a theme (history, flora, fauna…).

♦ **Chamina Voyages**
Naussac, BP 5, 48300 Langogne. ✆04 66 69 00 44. www.chamina-voyages.com. Organises walks with or without guide in the southern part of the Massif Central and in the Pyrénées.

DONKEY TREKS

Fédération nationale ânes et randonnées – ✆06 33 97 91 54. www.ane-et-rando.com. FNAR

Orientation table, Pic du Canigou

© Jean-Paul Garcin / Photononstop / Tips Images

can advise on how to go hiking in Pyrénées-Orientales accompanied by a pack donkey.

CLIMBING

The geography of the Pyrénées makes the mountain range a paradise for climbers. Tourist information offices can advise on clubs and other organisations that organise activities, including introductory climbing sessions.

Beginners should take advantage of the numerous courses available to learn a few basic techniques.

For additional information, contact this federation which provides the location of all the rock-climbing sites in France:

- **Fédération Française de la Montagne et de l'Escalade**, 8–10 quai de la Marne, 75019 Paris; ℘01 40 18 75 50; www.ffme.fr.

MOUNTAIN SAFETY

Safety first is the rule for beginners and old hands alike. The risk associated with avalanches, mud slides, falling rocks, bad weather, fog, glacially cold waters, the dangers of becoming lost or miscalculating distances, should not be underestimated.

Avalanches occur naturally when the upper layer of snow is unstable,

in particular after heavy snowfalls, and may be set off by the passage of numerous skiers or walkers over a precise spot. A scale of risk, from 1 to 5, has been developed and is posted daily at resorts and bases for walking trails. It is important to consult this *Bulletin Neige et Avalanche* (BNA) before setting off on any expeditions cross-country or off-piste. You can also call toll free ℘08 92 68 10 20 *(in French)*.

Lightning storms are often preceded by sudden gusts of wind, and put climbers and walkers in danger. In the event, avoid high ground, and do not move along a ridge top; do not seek shelter under overhanging rocks, isolated trees in otherwise open areas, at the entrance to caves or other openings in the rocks, or in the proximity of metal fences or gates.

For general information on mountain sports in the Pyrénées, apply to:

Hautes-Pyrénées Tourist Office 11 rue Gaston Manent, 65950 Tarbes; ℘05 62 56 70 00; www.tourisme-hautes-pyrenees.com.

Mountain guides suggest a choice of guided activities.

- **Bureau des guides de Luchon** 18 allée d'Étigny, 31110 Luchon. ℘05 61 89 56 08. www.bureau-guides-luchon.com

- **Bureau des guides de St-Savin**
  1 place du Trey, 65400 St-Savin.
  ✆05 62 97 91 09.
- **Bureau des guides de la vallée de Cauterets**
  2 place Georges-Clemenceau, 65110 Cauterets.
  ✆05 62 92 62 02.
- **Bureau des guides de la vallée de Luz**
  ✆05 62 92 96 10.
  www.pointapic.com
- **Bureau des guides de la vallée d'Aure** 65170 St-Lary-Soulan.
  ✆05 62 40 02 58. www.guides-saintlary.com
- **Bureau des guides des vallées d'Ax**
  Gare Aval Téléporté, Camp de Granaou, 09110 Ax-les-Thermes.
  ✆05 61 01 90 62.

ITINERARIES

Tourist authorities and heritage organisations in France have helpfully mapped out travel itineraries to help you discover particular regions or traditions. You will find brochures in tourist offices, and the routes are generally well marked and easy to follow (⌖*signs posted along the roads*).

HISTORY

Some of these itineraries are managed by the **Fédération Nationale des Routes Historiques** *(www.routes-historiques.com)*. Apply to local tourist offices for leaflets with mapped itineraries. The list below includes a local contact:

- **Route historique en Terre Catalane: de l'Homme de Tautavel à Picasso** (Réseau culturel Terre catalane, 110 rue du Théâtre, BP 60244, 66002 Perpignan Cedex, ✆04 68 64 93 54).
- **Via Domitia** – Association régionale Via Domitia - CRT Languedoc-Roussillon - Acropolis - 980 av. J.-Mermoz - 34000 Montpellier – ✆04 67 22 81 00.
- **Fédération nationale des routes historiques** – www.routes-historiques.com.

ROUTES DES VINS

The premises of wine producers are generally open to visitors and often offer tastings. Most vineyards and wine-making estates are included on "wine routes" which combine finding out about wine with visiting historical and natural sights. Various events are organised in connection with these routes during the year.

Listed below are some useful addresses and sources of information.

Vins de pays d'Oc – Wines denominated Pays d'Oc are available from over 800 private wine estates or producers' cooperatives. For addresses, contact the Syndicat des producteurs de vin de pays d'Oc, Domaine de Manse, av. Paysagère, Maurin CS 7026 34973 Lattes Cedex. ✆04 67 13 84 20. www.paysdoc-wines.com.

Minervois – Themed routes allow you to discover the Minervois AOC, while also getting to know its historical, cultural, and natural attractions.

Syndicat du cru minervois – Le Chai Port Minervois, 35 quai des Tonneliers 11200 Homps. ✆04 68 91 29 48. www.leminervois.com.

Vins du Roussillon – **Le Conseil interprofessionnel des vins du Roussillon** offers a wide range of routes and events to do with wine. There is a choice of four routes: in the Vallée de l'Agly and the Fenouillèdes, in Les Aspres, from Aspres to the Massif des Albères, and the vineyards of Collioure and Banyuls. In summer, meals are organised in the vineyards. There are festivals in January, May, June, July, October and November. 19 av. de Grande-Bretagne BP 649 66006 Perpignan Cedex. ✆04 68 51 21 22. www.vinsduroussillon.com.

Blanquette de Limoux – ♿*p114, 119*.

Vins des Corbières – Everything you want to know about the wines of the Corbières can be found at : www.20decorbieres.com.

Syndicat du cru Fitou – You can find information on this wine region and the addresses of wine producers

Houseboat on Canal du Midi

© L. Cazenave / MICHELIN

here: N 9 Aire de la Via-Domitia 11480 La Palme. Mon–Fri 8am–noon, 2–6pm. ℘04 68 40 42 70. www.cru-fitou.com.

DO-IT-YOURSELF ITINERARIES

France is extremely good at showing off its heritage and certain organisations exist to draw tourists' attention to what is on offer. The following organisations all offer a select list of towns, villages and monuments fulfilling certain criteria that can be put together to make an itinerary:

- **Les Plus Beaux Villages** www.les-plus-beaux-villages-de-france.org.
- **Villes et Pays d'Art et de l'Histoire** www.vpah.culture.fr
- **Villes et Villages Fleuries** www.cnvvf.fr.
- **Les Plus Beaux Detours de France** www.plusbeauxdetours.com.

RIDING TOURS

There are numerous marked riding trails throughout the region, crossing garrigue, forest and high plateaux, and climbing to mountain passes and peaks. To get to know them, and to find the relevant maps and guides, contact the departmental branches (CDTE) of the **Comité national de tourisme équestre** – ℘02 54 94 46 80, www.ffe.com. This organisation

publishes an annual brochure, *Cheval nature, l'officiel du tourisme équestre*, listing facilities for horseback trekking, especially places to stay which will accommodate riders and their horses. Various farms and riding schools offer guided rides taking one or more days, as well as riding lessons.

Comité régional du tourisme équestre Languedoc-Roussillon (ATECREL) – 14 r. des Logis 34140 Loupian. ℘04 67 43 82 50. www.telr.net.

Compagnie des guides des Pyrénées catalanes – Av. Serrat-de-l'Ours 66210 Bolquère. ℘04 68 30 39 66, or 06 14 84 92 99.

SKIING

Skiing in the Languedoc-Roussillon is remarkably cheap compared with the Alps, but they are just as well equipped, and offer downhill skiing, cross-country skiing, tobogganing and sledging, country snow hiking, and even treks with dog sleighs for the very fit.

Among the Pyrénées in particular, there is remarkably little evidence of the overcrowding experienced in the Alps (except at weekends), and so these dramatic mountains offer a carefree skiing experience amid scenery every bit as dramatic and inspiring as the Alps. Because development to accommodate skiers has been gradual, most Pyrénéan resorts have avoided descending into unsightly, charmless places, and many retain an atmosphere of village identity and beauty. Significant investment in lift systems and the improved quality of the accommodation means the gap between the Alps and the Pyrénées is closing all the time.

In the Pyrénées there are over 50 skiing resorts to choose from, most notably Tourmalet and La Mongie, the biggest linked resort with more than 100km/62mi of slopes and a 1,000m/3,281ft off-piste descent from the Pic du Midi observatory. Font-Romeu is one of the oldest ski resorts not only in the Pyrénées but in Europe, dating back to the 1920s, and it remains a justly popular destination today.

The principality of **Andorra** has long been a popular goal for skiers originally drawn by the duty-free status looking for cheap *après ski* and budget holiday destinations. Andorran ski schools have an excellent reputation for good English-speaking instructors, and the result of continuing investment in the facilities and infrastructure has been to provide Andorra with some of the most modern, efficient lift systems in Europe. Grand Valira is the linked ski area of Pas de la Casa and Soldeu el Tarter, and has just started expanding into France. The other linked area is Vallnord, which includes Pal-Arinsal,

☺ Useful Tips ☺

Always bear ski-slope etiquette in mind when out on the piste: never set off without checking that the way uphill and downhill is clear; never ignore signposts; beware of the danger of avalanches on loosely packed snow (especially skiing off-piste). If in any doubt, check the rules at the ski resort before setting off.

Ordino-Arcalis and La Massana. You can also try cross-country skiing at La Rabassa.

SPAS

France has long been renowned for its health spas, a popular retreat for many, who can sometimes receive spa treatment on the French national health service. The Pyrénées have numerous springs, some thermally heated, which have brought fame to the area for their health restoring qualities since Antiquity. Pyrénéan spas fall into two categories: sulphurated or mineral-water springs.

SULPHUR WATER SPRINGS

Some spas in the eastern Pyrénées and their foothills exploit thermally heated water that comes out of the ground at up to 80 °C/176°F. The waters are used in baths and showers to treat a number of conditions.

Snowboarding in the Pyrénées

© Cédric Villegier / Fotolia.com

Useful Contacts for Skiers

Comprehensive information about skiing localities in Languedoc-Roussillon is listed on **www.sunfrance.com**, in great detail. The principal organisation in the UK for skiing is the **Ski Club of Great Britain** (The White House, 57–63 Church Road, Wimbledon, London SW19 5SB. ☎0208 410 2000. www.skiclub.co.uk).
But a number of other website-based organisations maintain accurate, up-to-date information, e.g. www.snowheads.com, and the **Eagle Ski Club**, the UK's largest and most active ski-touring and ski-mountaineering club (www.eagleskiclub.org.uk).

The main spas are **Amélie-les-Bains, Molitg-les-Bains, La Preste-les-Bains, Rennes-les-Bains** and **Vernet-les-Bains**.

OPEN-AIR HOT BATHS
In Pyrénées-Orientales there are naturally-heated, open air baths, either still in their wild state or managed. Without proven curative properties they are certainly relaxing and can be made use of by anyone (some requiring payment). See chapters on the **Cerdagne** and **Conflent**.

MINERAL-WATER SPRINGS
Waters containing bicarbonate of soda are said to be "sedatives". They are found at **Alet-les-Bains**.

USEFUL ADDRESSES
Centre d'informations thermales – 1 r. Cels 75014 Paris. ☎0 811 908 080 (charged at local rate). www.france-thermale.org.
Fédération thermale et climatique française – 71 ter r. Froidevaux 75014 Paris. ☎01 40 47 57 33. www.federationthermale.org.
Chaîne thermale du soleil / Maison du thermalisme – 32 av. de l'Opéra 75002 Paris. ☎0 800 050 532 (free). www.chainethermale.fr.

SPECTATOR SPORT – RUGBY
Rugby is big in the southwest. Every town and village has its team, and passions run high as enthusiastic supporters follow their team's progress in the weekly Sunday matches which take place from October to May. More information is available from the **Fédération Française de Rugby**, 3 rue Jean de Montaigu, 91463 Marcoussis; ☎01 69 63 64 65; www.ffr.fr.

SEA-WATER THERAPY
Known as *thalassothérapie* in French, this kind of cure has increased in popularity in recent years. The great centres for *thalassothérapie* on the

Petit Train Jaune running near Latour-de-Carol

© Jordi Puig / Photolibrary

coast of Roussillon are **Port-Barcarès** and at **Banyuls-sur-Mer**. These resorts are equipped for extended rest-cures but also offer tariffs for a day's or weekend's visit, with or without accommodation.
Syndicat national de la thalassothérapie – ✆01 44 70 07 57, or 02 40 11 72 35. www.france-thalasso.com.

TOURIST TRAINS

The **Petit Train Jaune** (Little Yellow Train) offers a picturesque journey through the Cerdagne and Conflent regions; it runs between Latour-de-Carol and Villefranche-de-Conflent, once a day each way. www.ter-sncf.com.
The **Train du Pays Cathar et de Fenouilledes** is a red train travelling from Saint Paul to Axat, in the Eastern Pyrénées. www.tcpf.fr.

Activities for Kids

This section gives a few ideas for families planning a holiday with plenty of sights and activities of interest to children. More can be found in the Discovering section of the guide by looking for the 👥 symbol.

STORYTELLING VISITS

Réseau Culturel Terre Catalane – *www.reseauculturel.fr*. The Réseau Culturel Terre Catalane organises entertaining and educational visits to sights, led by a guide in historical costume. Sights that can be visited in this manner include the abbey at Arles-sur-Tech; the Palais des Rois de Majorque in Perpignan; the Château de Castelnou; Elne cathedral; Fort Lagarde (Prats-de-Mollo); the Orgues d'Ille-sur-Têt; the church and treasury in Prades; the abbey of St-Génis-des-Fontaines, the Fort de Salses and the Fauvisme route in Collioure.

QUALITY MARKS

Famille Plus – *www.familleplus.fr*. This quality mark is given to towns that cater particularly well for families. Destinations incuded in this guide are: Argelès-sur-Mer, Leucate, Port-Barcarès, Saint-Cyprien and Font-Romeu.
Stations Vertes – *www.stationverte.com*. This quality mark is awarded to natural attractions that demonstrate

respect for the environment, have good facilities and a variety of outdoor activities. The following sights in this guide are classed as Stations Vertes: Quillan, Rennes-les-Bains, Sallèles-d'Aude, Vernet-les-Bains, Osséja and Torreilles.
Villes et Pays d'art et d'histoire – *www.vpah.culture.fr*. The Villes et Pays d'art et d'histoire *(see guided tours)* offer guided visits and workshops for children on Wednesdays, Saturdays and during school holidays. Provided with booklets, games and other educational tools suitable for their ages, children get to know about history and architecture while they actively participate in discovering the town. In the workshops they can express themselves in various media (models, engravings, videos) and meet professionals working in the field: architects, stone masons, storytellers, actors etc.

Handcrafted espadrilles

J. Malburet/MICHELIN

Shopping

MARKETS

Major shopping centres are few and far between. Elsewhere there are numerous shopping opportunities in the narrow streets of Narbonne, Perpignan and Carcassone.

But the best shopping experience comes from the countless local and regional markets held every week in virtually every town and village, and which range from small stalls offering produce grown by the man selling it to you, to some of the finest, freshest food and drink produce available. Just walking round the markets is a memorable and aromatic experience. Traditional markets, known as *marchés au gras* are still held in a few places in winter months for the sale of ducks, geese and their livers.

REGIONAL PRODUCE

Preserved foodstuffs – To leave Collioure without buying a jar of salted anchovies is like leaving Castelnaudary without buying some (tinned) cassoulet. You might also want to take home a selection of charcuterie from the Cerdagne.

Fruit – In season you can by whole crates of red apricots and peaches in Roussillon. To make clafoutis, there is nothing better than some cherries from Céret. And for a spontaneous addition, why not add some russet apple from Le Vigan, in the Gard.

Sweets – Give in to the temptation for a crema catalana or some alléluias (cakes) from Castelnaudary. For a sweet snack try some croquants (dry biscuits made with almonds), rousquilles (round biscuits flavoured with anise or lemon) from Amélie-les-Bains, nougat from Limoux or some Catalan touron.

Alcohol – There is a wide range of wines to choose from, including vins doux naturels (fortified wines). Muscat from Maury, Carthagène from Narbonne or Byrrh from Thuir all make good choices as aperitifs.

CLOTHING AND ACCESSORIES

Espadrilles – These traditional canvas and rope-soled shoes are worn by sardana dancers. Try on a pair and you will discover how comfortable they are – ideal for summer.

Jewellery – In Perpignan garnets can be mounted on a ring, ear rings, necklace or – in local tradition dating from the 18C – on a Badine cross.

CRAFTS

For **household linen**, head for the Cerdagne where you will find a range of napkins, tea towels and towels in bright yellow and red. Some motorway service areas have gift shops useful for last minute present buying, such as the **Village Catalan** near Boulou on the A9.

Église Notre-Dame-des-Anges, Collioure, Côte Vermeille
© Bertrand Gardel / hemis.fr

Books

Travels with a Donkey in the Cévenne - Robert Louis Stevenson, 1879. One of the classic travel books. Penned by Stevenson while still in his 20s, it tells of his epic 12-day 120-mile hike with a donkey through the mountains of the Cévennes.

Notes from the Languedoc - Rupert Wright, 2003. A beautifully crafted collection of anecdotes about Languedoc, originally written as letters for the author's grandmother. A gem!

Virgile's Vineyard - Patrick Moon, 2003. The story of a year in the Languedoc wine country; enthusiastic, informative, and above all thoroughly entertaining.

Rick Stein's French Odyssey - Rick Stein, 2005. The TV chef's account of his sedate journey at 4mph on a canal barge called 'The Anjodi' through the Languedoc-Roussillon along the Canal du Midi. Stein focuses on country food prepared from ingredients found in local markets.

French Leaves: Letters from the Languedoc - Christopher Campbell Howes, 2002. Retired headmaster from Scotland evokes the scents, sights and sounds, the vibrant colours and earthy vitality of the area with British detachment.

In the High Pyrénées: A new life in a mountain village - Bernard Loughlin, 2003. A loving and hilarious account of the sensations and intrigues of a mountain village.

Films

Bernadette, 1988. Actress Sydney Penny gives a poignant performance as the teenager Bernadette Soubirous, who has visions of the 'Lady in White' – the Virgin Mary – in a cave at Lourdes. Shot in and around the pilgrimage site and the local Pyrénéan villages in winter.

CARCASSONNE

Les Visiteurs (The Visitors) 1993. A time-travelling farce by Jean-Marie Poiré, with Christian Clavier and Jean Reno.

GRUISSAN-PLAGE

37°2 le matin (Betty Blue) 1986, by Jean-Jacques Beineix, with Béatrice Dalle and Jean-Hugues Anglade.

NARBONNE

Le Père Noël a les yeux bleus (Santa Clause has Blue Eyes) 1966, by Jean Eustache, with Jean-Pierre Léaud.

PERPIGNAN

Le Retour de Martin Guerre, 1982, by Daniel Vigne, with Nathalie Baye and Gérard Depardieu.

Calendar of Events

Many regional tourist offices publish brochures listing local fêtes, fairs and festivals. Most places hold festivities for France's National Day (14 July) and 15 August, a public holiday, but almost all towns and villages enjoy a plethora of reasons for dropping everything and having a party. Enquire locally.

FEBRUARY
Limoux
Traditional carnival every weekend (and Shrove Tuesday). All-night *'Blanquette'* party follows. ✆04 68 31 11 82. www.limoux.fr.

Prats-de-Mollo, St-Laurent-de-Cerdans, Arles-sur-Tech
Traditional carnival. ✆04 68 39 70 83. www.pratsdemollolapreste.com.

EASTER - APRIL
Arles-sur-Tech
Night-time procession of black penitents (Good Friday). ✆04 68 39 11 99. www.tourisme-haut-vallespir.com.

Collioure
Procession of penitent brotherhoods (Good Friday). ✆04 68 82 15 47. www.collioure.com.

Montolieu
Antiquarian book fair (Easter weekend). ✆04 68 24 82 70. www.montolieu-livre.fr.

Perpignan
Festival of sacred music (2nd week). ✆04 68 66 33 54. Procession of the Pénitents de la Sanch (Good Friday). ✆04 68 66 30 30. www.perpignantourisme.com.

MAY
Céret
Cherry festival (Third weekend). ✆04 68 87 00 53. www.ot-ceret.fr.

JUNE
Amélie-les-Bains
Fête of the Muleteers (Saturday close to Jun 24). ✆04 68 39 01 98.

Perpignan
Saint-Jean Festa Major (with mid-summer bonfires around 21 June). ✆04 68 66 30 30. www.perpignantourisme.com.

Carnival in Limoux

Total Festum
> Festival of the Occitan and Catalan Cultures (all month, in various locations in Roussillon).

JULY

Bastille Day
> There are celebrations everywhere for France's national holiday, 14 July.

Bize-Minervois
> Olive festival (Third Sunday).

Carcassonne
> Festival of the City: Medieval Cité is 'set alight' by an evening firework display; classical music concerts, theatre, opera, dance, jazz (14 July).
> ✆04 68 11 59 15.
> www.festivaldecarcassonne.com.

Céret
> Feria: "Céret Bullfighting" (Second weekend).
> ✆04 68 87 00 53.
> International Sardana festival 400 dancers in costume. (2nd fortnight.)
> ✆04 68 87 00 53.

Osséja
> International sheep dog competition (last Sunday).
> ✆04 68 04 53 86.

Perpignan
> Les Estivales: theatre festival.
> ✆04 68 66 30 30.
> www.estivales.com.

Prades
> Ciné-Rencontres (second fortnight): cinema festival.
> ✆04 68 05 20 47.
> www.cine-rencontres.org.

Tour de France
> The famous cycle race often passes through the region. It always includes a hill climb to at least one of the passes of the Pyrénées.

JULY–AUGUST

Limoux
> Nava theatre festival (end Jul-beginning Aug). ✆04 68 31 99 48.

Lastours
> *Son et lumière* show at the chateau.
> ✆04 68 77 56 02.

Prades: St-Michel-de-Cuxa
> Pablo Casals festival. Concerts in the abbey (mid-July to mid-August). ✆04 68 96 33 07.
> www.prades-festival-casals.com.

St-Génis-des-Fontaines
> Prieuré Santa Maria del Vilar: International song and medieval festival. ✆04 68 89 64 61.

AUGUST

Amélie-les-Bains
> International folklore festival (second week). ✆04 68 39 01 98.
> www.festival-amelie.com.

Banyuls-sur-Mer
> Sardana festival (2nd weekend).
> ✆04 68 88 00 62.
> www.banyuls-sur-mer.com.

Castelnaudary
> Fête du cassoulet (last weekend).
> ✆04 68 23 05 73.
> www.feteducassoulet.com.

Pennautier
> Les Cabardièses de Pennautier: piano festival (mid-Aug).
> ✆04 68 25 35 79.
> www.lescabardieses.com.

AUGUST-SEPTEMBER

Perpignan
> Festival Visa pour l'image (end Aug–mid-Sep): Photography exhibitions, screenings.
> ✆04 68 62 38 00.
> www.visapourlimage.com.

SEPTEMBER

Journées du Patrimoine
> Historic monuments and heritage sites open day.

Principauté d'Andorre
> National Day of Andorra (8): pilgrimage to Notre-Dame de Meritxell.

OCTOBER

Perpignan
> Jazz festival. ✆04 68 35 37 46.
> www.jazzebre.com.

Know Before You Go

USEFUL WEBSITES

www.sunfrance.com

A dedicated, multilingual website for Languedoc-Roussillon. All the practical information you might need for a stay in the region.

www.franceguide.com

The French Government Tourist Office/Maison de la France site is packed with practical information and tips for those travelling to France. The home page has a number of links to more specific guidance, for American or Canadian travellers for example, or to the FGTO's London pages.

www.FranceKeys.com

This site has plenty of practical information for visiting France. It covers all the regions, with links to tourist offices and related sites.

www.franceway.com

This is an online magazine which focuses on culture and heritage. For each region, there are also suggestions for activities and practical information on where to stay and how to get there.

www.ambafrance-uk.org

The French Embassy's website provides basic information (geography, demographics, history), a news digest and business-related information. It offers special pages for children, and pages devoted to culture, language study and travel, and you can reach other selected French sites (regions, cities, ministries) with a hypertext link.

www.F-T-S.co.uk

The French Travel Service specialises in organising holidays in France using the rail network. Let FTS organise your travel and hotels anywhere in France.

www.pyrenees-online.fr

This regional site has a mine of information about accommodation, ski resorts and activities in the Pyrénées.

www.tourisme.fr

The way to find the address and website of any tourist information office anywhere in France.

www.pagesjaunes.fr

The French yellow pages, indispensable for finding the phone number of a particular hotel, restaurant or shop. It also supplies a range of additional information.

www.geoportail.fr

An impressive French government mapping system. Zoom in on any part of France that takes your fancy. It even shows up hamlets and fields.

TOURIST OFFICES ABROAD

Australia and New Zealand

♦ **Sydney** – Level 13, 25 Bligh Street, Sydney, New South Wales 2000
  ☏ (02) 9231 5244
  www.au.franceguide.com

Canada

♦ **Montreal** –
  1800 Avenue McGill College
  Suite 1010, Montreal,
  Quebec H3A 3J6
  ☏ (514) 288-2026
  www.ca.franceguide.com

South Africa

3rd floor, Village Walk, Office Tower, cnr Maude and Rivonia, Sandton, Johannesburg
☏ (0) 11 523 82 92
http://za.franceguide.com

United Kingdom and Ireland

London Maison de France –
  Lincoln House, 300 High Holborn,
  London WC1V 7JH
  ☏ (09068) 244 123
  http://uk.franceguide.com

United States

Three offices are available, but the quickest way to get a response is by phone. ☏ 514-288-1904. http://us.franceguide.com.

TOURIST OFFICES

Local tourist offices are referenced throughout the *Discovering* section of this guide.

Three towns and areas, labelled **Villes et Pays d'Art et d'Histoire** by the Ministry of Culture, are mentioned in this guide (Narbonne, Perpignan and the Têt Valley). More information is available from local tourist offices and from *www.vpah.culture.fr*.

Département Offices
- **Aude**
  Allée Raymond Courrière
  Carcassonne Cedex 9
  ✆ 04 68 11 66 00
  www.audetourisme.com
- **Pyrénées-Orientales**
  16 avenue des Palmiers, BP 80540
  66005 Perpignan Cedex
  ✆ 04 68 51 52 53
  www.tourisme-pyrenees
  orientales.com

Région Offices
- **Languedoc-Roussillon:**
  954, Avenue Jean Mermoz
  34960 Montpellier,
  ✆ 04 67 20 02 20
  www.sunfrance.com
- **Midi-Pyrénées:**
  54 boulevard de l'Embouchure,
  BP 52166, 31022 Toulouse 2,
  ✆ 05 61 13 55 48
  www.tourisme-
  midi-pyrenees.co.uk

INTERNATIONAL VISITORS
EMBASSIES AND CONSULATES
- **Australia Embassy**
  4 rue Jean-Rey, 75724 Paris Cedex.
  ✆ 01 40 59 33 00.
  france.embassy.gov.au.
- **Canada Embassy**
  35 avenue Montaigne, 75008 Paris.
  ✆ 01 44 43 29 00.
  www.france.gc.ca.
- **Ireland Embassy**
  4 rue Rude, 75116 Paris.
  ✆ 01 44 17 67 00.
  www.dfa.ie.
- **New Zealand Embassy**
  7 ter rue Léonard-de-Vinci, 75116
  Paris. ✆ 01 45 01 43 43.
  www.nzembassy.com/fr/france.
- **UK Embassy**
  35 rue du Faubourg St-Honoré,
  75383 Paris Cedex 08.
  ✆ 01 44 51 31 00.
  www.ukinfrance.fco.gov.uk.
- **UK Consulate**
  1b bis, rue d'Anjou,
  75008 Paris.
  ✆ 01 44 51 31 00.
  www.ukinfrance.fco.gov.uk.

- **USA Embassy**
  2 avenue Gabriel, 75382 Paris
  Cedex. ✆ 01 43 12 22 22.
  www.amb-usa.fr.
- **USA Consulate**
  2 rue St-Florentin, 75382 Paris.
  ✆ 01 43 12 22 22. www.amb-usa.fr.

ENTRY REQUIREMENTS
Passport
Nationals of countries within the
European Union entering France
need only a national identity card.
Nationals of other countries must
be in possession of a valid national
passport. In case of loss or theft,
report to your embassy or consulate
and the local police.

Visa
No **entry visa** is required for UK,
Canadian, US or Australian citizens
travelling as tourists and staying fewer
than 90 days, except for students
planning to study in France.
If you think you may need a visa, apply
to your local French Consulate.
US citizens should obtain the booklet
Safe Trip Abroad, which provides useful
information on visa requirements,
customs regulations, medical care etc
for international travellers.
Published by the **Government
Printing Office**, it can be ordered
by phone (✆ (202) 512-1800) or
consulted online (www.access.gpo.
gov). General passport information
is available by phone toll-free from
the **Federal Information Center**,
✆ 1-877-487-2778 .
US passport application forms can
be downloaded from *http://travel.
state.gov.*

CUSTOMS REGULATIONS
UK: Apply to the Customs Office for
a leaflet on customs regulations and
the full range of duty-free allowances;
available from **HM Revenue and
Customs**, *Crownhill Court, Tailyour Rd,
Plymouth PL6 5B2;* ✆ *08450 109 000*;
www.hmrc.gov.uk.
- **US:** www.cbp.gov
- **Canada:** www.cbsa.gc.ca

- **Australia:** www.customs.gov.au
- **New Zealand:** www.customs. govt.nz

There are no customs formalities for holidaymakers bringing their caravans or pleasure boats into France for a stay of less than six months but the registration certificate should be available. When in doubt counsult the **French Customs and Excise Service** at ✆08 20 02 44 44 or www. douanne.gouv.fr. Residents from a member state of the European Union are not restricted with regard to purchasing goods for private use, but the recommended allowances for alcoholic beverages and tobacco are as follows: Duty-free allowances: Spirits (10ltr), Fortified wines (20ltr), Wine (90ltr), Beer (110ltr), Cigarettes (100), Cigarillos (400), Cigars (200), Smoking tobacco (1kg).

HEALTH

First aid, medical advice and chemists' night service rota are available from chemists/drugstores *(pharmacie)* identified by the green cross sign. You should take out comprehensive insurance coverage as the recipient of medical treatment in French hospitals or clinics must pay. **Nationals of non-EU countries** should check with their insurance companies about policy limitations.

British and **Irish citizens** (and all EU citizens) should apply for a European Health Insurance Card (EHIC), which entitles the holder to treatment for accident or unexpected illness in EU countries. **British citizens** apply online at www.ehic.org.uk, or telephone 0845 606 2030. **Irish citizens** should consult www.ehic.ie.

Americans and **Canadians** can contact the **International Association for Medical Assistance to Travelers**, which can also provide details of English-speaking doctors in different parts of France: ✆ for the US (716) 754-4883; for Canada (416) 652 0137. www.iamat.org.

The American Hospital of Paris is open 24hrs for emergencies as well as consultations, with English-speaking staff. Accredited by major insurance companies. 63 boulevard Victor-Hugo, 92200 Neuilly-sur-Seine, ✆01 46 41 25 25. www.american-hospital.org.

The British Hospital is just outside Paris in Levallois-Perret, 3 rue Barbès, ✆01 46 39 22 22. www.british-hospital.org.

All prescription drugs should be clearly labelled; it is essential that you carry a copy of prescriptions.

ACCESSIBILITY

The sights described in this guide which are easily accessible to people of reduced mobility are indicated in the *Admission times and charges* by this symbol: &. Since 2001, the designation **Tourisme at Handicap** has applied to a thousand sites accessible to the disabled: go to www.franceguide.com.

The principal French source for information on facilities are the **Association des Paralysés de France**, (www.apf.asso.fr) and the **Association pour la défense des Handicapés de France** (www.adh-asso.org). On **TGV and Corail trains**, operated by national railway (SNCF), there are special wheelchair slots in 1st class carriages available to holders of 2nd-class tickets. On **Eurostar** and Thalys, special rates are available for accompanying adults. A Disabled Persons Travel Helpline is available on ✆08717 818179 at **Eurolines (National Express)**. A textphone is provided for customers who are deaf or hard of hearing on ✆0121 455 0086. All **airports** are equipped to receive less abled passengers.

Web-surfers can find information for slow walkers, mature travellers and others with special needs at www.access-able.com.

For information on museum access for the disabled contact La Direction, Les Musées de France, Service Accueil des Publics Spécifiques; 6 rue des Pyramides, 75041 Paris Cedex 1; ✆01 40 15 73 00.

Getting There and Getting Around

BY PLANE

Various international and other independent airlines operate services to **Paris** (Roissy-Charles de Gaulle and Orly airports), **Montpellier** and **Toulouse**. Check with your travel agent, however, before booking direct flights, as it may be cheaper to travel via Paris. Air France (✆*09 69 39 02 15; www.airfrance.fr)*, links Paris to Montpellier, Béziers-Agde and Toulouse several times a day. Other airlines offering flights to several towns in the region include British Airways, Flybe, easyJet and Ryanair. Contact airline companies and travel agents for details of package tour flights with a rail or coach link-up as well as fly-drive schemes.

BY SHIP

There are numerous **cross-Channel services** (passenger and car ferries) from the United Kingdom and Ireland, as well as the rail Shuttle through the Channel Tunnel (**Le Shuttle-Eurotunnel**, ✆0844 35 35 35 (UK only) and ✆08 10 63 03 03 (France) www.euro-tunnel.com).
To choose the most suitable route between your port of arrival and your destination use the Michelin Tourist and Motoring Atlas France, Michelin map 726 (which gives travel times and mileages) or Michelin maps from the 1:200 000 series (with the yellow cover). For details apply to travel agencies or to:

- **P&O Ferries** ✆08716 642 121 (UK), or 0825 120 156 (France), www.poferries.com. Service, between Dover and Calais.
- **Norfolk Line** ✆0871 574 235 (UK). www.norfolkline.com. Service, between Dover and Dunkerque.
- **Brittany Ferries** ✆0871 244 0744 (UK); 0825 828 828 (France).

www.brittanyferries.com. Services from Portsmouth, Poole and Plymouth.
- **LD Lines** ✆0844 576 8836, www.ldlines.co.uk. Services from Portsmouth, and Newhaven.
- **Condor Ferries** ✆01202 207216, www.condorferries.co.uk. Services from Weymouth, Poole and Portsmouth.
- **Seafrance** ✆0871 423 71 19. www.seafrance.com. Services between Dover and Calais.

BY TRAIN

All rail services throughout France can be arranged through **Rail Europe** in the UK, online (www.raileurope.co.uk), by telephone ✆0844 848 4064, or call into the Rail Europe Travel Centre at 1 Regent Street, London SW1. Rail Europe can also book Eurostar travel. **Eurostar** runs from **London** (St Pancras) to **Paris** (Gare du Nord) in under 3hr (up to 20 times daily). In Paris it links to the high-speed rail network (TGV) which covers most of France. There is fast inter-city service from **Paris** (Gare Montparnasse) to **Vendôme** *(45min)*, **Le Mans** *(50min)*, **Tours** *(1hr)* and **Angers** *(1hr 30min)* on the TGV. Bookings and information ✆0892 353 539 in the UK, www.eurostar.com.
Citizens of non-European Economic Area countries will need to complete a landing card before arriving at Eurostar check-in. These landing cards can be found at dedicated desks in front of the check-in area and from Eurostar staff. Once you have filled in the card please hand it to UK immigration staff.
France Rail Pass and Eurail Pass are travel passes which may be purchased by residents of countries outside the European Union. In the US, contact your travel agent or **Rail Europe** 44 South Broadway, White Plains NY 10601, ✆1-800-622-8600 (US) and ✆1-800-361-7245 (Canada). If you are a European resident of another country, you can buy an individual country pass.

Information on schedules can be obtained on websites for these agencies and the **SNCF**, respectively: www.raileurope.com, www.eurail. on.ca, www.sncf.fr. At the SNCF site, you can book ahead, pay with a credit card, and receive your ticket in the mail. There are numerous **discounts** available when you purchase your tickets in France, from 25–50 percent below the regular rate. These include discounts for using senior cards and youth cards, and seasonal promotions. There are a limited number of discount seats available during peak travel times, and the best discounts are available for travel during off-peak periods.

Tickets for rail travel in France must be validated (*composter*) by using the (usually) automatic date-stamping machines at the platform entrance (failure to do so may result in a fine). The French railway company **SNCF** operates a telephone information, reservation and prepayment service in English from 7am to 10pm (French time). To buy train tickets in France call ℘3635. More useful advice on rail travel in France is available at www.seat61.com.

BY COACH/BUS

- ♦ **Eurolines (National Express)**
  4 Cardiff Road, Luton, Bedfordshire LU1, 1PP. ℘0871 78 81 81 78. Their website www.eurolines.com has information about travelling all over Europe by coach (bus).
- ♦ **Eurolines (Paris)**
  28 ave du General de Gaulle 93177 Bagnolet. ℘0892 89 90 91. www.eurolines.fr

BY CAR
ROUTE PLANNING

The area covered in this guide is easily reached by main motorways and national routes. **Michelin map 726** indicates the main itineraries as well as alternate routes for avoiding heavy traffic during busy holiday periods, and gives estimated travel times. **Michelin map 723** is a detailed atlas of French motorways, indicating tolls, rest areas and services along the route; it includes a table for calculating distances and times. The Michelin route-planning service is available at **www.viamichelin.com**. Travellers can calculate a precise route using such options as shortest route, route avoiding toll roads, Michelin-recommended route and gain access to tourist information (hotels, restaurants, attractions).

The roads are very busy during the holiday period (particularly weekends in July and August) and, to avoid traffic congestion it is advisable to follow the recommended secondary routes (signposted as *Bison Futé – itinéraires bis*). The motorway network includes rest areas (*aires de repos*) and petrol stations (*stations-service*), with restaurant and shopping complexes attached, about every 40km/25mi. For information about traffic conditions look at www.bison-fute.equipement. gouv.fr.

DOCUMENTS

Travellers from other European Union countries and North America can drive in France with a valid national or home-state **driving licence.**
An **international driving licence** is useful because the information on it appears in nine languages (keep in mind that traffic officers are empowered to fine motorists). A permit is available (US$10) from the **National Automobile Club**, 1151 East Hillsdale Blvd., Foster City, CA 94404, ℘650-294-7000 or www. nationalautoclub.com; or contact your local branch of the **American Automobile Association**. For the vehicle, it is necessary to have the registration papers and a nationality plate of the approved size.

INSURANCE

Certain motoring organisations (AAA, AA, RAC and The Caravan Club) offer accident **insurance** and breakdown service schemes for members. Check with your insurance company in regard to coverage while abroad. If you plan to hire a car using your credit card, check with the company, which may provide liability insurance automatically (and thus save you having to pay the cost for optimum coverage).

ROAD REGULATIONS

The minimum driving age is 18. Traffic drives on the right.
All passengers must wear **seat belts**. Children under the age of 10 must ride in the back seat. Headlights must be switched on in poor visibility and at night; dipped headlights should be used at all times outside built up areas. Use side-lights only when the vehicle is stationary. In the case of a **breakdown**, a red warning triangle or hazard warning lights are obligatory as are reflective safety jackets.
In the absence of stop signs at intersections, cars must **give way to the right**.
Traffic on main roads outside built-up areas (priority indicated by a yellow diamond sign) and on roundabouts has right of way. Vehicles must stop when the lights turn red at road junctions and may filter to the right only when indicated by an amber arrow. The regulations on **drinking and driving** (limited to 0.50g/l) and **speeding** are strictly enforced – usually by an on-the-spot fine and/or confiscation of the vehicle.
From Spring 2012, all cars must carry a compulsory portable alcohol breathalyzer kit.

Speed limits

Although liable to modification, these are as follows:
♦ **toll motorways** (autoroutes) 130kph/80mph (110kph/68mph when raining);
♦ **dual carriageways and motorways without tolls** 110kph/68mph (100kph/62mph when raining);
♦ **other roads 90kph/56mph** (80kph/50mph when raining) and in towns 50kph/31mph;

♦ **outside lane on motorways** during daylight, on level ground and with good visibility – minimum speed limit of 80kph/50mph.
♦ **built-up areas** (50kph/30mph)

CAR RENTAL

There are car rental agencies at airports, railway stations and in all large towns throughout France. European cars have manual transmission; automatic cars are available in larger cities only if an advance reservation is made. Drivers must be over 21; between ages 21–25, drivers are required to pay an extra daily fee; some companies allow drivers under 23 only if the reservation has been made through a travel agent. Take advantage of **fly-drive offers when you buy your ticket**, or seek advice from a travel agent, specifying requirements.
There are many online services that will look for the best prices on car rental around the globe. **Nova** can be contacted at *www.novacarhire.com* or *✆0800 018 6682 (freephone UK)*.

RENTAL CARS – CENTRAL RESERVATION IN FRANCE	
Avis:	✆08 44 581 0147
Europcar:	✆08 71 384 1087
Budget France:	✆08 25 00 35 64
Hertz France:	✆01 39 38 38 38
SIXT-Eurorent	✆08 20 00 74 98
National-CITER	✆0825 16 12 12

PETROL/GASOLINE

French service stations dispense:
♦ *sans plomb 98* (super unleaded 98)
♦ *sans plomb 95* (super unleaded 95)
♦ *diesel/gazole* (diesel)
♦ *GPL* (LPG).
Prices are listed on signboards on the motorways; fill up off the motorway for better prices; check hypermarkets on the outskirts of towns.

Where to Stay and Eat

Hotel & Restaurant listings fall within the Address Books within the Discovering section of the guide.

WHERE TO STAY

The Green Guide is pleased to offer descriptions of selected lodgings for this region. The Address Books in the *Discovering* section of the guide give descriptions and prices *(based on double ocupancy)* of typical places to stay with local flair. The Legend on the cover flap explains the symbols and prices used in the Address Books. For an even greater selection, use the **Michelin Guide France**, with its famously reliable star-rating system and hundreds of establishments all over France. Book ahead to ensure that you get the accommodation you want. Some places require an advance deposit or a reconfirmation. Reconfirming is especially important if you plan to arrive after 6pm. For further assistance, **Loisirs Accueil,** (www.loisirsaccueilfrance.com), is a booking service that has offices in some French *départements* – contact the tourist offices listed above for further information.

A guide to good-value, family-run hotels, **Logis et Auberges de France**, (www.logisdefrance.fr), is available from the French Tourist Office, as are lists of other kinds of accommodation such as hotel-châteaux, bed-and-breakfasts, etc.

Relais et châteaux (www.relais chateaux.com), provides information on booking in luxury hotels with character: 33 bvd Malesherbes, 75008 Paris, ℰ08 25 82 51 80 (within France) or ℰ00 800 2000 00 02 (UK)

Economy Chain Hotels

If you need a place to stop en route, these can be useful, as they are inexpensive and generally located near the main road. While breakfast is available, there may not be a restaurant; rooms are small, with a television and bathroom. All chains have on-line reservations. Central reservation numbers and websites:
- **Akena** ℰ01 69 84 85 17, www.hotels-akena.com
- **B&B** ℰ02 98 33 75 29, www.hotel-bb.com
- **Etap** ℰ0 892 68 89 00, www.etaphotel.com
- **Mister Bed** www.misterbed.fr
- **Villages Hôtel** ℰ03 80 60 92 70

The hotels listed below are slightly more expensive, and offer a few more amenities and services:
- **Campanile** www.campanile.fr
- **Kyriad** kyriad.com
- **Ibis** www.ibishotel.com

RENTING A COTTAGE, BED AND BREAKFAST

The **Maison des Gîtes de France** is an information service on self-catering accommodation in France. Gîtes usually take the form of a cottage or apartment, or bed and breakfast accommodation *(chambres d'hôtes)*. Contact the **Gîtes de France** office in Paris: 59 rue St-Lazare, 75439 Paris Cedex 09; ℰ01 49 70 75 75; www.gites-de-france.fr, or their representative in the UK, **Brittany Ferries** *(address above)*. From the site, you can order catalogues for different regions illustrated with photographs of the properties, as well as specialised catalogues (bed and breakfasts, farm stays etc). You can also contact the local tourist offices.

The **Fédération nationale Clévacances**, 54 boulevard de l'Embouchure, BP 52166, 31022 Toulouse Cedex 2; ℰ05 61 13 55 66; www.clevacances.com, offers a wide choice of accommodation throughout France. It publishes a brochure for each *département*.

The **Fédération des Stations vertes de vacances** (6 rue Ranfer-de-Bretenières, BP 71698, 21016 Dijon Cedex; ℰ03 80 54 10 50; www.

stationsvertes.com) is an association which promotes 880 rural localities throughout France, selected for their natural appeal as well as for the quality of their environment, of their accommodation and of the leisure activities available.

FARM HOLIDAYS

The guide *Bienvenue à la ferme,* lists the addresses of farms providing guest facilities, which have been vetted for quality and for meeting official standards. For more information, apply to local tourist offices *(addresses above)* or to Service Agriculture et tourisme, 9 avenue George-V, 75008 Paris; ✆01 53 57 11 50; www.bienvenue-a-la-ferme.com.

HOSTELS, CAMPING

To obtain an **International Youth Hostel Federation** card (there is no age requirement) you should contact the IYHF in your own country for information and membership applications (US ✆1-301-495 12 40, www.hiusa.org; England ✆01707 324170; Scotland ✆01786 891400; Canada ✆613-273 7884; Australia ✆61-2-9883-7195, www.yha.com. au). There is a booking service, www. hihostels.com, which you may use to reserve rooms as far as six months in advance.
The main youth hostel association *(auberges de jeunesse)* in France is the **Ligue Française pour les Auberges de la Jeunesse**, 67 rue Vergniaud, 75013 Paris; ✆01 44 16 78 78; www.auberges-de-jeunesse.com. There are numerous officially graded **campsites** with varying standards of facilities throughout the Languedoc-Roussillon region. The **Michelin Camping France** guide lists a selection of campsites. The area is very popular with campers in the summer months, so it is wise to reserve in advance.

WALKERS

Walkers can consult the guide, *Gîtes d'Étapes et Refuges* by A and S Mouraret, which can be ordered from: www.gites-refuges.com.
This guide, which lists 4,000 places to stay, also contains much information to help with planning itineraries and is intended for those who enjoy walking, cycling, climbing, skiing, canoeing and kayaking holidays.

WHERE TO EAT

The Green Guide is pleased to offer a selection of restaurants for this region. The Address Books in the *Discovering* section of the guide give descriptions and prices of typical places to eat with local flair. The Legend on the cover flap explains the symbols and prices used in the Address Books. Use the red-cover **Michelin Guide France**, with its famously reliable star-rating system and descriptions of hundreds of establishments all over France, for an even greater choice. In the countryside, restaurants usually serve lunch between noon and 2pm and the evening meal between 7.30 and 10pm. The 'non-stop' restaurant is still a rarity in small towns in the provinces.

- ⓘ *For information on local specialities, see the Introduction.*
- ⓘ *For assistance in ordering a meal in France, see the Menu Reader, under Useful Words and Phrases.*

Gourmet guide

The Languedoc region boasts some spots which appeal to the gourmet tourist interested in discovering local specialities. Among the places which have been awarded the *Site remarquable du goût* (for 'remarkable taste sensations') distinction are the Aubrac area for its Laguiole and Fourme cheeses, the Rocher de Combalou for its Roquefort cheese, the Étangs de Thau for their production of oysters, and mussels, Banyuls for its sweet wine, and Collioure for its anchovies.

Basic Information

BUSINESS HOURS

In the provinces the banks open from 10am–12.30pm and 2.30–4.30 Tue–Sat. (They often close early the day before a Public Holiday). Most of the larger shops are open Mondays to Saturdays from 9am to 6.30 or 7.30pm. Smaller, individual shops may close during the lunch hour. Hypermarkets usually stay open non-stop from 9am until 9pm or later.

COMMUNICATIONS

All towns and many villages have at least one public call box, mostly used for emergencies. These use prepaid phone cards *(télécartes),* rather than coins. *Télécartes* can be bought in post offices, branches of France Télécom, *bureaux de tabac* (cafés that sell cigarettes) and newsagents.

NATIONAL CALLS

French telephone numbers have 10 digits. Paris and Paris region numbers begin with 01; 02 in northwest France; 03 in northeast France; 04 in southeast France and Corsica; 05 in southwest France.

INTERNATIONAL CALLS

To call France from abroad, dial the country code (33) + 9-digit number (omit the initial 0). When calling abroad from France dial 00, then dial the country code followed by the area code and number of your correspondent.

INTERNATIONAL DIALLING CODES ☎ (00 + code)			
Australia	☎ 61	New Zealand	☎ 64
Canada	☎ 1	United Kingdom	☎ 44
Eire	☎ 353	United States	☎ 1

International information:
US and Canada: 00 33 12 11
International operator:
00 33 12 + country code
Local directory assistance: 12

TO USE YOUR PERSONAL CALLING CARD	
AT&T	☎ 0-800 99 10 11
Sprint	☎ 0-800 99 00 87
MCI	☎ 0-800 99 00 19
Canada Direct	☎ 0-800 99 00 16

MOBILE PHONES

Any standard mobile phone bought in Europe will work in France as long as roaming is enabled. Phones need to be GSM 90 or GSM 1800 to work in France. Companies that rent mobile phones and computers include:

◆ **Euroteknic Location**
08 20 32 08 12
www.location-telephone.com
◆ **Eurolocation Informatique**
01 44 38 00 40
www.eurolocation.fr

MAIL/POST

Post Offices in the provinces are open from 9am–12.30pm and 2.30–4.30pm. Note that if a Public Holiday falls on a Tuesday or Thursday then the nearest Monday or Friday will be taken also. Stamps are also available from newsagents and tobacconists.

POSTAGE VIA AIR MAIL TO:	
UK	Letter (20g) 0.77€
North America	Letter (20g) 1.00€
Australia	Letter (20g) 1.00€
New Zealand	Letter (20g) 1.00€

DISCOUNTS

Significant discounts are available for senior citizens, students, young people under the age of 25, teachers, and groups for public transportation, museums and monuments and for some leisure activities such as the cinema (at certain times of day). Bring student or senior cards with you, and bring along some extra passport-size photos for discount travel cards.

The **International Student Travel Confederation** (www.isic.org), global administrator of the International Student and Teacher Identity Cards, is an association of student travel organisations. ISTC members collectively negotiate benefits with airlines, governments, and providers of other goods and services for the student and teacher community. The corporate headquarters address is Keizersgracht 174-176, 1016 DW Amsterdam, The Netherlands; ℘31 20 421 28 00.

Pass Inter-sites, Reseau Culturel Terre Catalane – This 'passport' is available at many sites in the area where the Catalonia culture and traditions are still strongly felt. The network has different routes organised by themes (Prehistory, Baroque, Medieval Churches, Chateaux, Natural and Scientific Heritage, Ethnic and Ethnological Heritage and Modern Art). Some of the routes are geared up for children and the price of the pass varies according to the sites. See *www. reseauculturel.fr.*

Carte Intersites Pays Cathare – This is a similar offer covering 16 sites of Cathar heritage: the châteaux of Lastours, Arques, Quéribus, Puilaurens, Termes, Villerouge-Termenès, Saissac, Peyrepertuse and Usson; the château Comtal de Carcassonne; the abbeys of Caunes-Minervois, Saint-Papoul, Saint-Hilaire, Lagrasse and Fontfroide; and the Musée du Quercorb in Puivert. It also gives free admission for one child. www.payscathare.org.

ELECTRICITY

The electric current is 220 volts. Circular two-pin plugs are the rule. Adapters and converters should be bought before you leave home. If you have a rechargeable device read the instructions carefully or contact the manufacturer or shop. You may need a voltage converter.

EMERGENCIES

EMERGENCY NUMBERS

Police: ℘17

SAMU (Paramedics): ℘15

Fire (Pompiers): ℘18

MONEY
CURRENCY

There are no restrictions on the amount of currency visitors can take into France. Visitors carrying a lot of cash are advised to complete a currency declaration form on arrival, because there are restrictions on currency export.

NOTES AND COINS

The **euro** is the only currency accepted as a means of payment in France. It is divided into 100 cents or centimes.

BANKS

For opening hours see section on business hours above. A passport is necessary as identification when cashing travellers cheques in banks. Commission charges vary and hotels usually charge more than banks for cashing cheques.

One of the most economical ways to use your money in France is by using **ATM machines** to get cash directly from your bank account either with a debit or credit card. Code pads are numeric; use a telephone pad to translate a letter code into numbers. Pin numbers have 4 digits in France; inquire with the issuing company or bank if the code you usually use is longer. Visa is the most widely accepted credit card.

Before you leave home, check with the bank that issued your card for **emergency replacement procedures**. Carry your card number and emergency phone numbers separately. You must report any loss or theft of credit cards or traveller's cheques to the French police, who will issue you with a certificate (useful proof to show the issuing company). **24-hour hotline numbers** are posted at most ATM machines.

TAXES

In France a sales tax (TVA or Value Added Tax from 5.5 per cent to 19.6 per cent) is added to almost all retail goods – it can be worth your while to recover it. VAT refunds are available to visitors from outside the EU only if purchases exceed 175 euros per store.

PUBLIC HOLIDAYS

Public services, museums and other monuments may be closed or may vary their hours of admission on public holidays:
National museums and art galleries are closed on Tuesdays; municipal museums are generally closed on Mondays. In addition to school holidays at Christmas and in spring and summer, there are long mid-term breaks in February and early November.

1 January	New Year's Day (Jour de l'An)
	Easter Day and Easter Monday (Pâques)
1 May	May Day (Fête du Travail)
8 May	VE Day (Fête de la Libération)
Thurs 40 days after Easter	Ascension Day (Ascension)
7th Sun–Mon after Easter	Whit Sunday and Monday (Pentecôte)
14 July	France's National Day (Fête de la Bastille)
15 August	Assumption (Assomption)
1 November	All Saint's Day (Toussaint)
11 November	Armistice Day (Fête de la Victoire)
25 December	Christmas Day (Noël)

SCHOOL HOLIDAYS

French schools close for vacations five times a year: one week at the end of October, two weeks at Christmas, two weeks in February, two weeks in Spring and the whole of July and August. In these periods, all tourist site and attractions, hotels, restaurants and roads are busier than usual.

SMOKING

Smoking is now banned in shopping malls, schools, offices and other public places, including restaurants, bars and cafés, if not on the terrace.

TIME

France is 1hr ahead of Greenwich Mean Time (GMT). France goes on daylight-saving time from the last Sunday in March to the last Sunday in October.

WHEN IT IS **NOON IN FRANCE**, IT IS	
3am	in Los Angeles
6am	in New York
11am	in Dublin
11am	in London
7pm	in Perth
9pm	in Sydney
11pm	in Auckland

In France 'am' and 'pm' are not used but the 24hr clock is widely applied.

TIPPING

Since a service charge is automatically included in the prices of meals and accommodation in France, it is not necessary to tip in restaurants and hotels. Restaurants usually charge for meals in two ways: a *menu* that is a fixed-price menu with 2 or 3 courses all for a stated price, or à la carte with each course ordered separately.
Cafés have very different prices, depending on where they are located. The price of a drink or a coffee is cheaper if you stand at the counter.

Useful Words and Phrases

Sights

	Translation
Abbaye	Abbey
Beffroi	Belfry
Chapelle	Chapel
Château	Castle
Cimetière	Cemetery
Cloître	Cloisters
Cour	Courtyard
Couvent	Convent
Écluse	Lock (Canal)
Église	Church
Fontaine	Fountain
Halle	Covered Market
Jardin	Garden
Mairie	Town Hall
Maison	House
Marché	Market
Monastère	Monastery
Moulin	Windmill
Musée	Museum
Parc	Park
Place	Square
Pont	Bridge
Port	Port/harbour
Porte	Gate/gateway
Quai	Quay
Remparts	Ramparts
Rue	Street
Statue	Statue
Tour	Tower

On The Road

	Translation
Car Park	Parking
Diesel	Gazole
Driving Licence	Permis de Conduire
East	Est
Garage	Garage
Left	Gauche
Highway	Autoroute
North	Nord
Parking Meter	Horodateur
Petrol/gas	Essence
Petrol/gas Station	Station Essence
Right	Droite
South	Sud
Toll	Péage
Traffic Lights	Feu Tricolore
Tyre	Pneu
Unleaded fuel	Sans Plomb
West	Ouest
Wheel Clamp	Sabot
Zebra Crossing	Passage Clouté

Time

	Translation
Today	Aujourd'hui
Tomorrow	Demain
Yesterday	Hier
Winter	Hiver
Spring	Printemps
Summer	Été
Autumn/fall	Automne
Week	Semaine
Monday	Lundi
Tuesday	Mardi
Wednesday	Mercredi
Thursday	Jeudi
Friday	Vendredi
Saturday	Samedi
Sunday	Dimanche

Numbers

	Translation
0	zéro
1	un
2	deux
3	trois
4	quatre
5	cinq
6	six
7	sept
8	huit
9	neuf
10	dix
11	onze
12	douze
13	treize
14	quatorze
15	quinze
16	seize
17	dix-sept
18	dix-huit
19	dix-neuf
20	vingt
30	trente
40	quarante
50	cinquante
60	soixante
70	soixante-dix
80	quatre-vingt
90	quatre-vingt-dix
100	cent
1000	mille

Food and Drink

	Translation
Beef	Bœuf
Beer	Bière
Bread	Pain
Breakfast	Petit-déjeuner
Butter	Beurre
Cheese	Fromage
Chicken	Poulet
Dessert	Dessert
Dinner	Dîner
Fish	Poisson
Fork	Fourchette
Fruit	Fruits
Glass	Verre
Ham	Jambon
Ice Cream	Glace
Ice Cubes	Glaçons
Knife	Couteau
Lamb	Agneau
Lettuce Salad	Salade
Lunch	Déjeuner
Meat	Viande
Mineral Water	Eau Minérale

Mixed Salad	Salade Composée
Orange Juice	Jus D'orange
Plate	Assiette
Pork	Porc
Red Wine	Vin Rouge
Restaurant	Restaurant
Salt	Sel
Spoon	Cuillère
Sugar	Sucre
Vegetables	Légumes
Water	De L'eau
White Wine	Vin Blanc
Yoghurt	Yaourt

Useful Phrases

	Translation
The bill, please	L'addition, s'il vous plaît
Goodbye	Au Revoir
Hello/good Morning	Bonjour
How	Comment
Excuse Me	Excusez-moi
Thank you	Merci
Yes/No	Oui/Non
I'm sorry	Pardon
Why?	Pourquoi?
When?	Quand?
Please	S'il Vous Plaît

MENU READER

La Càrte

The Menu

ENTRÉES
Crudités
Terrine de lapin
Frisée aux lardons
Escargots
Cuisses de grenouille
Salade au crottin

STARTERS
Raw vegetable salad
Rabbit terrine (pâté)
Curly lettuce with bacon bits
Snails
Frog's legs
Goat cheese on a bed of lettuce

PLATS (VIANDES)
Bavette à l'échalote
Faux filet au poivre
Côtes d'agneau
Filet mignon de porc
Blanquette de veau
Nos viandes sont garnies

MAIN COURSES (MEAT)
Flank steak with shallots
Sirloin with pepper sauce
Lamb chops
Pork fillet
Veal in cream sauce
Our meat dishes are served with vegetables

PLATS (POISSONS, VOILAILLE)
Filets de sole
Dorade aux herbes
Saumon grillé
Coq au vin
Poulet de Bresse rôti
Omelette aux morilles

MAIN COURSES (FISH, FOWL)
Sole fillets
Sea bream with herbs
Grilled salmon
Chicken in red wine sauce
Free-range roast chicken from the Bresse
Wild-mushroom omelette

PLATEAU DE FROMAGES

SELECTION OF CHEESES

DESSERTS
Tarte aux pommes
Crème caramel
Sorbet: trois parfums

DESSERTS
Sticky apple tart
Cooled baked custard with caramel sauce
Sorbet: choice of three flavours

BOISSONS
Bière
Eau minérale (gazeuse)
Une carafe d'eau
Vin rouge, vin blanc, rosé
Jus de fruit

BEVERAGES
Beer
(Sparkling) mineral water
Tap water (no charge)
Red wine, white wine, rosé
Fruit juice

MENU ENFANT
Jambon
Steak haché
Frites

CHILDREN'S MENU
Ham
Ground beef
French fried potatoes

Well-done, medium, rare, raw = bien cuit, à point, saignant, cru

Cherries from Céret

© Martine Wagner / Fotolia.com

CONVERSION TABLES

Weights and Measures

		⊠⊠	
1 kilogram (kg) 6.35 kilograms 0.45 kilograms	**2.2 pounds (lb)** 14 pounds 16 ounces (oz)	**2.2 pounds** 1 stone (st) 16 ounces	*To convert kilograms to pounds, multiply by 2.2*
1 metric ton (tn)	**1.1 tons**	**1.1 tons**	
1 litre (l) 3.79 litres 4.55 litres	**2.11 pints (pt)** 1 gallon (gal) 1.20 gallon	**1.76 pints** 0.83 gallon 1 gallon	*To convert litres to gallons, multiply by 0.26 (US) or 0.22 (UK)*
1 hectare (ha) **1 sq kilometre (km²)**	**2.47 acres** 0.38 sq. miles (sq mi)	**2.47 acres** 0.38 sq. miles	*To convert hectares to acres, multiply by 2.4*
1 centimetre (cm) **1 metre (m)** **1 kilometre (km)**	**0.39 inches (in)** 3.28 feet (ft) or 39.37 inches or 1.09 yards (yd) **0.62 miles (mi)**	**0.39 inches** **0.62 miles**	*To convert metres to feet, multiply by 3.28; for kilometres to miles, multiply by 0.6*

Clothing

Women	⊙	▤	⊠⊠
		35	4	2½
	36	5	3½
	37	6	4½
Shoes	38	7	5½
	39	8	6½
	40	9	7½
	41	10	8½
	36	6	8
	38	8	10
Dresses	40	10	12
& suits	42	12	14
	44	14	16
	46	16	18
	36	6	30
	38	8	32
Blouses &	40	10	34
sweaters	42	12	36
	44	14	38
	46	16	40

Men	⊙	▤	⊠⊠
	40	7½	7
	41	8½	8
	42	9½	9
Shoes	43	10½	10
	44	11½	11
	45	12½	12
	46	13½	13
	46	36	36
	48	38	38
Suits	50	40	40
	52	42	42
	54	44	44
	56	46	48
	37	14½	14½
	38	15	15
Shirts	39	15½	15½
	40	15¾	15¾
	41	16	16
	42	16½	16½

Sizes often vary depending on the designer. These equivalents are given for guidance only.

Speed

KPH	10	30	50	70	80	90	100	110	120	130
MPH	6	19	31	43	50	56	62	68	75	81

Temperature

Celsius (°C)	0°	5°	10°	15°	20°	25°	30°	40°	60°	80°	100°
Fahrenheit (°F)	32°	41°	50°	59°	68°	77°	86°	104°	140°	176°	212°

To convert Celsius into Fahrenheit, multiply °C by 9, divide by 5, and add 32.
To convert Fahrenheit into Celsius, subtract 32 from °F, multiply by 5, and divide by 9.
NB: Conversion factors on this page are approximate.

*Fortified village of Castelnou with Mont
Canigou in the background*
© Franz Waldhäusl / age fotostock

The Region Today

This sun-soaked corner of southwest France sits on the Spanish border and borrows much of its character from both countries.

People here remain very attached to their traditions and heritage, which are rich in Mediterranean flavours. Wine-making, fruit and vegetable growing, fishing, livestock farming and tourism are all the key elements of the local economy.

Taking advantage of the climate and natural resources, renewable energy is also playing an increasingly important role.

TRADITIONAL EVENTS

Whether religious or pagan in origin, the festivals of the region draw on ancient beliefs. To this day Catalonia remains resolutely Catholic.

PROCESSIONS AND CARNIVALS

Pénitents de la Sanch

On **Good Friday** in Perpignan a procession is held by the **Sanch**, the Brotherhood of the Holy Blood. The brotherhood was founded in the 15C by the Spanish Dominican friar St Vincent Ferrer, with the purpose of accompanying condemned criminals on their last journey.

The procession, which aims to bring the Passion of Christ to life, goes from the church of St-Jacques to the cathedral, singing *goigs* (hymns) and carrying *mistèris*, sculpted images of the Passion. Preceded by a *regidor* dressed in red, the lines of the **pénitents de la Sanch** in their black robes and tall pointed hoods (*caperutxas*) walk solemnly through the streets to the sound of drums.

Other processions take place on the same day in other Catalan towns, notably **Collioure** and Arles-sur-Tech.

Carnaval de Limoux

In the Aude, a straw dummy representing carnival was once paraded through the streets and then judged, often in Occitan (*see p61*), for being responsible for all the ills of the village. He was then hung or burned in the middle of a circle of singing people.

Today, carnival is especially celebrated in Limoux and without constraint; the festival takes up all of the weekends between January and Easter. The **fécos**, in Pierrot costumes, go slowly in parade holding a *carabena* (decorated wand). These are followed by the *godils*; men and women dressed as different characters. Limoux carnival ends with the Nuit de la Blanquette, during which the straw dummy is burned.

Solar furnace, Odeillo, with more than 9,000 mirrors on its parabolic surface
© Albrecht Weißer / image / imagebroker / age fotostock

Bear Festivals in the Vallespir

The Vallespir was once full of bears and festivals are still held in their honour in **Arles-sur-Tech**, **St-Laurent-de-Cerdans** and **Prats-de-Mollo**. That of **Arles-sur-Tech** takes place in February/March and again in summer. A man disguised as a bear is set loose, supposedly recently awakened from hibernation. A hunt is organised with a beautiful young girl as bait. Drawn by her charms, the bear lets himself be steered, to the sound of the **cobla** (band of musicians), to the village square, where he is subdued.

FEAST DAYS

Many villages celebrate the Feast day of their patron saint.

On the coast, the patron saint of fishermen, **St Peter**, is honoured on 29 June. A bust of the saint is carried through the town of **Gruissan**, preceded by a model boat on a pole and the fishermen's flag. After the mass, the procession goes to the harbour where the fishing boats are assembled. Bunches of flowers are thrown into the water in memory of sailors lost at sea.

Back on land, there is an abundance of harvest festivals, including the grape harvest. Saints' feast days follow one another from the beginning of August to the middle of October, each lasting up to a whole week. Some are followed by renewed celebrations, after a few days of rest, with the "**revivre**". During these celebrations, dances, activities, various games and bull running liven up the streets and squares.

BULLFIGHTING

The word *feria* originally referred to an agricultural fair, to which various festivities became attached, notably bullfighting. A tradition imported from nearby Spain, the **feria** in Carcassonne draws thousands of visitors. It lasts for three days at the end of August.

LAND OF THE OVAL BALL

This sport rapidly gained popularity among Catalans and Occitans following its invention in England in 1823. Their love of fraternity, amusement and "rough and tumble" are freely expressed in this *"ruffian's game played by gentlemen"*.

The most popular variant is 15-a-side rugby union (known as **rugby à XV**), in which passing the ball forwards leads to a "scrum" when the players huddle tightly together. Among the most successful regional teams is the Union sportive Arlequins Perpignan-Roussillon (USAP), which plays at the highest level. The Racing-Club Narbonne-Méditerranée (RCNM) and the Union Sportive Carcassonnaise (USC) also fill stadiums and have loyal supporters.

In rugby league (**rugby à XIII** or **jeu à XIII**), there are just 13 players and the scrum is formed when the ball goes out of play. The teams of Carcassonne, Perpignan (XIII Catalan), Pia, Lézignan and Limoux are the elite of this "heretic rugby", also known as the "sport of the Cathars".

The fervour for the oval ball is fed by the weekly newspaper *Midi Olympique,* traditionally printed on yellow paper.

THE SARDANA, EMBLEMATIC DANCE

Symbol of fraternity, the **sardana** is an affirmation of Catalan identity. Derived from an earlier dance, the *contrepàs*, it was codified in the 19C by a musician from Figueras, **Pep Ventura**, and an instrument maker of Perpignan named Turron.

The sardana is danced to the music of a **cobla**, a group of eleven instruments (*flabiol-tambori*, *tibles*, *tenores*, *fiscorns*, trumpet, trombone and three-stringed double bass), which is capable of expressing the softest moods, as well as the most passionate. The dance subtly alternates eight measures of short steps and sixteen long ones. It is danced in teams, or *colles*. In a competition of a festival (**Céret**, **Argelès**), the sardana is danced with the arms raised and as a finale the participants form concentric circles to perform a "sardana of friendship". You'll probably get a chance to experience its subtleties yourself if you join the dancers in the square of a Catalan village on a Sunday morning.

CASTELLS, HUMAN CASTLES

Another distinctive Catalan tradition is the building of human towers by teams of *castellers*, who stand on each other's shoulders to reach several storeys high. The **castell** is crowned by a child perched on the summit, the whole thing symbolising co-operation between the generations. Competitions between clubs of castellers increased after the Olympic Games in Barcelona popularised this activity, which was traditionally practised south of the Catalan capital.

FOOD AND DRINK

Drawing on both land and sea, the region's cuisine is much influenced by the warmth of the Mediterranean sun. Rich and varied, it differs between the coast and inland. A lot of vegetables (aubergines, tomatoes, courgettes, peppers…) and fruit (cherries, peaches, pears, melons) are grown here, all swollen by the light and heat of the sun.

THE CUISINE OF THE COAST AND INLAND

On the **coast**, there is an abundance of fish and seafood: daurade, grouper, sea bass, conger eel – grilled à la *plantxa*; fish soup; oysters (Etang de Leucate); sardines (Port-Barcarès, Saint-Cyprien); anchovies (Collioure); prawns (Banyuls-sur-Mer), cuttlefish à la rouille or in macaronade…

Inland, whether on the plain or in the mountains, there is a robust traditional cuisine. The **Cerdagne** and **Capcir** are known for their **charcuterie** (sausages, ham) and their mountain **cheeses**, most often made with goat's milk, and for their perfumed **honey**.

The Aude's signature dish is **cassoulet**, which used to be made in a *cassole*, a pottery dish made with clay from Issel. Beans, goose fat, garlic and pork rind are cooked with either breast of lamb and pork in Castelnaudary, or leg of lamb and braised partridge in **Carcassonne**.

CATALAN CUISINE

Savoury

Mediterranean in influence, Catalan cuisine is a marvellous combination of **olive oil**, **garlic**, **aromatic herbs** and *sagi*, lightly rancid lard that gives a unique taste to dishes.

Sauces are very important. They include *picada* (almonds, toasted bread, olive oil and red wine), *romesco* (tomatoes, peppers, grilled almonds, fried bread, olive oil) and **aïoli**, made with olives and garlic. Vegetables and starchy foods, short-grained rice, haricots beans and broad beans are served with fish and meat.

Other delicious dishes are **bouillinade**, a local bouillabaisse made with fish and potato stock; **anchoïade** (based on anchovies), a speciality of **Collioure**; **prawn stew** in **Banyuls**; *ollada* (soup of pork, cabbage, potatoes, haricot beans and *sagi*); *boles de picolat* (meat dumplings); and **partridge**.

At Easter and Pentecost people get together to eat **cargolade of snails** accompanied by aïoli and grilled sausages, lamb chops and *botifares* (boudins, black sausages), all washed down with a red wine served by the carafe or in a **borratxa** (leather drinking bottle).

Sweet

To finish your meal with something sweet you also have an ample choice: an abundance of **fresh fruit** ripened in the Roussillon sun, **crema catalana**, **bunyetes** (fried flatcakes) flavoured with orange blossom, **almond rousquilles** from **Amélie-les-Bains** (shortbread biscuit in the form of a ring), *pessigoles de xocolata* (chocolate meringues), **alléluias de Castelnaudary** (small cakes with candied fruit), **marrons glacés** from **Carcassonne**, and last but not least **tourons**.

WINES

Viticulture is an ancestral tradition in the region. From Narbonne to the Minervois and from Collioure to Rivesaltes, the sunny hillsides are famous for their vineyards. The grape varieties grown, often prestigious and very old, give the various wines their subtle flavours and nuances. The appellation régionale **coteaux-du-languedoc** brings together the appelation d'origine contrôlée (AOC) of Languedoc and a small part of Roussillon.

Minervois

The highly rated **Minervois vineyards** extend from the slopes of the Montagne Noire to the Aude and produce wines of exceptional variety. Wines include fruity cherry-red **Mourels** and **Serres** and fine whites that are long on the palate, with flavours of honey and limeflower. Supple reds with a spicy accent and fresh whites are made in **Balcons de l'Aude**.

Corbières

The vineyards of the **Corbières** (AOC) hug the contours of the hills. Wines from the Montagne de l'Alaric are delicate and flowery; those made between Berre and the Barrou are spicy; and along the Orbieu they are rounded and alluring. Several charming grape varieties are grown in this region: Carignan, Syrah, Grenache Noir and Cinsault for reds; Mourvèdre for rosés; Grenache, Bourboulenc, Marsanne, Roussanne, Vermentino and Maccabéo for whites.

Fitou

Fitou (**AOC**), between Narbonne and Perpignan, is divided into two zones: the vineyards of the Hautes Corbières, at the foot of Mount Tauch, and those of the coast, above the Etang de Leucate.

Blanquette de Limoux

The famous **Blanquette de Limoux** (AOC) is thought to be the oldest sparkling wine in the world. The first recorded mention of it comes from 1531 when the monks of St-Hilaire abbey made it in glass flasks. The selected grape varieties (Mauzac, Chenin and Chardonnay) give it a fresh and distinguished fizz, as in **crémant** (AOC). Both go well with Limoux's pepper biscuit and nougat.

Cabardès and Malepère

These two appellations, located near Carcassonne, are perfect accompaniments to game and red meats.

Clape and Quatourze

East of Narbonne, these two wine regions produce very elegant whites and reds that are both powerful and full of flavour.

Roussillon

The burgeoning vineyards of Roussillon produce a large range of wines including whites with a sparkle of green, pale rosés and garnet-tinted reds that come from the Agly, the Glacis des Aspres and the Côte Vermeille.

Collioure is the best known of the region's AOCs. **Côtes-du-Roussillon** contribute dark, full-bodied reds perfumed with mature fruits and spices. Over 30 communes are classed under the denomination **Côtes-du-Roussillon-Villages** for their robust red wines.

Fortified wines

Sweet fortified wines (*vins doux naturels*) are typical of the Mediterranean. Alcohol is added to the must (grape juice), while it is fermenting, to maintain the desired quantity of sugar in the wine. A distinction is made between muscats, made from Muscat of Alexandria or Muscat *à petits grains grapes* and wines made with other grape varieties such as Grenache, Maccabéo, Carignan and Malvoisie.

Muscat de **Rivesaltes**, drunk chilled while still young, has a beautiful golden colour and develops aromas of citrus fruit and honey.

Amber or garnet in colour, the other wines are darker due to the oxidation that takes place while they are being matured in oak barrels or glass demijohns exposed to the sun (as in the *paillé* wine of Banyuls). **Banyuls**, **Rivesaltes** and **Maury** go perfectly with chocolate desserts and blue cheeses. **Byrrh** is an aperitif derived from wine and fortified wine: its name is a composite of *bi* ('wine' in Catalan) and **Thuir**, the town where it is made. In the same town Ambassadeur, Dubonnet and Cinzano, an Italian speciality, are made.

ECONOMY

As the climate of the region is so favourable to agriculture, cultivation is omnipresent on the plains and on medium-high slopes up to 600m/2,000ft. Grapes are the most common crop, followed by fruit and vegetables. Livestock farming also plays an important role. There is little by way of industry in the region; in contrast, tourism is a key element in the economy.

VITICULTURE

Despite difficult conditions, wine growing remains dominant: vines cover 40 per cent of the land available for farming. Competition from New World wines, a decline in national consumption and a slump in prices have all made things difficult for wine makers. The Languedoc wine industry has been suffering for decades. Over thirty years, restructuring has led a loss of more than a third of vineyards.

In parallel to a policy of reducing the planted area, the wine-producers of Roussillon, along with those of the Languedoc, have decided over the last few years to improve **quality** by replacing mediocre grape varieties with Cabernet, Merlot and Chardonnay. This **policy of improvement** has produced encouraging results.

Another significant change to the wine industry is its response to **environmental constraints**. The reduction of chemical fertilisers and pesticides has become a priority for grape growers. This has encouraged them to carry out better initial soil analyses and use organic farming techniques to protect their vines. Inter-planting between rows of vines, which among other things helps prevent pesticide run-off, is increasingly common in the region. Don't be surprised to see vineyards with green paths running between the vines.

AGRICULTURAL RESOURCES

Influenced by the Mediterranean climate, the region is divided into three broad zones: coast, plains and mountains. The agricultural area along the coast and on the plains is mainly dedicated to market gardens and fruit orchards, whereas higher up the land is more suitable for livestock grazing. Mediterranean produce (wine, fruit and vegetables) and livestock and farm produce from the Pyrénées vary in quality.

Fruit and vegetables

The fruit and vegetable sector is the second most important agricultural sector in Roussillon. **Nectarines** are the vanguard product (the department of Pyrénées-Orientales is the leading producer in France), while **cherries** are abundant in Céret, **apricots** are grown in Salanque and in the valley of the Têt.

The region also grows a large quantity of **apples** and **pears**.
Pyrénées-Orientales is one of the leading areas for market garden produce in France. The main areas of production are concentrated around Perpignan and along the coast between Salanque and Argelès. **Lettuces**, **artichokes**, **asparagus**, **tomatoes** and **potatoes** are among the main vegetables cultivated. **Europe's largest fruit and vegetable distribution centre** is located at Perpignan. The centre manages the fluctuations in supply from the region and other centres of production, chiefly Spain and the Maghreb countries (Morocco). It is a veritable **business hub** being the biggest employer in the département (600 companies and almost 9,000 jobs).

Extensive livestock grazing

Livestock grazing is ubiquitous in the Catalan Pyrénées, following a seasonal transhumance pattern that favours high-quality products and also helps to preserve landscapes. Calves and heifers, reared in liberty and fed on their mother's milk, are slaughtered between five and eight months to yield a much-prized meat classed as *rosée des Pyrénées*. Other products linked to extensive livestock farming are Cerdagne-Capcir beef, Catalan lamb and farmhouse cheeses, essentially goat's milk cheese.

FOOD INDUSTRY

At the intersection between industry and agriculture, the food industry has become a key component of the regional economy. Some large companies have chosen this part of France to install their factories. Companies that stand out for their products include Cémoi-Cantalou, a manufacturer of chocolates and chocolate-based sweets, which has a factory near Perpignan. **Spanghero**, founded by a renowned rugby player who played for RC Narbonne and France, specialises in dishes cooked in the Aude, while La Belle Chaurienne is a cassoulet specialist in Castelnaudary.

FRUITS OF THE SEA

Between Leucate and the Cap Cerbère, the Aude and Pyrénées-Orientales have 110km/70mi of coastline, 70km/45mi of sandy beach and 40km/24mi of rocky shore punctuated by seven fishing ports.

Trawling

Trawling is centred on **Port-la-Nouvelle** and **Port-Vendres**. The **trawlers** catch sardines, mackerel and anchovies ("blue fish"), using large encircling purse nets. However, the fishing industry has found it hard to survive and the number of trawlers on the Gulf of Lion has been reduced by increases in the price of diesel and the diminishing size of the fish. At Port-la-Nouvelle, for example, the tonnage of blue fish declined from 2,600 to 400 between 2008 and 2011 and at Port-Vendres, from 1,200 to 700. The fleet of **tuna boats** also faces problems caused by over-fishing of red tuna and the consequent imposition of quotas, which could end in a ban on fishing this species altogether.

Traditional fishing

Small fishing boats are generally less than 12m/40 ft and are equipped with gill nets, trammels and longlines. Traditional fishing methods are practised at sea and in the lagoons, where clams, sea bass, eels, sole, whiting and grey mullet are found. Catches are estimated at 5,000 tonnes per year for the entire region of Languedoc-Roussillon. Even so, the number of boats has halved in twenty years due to the scarcity of resources.
Shellfish gathering is done standing up and raking the shellfish from the sandy bottom with a special net. This activity provides a livelihood for dozens of families.
Lampara fishing, undertaken at night to lure blue fish towards the light, is no longer widespread. A few Catalan boats are still to be seen in the small harbours of the Côte Vermeille. The former brownfield **Site des Paulilles**, south of Port-Vendres, has returned to its natural beauty and now has a workshop where these fishing boats are restored.

Shellfish cultivation

Farms for raising oysters, mussels and other shellfish have reshaped the coastal lagoons. **Oyster farming** is carried out in the Etang de **Leucate** (30ha/74 acres) and Etang de **L'Ayrolle** (25ha/62 acres) where the absence of tides necessitates a system of suspension, using tables planted in the sediment of the lagoons. Particularly sensitive, these wetlands are subject to constant health and safety checks. Producers are therefore looking towards the open sea, which offers new possibilities. The farming of **mussels**, notably, is carried out around Gruissan and Fleury in the Aude.

Fish farming

Aquaculture has developed enormously over the last decade in response to the decline in natural fish stocks. **Sea bass**, **daurade** and **prawns** are the most common products of these farms, which are located near the edges of the lagoons. The sea offers new opportunities for fish farming, but also provokes opposition. In one such case a proposed tuna farm was to be sited near the Cerbère-Banyuls marine nature reserve. The project was abandoned after campaigners pointed out the pollution risks it entailed.

Working Ports

The two principal commercial ports, **Port-la-Nouvelle** and **Port-Vendres**, handle several million tonnes of cargo each year. **Port-Vendres** specialises in the import of fruits, while the traffic into and out of **Port-la-Nouvelle** is mainly concerned with fuel oil and cereals.

TRADITIONAL CRAFTS

Most trades are now connected to the building industry and the service sector, but some traditional crafts endure. Some specialised arts and crafts businesses in the region keep ancestral know-how alive. Such is the case of the textiles of the **Haut Vallespir**, cotton or linen cloth in bands of colours which are mainly used in the manufacture of the *espardinya* or **espadrille**. The last factory making these shoes in the traditional way is located in **St-Laurent-de-Cerdans**. Elsewhere, craftsmen attempt to adapt old traditions to modern tastes. This is especially the case in Perpignan where it is the tradition in each family to have a piece of **garnet jewellery**. Even if the stones themselves don't come from the mines of Pyrénées-Orientales, local jewellers still use them to make contemporary-style pieces.

TOURISM

With 15 million visitors a year – a third of them from abroad – tourism is of great local importance. Indeed tourism is indispensable to the Languedoc-Roussillon, the fourth most popular French tourist destination after Paris/Île-de-France, Provence and the Côte d'Azur, and Rhône-Alpes.

Tourism is especially important to the economy of Roussillon (French Catalonia) and the Aude (Cathar Country). On the coast, the Côte Vermeille, made famous by painters of the early 20C, attracts many visitors. To the north, the "new" resorts built in the 1960s (Port-Leucate, Port-Barcarès, Canet, St-Cyprien), draw summer holidaymakers. In the **mountains**, the valleys are also brought alive by visitors. The development of winter sports and spas bring income to health resorts and other towns inland. Such is the case for the Cerdagne and the Capcir, favourite destinations for nature lovers, ski-enthusiasts and hikers, but also for people interested in Romanesque churches, and in the Vallespir thanks to its spa Amélie-les-Bains.

As to the department of the Aude, it has astutely marketed its attractions under the brand "Pays Cathare", the charge being led by the vast Cathar stronghold of Carcassonne.

RENEWABLE ENERGY

Copious quantities of sunshine, steady winds and hot water springs have given rise to a fast developing renewable energy industry in Languedoc-Roussillon. A pioneer in "clean" energies, the **Cerdagne**, one of the sunniest corners of France, began experimenting in this field in 1953 with its first solar furnace at

Mont-Louis. A second one was built ten years later at **Odeillo**, which has become a reference-point for the world. In 1983, the **Thémis solar power station** came on-line, supplying the national power grid. The last oil crisis in 2008 has given impetus to projects for **photo-voltaic power stations** in the region, near to Narbonne and at Torreilles, for example. Today, more and more building projects, both public and private, include a component for the generation of solar power. The buildings of the Pôle Economique de Saint-Charles, a fruit and vegetable distribution centre outside Perpignan, has the largest photovoltaic roof in the world. **Windfarms** are also numerous in the region.

🔊 The wind farm at **Port-la-Nouvelle**, is easily accessible, making it possible to get close to the turbines.

CHALLENGES OF AN ATTRACTIVE REGION

Experiencing a sharp increase in population, the region must face up to the challenge of receiving new residents and the management of its natural areas. These challenges have encouraged a number of environmental initiatives.

INCREASE IN POPULATION AND EMPLOYMENT

The population increase in Languedoc-Roussillon has in recent years been twice the national average, thanks to a net gain in population (the difference between the number of immigrants and emigrants). With 25,000 more inhabitants per year (people retiring as well as working people attracted by the quality of life), this is the fastest growing region in France.

According to a forecast by INSEE (the National Institute for Statistics), assuming that recent tendencies continue, by 2030 the number of inhabitants will increase by one per cent per year in Pyrénées-Orientales and by 0.9 per cent in the Aude, which represents a demographic growth just below the regional average for Languedoc-Roussillon.

Unequal distribution

The majority of inhabitants are concentrated on the coast, especially close to the urban centres of Perpignan and Narbonne, whereas inland areas are comparatively less populous. The transfer of people from the mountain to the coast during the 20C has left small valleys as backwaters and isolated hamlets as the first victims of depopulation. In out-of-the-way areas communications can be difficult and mountain passes are often blocked by snow in winter.

High unemployment

The region has an unemployment rate above the national average, around 13 per cent in Pyrénées-Orientales and the Aude.

ENVIRONMENTAL CHALLENGES

The counterpart of demographic growth is that natural areas are threatened by an increase in rubbish produced and car journeys driven; intensified demands for water and the transformation of villages into dormitory settlements through building of housing estates. Only better planning controls can reverse these tendencies. Grants and loans are available for the protection of the environment.

Protection of the *littoral*

Contemporary development is destabilising the ecosystems of the coast, reducing biodiversity and altering the water cycle. Building pressure has reduced the capacity of the lagoons to act as reservoirs that prevent floods in built up areas. The sheer number of tourists, as well as the maintenance of beaches in summer, threatens the ecosystems of the sand dunes, which provide a habitat for many rare creatures. Plans for sustainable development include a programme for dealing with the erosion of beaches. Work is being carried out at the Site des Coussoules and the étang du Canet with the aim of their protection.

History

The region has been inhabited by humans since prehistoric times, as demonstrated by Tautavel Man, the oldest hominid ever found in Europe. After a brilliant period of prosperity, the Pax Romana, and an aftermath interrupted by barbarian invasion, in the 12C the Languedoc was convulsed with violence. This was the bloody military campaign against adepts of the Cathar religion, also known as the Albigensian Crusade. Later the region endured multiple struggles between France and Spain for the possession of Catalonia, as well as the Wars of Religion. These conflicts have nurtured an acute sense of freedom and a mistrust of centralised power.

A MELTING POT OF CIVILISATIONS

At first inhabited by hunters, later by herdsmen and farmers, this region between the sea and mountains has always been open to trade with the wider world: first it had contact with Phoenician cities then the Roman empire, which brought a unity and stability that evolved into the feudal arrangements of the Middle Ages.

PREHISTORIC PEOPLE

Two excavations, in 1971 and 1979, in the **Caune de l'Arago**, about 30km/18mi northwest of Perpignan, unearthed the cranium of the famous **Tautavel Man**. He lived in the Lower Palaeolithic era, around 450,000 years ago. This *Homo erectus* was 1.65m/5ft 5in tall. He had a flat receding forehead, high cheekbones and rectangular eye sockets, was a hunter and ate his meat raw. Some of the tools he used have been discovered, notably scrapers.

Some 440,000 years later, at the start of the Neolithic, another prehistoric population left behind remains of their existence in the rock shelter of

Font-Juvénal, between the Aude and the Montagne Noire. They were an agricultural and herding people living in sophisticated dwellings (cooking hearths, posts, slab floor and silos). They preferred to live on slopes of medium altitude as witnessed by arms (arrows, axes and knives), jewellery (necklaces and bracelets) and pottery (bowls and vases) that have been found.

There are many **megaliths** in the Aude and Pyrénées-Orientales, dating from the middle-to-late Neolithic. Three quarters of the **dolmens** are situated at altitudes of between 600 and 1,000m (1,970–3,280ft). Originally they were covered by earth tumuli, or piles of stones, and served as tombs. The largest dolmens, built in areas with stable populations, contained the remains of hundreds of people. In the higher pastures they are smaller and were replaced later by **cists**, stone boxes which contained the remains of individual herdsmen.

RISE AND FALL OF GALLIA NARBONENSIS

When the Romans arrived in the region they found a land already influenced by the Celts (the **Volques Tectosages** tribe), Greeks (at Port-Vendres and Collioure) and the Carthaginians – Hannibal's army had passed through the Pyrénées and Roussillon in 214BC. In 122BC, the Roman general **Domitius Ahenobarbus** pushed the Arverni tribe back to the Massif Central, defeated the Volques and created Transalpine Gaul, a province taking in Marseille, Narbonne (Narbo), Toulouse (Tolosa) and stretching up the Rhone valley to Vienne and Geneva. Reorganised in 27 BC, after **Caesar**'s conquest of Gaul (5-51), it became Gallia Narbonensis.

First to make conquest easier, then with the aim of facilitating trade, the Romans build numerous roads. The two main roads in this region were the **Via Domitia** – from the Rhône to Tarragona in Spain via Narbonne and the oppidum of Ruscino (now Chateau-Roussillon near Perpignan) – and the Aquitaine

Important Dates

- **450,000 BC**: Tautavel man lives near Perpignan.
- **122 BC**: Foundation of Transalpine Gaul, which becomes Gallia Narbonensis.
- **878**: Foundation of the county of Barcelona by **Wilfred the Hairy**.
- **1140–1200**: Spread of the Cathar heresy.
- **1209**: Start of the first crusade against the **Cathars**.
- **1213**: Death of king Peter (Pere) of Aragon at the battle of Muret.
- **1250–1320**: The Inquisition eradicates the last vestiges of Catharism.
- **1276**: Perpignan becomes the capital of the kingdom of Mallorca, provisionally attached to Aragon and also composed of the Cerdagne (Cerdanya), Roussillon and Montpellier.
- **1344**: Disappearance of the kingdom of Mallorca. Roussillon and Cerdagne are integrated into the principality of Catalonia, an autonomous entity under the kingdom of Aragon.
- **1539**: The Edict of **Villers-Cotterêts** makes French the only legal language in the kingdom. Occitan can only be spoken by the people.
- **1659**: Under the Treaty of the **Pyrénées**, Roussillon and the Cerdagne are attached to the kingdom of France. Perpignan becomes definitively French.
- **1666–1680**: Construction of the canal du Midi.
- **1685**: Revocation of the Edict of Nantes.
- **1790**: Creation of the department of Roussillon, which soon takes the name of Pyrénées-Orientales.
- **1871**: Revolutionary movements during the Commune de Narbonne.
- **1907**: A crisis in the wine industry unleashes the revolt of the *gueux*.
- **1940–1944**: Vichy regime. French Resistance active in the Pyrénées.
- **1963**: Plan for the development of the Mediterranean coast, which creates resort-spas in Languedoc-Roussillon.
- **1970**: Inauguration of the Solar Furnace at Odeillo (Font-Romeu) in the Cerdagne.
- **1996**: Opening of the Paris-Perpignan TGV rail line.
- **1996–1997**: The **Canal du Midi** and after it the Cité of Carcassonne, are classed as World Heritage Sites by UNESCO.
- **2013**: Opening of the TGV line between Perpignan and Barcelona (1hr).

way, which linked Narbonne to Toulouse and Bordeaux. Gallia Narbonensis rapidly integrated into the Roman world, adopting its administration, its lifestyle and its culture. A long period of prosperity began, know as the **Pax Romana**. The province was divided into *pagi* (which would become counties in the middle ages). Each *pagus* had its administrative *civitae* (Narbonne, Carcassonne, Castelnaudary), its *vici* or rural centres (Eburomagnus which became Bram) and its *villae* or agricultural estates. Rome gave the people of Gaul its law and the Latin language, both of which would shape France several centuries later.

BARBARIAN INVASIONS

Between the 3C and 5C, successive invasions of **Alemanni**, Vandals and Visigoths brought to an end the Roman presence in the region.

Pushed back by **Clovis** in 507, the **Visigoths** established themselves in **Septimanie** (Carcassonne, Narbonne, Béziers, Agde, Nîmes, Maguelone, Elne). But the Visigoth kingdom faced a threat from the south: the **Saracens** (or Moors) who, having overrun Spain, took Narbonne in 719. They were driven out some forty years later by the Franks led by **Pepin the Short**.

COUNTS OF BARCELONA

The reconquest of Catalonia by the Christians was followed by the installation of a dynasty of local overlords under **Wilfred the Hairy**. In 878 he carved out a fief for himself that included Barcelona and Girona, the Capcir, Conflent, Fenouillèdes and Roussillon. The counts of Barcelona became kings of Aragon in 1137 and went on to extend their power over Provence, Valencia, Sicily, Montpellier and the Gévaudan (1204–1349).

THE CATHAR ERA

In the 12C and 13C, the success of a heresy, Catharism, brought disaster to the county of Toulouse. The crusade against the Cathars (or Albigensians) unleashed unimaginable political consequences, beginning with the political attachment to the French crown of what seemed like an incipient rival to its power. The violence of the crusade traumatised the people of the Languedoc and undoubtedly contributed to their mistrust of all things emanating from centralised power.

THE CATHAR HERESY

Brought from the orient (in particular Bulgaria, its adepts sometimes being known as *Boulgres*), Catharism derives its name from the Greek katharos ("pure"). Nicetas, bishop of Constantinople founded "radical dualism" in 1167 at the council of St-Félix-Lauragais. Growing out of Catholicism but denying the divinity of Christ, Catharism distinguished between a spiritual world of light and beauty and the material world in which Satan had imprisoned man. In addition, the Cathars refused the traditional rites (baptism and marriage), thus attracting the wrath of the clergy. The only sacrament administered was the **consolamentum**, performed for the ordination of a 'perfect 'or as a blessing given to a believer at the moment of his death.

Perfects and believers

The Cathar church was governed by four bishops (those of Albi – from which derives the name of Albigensians – Toulouse, Carcassonne and Agen). But it was the **perfects** or **bonshommes** who spread the belief to the ordinary Cathar **faithful**. The perfects lived lives of austerity to free themselves of the grip of evil and attain divine purity. The heresy was at first successful in towns amongst artisans and merchants. It then spread through the countryside under the protection of the seigneurs Raymond-Roger Trencavel, viscount of Béziers and of Carcassonne, and Ray-

Death of Simon de Montfort who fought against the Albigensans in the early 13C

©DEA / G DAGLI ORTI / De Agostini Editore / age fotostock

Historical Figures

People who played a key role in history, in order of appearance:

Wilfred the Hairy (c840–897) – Considered the founder of Catalonia for uniting Barcelona, Girona, the Capcir, the Conflent, the Fenouillèdes and Roussillon in the late 9C.

Raymond-Roger Trencavel (1185–1209) – Count of Carcassonne who led the resistance to the invasion of Simon de Montfort. Imprisoned after the fall of the city, he died in prison – murdered, some people allege.

Raymond VI (died 1222) – Count of Toulouse in 1195, the unhappy hero of the Albigensian crusade.

Guillaume Bélibaste (died 1321) – The last Cathar, burnt at the stake in Villarouge-Termenès (Aude).

Pierre Paul Riquet (1604–1680) – Designer of the Canal du Midi.
See Canal du Midi p83 and Montagne Noire, p109.

François Arago (1786–1853) – Polymath and politician.

---

mond-Roger, count of Foix. Meanwhile, the count of Toulouse, **Raymond VI**, turned a blind eye.

WAR AND REPRESSION

The Catholic church sought to reimpose its authority by preaching to Cathar believers through **Saint Dominic** and by trying to persuade Raymond VI to stop protecting heretics. But its efforts were in vain. In March 1208, the assassination near St-Gilles of Pierre de Castelnau, legate from Pope Innocent III to the county of Toulouse, unleashed the crusade. This was orchestrated by the "northern barons", led by **Simon de Montfort** and **Gui de Lévis**. To general surprise, **Raymond VI** took the cross. This was a shrewd decision since by joining the crusade he avoided having his lands confiscated and given to the crusaders.

The campaign against the Cathars was punctuated by atrocities: the inhabitants of Beziers were massacred and **Carcassonne** fell in 1209. **Trencavel**, who lacked the prudence of his suzerain, died in prison. The crusaders captured the fortified towns of Minerve, Termes, Puivert (1210) and Lastours (1211). **Raymond VI** appealed to his brother-in-law the king of Aragon, **Peter (Pere) II** who gave assistance but was killed in

the battle of Muret (1213). **Simon de Montfort**, meanwhile, had taken control of the county of Toulouse but he was killed in his turn while besieging the city (1218).

FROM COUNTS OF MONTFORT TO THE KINGDOM OF FRANCE

Succeeding his father in 1222, **Raymond VII** set about the reconquest of his lost territories, which had passed to Amaury de Montfort, son of Simon. Overwhelmed by the task of defending his lands , Amaury passed his rights over them to the king of France in 1224.

The fight now changed character. **Louis VIII** led the next campaign in person: this was the north against the south, the kingdom of France against the Occitan counties. The **Treaty of Meaux** (1229) concluded a continuation of the "holy war" which is known as the Second Albigensian Crusade. Raymond VII was forced by Louis IX (known in France as **Saint Louis**) to sign the Treaty of Lorris (1243), by which his only daughter, Jeanne, was married to the king's brother, Alphonse de Poitiers. This union was without offspring and resulted in the eventual annexation of the possessions of the count of Toulouse.

The last Cathar strongholds were overcome one by one. After four inquisitors were murdered at Avignonet in 1244, an army of crusaders laid siege to the stronghold of **Montségur** which ended with the burning alive of 225 unrepentant Cathars (◐ *see p131*). The war only ended with the fall of another formidable castle, Quéribus, in 1255. In 1258 the **Treaty of Corbeil** was signed between the kings of France and Aragon delineating their respective dominions. The castles guarding the frontier on the French side – Peyrepertuse, Puilaurens, **Termes**, **Aguilar** and **Quéribus** – formed a formidable barrier and became known as the Five Sons of Carcassonne.

The end of military operations did not mean a return to peace for the people of the Languedoc. Now came the time of repression.

The Inquisition got to work with its investigations, questions and condemnations all of which exacerbated the deep wound in the region's psyche. The era of persecution only came to an end in 1321 when **Guillaume Bélibaste**, the last known Cathar perfect, was burned at the stake in Villerouge-Termenès.

14–18TH CENTURY

War, recurring Spanish skirmishes, famine and epidemics characterise the changing times of the 14–15C in the Pyrénées and the Languedoc. The Franco-Spanish struggle erupted again at the end of the 18C.

THE FATE OF CATALONIA

Attached to the Aragonese crown in 1137, an integral part of the kingdom of Mallorca founded by **James I of Aragon**, with its capital established at Perpignan, Roussillon and Cerdagne were seized briefly by the French crown between 1462 and 1492. But in 1493, Charles VIII, principally interested in Italy, restored these two counties to the kingdom of Spain. During the reign of the kings of Mallorca and Aragon, "Catalan" Perpignan enjoyed its golden age: the Palais des Rois de Majorque date from this period.

Only by the Treaty of the Pyrénées (1659) were the Catalan provinces (Roussillon, the Vallespir, the Conflent and half of the Cerdagne) definitely joined to France.

WARS OF RELIGION

Protestantism became established in the Languedoc and the region was plunged into more trouble in 1559 when war broke out between Protestants and Catholics. The **Edict of Nantes** returned peace in 1598, even if the tensions resurfaced after the death of Henri IV. The **Peace of Alès** (1629) guaranteed a time of freedom of conscience for Protestants. It was only a short-lived truce, however, because Louis XIV "favoured" for the Catholic cause, increasing persecutions before revoking the Edict of Nantes in 1685. Economic difficulties exacerbated the situation and the conflict defined the political landscape for more than two centuries. The persecutions didn't come to an end until 1787, with the signature of the Edict of Tolerance by Louis XVI.

From an economic point of view, the region was given a major boost at the end of the 17C by the building of the **Canal du Midi** (a canal joining "the two seas" of the Atlantic and Mediterranean) by **Pierre-Paul Riquet** between 1666 and 1680.

In 1790, the Languedoc was divided into départements. The province of Roussillon and the Fenouillèdes became Pyrénées-Orientales, while the area around Carcassonne became the Aude, named after its principal river.

A new Franco-Spanish war broke out between 1793 and 1795, when Spain tried, unsuccessfully, to retake Roussillon and the Cerdagne.

THE MODERN WORLD

Roussillon and the Aude are still rooted in agriculture, the cultivation of the vine in particular, but they have been transformed by the development of tourism.

THE REVOLT OF THE *GUEUX* IN 1907

The local wine industry has been hit by two episodes of vine disease. First phylloxera (1868–1872) ruined many grape growers. This was followed by the discovery of another plague, mildew, a fungus that rots vines. In addition, the beginning of the 20C brought economic difficulties to the wine industry. The grafting of American plants, resistant to phylloxera, led to an overproduction of wines of poor quality and encouraged the practice of chaptalisation (the addition of sugar). Severe competition from wines from Algeria and other imports led to a fall in prices.

The region, which had already proved its capacity for resistance (opposition to the coup d'État de **Napoléon III** in December 1851, Commune de Narbonne in 1870–1871), did not react to the crisis in the wine industry with passivity. In 1907 protests grew and demonstrations were held in the main towns of the Languedoc called by *Tocsin*, a newspaper run by a cafe owner from Argeliers (Aude), **Marcellin Albert**. The forthright mayor of Narbonne, **Ernest Ferroul**, along with more than 600 other mayors of the region, resigned. He took the side of the disaffected wine growers against the government and became leader of the protesters who called themselves the *gueux*.

The crisis deepened when a million people assembled in Montpellier. The government ordered the arrest of the leaders of the movement. Soldiers opened fire in Narbonne and six demonstrators were killed. However, the soldiers of the 17th infantry regiment, based at Agde, were for the most part sons of grape growers themselves and sympathised with the protestors. They mutinied and marched on Béziers. The situation had become quasi-revolutionary. Marcellin Albert went to Paris to negotiate with the prime minister, **Clemenceau**, but the brave cafe-owner wasn't used to the devious nature of politics. At the end of the meeting Clemenceau gave him a few francs to pay his fare home and Albert was entirely discredited in the eyes of his former comrades.

Meanwhile, parliament voted through measures that would prevent fraud (*mouillage* and *sucrage*), and this gave rise to the system of quality control that continues today, including the setting up of the system of vins d'appellation d'origine (1919), ancestor of the AOC. With the aim of cutting their losses, wine-makers organised themselves into co-operatives: the first was created in Lézignan in 1909. The members of these co-operatives mutualised the burden of cost and equipment for wine making and marketing their wines.

URBAN GROWTH

In 1936 the Spanish Civil War broke out and this led to republicans seeking refuge in France. In 1939 the **exodus** reached its height. Almost 500,000 people crossed the frontier of the Pyrénées in appalling conditions, in an episode of history known as *la Retirada*. Later, in 1962, the Évian agreements led to a massive influx of refugees from Algeria into Languedoc-Roussillon. Many of them arrived at Perpignan and Port-Vendres in Pyrénées-Orientales. Suburbs were built hastily by these municipalities to cater for the new inhabitants.

At the same time, the plan to develop the Languedoc-Roussillon coastline, decided in 1963, created **new resorts** from scratch: **Port-Barcarès**, **Canet-Plage** and **St-Cyprien-Plage**…

TOURISM

A new activity appeared in the 19C; **tourism**. Spa cures at Amélie-les-Bains were all the rage under Louis-Philippe, as was the taste for climbing in the Pyrénées. At the same time, the **Catalan forges**, known since the 12C, disappeared.

In the 1960s, tourism became the principal motor of the regional economy, to such an extent that traditional occupations suffered. Winemaking, in particular, went from crisis to crisis. Today the region profits from its tourist attractions – the Mediterranean, spa holidays, the Pyrénées, Cathar chateaux, Carcassonne – and is distinguishing itself in the sector of alternative energy.

For the contemporary period see "Renewable Energy" p50 and "Challenges of an Attractive Region" p51.

Art and Culture

Route of passage and melting pot of civilisations, the region has absorbed many influences and with them forged an art of its own: Romanesque churches elegant in their austerity, severe-looking Cathar fortresses perched on crags as if they were themselves extensions of the rock, and astounding Catalan Baroque altarpieces. The harmonious forms of the landscapes, sculpted by light, have beguiled painters and in the early 20C gave birth to Fauvisme.

ART AND ARCHITECTURE
LEGACY OF THE ROMANS

The region was quickly and extensively Romanised, but continuous and rapid urban development in the cities, notably Narbonne, capital of the province, meant a constant recycling of Roman buildings. However some traces of five centuries of Roman presence remain.

Excavations carried out in Narbonne have revealed different kinds of houses, among them **patrician houses** richly decorated with mosaics and murals. The remains of an aqueduct have been found at Amélie-les-Bains, as well as baths, potteries and imperial coins.

At Angoustrine in the Cerdagne, beside the church of St-André, there is a Roman *cippus* (stele). This block of granite, carved with an inscription, would have been a votive offering. The Romans were great engineers and crisscrossed their empire with roads: the **via Domitia**, the principal road through Gallia Narbonensis, linked the Rhône (at Beaucaire) with Tarraconensis in Spain. Several stretches of this remarkable road have been preserved, such as in Narbonne for example.

See– **Narbonne**
(Musée archéologique, Horreum).

ROMANESQUE ART

An original form of art combining influences from Mozarabic art (Christian subjects treated in Islamic style) and Carolingian art, appeared in the Catalan Pyrénées in the middle of the 10C. The abbey of **St-Michel-de-Cuxa**, in Conflent, mixes various features (low and narrow transept, long chancel with an apse, side aisles) giving it a complex appearance, typical of the first Romanesque architecture.

The more simple style represented by **St-Martin-du-Canigou**, beautiful in its austerity, spread in the 11C. On occasion red marble and black schist, from the quarries of the Conflent and Roussillon, were placed together as a colourful counterpoint. The stone walls were enlivened with lesenes (Lombard strips), placed around the apses, façades and belltowers and joined at the top by numerous small arches.

Inside, penumbra reign: there are few openings in order not to weaken the walls of the nave, which was covered with a vault. Sculpture is almost absent from churches of the 11C although one example is the portal of St-Génis-des-Fontaines, where the finely worked white marble is separate from the facade, which is made of stone and mortar. However, the next century saw the apogee of Romanesque sculpture in Roussillon, notably in the cloister of St-Michel-de-Cuxa and in the works of the **master of Cabestany**, seen in the arcades at Elne and the rose-red tribune of Serrabone. The style of this itinerant sculpture and his workshop in Boulou, can be seen in Lagrasse, Rieux-Minervois, St-Hilaire and, especially, in Monastir-del-Camp. His distinguishing mark: the enormous hands of the characters he portrays.

Mural painting had an important place in the art of this period. The decorations of the apses depict Christ in glory, the Apocalypse and the Last Judgement.

See – The abbeys of **St-Martin-du-Canigou** and of **St-Michel-de-Cuxa** (*illustrated on p62*), Prieuré de **Serrabone**, cloister at **Elne**, abbeys of **St-Hilaire** and **Lagrasse**.

ONE GOTHIC TO ANOTHER

Attached as they were to Romanesque forms, the architects of the Midi only adopted innovations from northern

Abbaye St-Michel-de-Cuxa

© F. Guiziou / hemis.fr

France with reluctance. Their research had led them towards a southern Gothic style, enriched by a Romanesque past, which it transformed into something new. Their attempts to introduce this northern form were nonetheless impressive. This can been in the style of *rayonnant* Gothic found in the choir of **St-Nazaire in Carcassonne**, a worthy successor to the Sainte-Chapelle (renowned for its superb stained glass windows), and in **Narbonne cathedral**: vast, soaring, luminous. However, the influence of the north is little visible : Romanesque preferences for large expanses of wall without sculpture or stained glass and the single sturdily built nave were preferred to Gothic styles.

See – Carcassonne (Basilique St-Nazaire), Narbonne (cathedral).

MILITARY ARCHITECTURE

The insecurity of a coastline exposed to the Saracen dangers and then – once the Cathar resistance had been quashed – the king of France's need to affirm his presence in the region, gave rise to some formidable defensive constructions.

Châteaux and fortifications

Abandoned or rebuilt by the victors in the war against heresy, the **Cathar chateaux** are all in ruins today, as seen at **Quéribus**, **Puilaurens** and **Peyrepertuse**. Rebuilt after the conquest, they have all the features of royal castles, of which bosses on the stonework are most characteristic. **Carcassonne** is the paragon of this military architecture of the second half of the 12C that was not limited to royal constructions. Examples of this are all the chateaux built by the craftsmen of the conquest of which **Puivert** is a fine example, with a master tower enclosing a great hall vaulted with ogive arches with sculpted bases.

Modern fortresses

Built by the Spanish crown to protect the northern frontier of Roussillon, **Salses** is the first modern fort in the sense of having studiously designed defences and an internal arrangement specially intended to house a garrison. In the 17C, **Vauban** conceived defensive systems adapted to difficult mountain conditions, notably in the Conflent: the forts of **Villefranche-de-Conflent** and **Mont-Louis** are still intact as admirable examples of his skill.

See – **Châteaux**: Quéribus, Puilaurens, Peyrepertuse, Puivert…
Fortified town: Carcassonne.
Modern forts: Mont-Louis, Villefranche-de-Conflent.

CATALAN BAROQUE

Deriving from, and influenced by Spain, Catalan baroque art developed during a time when Catalonia was experiencing a serious territorial crisis (1640–1660) that would end with partition between Spain and France. Catalan baroque was primarily sacred in nature but it served as a form of artistic expression that could bring together a people being torn apart. Catalonia is still marked by this 17C religious fervour: there isn't a church or chapel that did not commission its own altarpiece, invariably more sumptuous than that of the adjacent parish.

Marriage between sculpture and architecture

These altarpieces, entirely sculpted, reached enormous proportions at the end of the 17C, as can be seen in the works of **Lluis Generès** in Baixas and **Josep Sunyer** in Prades. Tiers and sculptures multiplied: little by little a crowd of saints and angels found their way into niches and onto pediments. Architecture sprang to life, pediments were broken, columns were twisted and became fluted. In the 18C, this exuberance spread to architecture. The sense of exuberance can be seen in the statues: the saints in the bas-reliefs on the Rosary altarpiece in the church of Espira-de-Conflent swirl in ecstatic poses worthy of Bernini. The object of this splendour was to glorify God, stunning the faithful through the richness of materials used: marbles from **Caunes-Minervois** and Villefranche-de-Conflent, gold from the Americas… it was an outpouring of light and colour and included statues painted and gilded by specialist workshops such as that of the Guerra. A unique example of this art can be seen in **Collioure**: the altarpiece of Notre-Dame-des-Anges, orchestrated by Josep Sunyer.

Mirrors of faith

But why was there such a need for so many statues, so many portraits of saints, so many scenes of martyrdom, so many miracles and mysteries? Because the austerity of Protestantism was never far away and it had to be repudiated. Instead, Catalan baroque proclaimed the richness of dogma, exalted faith and transmitted models of piety. To create the altarpiece of the Rosary that can be seen today in the church of St-Jacques in Perpignan, **Lazare Tremullas** followed the detailed instructions of his Dominican patrons. In it can be seen a representation of the joyous mysteries, painful and glorious, accompanied by figures representing three theological virtues. It is a masterwork by a Catalan sculptor that would start a school. In many churches and chapels you can see the intensity of popular devotion: **Joan-Perre Geralt** echoes it in his sculpting of St Acislus and St Victoria for the main altar in the church of **Trouillas**.

See – Altarpieces in Collioure, Prades, Baixas, Perpignan…

PAINTING AND SCULPTURE

The Catalan portrait painter **Hyacinthe Rigaud** (1659–1743) and the Narbonnais **Antoine Rivalz** were among the leading artists of the 17C and 18C.

Later, the Catalan **Aristide Maillol** (1861–1944), native of Banyuls, translated his admiration for Gauguin into his graceful feminine sculptures. He spent much time in his farmhouse near **Banyuls**, where he rests today. The sculptor from Lodève (in Hérault), **Paul Dardé** (1888–1963) became know for his very personal style before being largely forgotten. He is little remembered today.

THE "BEASTS" OF COLLIOURE

"Collioure? That's women, boats, the sea and the mountain […]. But above all it is the light. A yellow light, golden, that chases away the shadows."

This is how **Derain** described the little fishing port where he worked with **Matisse** in 1905. The two of them explored the village, the harbour and the fishing boats in their canvases, in oranges, reds and other luminous colours, the brush strokes melting in contrasting blocks of colour. Only the drawing allowed the viewer to recognise certain objects drowning in an unreal polychrome universe. During the Salon d'Automne of 1905, the violence of these canvases drew criticism and unleashed the scandal of the fauves – "wild beasts", as these painters were dubbed.

CÉRET, MECCA OF CUBISM

With these words, the critic André Salmon baptised the Catalan village which saw the arrival of **Picasso** and **Braque** in

1911. They dreamed up canvases of perfect architectural structure, into which seeped the atmosphere of Catalonia. Céret subsequently attracted many other artists, including **Juan Gris**. In 1950, the painter **Pierre Brune** founded a museum confirming the town's connection to modern art.

⏺See – Métairie Maillol at Banyuls, the museums in Céret and Collioure.

LOCAL LANGUAGES

Keep an ear open for how the locals talk. French is the lingua franca but it is coloured by two sister languages, Catalan and Occitan (the *langue d'oc*).

CATALAN

Close to Occitan and also heir to the Roman presence, Catalan is a cultural link to the county of Barcelona (9C–10C). Its apogee came in the 13C, with the writings of **Ramon Llull**. From the 16C, it entered into decline. The centralising king of Spain, Felipe (Philip) II decreed that Castilian (Spanish) must be used. Then came the Treaty of the Pyrénées (1659) which forbade its use in Roussillon. However, Catalan proved tenacious. It survived for a long time as an oral language and enjoyed a literary renaissance in the 19C. An essential component of the cultural identity of Roussillon, its use began to be affirmed once again from the 1980s, in infant schools, the publishing industry and, today, on road signs.

CATALAN IDENTITY TODAY

Catalan is the official language of Andorra and of the Spanish region of Catalonia. On the French side of the border, thanks to help coming from the south, it is enjoying something of revival. Proof of renewed interest in learning Catalan include changes in education such as through the **bressolas**, schools in which the teaching is entirely in Catalan. Theatre, literature and poetry are also encouraging the use of the language.

There are numerous organisations that exist to promote Catalan, in France and Spain, of course, but also in Italy, Canada and other countries.

OCCITAN

This is the modern name for what used to be called the *"langue d'oc"*. The langauges of "d'oïl" (which became French) and "d'oc " derive their names from the way in which the word "yes" was pronounced in each of them. The dividing line between their areas of dominance passes through the Massif Central, with Occitan being spoke to the south. It is divided into dialects including languedocien, gascon, limousin, auvergnat, provençal and nissard (spoken near Nice). The name Languedoc appeared in the 13C to designate the royal domains from the Rhône to the Garonne, territories which had formerly belonged to the count of Toulouse and the king of Aragon.

Today, it is hard to imagine the prestige that this language once enjoyed. **Dante** dreamed of being able to write the *Divine Comedy* in the language of the troubadours.

Nevertheless, after the crusades against the Cathars, the use of Occitan declined, at least among the aristocracy. In 1323, some poets of Toulouse attempted to restore it to greatness with the Jeux Floraux, in pure medieval tradition. In 1539, the **Ordinance of Villers-Cotterêts** delivered a coup de grâce to Occitan, ruling that administrative documents had to be written in the dialect of the Île-de-France. After that, Occitan was spoken mainly in the countryside, and was referred to as "patois" to deride both the language and the culture. The teachers of the Third Republic aimed to eradicate it but it was the First World War that dealt the most severe blow.

Occitan, however, has occasionally defied the trend: in 1819, with the publication by Rochegude, of an anthology of poems by troubadours; and in 1854, when the **Félibrige** reformed the spelling of Provencal. The Escòla Occitana (1919) and the Institute of Occitan Studies in Toulouse (1945) played a decisive role in the renewal of the language, giving it a written form more like accepted languages. Only recently has Occitan been accepted into the school curriculum (1997).

ABC OF ARCHITECTURE

From Romanesque churches to medieval chateaux, the area covered by this guide is not lacking in architectural masterpieces. These illustrations provide a visual key to the architecture of the region, explaining specialised technical terms (some of only local application) to help you to get the most out of a visit to the most emblematic buildings of the Aude and Pyrénées-Orientales.

ST-MICHEL-DE-CUXA – Bell-tower of the abbey church (11C)

The Romanesque churches in Roussillon and Catalonia nearly all feature one or two Lombard bell-towers. This style was probably imported from Italy in the 11C, making its earliest appearance at St-Michel-de-Cuxa, and later became typical of the architecture of this region. The bell-tower at Cuxa stands at the far south end of the transept (originally, there was a matching tower at the far north end).

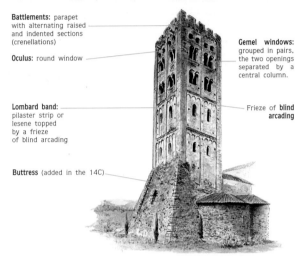

Battlements: parapet with alternating raised and indented sections (crenellations)

Oculus: round window

Lombard band: pilaster strip or lesene topped by a frieze of blind arcading

Buttress (added in the 14C)

Gemel windows: grouped in pairs, the two openings separated by a central column.

Frieze of **blind arcading**

ELNE – Cloisters of the cathedral of Ste-Eulalie-et-Ste-Julie (12-14C)

The cloisters are a set of four roofed galleries around a central quadrangle, enabling monks to walk under cover from the conventual buildings to the church.

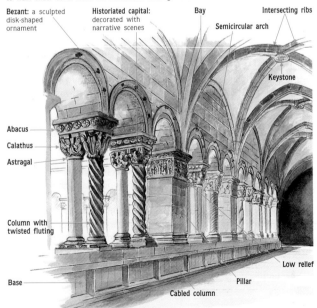

Bezant: a sculpted disk-shaped ornament

Historiated capital: decorated with narrative scenes

Bay

Intersecting ribs

Semicircular arch

Keystone

Abacus

Calathus

Astragal

Column with twisted fluting

Base

Low relief

Pillar

Cabled column

R. Corbel/MICHELIN

NARBONNE – Cathedral of St-Just-et-St-Pasteur (13-14C)

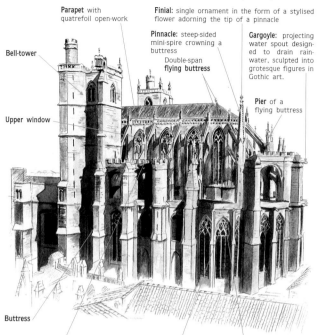

Parapet with quatrefoil open-work

Finial: single ornament in the form of a stylised flower adorning the tip of a pinnacle

Pinnacle: steep-sided mini-spire crowning a buttress

Double-span **flying buttress**

Gargoyle: projecting water spout designed to drain rainwater, sculpted into grotesque figures in Gothic art.

Bell-tower

Upper window

Pier of a flying buttress

Buttress

Watch-path with battlements

Tracery: stone open-work decorating the upper part of the windows

Lanceolate or spearhead motif in the undulating ornamentation of a Flamboyant Gothic window

R. Corbel/MICHELIN

RURAL DOMESTIC ARCHITECTURE

R. Corbel/MICHELIN

CARCASSONNE – East gateway of the Château Comtal (12C)

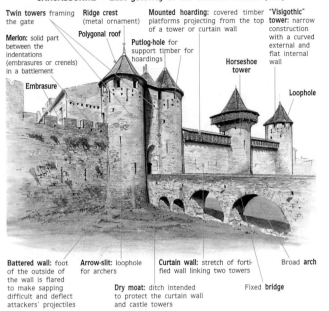

Twin towers framing the gate

Merlon: solid part between the indentations (embrasures or crenels) in a battlement

Embrasure

Ridge crest (metal ornament)

Polygonal roof

Putlog-hole for support timber for hoardings

Mounted hoarding: covered timber platforms projecting from the top of a tower or curtain wall

"Visigothic" tower: narrow construction with a curved external and flat internal wall

Horseshoe tower

Loophole

Battered wall: foot of the outside of the wall is flared to make sapping difficult and deflect attackers' projectiles

Arrow-slit: loophole for archers

Curtain wall: stretch of fortified wall linking two towers

Dry moat: ditch intended to protect the curtain wall and castle towers

Broad **arch**

Fixed **bridge**

R. Corbel/MICHELIN

Fort de SALSES (15-17C)

Salses fortress is a typical example of a half-buried fortification.

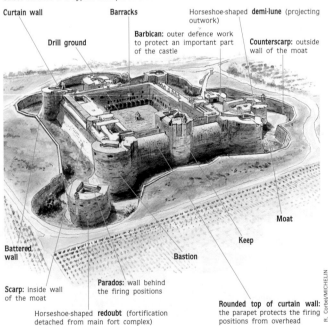

Curtain wall

Drill ground

Barracks

Barbican: outer defence work to protect an important part of the castle

Horseshoe-shaped **demi-lune** (projecting outwork)

Counterscarp: outside wall of the moat

Moat

Keep

Battered wall

Bastion

Scarp: inside wall of the moat

Parados: wall behind the firing positions

Horseshoe-shaped **redoubt** (fortification detached from main fort complex)

Rounded top of curtain wall: the parapet protects the firing positions from overhead

R. Corbel/MICHELIN

Nature

Remarkable for its sunshine – even in upland valleys – the region is composed of sea coast, plain and mountain. It is delimited to the west by the central Pyrénées, to the east by the Mediterranean, to the north by the Montagne Noire and the mouth of Aude, and to the south by the Spanish frontier.

The beaches, lagoons and coves of the coast attract crowds in summer. The vineyards, garrigue scrub and snow covered summits of the Pyrénées and its foothills create a wide variety of landscapes.

THE COAST
LOW COAST TO THE NORTH : SANDY BEACHES AND LAGOONS

From the mouth of the Aude to that of the **Têt** near Perpignan, the coast of the **Gulf of Lion** is a 70km/42mi strip of **low-lying coast**. This southern part of the **Bas-Languedoc** is a sandy plain planted with **vineyards** and given relief by a few chalky hills (Montagne de la Clape near Narbonne).

Beside the coast are numerous **étangs**, **saltwater** lagoons formed by marine currents and sediments carried by the rivers. They are sprinkled with sandbanks. The étangs are separated by **sandbars** (or **lidos**), formed by waves, currents and rivers. One main determinant is the **Rhône**, which carries sands and gravels towards the Languedoc coast. Less powerful rivers including the Vidourle, the Orb and the Aude have also played their part in shaping the coast. When the bars emerged from under the water they cut off the bays behind them creating lagoons.

Harbours that are today inland (Port-Leucate and Port-Barcarès), are evidence of this incessant modification of the coast. The sea is still modifying the coastal geography and dykes are used to try to tame natural processes, but with mixed results.

The sandbars are pierced by **graus**, natural channels by which the rivers find a way out to the sea.

The **lagoons** provide a habitat for many fish and shellfish, including eels, mullet, bass, daurade and clams.

The shoreline itself is a long sandy beach, punctuated by resorts and harbours. At the end of the 1960s, the development of the coast led to the remodelling of the area around the Etang de Leucate, creating the resorts of **Port-Leucate**, Port-Barcarès, as well as Canet and St-Cyprien.

The result of a policy concentrating on mass tourism is an almost continuous built-up area along the coast as far as Argelès, a road network that becomes gridlocked as soon as the weather turns

Deer of the Pyrénées

© Pierre Crétu / Fotolia.com

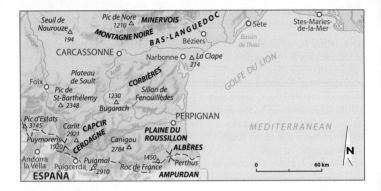

fine and a landscape damaged in places with only a few natural spaces preserved.

SOUTHERN ROCKY COAST : THE CÔTE VERMEILLE

For around 40km/24mi south of Argelès, up to the Spanish frontier at Port-Bou, the **rocky coast** is known as the **Côte Vermeille**. Wild and twisting, the hillsides covered with terraced vineyards, this section of coast contrasts sharply with the low-lying coast to the north. Charming fishing harbours and villages are discreetly located in narrow bays: Collioure, Port-Vendres, Banyuls-sur-Mer, Cerbère. The coast is particularly renowned for its rocky coves suitable for adventurous swimmers, snorkellers and scuba divers.

COASTAL FLORA AND FAUNA

The flora of the northern **coast, with its lagoons and marshes,** is dictated by the wind and salty sea spray. A mixture of grasses, rushes, reeds, marram grass and scrub fix little heaps of sand into **montilles**. On the edges of the lagoons, oraches, sea lavender and glasswort grow in the hard, cracked, salty soil.

A few hundred metres back from the lagoons grow tamarisk, rosemary and Aleppo pines (recognisable by their light green foliage and twisted trunks of grey bark). Here too are isolated stone pines, their trunks sometimes twisted by the wind.

Flocks of ducks and other water birds take refuge in the **étangs**: coots, snipe, grey herons, flamingoes, migrating storks, elegant white egrets, and gulls.

The beaches are inhabited by smaller, often inconspicuous creatures: dragonflies, lizards and earwigs.

INLAND
PLAINS OF THE BAS-LANGUEDOC

Behind the lagoons another sea stretches out: that of **vineyards** that continue to provide a livelihood for many villages despite the decline of recent years. The region is still "the largest vineyard in France", going by extent of planted area (the plain around Narbonne, the valleys of the Corbières, the Minervois). Here also are **olive groves**, mainly on the plain around Perpignan where the **picholine**, a variety of olive, often served pickled, is grown. The Minervois is the kingdom of the **lucque**, an olive with an elongated form.

THE CORBIÈRES

Further away from the coast, as the vineyards disappear, **garrigue** (Mediterranean scrub) takes over the stony limestone soils. It covers the hills of the **Corbières**, out of which protrude great blocks of rock. A sparse vegetation adapted to drought it is characterised by plants such as holm oak, dwarf Kermes oaks (*garric*, in Occitan, thought to be the origin of the word garrigue), box, spiny broom, pink rockroses and strawberry tree. Thyme, rosemary and juniper grow in scented clumps amongst a greyish grass, brachypodium, much sought after by sheep.

These hills, land of "Cathar" chateaux, are overflown by a number of birds of prey, including hawks, sparrowhawks and Bonelli's eagles.

The garrigue is the universe of the ocellated green lizard and of the longest snakes indigenous to France, the Montpellier snake (2m long). Occasionally its long sloughed skin can be found entwined in the bushes. Not dangerous to man, it cohabits with the viper and is at home on rocks and scree slopes.

MONTAGNE NOIRE

Northwest of the Corbières, in the hinterland of Carcassonne, is the Montagne Noir. This is the southwest extremity of the Massif central and marks the separation between the departments of Aude, Haute-Garonne, Hérault and Tarn. The highest point, the Pic de Nore (1,210 m/3,970 ft) emerges from a landscape of rounded forms and offers a view as far as Canigou. The Montagne noire range is characterised by a sharp contrast between its northern slopes, which rise steeply above the Thoré, and the southern slope, gently sloping towards the plains of the **Lauragais** and **Minervois**, in view of the Pyrénées.

Habitat – The farmhouses of the Montagne Noire incorporate the family living quarters, the barns and the storerooms all under the same roof. On larger farms these three are separate buildings arranged in a horse shoe.

Many houses have their own dovecote (**pigeonnier**). The most characteristic of these are in stone or are half-timbered. They are often raised on pillars topped by round stones to prevent predators from climbing up. Generally square in plan, these dovecotes are surmounted by a lantern pierced with holes to allow the birds to get in and out.

INLAND CATALONIA, THE "GARDEN" OF ROUSSILLON

The **plain du Roussillon**, extending for 40km/24mi, is an ancient gulf filled in with debris torn from the Pyrénées. The dry and stony terraces (**Aspres** region), cut with wide valleys and sprinkled with small hills, are the domain of the fruit tree and vine. Taking advantage of the sunshine and the protection of neighbouring mountains, inland Catalonia is one big market garden and fruit orchard.

THE EASTERN PYRÉNÉES

A natural frontier between France and Spain, the Pyrénées form a barrier that is difficult to cross. They are backed to the north by the adjacent Corbières. The ruggedness of the crystalline rock and the softness of the Mediterranean form a pleasing contrast.

MEDITERRANEAN PYRÉNÉES

East of **Canigou** (2,784 m/9134 ft), the mountains descend to the sea. A spur of crystalline rock, the **Albères**, separates Empordà in Spain, to the south, and Roussillon, to the north.

Heading westwards from Canigou, the mountains continue in the **Cerdagne** (1,200 m/3,937 ft), a wide valley surrounded by high mountains with a rich vegetation, and the **Capcir** (1,600 m/5,250 ft), the highest region of French Catalonia

Pic du Canigou

© Tilio & Paolo / Fotolia.com

in which the mountains are covered by dense forest.

Everywhere, streams hurtle down the mountains, feeding powerful **rivers** running down the middle of the valleys, such as the **Têt** and the **Tech**.

Between the Corbières, which advance to the north towards the Montagne Noire, and the central part of the Pyrénées, limestone buttresses create a singular landscape. Above Limoux and Quillan, a steep pass gives access to the **plateau de Sault** which owes its name to the fir trees (*saltis*) growing on the mountains that surround it. The plateau is divided in two by the fault line of the **Rebenty** that runs through spectacular gorges on its way into the valley of the Aude. Adjacent are the **Fenouillèdes**, a region of forests, garrigue and farmland, full of mysteries and histories.

The Pyrénées proper are full of interesting landscapes. Their characteristic sound is that of cow bells as herds of cattle are moved to their summer pastures from the Côte de Langarail, passing in front of the château de Montségur. The Pyrénées are also conjured up by the smell of saw mills. And they have their stories, constantly embellished, about the activities of the maquis in the mountains during the Occupation.

Remains of a way of life

Land use is still often decided by ancestral ways of farming. Fields and villages are strung out along the valleys. At a higher level there are forests and hay meadows. Highest of all are the pastures for grazing animals. Wheat, rye and maize are still grown in the high Vallespir, the Cerdagne and the Conflent. The plateau de Sault today specialises in potatoes. Lower down, broom and garrigue have little by little taken the place of holm oak woods, pines and beeches.

MOUNTAINS OF ANDORRA

Sculpted out of gneiss, an extremely resistant kind of rock, the mountains of Andorra mark the transition between the Mediterranean Pyrénées and the central Pyrénées. The lowest point in the principality is 840m/2,756 ft and most of its territory is unpopulated mountains making it a paradise for outdoor nature study, especially botany.

FLORA AND FAUNA OF THE PYRÉNÉES

There are two types of vegetation in the eastern Pyrénées. The Capcir, Cerdagne and Andorra are characteristic of the central Pyrénées. In the east, meanwhile, the flora becomes increasingly Mediterranean as it approaches the sea. In the **Capcir** and the **Cerdagne**, the forests principally occupy the shaded northern slopes of the mountains, while the *soula* (southern slopes) are dedicated to crops and pastures. Fir trees grow on the high slopes of the Aude. From around 2,400m/7,800ft there are subalpine pastures covered with flowers, several of them endemic: Pyrénéan lily (yellow or red), a deep blue delphinium, vivid yellow tormentil, and multiple saxifrages growing in rosettes.

The mountains support a variety of wild animals: foxes that often approach villages, wild boar, deer, Pyrénéan chamois (or *isards*, the population of which is increasing), wild cats, marmots and otters. Birds include golden eagles, hawks and capercaillies.

The **brown bear** has been reintroduced to the mountains. The population is extremely small and mainly inhabits the centre of the range. Its presence is controversial, especially in sheep-herding communities.

The Mediterranean Pyrénées are lower and are characterised by the appearance of the Scots pine on higher, dry and sunny slopes in place of the fir, relegating the beeches to other locations. Under 800m/2,600ft, cork oaks grow in the warmth and humidity, as in the **Vallespir** where there is a cork-making industry. Above 1,700m/5,500ft, the mountain pines and the birch give way to delicate subalpine pastures where a number of flowers grow: the great yellow gentian, the oblong leaves of yellow-flowering wolf's bane and the almost violet bells of the toxic monkshood.

Vineyards of Rivesaltes
© Mick Rock / Cephas / Photononstop

Collioure, Côte Vermeille
© René Mattes / hemis.fr

*Barbarossa Tower in
the distance, Gruissan*
© Bertrand Rieger / hemis.fr

A broad geographical corridor separates the Pyrénées to the south from the Massif Central to the north. The corridor connects the Mediterranean with one of the most dramatic sights in France, the restored medieval citadel of Carcassonne. Along the valley flows the river Aude and beside it the Canal du Midi, an extraordinary work of 17th century engineering. The canal is highly scenic for much of its length and is as popular with pleasure boaters as with the walkers and cyclists that explore its tow paths. Set back from the coast is the historic city of Narbonne founded by the Romans. Once a seaport, it is now stranded inland. Vine growing and wine making are the principal economic activities here, along with beach-bound and cultural tourism.

Home Cooking

The extreme western part of Aude is consumed by the Pays du Lauragais, which centres on the town of Castelnaudary, arguably – and they really do argue – the cassoulet kingdom of the world. Like all French classics, cassoulet has a legion of 'genuine' recipes. This stick-in-the-ribs concoction is the very antithesis of junk food; it's mother's cooking, an icon of the simple life, a dish of white haricot beans, Toulouse sausage, duck and belly pork. Bon appetit!

Highlights

1 Visit the historic sites of **Narbonne** (p76)
2 Take a boat trip on the **Canal du Midi** (p84)
3 Explore the citadel of **Carcassonne** (p99)
4 Eat **cassoulet** (p88, 98, 107)
5 Relax on one of the sandy **beaches** on the coast (p90, 92, 110)

Étangs

The Languedoc coast is characterized by its étangs, shallow coastal lagoons, more than by its long, popular beaches. These were once bays until deposits accumulated as sand bars, cutting the étangs off from the open sea, to which they are now only connected by narrow openings called *graus*. Only navigable by small vessels, the lagoons are havens of wildlife and also used to catch and farm fish and seafood to supply the region's restaurants.

Vineyards around Carcassonne

© Sylvaine Poitou / Apa Publications

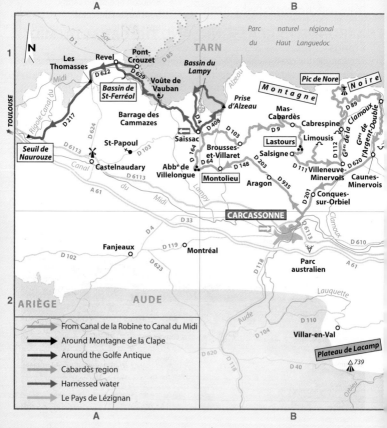

Notre-Dame de Colombier chapel and the vineyards of Montbrun-des-Corbières near Lagrasse
© Hervé Lenain / hemis.fr

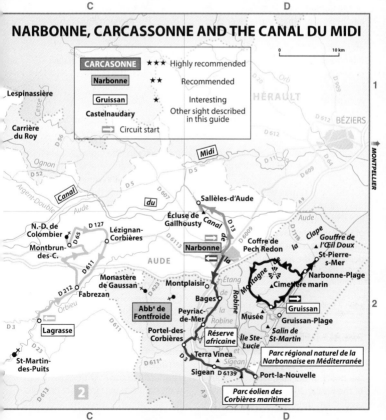

NARBONNE, CARCASSONNE AND THE CANAL DU MIDI

CARCASONNE	★★★	Highly recommended
Narbonne	★★	Recommended
Gruissan	★	Interesting
Castelnaudary		Other sight described in this guide
⇨	Circuit start	

0 ___ 10 km

Lespinassière

Carrière du Roy

HÉRAULT

BÉZIERS

MONTPELLIER

Cesse

Ognon

Argent-Double

Canal

du

Midi

Sallèles-d'Aude

Écluse de Gailhousty

N.-D. de Colombier

Lézignan-Corbières

Narbonne

Coffre de Pech Redon

Gouffre de l'Œil Doux

St-Pierre-s-Mer

Montbrun-des-C.

Monastère de Gaussan

Fabrezan

Montplaisir

Narbonne-Plage

Cimetière marin

Gruissan

Lagrasse

St-Martin-des-Puits

Abbᵉ de Fontfroide

Bages

Peyriac-de-Mer

Portel-des-Corbières

Musée

Gruissan-Plage

Salin de St-Martin

Île Ste-Lucie

Réserve africaine

Terra Vinea

Sigean

Port-la-Nouvelle

Parc régional naturel de la Narbonnaise en Méditerranée

Parc éolien des Corbières maritimes

AUDE

Étang de la Robine

Sigean

C D

75

Narbonne★★

Narbonne, which has been in its time the ancient capital of Gallia Narbonensis, the residence of the Visigoth monarchy and an archiepiscopal seat, is now a lively Mediterranean city playing an important role as a wine-producing centre and a road and rail junction.

A BIT OF HISTORY

A sea port – Narbonne may well have served as a harbour and market for a 7C BC Gallic settlement on the Montlaurès hill to the north of the modern city. The town of 'Colonia Narbo Martius', established in 118 BC by decree of the Roman Senate, became a strategic crossroads along the Via Domitia, as well as a flourishing port. It exported oil, linen, wood, hemp, cheeses and meat from the Cévennes – so was much appreciated by the Romans – and later on sigillated earthenware. Most of the river shipping business, however, was centred on the Italian, Iberian and then Gallic wine trade. During this period the city expanded dramatically and was embellished with magnificent buildings.

A capital city – In 27 BC, Narbonne gave its name to the Roman province created by Augustus. After the sack of Rome in 410 by the Visigoths, Narbonne became their capital. Later, it fell to the Saracens; in 759 Pépin the Short recaptured it and Charlemagne created the duchy of Gothie with Narbonne as the capital.

From the 14C, the change in the course of the Aude, the havoc wrought by the Hundred Years War and plague, and the departure of the Jews caused Narbonne to decline.

WALKING TOURS

PALAIS DES ARCHEVÊQUES★

2hrs. The Archbishops' Palace overlooks the lively **place de l'Hôtel-de-Ville**, in the heart of the city, where a section of the Roman Via Domitia was discovered. It has three square towers: fram-

- ▶ **Population:** 50,776.
- **Michelin Map:**
  Region map D2. 344: J3.
- **Info:** 31 r. Jean Jaurès, 11100 Narbonne. ℘04 68 65 15 60. www.narbonne-tourisme.com. Pick up a Monuments and Museum Pass for *9€*; combined ticket with musée d'Art et d'Histoire, musée lapidaire, and valid for 15 days.
- ▶ **Location:** 30km/19mi SW of Béziers by the N 9, and 60km/37.5mi E of Carcassonne by the A 61.
- **Parking:** There are plenty of parking areas along the canal, near the Quai Valière; do not be tempted to drive into the centre.
- **Don't Miss:**
  The Archaeological Museum, with its Roman paintings.
- **Timing:** Allow a full day.
- **Kids:** The Musée archéologique de Narbonne.

ing the Passage de l'Ancre, the Tour de la Madeleine (the oldest) and Tour St-Martial; farther to the left the Donjon Gilles-Aycelin. Between the last two, Viollet-le-Duc built the present Hôtel de Ville (town hall) in a neo-Gothic style. The Archbishops' Palace is an example of religious, military and civil architecture bearing the imprint of centuries, from the 12C to the 19C Hôtel de Ville.

Donjon Gilles-Aycelin★

Open Jun–Sep 10am–6pm; Oct–May 9am–noon, 2–6pm except Tue. Closed 1 Jan, 1 May, 1 and 11 Nov and 25 Dec. 4€ (or Monuments & Museums Pass). ℘04 68 90 30 65. Entrance on the left inside the town hall.

This fortified tower with its rusticated walls stands on the remains of the Gallo-Roman rampart that once protected the

Cathédrale St-Just-et-St-Pasteur

© cynoclub / Bigstockphoto.com

heart of the old town. It represented the archbishops' power as opposed to that of the viscounts, who occupied a building on the other side of place de l'Hôtel-de-Ville. From the sentinel path on the platform (162 steps), the **panorama★** stretches over Narbonne and the cathedral, the surrounding plain and away across La Clape summit, the Corbières and the coastal lagoons as far as the Pyrénées on the horizon.

◐ Walk through the town hall to the main courtyard of the Palais Neuf.

Palais Neuf (New Palace)

The New Palace complex surrounds the Cour d'Honneur and comprises the façade over the courtyard of the town hall, the Gilles-Aycelin keep, the St-Martial tower, the synods building and the north and south wings.

Musée Archéologique★★ – *Palais Neuf.* ◐*Open Apr–14 Jul 10am–noon, 2–5pm except Tue; 15 Jul–Oct 10am–1pm, 2.30–6pm; Nov–Mar except Tue 2–5pm.* ◉*4/6€.* ✆*04 68 90 30 66.* Narbonne undoubtedly possesses one of the finest collections of **Roman paintings★★** in France. For the most part the items came from the archaeological site of Clos de la Lombardia, north of the ancient city, where they once adorned the homes of the wealthy.

Musée d'Art★ – ◐*As for the Archaeological Museum. Same building as the*

Salle des Synodes, on the second floor. This museum occupies the old episcopal apartments where Louis XIII stayed during the siege of Perpignan in 1642. Many rooms are hung with portraits of Narbonne's consuls during the 16C, while the King's Chamber is decorated with a beautiful coffered ceiling representing the nine muses.

Salle des Consuls

Enter via the Cour d'honneur. Located on the ground floor of the synods building, the room is supported on part of the old Roman fortified city wall.

◐ Leave the Palais Neuf via the door on the north side of the courtyard and enter the Palais Vieux via the door opposite, on the other side of passage de l'Ancre.

Palais Vieux (Old Palace)

The Old Palace consists of two main buildings flanking the Madeleine tower. To the east, a square staircase tower divides a Romanesque façade pierced by arcades. Other monuments stand around Madeleine courtyard: the square Carolingian bell-tower of the church of St-Théodard, the apse of the Annonciade Chapel overlooked to the north by the imposing cathedral chevet, and the 14C **Tinal** (the canons' old storeroom), which has recently been restored.

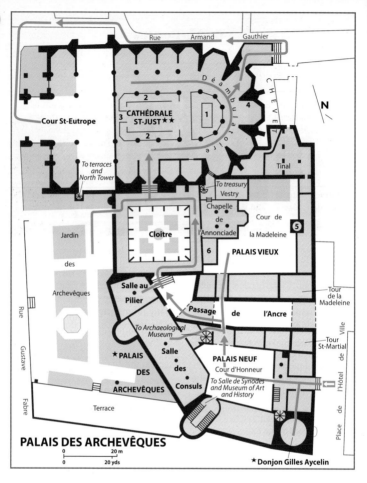

PALAIS DES ARCHEVÊQUES

★ Donjon Gilles Aycelin

Come out onto passage de l'Ancre and walk to the right.

Passage de l'Ancre

This almost fortified street with its impressive walls separates the old and new palaces and leads from place de l'Hôtel-de-Ville (between the St-Martial and Madeleine towers) to the cloisters.

Enter the Salle au Pilier via a door to the left of the stairs leading to the cathedral cloisters.

Salle du Pilier

Open Apr–14 Jul 10am–noon, 2–5pm except Tue; 15 Jul–Oct 10am–1pm, 2.30–6pm; Nov–Mar 2–5pm except Tue.

Closed 1 Jan, 1 May, 1 and 11 Nov, 25 Dec. ℰ04 68 90 30 65.

This 14C room houses the Palais shop, and owes its name to the enormous pillar that supports the vault.

Cathédrale St-Just-et-St-Pasteur★★

It is possible to enter the cathedral via passage de l'Ancre and through the cloisters.

The first stone was laid on 3 April 1272 and by 1332, the radiating chancel had been completed in the same style as the great cathedrals of northern France. Building the nave and the transept would have involved reaching the ancient rampart, which still served in

The Via Domitia

The Via Domitia is the oldest of the Roman roads built in Gaul. It was named after the Consul of the Roman province of Gallia Narbonensis, Domitius Ahenoarus, who had it built in 118–117 BC at the time the province was founded.

Following an ancient route once used by the Ligurians and Iberians, the Via Domitia ran from Beaucaire (Gard) to Le Perthus (Pyrénées–Orientales), forming a communications route between Rome and Spain. Beyond the Rhône, the Via Domitia led into the Via Aurelia. Spanned by ridges and punctuated along its length by milestones marking every Roman mile (1,481.5m) and staging posts, the Via Domitia linked Beaucaire (Ugernum), Nîmes (Nemausus), Béziers (Julia Baeterrae), Narbonne (Naro Martius) and Perpignan (Ruscino).

Originally intended for military use, to enable Roman legions to reach the furthest outposts of the empire, Roman roads also aided the transportation of commercial goods and, of course, the spread of new ideas.

---

troubled medieval times, so this was postponed. Today, the edifice consists of the chancel flanked by cloisters on the south side.

Cloître – The cloisters (14C) are at the foot of the south side of the cathedral. The west gallery gives access to the arch-bishops' gardens. From the 18C **Jardin des Archevêques**, there is a fine view of the flying buttresses, the south tower of the cathedral and the synods building. Inside, the strikingly well-proportioned chancel was the only part to be completed. The height of its vaulting (41m/134ft) is exceeded only by that in the cathedrals of Amiens (42m/137ft) and Beauvais (48m/157ft). The chancel houses numerous works of art (&see diagram). Located opposite the high altar is the **organ case** flanked by fine 18C **choir stalls**. The Lady Chapel dedicated to Ste-Marie-de-Bethléem has regained its large Gothic **altarpiece★**, discovered in 1981 under a coat of stucco.

Trésor – ⊙Open Jul–Sep 10–11.45am, 2–5.45pm (Sun 2–5.45pm); Oct–Jun 2–5pm except Tue. ⊙Closed 1 Jan,1 May, 1 and 11 Nov, 25 Dec. ☞4/6€. (or Monuments & Museums Pass) ℘04 68 90 30 65. The treasury includes illuminated manuscripts and, together with other church plate, a fine gilt chalice (1561). The most remarkable exhibit is a late-15C Flemish tapestry depicting the **Creation★★**, woven in silk and gold thread.

▷ Leave the cathedral via a door in the second radiating chapel from the left.

Exterior – Note in particular the chevet with its High Gothic lancets, the great arches surmounted by merlons with arrow slits overlooking the terraces of the ambulatory, the flying buttresses, the turrets and the powerful defensive buttresses, and the lofty towers.

OLD NARBONNE

&See town map. Start from place de l'Hôtel-de-Ville and follow pedestrianised rue Droite.

Place du Forum

Remnants of a 1C temple on the site of the Antique forum and Capitol.

Place de l'Hôtel-de-Ville

© Jean-Pierre Degas / hemis.fr

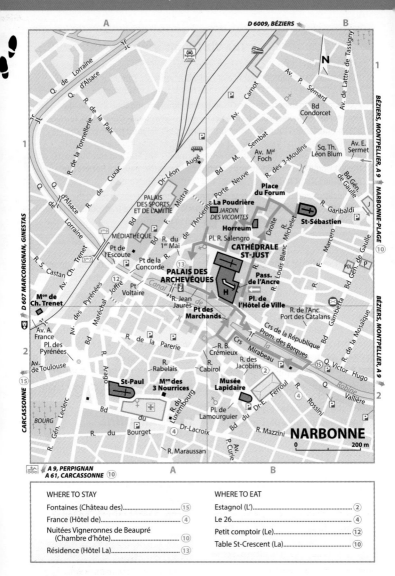

WHERE TO STAY		WHERE TO EAT	
Fontaines (Château des)	⑮	Estagnol (L')	②
France (Hôtel de)	④	Le 26	④
Nuitées Vigneronnes de Beaupré		Petit comptoir (Le)	⑫
(Chambre d'hôte)	⑩	Table St-Crescent (La)	⑩
Résidence (Hôtel La)	⑬		

▶ Turn right onto Rue Girard then left onto Rue Michelet.

Église St-Sébastien
This 15C church with 17C extensions, was built, according to legend, on the site of the saint's birthplace.

▶ Return to Place Bistan and, from the SW corner, follow Rue Rouget-de-l'Isle.

The itinerary takes you past the **Horreum**, a Roman warehouse.

▶ Turn right onto Rue du Lieut.-Col.-Deymes and right again onto Rue Armand-Gauthier, which leads to place Salengro.

La Poudrière
Situated behind the Jardin des Vicomtes, this 18C powder magazine houses temporary exhibitions.

Covered market in Narbonne

© fanou111 / Fotolia.com

◖ Return to Place Salengro; right on Rue Chenneier and left on Rue du Lion-d'Or to the embankment; turn left.

Banks of the Robine

The Robine canal links together the Sallèles-d'Aude junction canal to **Port-la-Nouvelle**.

◖ When you reach the end of Promenade des Barques, take Pont de la Lierté across the Robine canal. Note the fine metal-framed covered market. Follow the south bank to Pont des Marchands.

Pont des Marchands★

This picturesque bridge, a pedestrianised street lined with colourful shops overlooking the canal, follows the old Roman road (Via Domitia).

◖ Return to Place de l'Hôtel-de-Ville.

ADDITIONAL SIGHTS
Musée Lapidaire★

🕐 *Same details as for the Archaeological museum in the Palais Neuf.*
This is in the deconsecrated 13C church of Notre-Dame-de-la-Mourguié.

Basilique St-Paul

🕐 *Open daily except Sun afternoon.*

This basilica was built on the site of a 4C–5C necropolis near the tomb of the city's first archbishop.

Maison natale de Charles Trenet

13 av. Charles-Trenet. ↝ *Guided visits Jun–Sep 10am–6pm; Oct–May 10am–noon, 2–5pm except Tue.* 🕐 *Closed 1 Jan, 1 May, 1 and 11 Nov, 25 Dec.* ✦6€ (or Monuments & Museums Pass). *℘04 68 90 30 66.*
Birthplace of Charles Trenet, writer of fantasy songs and poetry, and much influenced by jazz.

🚗 DRIVING TOUR

From Canal de la Robine to Canal du Midi

⏱ *See region map. 16km/9.9mi. Allow 4hr.*

The architects of the Canal du Midi ignored Narbonne, but its people, not to be outdone, realised that an old canal, the Robine, could be connected to the Midi, bringing them within the canal's sphere of prosperity. This was done in 1787.

◖ Leave Narbonne to the N on the D 13 as far as Cuxac-d'Aude, then turn left onto the D 1626 towards Sallèles.

Canal de Jonction

Above and below Sallèles, this canal has many beautiful bays lined with pine.

 Take a narrow lane on the left before arriving in Sallèles in order to reach the locks of Gailhousty.

Écluse de Gailhousty

The lock allows the canal to cross the Aude; at this point there is a remarkable stonework pediment in bas relief.

◗ 11km/6.5mi to Sallèdes-d'Aude.

Sallèles-d'Aude

This agreeable village has a wine pro-ducing pedigree extending back 2,000 years to Gallo-Roman times.

ADDRESSES

🛏 STAY

⊖ **Hôtel de France** – *6 r. Rossini. ☎04 68 32 09 75. www.hotelnarbonne.com. Closed Jan. 16 rms. 55/79€. � 8€. Free wifi.* A hotel in a late-19C building located on a quiet street downtown. The rooms are rather plain; those on the back promise a good night's sleep.

⊖ **Chambre d'hôte Nuitées Vigneronnes de Beaupré** – *Rte d'Armissan. ☎04 68 65 85 57. www.domaine-de-beaupre.fr. 4 rms. 60/70€. Free wifi.* Wine buffs will delight in this small B&B on a wine estate close to the centre of Narbonne.

⊖⊖🍴 **Hotel la Résidence** – *6 r. du 1er-Mai. ☎04 68 32 19 41. www.hotel residence.fr. Closed 20 Jan–15 Feb. 26 rms. 97/135€. ⊂ 12€. Free wifi.* A fine hotel in a renovated 19C building.

NEARBY

⊖⊖🍴 **Château des Fontaines** – *2 av. de la Distillerie, 11200 Canet (14km/8.7mi W via the D 6113 in the direction of Lézignan-Corbières, then the D 11 from Villedaigne). ☎04 68 49 72 48. www.chateau-des-fontaines.com. Open Jun–Sep. 7 rms.*

97/160€. ⊂. A prestigious 19C house where luxury and serenity reigns. Choose an historically themed room – from Abbé Saunière to Alfons Mucha and Emma Calvé.

🍽 EAT

⊖⊖ **L'Estagnol** – *5 bis Cours Mirabeau. ☎04 68 65 09 27. www.lestagnol.fr. Closed 16–24 Nov, Sun and Mon eve. Set menu lunch 11.50/18€. 24/32€.* This lively brasserie situated near Les Halles, popular with the locals, specialises in traditional cuisine.

⊖⊖ **Le 26** – *8 bd Dr Lacroix. ☎04 68 4146 69. www.restaurantle26.fr. Closed Sun eve and Mon. Set menu lunch 14.50€. 26/37.50€.* The chef loves to cook things slowly, filling the restaurant with the appetising aromas of cooking.

⊖⊖🍴 **Le Petit Comptoir** – *4 bd du Mar.-Joffre. ☎04 68 42 30 35. www.petit comptoir.com. Closed 15 days in Jul, Sun–Mon. (May–Sep). Set menu lunch 15/18€. 37/47€.* Bistro-style restaurant where one can try local specialities.

⊖⊖🍴🍴 **La Table St Crescent** – *68 av. du Gén.Leclerc au Palais du vin. ☎04 68 41 37 37. www.la-table-saint-crescent.com. Set menu lunch 25€. 6580€. Closed Sat lunch, Sun eve and Mon.* Located at the edge of the town in a former oratory transformed into a temple of wine; inventive cuisine and superb wines.

SHOPPING

GOURMET

Les Halles – *1 bd du Dr-Ferroul. ☎04 68 32 63 99. www.narbonne.halles.fr. Free wifi.* A bright and lively renovated market hall containing 70 shops and bars.

Les Cuisiniers Cavistes – *1–5 pl. Lamourguier. ☎04 68 65 04 4. www. cuisiniers-cavistes.com. Open 8am–7.30pm. Closed Sun afternoon and Mon.* This location invites you to discover the wines of the region while offering local produce in jars ready to take away. Cookery workshops. Table d'hôte, should you want to taste first.

Canal du Midi★

Today's tourists enjoying the calm and beauty of the Canal du Midi have little idea of the phenomenal natural obstacles to building this canal which links the Atlantic to the Mediterranean.

A BIT OF HISTORY

Even the Romans envisioned a canal linking the Atlantic to the Mediterranean, yet by the time of François I, Henri IV and Richelieu, nothing had been achieved. Finally **Pierre-Paul Riquet**, Baron of Bonrepos (1604 80) began the project at his own expense, spending 5 million livres, burdening himself with debts and sacrificing his daughters' dowries to do it. He died exhausted in 1680, six months before the Canal du Midi opened. **Riquet's** descendants regained their rights to a share of the canal profits, and in 1897 sold the canal to the State.

Heritage and future projects – Riquet's 240km/150mi-long canal begins at Toulouse at the Port de l'Embouchure and runs into the Thau lagoon, through 91 locks. Today only pleasure-craft cruise this scenic waterway, and several companies rent houseboats or offer river cruises.

Canal architecture – Along the canal's banks are buildings erected to house engineers, workers and lock-keepers; buildings for technical and administrative tasks, as well as inns and mills. Canal du Midi lock-keeper's houses are rectangular, with one/two rooms on the ground floor. The façade's plaque indicates the distance to the nearest lock.

Ports – Ports usually have a stone pier and an inn, and in the past there were stables for the draught-horses, a washhouse, chapel and sometimes an ice house, as at Somail. Ports like Castelnaudary and Port St-Sauveur in Toulouse have dry docks for repairing boats.

Vegetation – The canal is lined with great trees which provide shade and beauty, but also limit the evaporation

- **Michelin Map:** Region map BC2. 343: AK1 and 339 AF9.
- **Info:** www.canalmidi.com, or www.canaldumidi.fr.
- **Location:** Between Naurouze and Béziers.
- **Timing:** To see as much as possible in a short time, take a driving tour of an hour or half day. For a sense of the leisurely life of the canal, explore its banks on foot or by bike. Best and slowest of all is to take to the water on a barge.
- **Don't Miss:** The cité de Carcassonne; the treasure of the church of Quarante; the three Malpas tunnels and Fonséranes locks.
- **Kids:** The Aiguille locks; the oppidum of Ensérune; a family cruise on the canal.

© A. Thuillier / MICHELIN

of canal water. Most are fast-growing species like plane trees, poplars and maritime pines. At points like Naurouze, landscaping is extensive.

🚗 DRIVING TOURS

SEUIL DE NAUROUZE TO CARCASSONNE
50km/31mi along N 113. Allow 1hr. From the watershed ridge, N 113 runs along

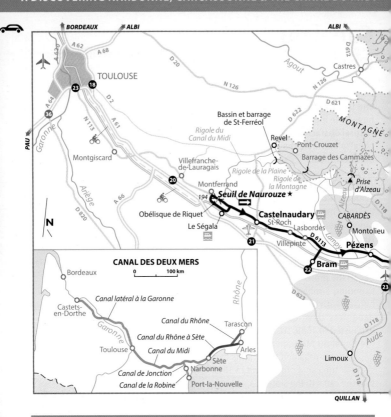

THE PRACTICAL CANAL
WHEN TO CRUISE ALONG THE
CANAL – March to November is the best time. During July and August boats for hire are difficult to find, lock traffic is intense, and prices are higher. May and June brighten the canal banks with irises and various water plants. September and October bring settled weather, mild temperatures and the countryside wears a beautiful russet mantle. Locks operate between June and August from 9am–12.30pm and 1.30–7.30pm. Some operate automatically, others manually (average time: 15min).

Hiring a boat – No licence is needed; instruction is usually provided by the boat-hire company just before departure. Maximum speed allowed: 6kph/3.7mph. Boats can be hired for a week or a weekend, for a one-way journey or for a return trip.

For summer cruising, book well in advance. Bikes are very useful to have on board for shore excursions (some boat-hire companies also hire bikes). For addresses of boat-hire companies, consult the *Planning Your Trip* section at the beginning of the guide.

Boat trips – Several companies organise trips along the Canal du Midi in season, with or without lunch.

Lou Gabaret (*Av.Pierre Semard, Carcassonne; &04 68 71 61 26. www.carcassonne-croisiere.com*). Some cruises, lasting between 1.30hr and 2.45hr, give views of the Cité.

Croisières du Midi (Luc Lines) (*35 quai des Tonneliers, Homps; &04 68 91 33 00. www.croisieres-du-midi.com*) offer 2hr trips aboard traditional *gabares*, starting from Homps, from April to late October. Bookings essential.

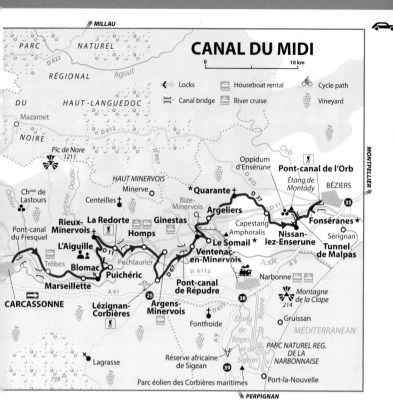

CANAL DU MIDI

the north bank of the canal all the way to Carcassonne.

Seuil de Naurouze★

Walk the shady path round the octagonal reservoir built 1669–1673 amidst an arboretum of Aleppo pines, nettle trees, sycamores, North-African cedars and wild cherry trees. The tour goes from the pumping station to the Canal du Midi and the Ocean lock (1671).

▷ Return to the parking area along an alleyway lined with plane trees.

The **Riquet obelisk**, raised in 1825 by his descendants, stands between the col de Naurouze (on the D 113) and the canal. It is surrounded by a ring of cedars and, according to legend, when the cracks in the stones close up, the society will sink into debauchery and the end of the world will arrive.

▷ Leave the Seuil de Naurouze heading southwards until you reach **Le Ségala**, a pretty canal port. Go back along the D 217 to Labastide-d'Anjou. Then take the D 6113 on the right. After **Castenaudary** take the D 6113 heading E towards Carcassonne. After Villepinte, turn right onto the D 4.

Bram

Birthplace of writer and journalist Jean Cau (1925–93), Bram is a typical example of urban planning in Languedoc, known as *circulades*, with villages built in concentric circles around the church.
Bram was the scene of one of the worst atrocities of the Albigensian crusade, when Simon de Montfort besieged the town in 1210. The siege lasted just three days, but de Montfort took revenge by cutting off the top lip of all his prisoners and blinding all but one. For the last he gouged out only one eye, so that he

could lead the others out of the town to the château of Lastours.

▶ Turn round and go back along the D 4 and then turn right onto the D 6113.

Pézens

Pézens has contrived to retain some vestiges of its ramparts and fortified gate.

▶ Head for Carcassonne on the D 6113.

LA PLAINE DU MINERVOIS

120km/75mi; allow a few extra miles for detours – half a day. ⓑ See Canal du Midi map, pp84–85.

▶ Leave Carcassonne to the N on the D 118. The road runs along the canal, and passes over the **Fresquel**. At the Bezons crossroads, take the D 620 on the right, then the D 201. After Villedubert, turn left onto the D 101.

Shortly before **Trèbes**, the canal passes over the Orbiel on a bridge built by Vauban in 1686.

▶ Leaving Trèbes, turn right on D 157.

Here is the so-called 'dry pond' of **Marseillette**, although this plain was formerly covered by the sea; today it is all orchards, vineyards and rice fields.

▶ After Marseillette turn right on the D 157, drive through B**lomac**, and follow the D 610 to Puichéric.

Puichéric is a place of narrow streets, ancient mansions, a church and castle burned down by the Black Prince in 1355. The road crosses the canal at the 🚶 **l'Aiguille** lock, which is surrounded by folk-art-inspired sculptures. **Rieux-Minervois★** is a large wine-producing village at the heart of the Minervois vineyards. Likewise is **La Redorte**, which was established in a loop in the canal. Continue on the D 11, and then take a left onto the D 610 to **Homps**, another village that was destroyed during the Albigensian crusade, and again during the Wars of Religion.

▶ Leave Homps by the D 65, and after 1.5km/1mi turn right on the D 124.

The route now runs alongside the canal towpath towards **Argens-Minervois**. The village clings to a hill on which stands the castle rebuilt in the 14C after its capture by Montfort.

Cyclists beside the Canal du Midi
© O. Fantuz / SIME / Sime / Photononstop

▷ Drive to **Lézignan-Corbières** to the south on the D 611. Drive to Paraza to the northeast on la D 67, which turns into the D 124 to **Paraza**. Leave your car and walk along the chemin de halage to Ventenac (🚶‍2.5km/1.2mi there and back).

The **Pont-canal de Répudre** was the first canal-bridge built in France, by Riquet in 1676.

▷ Follow the D 124.

The castle overlooking **Venténac-en-Minervois** offers a fine view of the canal and surrounding plain.

▷ Drive N along D 26.

Set among vineyards, the village of **Ginestas** has a **church** with a 17C gilded wood altarpiece and a 15C naïve polychrome statue of St Anne.

▷ Leave Ginestas via the D 926. Turn right onto the D 607 and head for the port of Le Somail.

The peaceful hamlet of **Le Somail★** has preserved its humpback bridge and inn dating from 1773. The **Musée de la Chapellerie** contains hats and

head-dresses from around the world, dating from 1885.

▷ Drive north on the D 607 then turn right onto the D 326 and head for Argeliers.

The medieval village of **Argeliers** has a grand fortified church.

▷ Leaving Argeliers, turn right onto the D 326, which extends the D 37E2 to Quarante.

Quarante★ is a hilltop village to the north, surrounded by vineyards. The beautiful **Église Ste-Marie** was consecrated here in 1053.

▷ Drive east on the D 37 towards Nissan-lez-Ensérune.

The former summer residence of the bishops of Narbonne, **Capestang** is today one of the Canal's busiest ports for river tourism. **Nissan-lez-Enserune** is home to the 14C gothic Église St-Saturnin.

▷ In the north of the village, cross the D609 and take the D162E opposite (signposted Oppidum d'Ensérune).

Canal du Midi

©Thieury/Fotolia.com

The **Oppidum d'Ensérune**★★ hill fort above the Béziers plain has a Mediterranean location, extraordinary pine wood and a fascinating story: in 1915, traces of an Iberian-Greek settlement and a crematorium dating from the 4C and 3C were uncovered. The hillfort encompasses a panorama of the Cévennes to Canigou and across the coastal plain. The **view**★ to the north takes in the **old Montady Lake**★, drained in 1247. The **museum**★ built on the ancient city's site contains artefacts of 6C–1C BC daily life.

▶ Returning from the oppidum, stop at the site of Malpas.

It's difficult to imagine, when driving through the small **Malpas** pass ('bad crossing'), the importance of this place that joins the Roman Via Domitia and three superimposed tunnels: The canal (165 m/180yd long, 17C) – a technical feat, the more so since it was drilled 'clandestinely' in a week (Colbert was opposed to this initiative of Riquet's, which he judged to be too dangerous given the nature of the terrain) – the railway (19C) and the drainage channel (13C) for the former wetland of the Etang de Montady.

▶ Continue to Colomiers.

The commune of **Colombiers** has a little harbour where you can hire boats.

▶ Head east on the D 162E then left onto D 609 and follow signposts to the Écluses de Fonséranes.

At the **Écluses de Fonséranes**★ a sequence of eight locks makes up a 312m/338yd-long 'staircase' enabling river craft to negotiate a drop of 25m/81ft. Today, locks have been replaced by a single lock, lying parallel to the original system.

🔖 At the **Pont-canal de l'Orb**, access is via the towpath downstream from the locks. Since 1857, a canal-bridge carrying the Canal du Midi over the Or provides an alternative to the somewhat daunting stretch of river.

ADDRESSES

🏨 STAY

😊😊 **Chambre d'hôte Villa les Cèdres** – 2 r. des Écoles. 11170 Alzonne. ℰ04 68 76 93 43. www.villalescedres.com. Closed Jan. 🅿. 3 rms and a suite 65/134€. 🍴 Rest. 20/30€. The immaculate decoration highlights the charm and authenticity of this elegant 19C townhouse. The rooms are personalized (fabrics, family furniture) and very comfortable. Dinner by candlelight under the garden arbour (don't miss the cassoulet!) will provide the finishing touch to a lovely day spent in Cathar country.

😊😊 **Chambre d'hôte La Marelle** – 19 av. du Minervois. 11700 La Redorte. ℰ04 68 91 59 30. www.chambres-la marelle.com. 🍴. 5 rms. 70€ 🍴. Free wifi.

This 16C house was a school in the 19C before becoming this lovely guest house. The rooms, furnished with flea-market finds, are named after the colour in which they are painted. Providing the sun doesn't play truant, you can take breakfast in the courtyard. Heated pool.

Chambre d'hôte Le Domaine du Parc – *3 r. du Barri. 11700 Douzens.* ℘06 77 88 48 53. 5 rms. *67/82€.* *Free wifi.* Set in a park of 5000 m2/1.2 acres, this former winemaker's house has five luxurious, soundproofed and air-conditioned rooms. The subtle decoration enhances the house's character. Sun loungers, hammocks, a boules pitch and a covered pool brighten up sunny days even more.

Chambre d'hôte La Baïsa – *Le Port. 11120 Argeliers.* ℘06 07 88 18 30. *www.peniche-chambres-hotes.com.* *3 rms. 85€.* *evening table d'hôte (by reservation only) 15/30€.* Go with the flow and treat yourself to a break aboard this lovely barge moored in the village's little harbour. Each cabin has its own private bathroom and the roof has been made into a solarium (with sun loungers), ensuring pleasant moments of relaxation. Traditional breakfasts with homemade cakes and jams; table d'hôte in the evening.

L'Appart des Anges – *Canal du Midi, 34500 Cers.* ℘04 67 26 05 57. *www.appartdesanges.com.* *3 rms.* *128/155€. Free wifi.* On the canal du Midi, shaded by 100-year-old palm trees, this barge has three immaculately decorated guest rooms. Pale wood, cosy linen, very comfortable bathrooms, spa: here's a place you'll feel good. On sunny days, breakfast/brunch is served on the terrace by the small pool.

ⵑ/EAT

Le Relais de Riquet – *12 espl. du Canal. Le Ségala. 11320 Labastide-d'Anjou.* ℘04 68 60 16 87. *www.lerelaisderiquet. com.* Set menu lunch *13€. 15/30€.* Stop for a meal here – you won't regret it. This inn, which is both restaurant and wine bar (22 products; you can also buy bottles or boxes), welcomes you with a rather retro ambiance, higlighted by the old photographs of the Canal du Midi. Homemade cassoulet and grills. A lovely terrace beside the canal.

Ferme-auberge du Pigné – *Domaine de Valgros. BP 12. 11150 Bram.* ℘04 68 76 10 25. *www.ferme-auberge-du-pigne.com.* *24/58€. 2 rm. 53€.* This lovely 18C farmhouse presides over a large farm. The dining room occupies an annex and opens onto an open terrace overlooking the garden planted with trees. Dishes are prepared using farm-reared meat and herbs from the garden, the charcuterie is also prepared here and desserts are homemade. Private pool. Preserves and farm produce for sale.

L'Ambrosia – *Carrefour de la Madeleine (D 613), 11170 Pézens.* ℘04 68 24 92 53. *Closed 5 wks Jan–Feb, Wed lunchtime, Sun evening and Mon.* 32€ (Mon–Fri lunch), *42/92€.* A young chef, Daniel Minet, is at the helm of this family restaurant, which has become a favourite stop for Aude food lovers, who are willingly won over by the joyful creativity of his cuisine. Try, in particular, when it's in season (Jul–Aug) the 'paella version 21e siècle'!

SHOPPING

GOURMET

Coopérative L'Oulibo – *Hameau de Cabezac. 11120 Bize-Minervois.* ℘04 68 41 88 88. *www.loulibo.com.* Jul–Aug Mon–Fri 8am–noon, 2pm–7pm, Sat 9am–noon, 2–7pm, Sun 10am–noon, 2–7pm; Sep–Jun Mon–Fri 8am–noon, 2–6pm. Sells olive oil, olives (hand-picked lucques de Bize and picholines) and local produce such as wine, honey, nougat, jam, crafts, etc. Guided tour (charged) of the cooperative by reservation, for groups; Jul–Aug hourly. Online sales: www.huile-olive-tapenade.fr.

Librairie ancienne du Somail – *28 allée de la Glacière. 11120 Le Somail.* ℘04 68 46 21 64. *www.le-trouve-tout-du-livre.fr.* May–mid-Nov 10am–12.30pm, 2.30–6.30pm; mid-Nov–Apr 2.30–6.30pm. *Closed Tue (except Jul–Aug).* At a picturesque location beside the Canal du Midi, the 'Le Trouve-tout-du-Livre' offers an impressive selection of works from all periods and on all subjects, as well as some prints and posters. A magical place!

EVENTS

Festival Convivencia – ℘05 62 19 08 08. *Mid-Jun–early Apr.* Touring festival along the canal. Ports of call: open-air café-bars and music from the Languedoc, Gascony and the Mediterranean.

Gruissan★

Gruissan once served as a point of defence for the port of Narbonne. The new resort adjoins the old village on the shores of the Grazel lagoon, and coastal houses are set on high stilts. Gruissan makes an ideal centre for exploring Languedoc beauty spots like the montagne de la Clape.

SIGHTS
Old Village
The old village was home to fishermen and salt-pan workers, and their houses form concentric circles around the ruins of the **Barbarossa Tower**.

Resort
The demands of tourism have thrown up hundreds of pastel-coloured apartments stacked like freight containers on a ship, plus all the trappings of a marina and popular beach-side holiday resort.

Gruissan-Plage
This resort has chalets built upon piles to protect them from floods.

EXCURSIONS
Cimetière marin
▶ 4km/2.5mi, then 30min on foot. Leave Gruissan on the D 32 towards

- **Info:** Bd. du Pech-Meynaud. ℘04 68 49 09 00. www.gruissan-mediterranee.com.
- **Location:** 20km/12.5mi SE of Narbonne on the D32
- **Don't Miss:** The ruins of the Barbarossa Tower.
- **Timing:** Allow 30 minutes to visit the town, and the same for Gruissan-Plage, where several houses have original façades. Note: At the end of the afternoon the traffic can be particular congested heading from Gruissan towards Narbonne-Plage.
- **Kids:** If the beach is not enough to keep them amused, try the saltpans of the Salins de l'Île St-Martin or bird-watching in the Parc Naturel nature reserve.

Narbonne; at the crossroads take the road for N.-D.-des-Auzils into the massif de la Clape. Keep left, and then leave the car in the parking area.
🚶 Along a stony path, among broom, pine, oak and cypress, moving headstones remind us of sailors lost at sea.

Salins de l'Île St-Martin
▶ Rte. de l'Ayrolle 3km/1.8mi S. ⬤ Guided visits on demand; écomusée ◷ open 10am–noon, 3–6pm. ◷ Closed Nov–Feb. ℘04 68 49 59 97.
Sea water invades this salt marsh along 35km/22mi of channels, and salt is harvested in September.

Le Parc Naturel★
▶ (RN9) Domaine de Montplaisir, 11100 Narbonne. 26.4km/16.4mi W on the D 32 and D105.
Maison du Parc naturel régional de la Narbonnaise – ◷ Open 8am–12.30pm, 2–6pm. ◷ Closed weekends; 25 Dec–1 Jan. ℘04 68 42 23 70. www.parc-naturel-narbonnaise.fr.

Salins de l'Île St-Martin

© Bertrand Rieger / hemis.fr

The Regional Natural Park of Narbonne in the Mediterranean extends from the Massif de Clape in the north to the Leucate plateau in the south, and embraces the massif de Fontfroide. Here, the extraordinary diversity of landscapes and natural environment is conducive to the development of flora and fauna of great richness. At the heart of the park, a vast lagoon complex is a major halt for migrating and wintering birds.

🚗 DRIVING TOUR

AROUND MONTAGNE DE LA CLAPE
👣 See region map. 36km/22.3mi. Allow about 2hrs.

The limestone massif of la Clape rises to 214m/702ft, dominating the coastal lagoons around Guissan.

▷ Leave Gruissan following the D 332 towards Narbonne-Plage.

Narbonne-Plage
This resort stretching along the coast is typical of the traditional Languedoc seaside resorts. There is sailing and water-skiing here.

▷ From Narbonne-Plage, continue N to St-Pierre-sur-Mer.

St-Pierre-sur-Mer
Family seaside resort. The chasm of l'Oeil-Doux to the north is a curious natural phenomenon. It is 100m/328ft wide and contains a salt water lake 70m/229ft deep into which the sea surges.

▷ Turn round and, at the exit of Narbonne-Plage, turn right onto the D 168 (direction Narbonne).

La montagne de la Clape
The winding and hilly road traverses a rocky terrain where pine forests compete with vineyards nestled in small valleys. From the high point of the 'mountain' there is an excellent view★ of Narbonne.

▷ After 14km/9mi, turn left onto a road returning you to Gruissan.

AROUND THE GOLFE ANTIQUE
👣 See region map (p74). 32km/20mi from Narbonne to Port-la-Nouvelle. Allow half a day.

Sprinkled with small islands, the lagoons (étangs) of Bages and Sigean once formed a gulf of the Mediterranean. On its shore the Romans built the city of Narbo Martius (Narbonne). The vagaries of the Aude river, however, and silt deposited by it (before it abruptly changed its course) turned this area into a vast wetland, its scenery resembling the Camargue.

Today, le **canal de la Robine**, which empties into the Mediterranean at Port-la-Nouvelle, after passing the Bages and Sigean lagoons on the right, and the lagoon of L'Ayrolle on the left, follows the old course of the river. Nearing Port-la-Nouvelle, it runs along the **île Ste-Lucie** which is renowned for the abundance and diversity of its wildlife, especially its flora (more than 300 recorded species). The best and most relaxing way to discover these landscapes is by boat.

▷ Leave Narbonne on the D 6009 heading south (towards Sigean and Salses). After 2km/1.5mi, take the minor road, D 105, beside the lagoon.

Bages
After 3.5km/2mi.
Standing on a rocky promontory, and looking out on to the lagoon to which it has given its name , this fishing village catches eels, in season.

Peyriac-de-Mer
5km further on.
The name of this little town, standing on the **étang de Bages-Sigean**, recalls the times when it stood on the sea coast. Formerly known for its salt pans, the town has at its heart a beautiful fortified 14C church, its portal ornamented with statues.

▶ The road leads back to the D 6009. Continue south but turn off right shortly afterwards towards Portel-des-Corbières on the D 611A, then left following signs to "Terra Vinea".

Portel-des-Corbières

This village once specialised in the production of gypsum and it has converted its quarries to new uses in an impressive manner.

Terra Vinea – *☎04 68 48 64 90. www. terra-vinea.com. ♿ ⏱ Guided tours 10.15am–6.15pm (departures every 30mn). ⊘1 Jan, 25 Dec. ⊛8.50€ (under 14 3.50€).* This old gypsum quarry has been rehabilitated as a cellar for ageing wines. A little train takes visitors on a journey back through time 80m/262ft underground, with a **son et lumière show** provided as an additional attraction. Among the themed stops on the trip are the age of ancient Rome – when wine was transported along the via Domitia – and the Middle Ages where you discover medieval habits of eating and drinking. The last stop is the shop where wines and other local produce can be sampled. There is also a restaurant.

To the south of the village, the little ruined chapel of Notre-Dame-des-Oubiels, lost among the vines, has a melancholy charm.

▶ In Portel, take the D3 towards Sigean.

Réserve africaine de Sigean★

👶 *See p93.*

👥 Parc éolien des Corbières maritimes★

To reach the windfarm, go into Sigean and head towards Port-la-Nouvelle. Turn right on the road towards Lapalme. At the first roundabout, take the road left over the main road to reach a little bridge. Park and continue on foot, taking the path heading upwards into the garrigue scrub.

This wind-farm on the summit of the hill of Castanière, between Sigean and Port-la-Nouvelle, feeds electricity into the national grid. It supplies around 25million kW, equivalent to the annual consumption of 10 000 people, excluding heating. Installed in 1991, the first five wind turbines of 660 kW each were joined by ten more in 2000. The blades reach up to 60m/197ft above the ground. Information panels on-site supply technical details. It is a futuristic scene that takes your breath away.

▶ Follow the D 6139 towards the sea.

Port-la-Nouvelle

Built at the mouth of the canal de la Robine, Port-la-Nouvelle is the only town on the Gulf of Lion between Sète and Port-Vendres to have an economic life outside the tourist season, thanks to its commercial port, which serves as a base for the distribution of oil throughout the southwest. The harbour is also equipped to receive leisure craft. A **beach** of fine sand extends for 13km/8mi.

ADDRESSES

🛏 STAY

◗◗ **Hôtel du Port** – *Bd de la Corderie. ☎04 68 49 07 33. www.hotel-gruissan.com. 🅿. 50rms. 39/185€. ⊑8/9.50€. Restaurant 20/32€. Free wifi.* The exterior may be somewhat austere but this contrasts with the pleasant and welcoming interior, which includes painted wooden furniture and southern colours in the bedrooms. The restaurant also has a southern spirit (wrought iron, sunny tones) and a pretty terrace shaded by a vine. Swimming pool and massage room.

◗◗ **Hôtel de la Plage** – *13 r. Bernard-l'Hermite à la plage des Chalets. ☎04 68 49 00 75. www.hotel-de-la-plage-gruissan. com. Closed 2 Nov–31 Mar. 🅿. 17rms. 62/68€ ⊑. Free wifi.* Tasteful bedrooms well maintained and equipped with a balcony, set in a quiet little street two minutes from the raised beach houses immortalised in the film *Betty Blue*. Warm welcome.

Réserve Africaine de Sigean★

This **safari park** (nearly 300ha/ 740 acres) owes much of its unique character to the wild landscape of coastal Languedoc, with its *garrigues* dotted with lagoons, and to the fact that for each species large areas have been set aside, which resemble their original native environment as closely as possible.

PARK TOUR
Visit by Car
Please observe the safety instructions displayed at the entrance. &🕐*Open Apr–Sep 9am–6.30pm; rest of the year: 9am–4pm.* ☜*25€ (children 4–14, 19€).* ☏*04 68 48 20 20. www.reserve africainesigean.fr.*

The route for visitors in cars goes through four areas, reserved for free ranging animals: the **African bush** with its red buffalo, ostriches, impalas, gnus, giraffes and greater kudus, the males of which species have long twisted horns; the enclosure of the **Asiatic black bear★**, identified by the white V on its chest; the **lion** enclosure, inhabited by a small pride of apparently peaceful males and females (but still be wary of them!); and the **African savannah** with its numerous antelopes (Cape elans, sita-tungas, blesboks etc…), where you can also admire **white rhinoceroses**, the elegant black and white markings of the zebras and the astonishing horns – almost horizontal – of the watusi.

Visit on Foot
3hr. Start from the central car parks, inside the safari park.
🚶Walking round the safari park, visitors will come across the fauna of various continents – Tibetan bears, dromedaries, antelopes, zebras, cheetahs, alligators – and, near the lagoon of L'Oeil de Ca, bird life such as pink flamingoes, cranes, ducks, white storks, sacred ibis, macaws, swans and pelicans.

◉ **Location:** 18km/11m S of Narbonne and 54km/34m N of Perpignan by the N9. After Sigean follow signs.

◈ **Don't Miss:** The Asiatic black bear, which sunbathes on the road; the impressive rhinoceroses in the African savannah and the chimpanzee's grooming sessions.

🕐 **Timing:** Allow half a day (there are picnic areas, refreshment stalls and restaurants).

👪 **Kids:** There is plenty for them to do here. The goat enclosure is a favourite with young children.

ADDRESSES

🛏 STAY

⬮**Chambre d'hôte la Milhauque –** *11440 Peyriac-de-Mer. 2km/1.25mi NW of Peyriac-sur-Mer.* ☏*04 68 41 69 76. www.la-milhauque.gites11.com.* 🅿☐ *4rms. 55/75€.* ☐ *Dinner 22€. Free wifi.* A restored sheepfold, tastefully restored, offers three rooms in a superb setting out in the *garrigue* and amid vineyards. *Bourride d'anguille* is a speciality dish.

⬮⬮ **Domaine de la Pierre Chaude –** *Les Campets, 11490 Portel-des-Corières. 6km/3.7mi W of Réserve Africaine, towards Duran by D 611 A.* ☏*04 68 48 89 79. www.lapierrechaude.com.* ☐ *Closed Jan–Mar. 5 self-catering gîtes. 275/1,400€ (week).* ☐ *depending on numbers and season.* This former *chai* (18C), nestled in a hamlet amid vines and garrigue, was renovated by a student of the architect Gaudí. Ravishing guest rooms and Andalusian-style patio shaded by fig trees.

🍴 EAT

◉ The safari park's panoramic restaurant is a chance to have lunch while enjoying a great view over the African plain.

Abbaye de Fontfroide★★

Fontfroide's spectacular **Cistercian abbey** enjoys a tranquil setting amidst cypress trees, and sunset lights up its flame-coloured ochre and pink Corbières sandstones.

ABBEY★★

The welcome centre contains the ticket office, bookstore, winery and restaurant. Guided tours: mid-Jul–Aug 10am–5.30pm; Apr–mid-Jul and Sep–Oct 10am– 5.30pm; Nov–Mar 10am–4pm. 9€ (children ages 10–18, 2.50€). ℘04 68 45 11 08. www.fontfroide.com.

In 1093 a Benedictine abbey was founded on land belonging to Aymeric I, Viscount of Narbonne, and the 12C and 13C saw great prosperity. Pope Pierre de Castelnau's legate, whose assassination sparked off the Aligensian Crusade, stayed here after his trip to Maguelone. Jacques Fournier, who reigned under the name of Benedict XII, was abbot here from 1311 to 1317. Most abbey buildings were erected in the 12C and 13C. The tour begins in the 17C Cour d'honneur,

- **Info:** ℘04 68 45 11 08. www.fontfroide.com.
- **Location:** 14km/8.75mi SW of Narbonne.
- **Timing:** In order to appreciate the acoustics of the nave, time your visit to attend a concert or to participate in one of the rare masses held here. At all other times, allow 1hr15min (guided visit). Note that the tour route in winter differs to the summer one so as to visit heated rooms.
- **Don't Miss:** The cloister and exquisite early 20C windows.
- **Kids:** Decipher the imagery in the stained glass windows with your kids.

moves through the 13C guard-room and on to the medieval buildings.

Cloisters★★★ – The cloisters are an example of architectural elegance. The oldest gallery (mid-13C) adjoins the church.

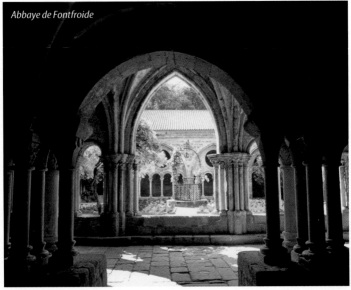
Abbaye de Fontfroide

© Kevin O'Hara / age fotostock

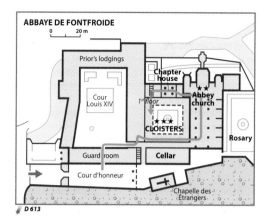

ABBAYE DE FONTFROIDE

0   20 m

Prior's lodgings

Chapter house

Cour Louis XIV

1st floor

★★ Abbey church

★★★ CLOISTERS

Rosary

Guard room   Cellar

Cour d'honneur

Chapelle des Étrangers

D 613

Abbey church★★ – Building began on the abbey church in the mid-12C and south chapels were added in the 14C–15C.

Chapter House – The Chapter house is roofed with nine Romanesque vaults supported on decorative ribs that spring from slender marble colonnettes.

Monks' dormitory – Set above the storeroom, the dormitory is roofed with 12C fine ribbed barrel-vaulting.

Exterior – The **Rose garden** contains about 3,000 rose bushes (11 varieties). Follow footpaths around the abbey to appreciate the charms of its setting.

EXCURSION
Abbaye N.-D.-de-Gaussan
▶ *8km/5mi W of Fontfroide along the D 423.*

The original buildings of this former abbey-farm were built 12C–14C, and the abbey remained in occupation until the Revolution. In the 19C, major restoration work was carried out, and a Benedictine monastic community has occupied the abbey since 1993. Mass is sung in Gregorian chant at 10am.

ADDRESSES

🛏 STAY

◷◷ **Chambre d'hôte Domaine de St-Jean** – *11200 Bizanet (10km/6mi southwest of Narbonne via N 9, N 113, D 613 then D 224). ℘04 68 45 17 31. www.domaine-de-saint-*

jean.com. ⚲. 4 rms. 65/80€ ⚬. Free wifi. This large house in a wine estate will suit anyone who likes peace and authenticity. The rooms are comfortable and some are air-conditioned *(25€/person supplement)*. They are enlivened by hand-painted motifs on the furniture and walls. One room has a private terrace with a beautiful view over the Massif de Fontfroide. Pleasant garden maintained by the proprietor.

◷◷◷ **Chambre d'hôte Demeure de Roquelongue** – *53 av. de Narbonne, 11200 St-André-de-Roquelongue. ℘04 68 45 63 57. www.demeure-de-roquelongue.com. Closed 16 Nov–28 Feb. 5 rms. 95/135€ ⚬. Restaurant 35€. Free wifi.* This elegant house in a wine estate (1885) has enchanting rooms decorated with antique furniture and equipped with beautiful bathrooms. Cosy sitting room with a charming atmosphere.

🍴 EAT

◷◷ **La Table de Fontfroide** – *Abbaye de Fontfroide. ℘04 68 41 02 26. www.fontfroide.com. Lunch Mar–Nov, dinner Jul–Aug, Wed–Sat. 18.50/22.50€.* Two gourmet menus are served in the old farmhouse of the abbey. Gîte accommodation is available. *(115€ per night).*

SHOPPING

Vin du domaine de Fontfroide – Wines are on sale in the reception building and the cellar below.

Lagrasse★

On the shores of the river Orbieu, the town owes its existence to its majestic abbey. An outpost of the Carolingian civilisation near Frankish Catalonia, the abbey's fortifications were added in the 14C and its embellishments added in the 18C. See the 11C humback bridge and covered market.

🐾 WALKING TOUR

MEDIEVAL CITY

Enter the walled town via Porte du Consulat and follow the street of the same name before turning left onto Rue Paul-Vergnes. The old medieval city developed around the monastery. Stroll the narrow streets lined with medieval houses where craftsmen have set up workshops.

Église Saint-Michel

This Gothic church is flanked by nine side chapels. Note the keystones decorated with the guilds' symbols.

▶ Retrace your steps and turn left onto rue de l'Église; cross place de la Bouquerie; follow rue des Mazels.

Place de la Halle

The 14C covered market has 10 stone pillars supporting a timber framework. Medieval façades, some half-timbered, surround the square (note the 14C **Maison Maynard**). See the 16C Maison Sibra in Rue Foy, then follow Rue des Deux-Ponts to **Pont Vieux**, for access to the abbey.

ABBAYE SAINTE-MARIE-D'ORBIEU★

Allow 45min. ⏱*Open Jul–Sep 10am–6pm; Apr–Jun and Oct 10.30am–11.30am, 2–5pm; Feb–Mar and Nov–mid-Dec 10–11.30am, 2–6pm.* ✆3.50€. ✆04 68 43 15 99.
The **abbot's chapel★** contains rare late-14C ceramic paving and traces of mural paintings. The Palais Vieux includes the oldest parts of the abbey. A lapidary

ℹ Info: 16 r. Paul-Vergnes, 11220 Lagrasse. ✆04 68 43 11 56. www.lagrasse.com.

◑ Location: 42km/26.25mi SW of Narbonne. The D 212 from Fabrézan offers a sweeping view of the fortified town.

🅿 Parking: Visitors are strongly urged to park outside the town in the two surfaced carparks provided. Out of season there is parking under the plane trees of the Promenade.

👁 Don't Miss: A walk along the Orbieu river; the architecture of the Abbaye Ste-Marie d'Orbieu and the view from the Plateau de Lacamp.

🕐 Timing: 30min is enough to explore the medieval city. On Saturday morning, the local producers' market is a good reason to extend your stay.

Abbaye Sainte-Marie-d'Orbieu

© brenkel / iStockphoto

Lagrasse

© Jean-Paul Azam / hemis.fr

museum displays fragments from the original cloisters. The lower level contains cellars, store rooms and bakery. The **Cloisters** were built in 1760 on the site of the visible remains of the 1280 cloisters. The 13C abbey church was built on the foundations of a Carolingian church. The 40m/131ft bell-tower built in 1537 affords an attractive view from the top.

EXCURSIONS
St-Martin-des-Puits
 8km/5mi S of Lagrasse on the D 23 then the D 212.
The church has a choir of the pre-Romanesque period, along with 12C murals.

Plateau de Lacamp★★
 27km/17mi SW on D 23 and D 212.
Between Caunette-sur-Lauquet and Lairière, the Louviéro Pass on D 40 gives access to the 'forest track' of the western Corbières. The Plateau de Lacamp, with an average altitude of 700m/2 300ft, forms a breakwater towards the Orbieu. The track runs along the southern edge of the causse for about 3km/2mi, with sweeping **views** of the Orbieu valley, the Bugarach and Canigou peaks, St-Barthélemy, the threshold of the Lauragais and the Montagne Noire.

Villar-en-Val
 17km/10.5mi W Lagrasse by the D 3 then, to the left, the D 603 towards Serviès-en-Val and the D 10.
The birthplace of poet Joseph Delteil (1894–1978). A Poetry Trail has been made through the forest and garrigue to the clearing where he spent his early years with his grandfather.

🚗 DRIVING TOUR

LE PAYS DE LÉZIGNAN★
 See region map. 52km/32.3mi. Allow about 2hrs. Leave Lagrasse on the D 212 to the N (direction Lézignan).

Fabrezan
Dominating the Orbieu valley, the village with its winding streets houses a small museum in the town hall dedicated to scientist and poet Charles Cros (1842–1888), who invented the paléophone, precursor of Edison's phonograph.

 Turn left twice, on the D 212, then the D 111. Before Moux, turn right. At Conilhac, turn left onto the D 165.

The road climbs a hill then opens out onto the **vineyards** of **Montbrun-des-Corbières** which it dominates.

▶ The D 127 and D 611 lead to Lézignan.

Lézignan-Corbières

9 cours de la République. ☎04 68 27 05 42 www.lezignan-corbieres.fr. Standing in the rugged landscapes of Corbières, halfway between Carcassonne and the sea, Lézignan largely depends on wine for its economic life. The medieval city, of which some traces remain, is dominated by the church of St-Félix, distinguished by its impressive fortified bell tower. The narrow streets, small squares and promenades bordered by old plane trees around the church are an invitation to take a stroll or have a rest in the shade.

▶ Regagnez Lagrasse par la D 611, puis la D 212 au sud.

ADDRESSES

🏨 STAY

⊖⊜⊟ **Hostellerie des Corbières** – *9 bd de la Promenade, 11220 Lagrasse. ☎04 68 43 15 22. www.hostellerie-des-corbieres.com. Closed 15–30 Nov and 10 Jan–10 Feb. 6 rms. 70/95€. �8€. Set menu lunch 17€. 27/37€. Free wifi.* This mansion situated at the heart of the village has well-equipped rooms in Louis Philippe style. The restaurant terrace looks on to a beautiful landscape of vines, olive trees and garrigue countryside. Traditional cuisine accompanied by panoramic views of the Corbières.

⊖⊜⊟ **Hôtel La Fargo** – *11220 St-Pierre-des-Champs. ☎04 68 43 12 78. www.la fargo.fr. Closed 21 Dec–23 Feb. ♿🅿. 12 rms. 75/125€. ⊐8€. Rest. 30€.* This former Catalan forge in a magnificent wooded park along the riverbank, is renovated with Colonial style furnishings.

⊖⊜⊟ **Chambre d'hôte M. et Mme Tenenbaum** – *5 av. du Minervois, 11700 Azille. ☎04 68 91 56 90. www.pierreet claudine.com. Closed 1–15 Nov. 🅿 ⊠ 4 rms. 68/71€⊐.* Free wifi. A charming welcome and a swimming pool sheltered by the high walls of the terrace-garden are among the attractions of this mansion built in 1835. The rooms (one of which is air-conditioned) are equipped

with a variety of furniture. There is one family room (4/5 people) and one room with a private terrace looking on to the swimming pool.

⊖⊜⊟ **Le Clos des Souquets** – *47 av. de Lagrasse, 11200 Fabrezan. ☎04 68 43 52 61. www.leclos-des-souquets.com. 🅿. 5 rms. 60/90€. ⊐9€. Restaurant 19.50/30€. Free wifi.* This small auberge offers traditional cuisine, along with a choice of hotel or B&B. A true find.

⊖⊜⊟ **Chambre d'hôte La Bastide de Donos** – *11200 Thézan-des-Corbières. ☎04 68 43 32 11. www.chateaudonos.com. Closed 1 Nov–Easter. 🅿 3 rms and 2 suites. 105/125€. ⊐Table d'hôte by reservation. Free wifi.* Offers superb view of the chateau and the old washing place. On-site wine tasting. Access to private lake.

🍴EAT

⊖ **La Balade Gourmande** – *B d Léon-Castel, D 6113, 11200 Lézignan-Corbières. ☎04 68 27 22 18. Closed weekends and two weeks in Feb. Reservations recommended. ♿🅿. Set menu lunch 15€. 12/30€.* Two dining rooms decorated in southern colours. The perfect place to try cassoulet.

⊖⊜ **L'Affenage** – *32 bd de la Promenade – ☎04 68 43 16 59. ♿ Closed Sun eve and Mon. "Hiker's lunch" 12€ . 18/25€.* A large dining room, extended by a terrace under the plane trees. Salads and dishes of the day. Corbières wines.

⊖⊜ **Le Tournedos** – *Pl. de Lattrede-Tassigny, 11200 Lézignan-Corbières. ☎04 68 27 11 51. Closed Sun pm and Mon. Set menu lunch 14. 17/46€. Rms 46/48€ . ⊐8€.* Grills and tournedos are the chef's specialities, served in a bright and airy dining room. 19 bedrooms also available.

SHOPPING

La Maison du Terroir – *6 bd de la Promenade. ☎04 68 43 11 43. Apr–Oct. 10am–12.30pm, 3–7pm.* AOC wines, cooked dishes, jams, farmhouse cheeses: the best produce of the Corbières.

EVENTS

Le Banquet du livre – *Août, à l'abbaye.* Talks and conferences with writers. *(rens. Association Marque Page et Bistrot du Livre – ☎04 68 32 63 89).*

Carcassonne★★★

A visit to Carcassonne is like stepping back to the Middle Ages. On Bastille Day (14 July), a dramatic fireworks display seems to set the citadel of this UNESCO World Heritage Site alight. The romantic old town contrasts sharply with the commercial Ville Basse (lower town), a *bastide* town, where Carcassonne shows off its role as the centre of the Aude's wine-growing industry.

A BIT OF HISTORY

Carcassonne commands the main communication route between the Mediterranean and Toulouse. For 400 years, Carcassonne remained the capital of a county, then of a viscountcy under the suzerainty of the counts of Toulouse. After the annexation of Roussillon under the Treaty of the Pyrénées, Carcassonne's military importance dwindled to almost nil, as some 200km/125mi separated it from the new border, guarded by Perpignan. Carcassonne was abandoned and left to decay until the Romantic movement brought the Middle Ages back into fashion.

Prosper Mérimée, appointed general inspector of Historical Monuments, celebrated the ruins in his memoir, *Notes d'un voyage dans le Midi de la France*, 1835. Local archaeologist Jean-Pierre

- ▶ **Population:** 43,950.
- **Michelin Map:** 344: F3.
- **Info:** 28 rue de Verdun, 11000 Carcassonne. ℰ04 68 10 24 30. www. carcassonne-tourisme.com.
- **Location:** 96km/60mi SE of Toulouse, 60km/37.5mi W of Narbonne.
- **Timing:** Allow a half day for the town. Take advantage of the morning light to enjoy the stained glass windows of St-Nazaire. The tour of the Cabardès requires a day.
- **Don't Miss:** The château comtal, the walk around the Cité along the "lices", the stained glass and statues of the basilique St-Nazaire.
- **Kids:** The musée de l'École and the Parc Australien.

Cros-Mayrevieille was passionately committed to the restoration of his native town. After visiting Carcassonne, **Viollet -le-Duc** returned to Paris with such an enthusiastic report that the Commis-

Aerial view of Carcassonne

© P. Blot / MICHELIN

sion of Historical Monuments agreed to undertake the Cité's restoration in 1844.

⚫🐾WALKING TOURS

LA CITÉ★★★

The 'Cité' of Carcassonne on the Aude's east bank is the largest fortress in Europe. It consists of a fortified nucleus, the Château Comtal, and a double curtain wall: the outer ramparts, with 14 towers, separated from the inner ramparts (24 towers) by the outer bailey, or lists *(lices)*. A resident population of 139 and school and post office saves Carcassonne from becoming a ghost town.

⚫ Leave the car in one of the car parks outside the walls in front of the gateway to the east, Porte Narbonnaise.

Porte Narbonnaise

On either side of the gateway to the original fortified town are two massive Narbonne towers, and between them, a 13C statue of the Virgin Mary. Inside, the 13C rooms restored by Viollet-le-Duc house **temporary exhibitions** of modern art.

Rue Cros-Mayrevieille

This street leads directly to the castle, although you might prefer to get there by wandering the narrow winding streets of the medieval town, with its many crafts and souvenir shops.

TOURS

2hr tour of the ramparts aboard a **tourist train** (⚫⚫ *open May–Sep tours, 25min, leaving from the Porte Narbonnaise with explanation of the defence system 10am-noon, 2–6pm;* ⚫ *7€, children 4€;* ☎*04 68 24 45 70)* or a **horse-drawn carriage** (⚫ *open Apr–Nov: discovery of the ramparts in a caleche, 20min, with historical commentary;* ⚫ *7€, children 4€; Route de la Cavayère, Montlegun, Carcassonne;* ☎*04 68 71 54 57; www.carcassonne-caleches.com).*

Château Comtal

⚫🐾*Apr–Sep 10am–6.30pm; Oct–Mar 9.30am–5pm. Last admissions 45min before closing.* ⚫*Closed 1 Jan, 1 May, 1 and 11 Nov, 25 Dec.* ⚫*8.50€.* ☎*04 68 11 70 72. www.carcassonne. monuments-nationaux.fr.*

The castle was originally the palace of the viscounts, and built in the 12C by Bernard Aton Trencavel. It became a citadel after Carcassonne was made part of the royal estate in 1226. Since the reign of St Louis IX, it has been defended by a large semicircular barbican and formidable moat.

The tour begins on the first floor, now an archaeological museum (**Musée lapidaire**). This museum exhibits archaeological remains from the fortified town and local region, including a 12C marble lavabo from the abbey of Lagrasse, late 15C stone **calvary★** from Villanière and the recumbent figure of a knight killed in battle. A collection of prints shows the fortified town as it was before Viollet-le-Duc's restoration.

Cour d'honneur – The buildings surrounding the large main courtyard have been restored.

The building to the south has an interesting façade reflecting its three periods of construction: Romanesque, Gothic and Renaissance.

Cour du Midi – The tallest of the fortress' watchtowers, the Tour de Guet, affords a view of up to 30km/19mi away.

⚫ Leave the castle and follow rue de la Porte d'Aude on the left.

Porte d'Aude

A fortified path, the Montée d'Aude, weaves from the church of St-Gimer up to this heavily defended gateway.

The **Tour de l'Inquisition** was the seat of the Inquisitor's court, and its central pillar with chains and cell bear witness to the tortures inflicted upon heretics. The Bishop's **Tour carrée de l'Évêque** was appointed much more comfortably.

⚫ Return towards the Porte d'Aude and continue along the Lices Basses.

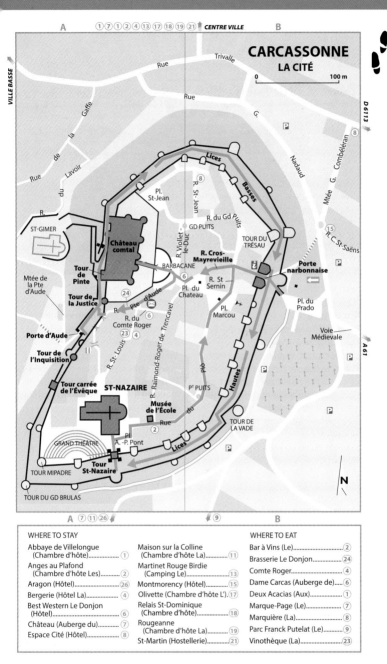

CARCASSONNE
LA CITÉ

WHERE TO STAY

Abbaye de Villelongue
(Chambre d'hôte).................. ①

Anges au Plafond
(Chambre d'hôte Les)......... ②

Aragon (Hôtel)....................... ㉖

Bergerie (Hôtel La)................ ④

Best Western Le Donjon
(Hôtel)................................... ⑤

Château (Auberge du)........... ⑦

Espace Cité (Hôtel)............... ⑧

Maison sur la Colline
(Chambre d'hôte La)............. ⑪

Martinet Rouge Birdie
(Camping Le)........................ ⑬

Montmorency (Hôtel)........... ⑮

Olivette (Chambre d'hôte L').. ⑰

Relais St-Dominique
(Chambre d'hôte)................ ⑱

Rougeanne
(Chambre d'hôte La)........... ⑲

St-Martin (Hostellerie)........ ㉑

WHERE TO EAT

Bar à Vins (Le)........................ ②

Brasserie Le Donjon................. ㉔

Comte Roger........................... ④

Dame Carcas (Auberge de)..... ⑥

Deux Acacias (Aux)................. ①

Marque-Page (Le).................... ⑦

Marquière (La)........................ ⑧

Parc Franck Putelat (Le)......... ⑨

Vinothèque (La)...................... ㉓

The itinerary takes you past the **Tour de la Justice**. The Trencavels, protectors of the Cathars, sought refuge here with the count of Toulouse during the Albigensian Crusade. This circular tower has windows whose tilting wooden shutters enabled those inside to see (and drop things on) attackers.

▶ Walk beneath the drawbridge by the Porte Narbonnaise and continue SE.

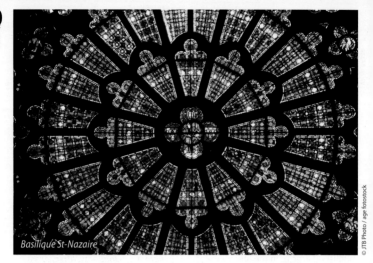

Basilique St-Nazaire

© JTB Photo / age fotostock

'Lices basses' and 'Lices hautes'

These wide gaps between the inner and outer ramparts, edged with moats, were used for weapons practice and jousting. The '**lices basses**' are the part contained between the two main walls, between the Porte d'Aude and the Porte Narbonnaise at the northern end of the city. The '**lices hautes**' run south from Porte Narbonaise to the Tour St-Nazaire.

Beyond Porte Narbonnaise, note the three-storey Tour de la Vade on the outer curtain wall to the left. This fortified tower kept watch over all of the eastern ramparts.

Carry on to the Tour du Grand Brulas, on the corner opposite the Tour Mipadre.

Tour St-Nazaire

This tower's postern was only accessible by ladders. A well and an oven are still in evidence on the first floor. At the top of the tower is a viewing table.

▶ Enter the Cité through the Porte St-Nazaire.

Basilique St-Nazaire★

All that remains of the original church is the Romanesque nave. The basilica's **stained-glass windows★★** (13C–14C) are considered the most impressive in the south of France. Remarkable

statues★★ adorn the pillars around the chancel walls, and one of the most eye-catching bishops' tombs is that of Pierre de Roquefort (14C).

Viollet-le-Duc is responsible for the modifications to the west: he wrongly believed that the church belonged to a "Visigothic " fortification that justified the belltower-wall being crowned with crenellations.

▶ Return to Porte Narbonnaise on rue du Plô.

▲♟ Musée de l'école

3 r. du Plô. ♿ ⏱*Open 10am-6pm (7pm in summer), by reservation (apply one month in advance). Closed 1 Jan, 25 Dec.* ✆*3.50€ (students and the unemployed 3€, under-12s free).* ✆*04 68 25 95 14.*
Occupying an old school, this museum consists of documents, materials and furniture evoking education at the beginning of the 20th century. Desks, satchels and blackboards are complemented by instructive posters. In one of the classrooms you can practise writing with a dip pen.

LOWER TOWN

Founded by Saint Louis on the left bank of the Aude river and flanked to the north by the **Canal du Midi**, the lower town has preserved its street grid plan typical of bastide towns. It is organised around a central square, place Carnot.

Maison des Mémoires Joë-Bousquet

53 rue de Verdun. ⟨⟩ *Daily except Sun, Mon and public holidays 9am–noon, 2–6pm.* ⟨⟩ *No charge.* ⟨⟩ *04 68 72 45 55.*
Paralysed during World War II, Joë Bousquet lived in this house from 1918 to 1950 and never left his closed-shutter first floor bedroom. Here he wrote his poetry and letters and received the famous writers and artists of his time – André Gide, Paul Valéry, Aragon, Michaux, Paul Éluard and Max Ernst. He founded the Carcassonne Group with two local writers and published articles in the literary magazine *Cahiers du Sud.*

Musée des Beaux-Arts

1 rue de Verdun. Entrance: sq Gambetta. ⟨⟩ *Open mid-Jun–mid-Sep 10am–6pm; mid-Sep–mid-Jun Tue–Sat 9am–noon, 2–6pm (1st Sun 2.30–5.30pm).* ⟨⟩ *Closed public holidays.* ⟨⟩ *04 68 77 73 70.*
On display are 17C and 18C paintings of French, Flemish and Dutch masters, and faïence from Moustiers, Marseille and elsewhere. Works of Carcassonne painter Jacques Gamelin (1738–1803) add local interest. Note Chardin's *Les Apprêts d'un déjeuner.* Works by Courbet and other artists from the French Academy represent 19C painting.

EXCURSIONS
Parc australien

Chemin des Bartavelles. 👥👶 ⟨⟩ *Open Jul–Aug 10.30am–7pm; Oct Wed and Sat 2–6, Sun and public holidays 10.30am–7pm); rest of the year daily except Sun 2am–6pm* ⟨⟩ *9€ (children, 4–12, 6.50€).* ⟨⟩ *04 68 25 05 07. www.leparcaustralien.free.fr.*
A French take on the beasts of Australia, with wallabies, kangaroos and emus.

Montréal

▶ *16km/10mi W of Carcassonne.*
This village overlooks the vineyards of the Carcassès and the vast plains of Razè and Lauragais; it's dominated by 14C St Vincent's collegiale, built in the southern Gothic style.

Fanjeaux

▶ *9km/5.5mi further, along the D 119.*
A sacred place since Roman times – the name comes from Fanum Jovis, the Temple of Jupiter – the village is closely linked with the Cathar story.

🚗 DRIVING TOURS

CABARDÈS REGION★
Round trip from Carcassonne 165km/ 103mi – Allow 1 day. ⟨⟩ *See region map.*
▶ *Leave Carcassonne along N 113 towards Castelnaudary. After Pezens, turn right onto D 629.*

Aragon

Proudly standing on its rocky outcrop, this little jewel of Cabardès is a place of narrow streets, charm and heritage, with a 16C castle that now serves as a B&B.

▶ Take the D 203 NW towards Fraisse-Cabardès then the D 148 to the left (direction Montolieu).

Montolieu★

This village in the Cabardès region is devoted to the world of books, with 20 or so bookshops, craft workshops (bookbinder's, copyist's, engraver's) and a **Conservatoire des Arts et Métiers du livre** dedicated to book design and production (⟨⟩ *open Apr–Oct 10am– noon, 3–6pm, Sat–Sun 3–6pm; rest of the year weekdays 2–5pm.* ⟨⟩ *Closed 1 Jan, 25 Dec;* ⟨⟩ *2€;* ⟨⟩ *04 68 24 80 04).*

▶ A small road (D 64) S of the village leads to Villelongue Abbey.

Ancienne Abbaye de Villelongue

⟨⟩ *Open Easter–Jun and Sep–Oct daily except Mon 10am–noon, 2–6.30pm (Sat 4pm); Jul–Aug daily except Mon 10am–noon, 2–7pm).* ⟨⟩ *5€.* ⟨⟩ *Closed Nov–Apr.* ⟨⟩ *04 68 24 90 38. www. abbaye-de-villelongue.com.*

This old abbey church was built to a Cistercian design and rebuilt in the 13–14C. It's interesting for its refectory with ribbed vaulting, the south gallery of the cloisters and its chapter-house.

▶ D 164 on the right leads to Saissac.

Saissac

This village high over the Vernassonne ravine is shadowed by the ruins of a 14C castle. The largest tower in the old curtain wall affords a beautiful panorama of the site.

▶ Drive E along D 103.

Brousses-et-Villaret

An 18C **paper mill** manufactures paper the traditional way, and its **Gutenberg Museum** (○☀♛*open Jul–Aug guided tours (1hr) on the hour 11am–7pm; rest of the year 10am–noon, 2–6pm; ○closed 1 Jan, 25 Dec; ☞7€; ♪04 68 26 67 43 www.moulinapapier.com) relates the history of printing techniques.

▶ Continue on D 103 to D 118 and turn right. Beyond Cuxac-Cabardès, turn right onto D 73, follow D 9.

Mas-Cabardès

The ruins of a fortified castle tower over this village and its narrow streets. Near the **church** belfry topped by a 15C octagonal tower of Romanesque appearance, look for a 16C stone cross carved with a shuttle, emblem of the Orbiel valley weavers.

▶ Drive S along D 101.

Les Quatre Châteaux de Lastours★

Departure from the village centre, at the 'Accueil Village'. ○*Open Jul–Aug 9am–8pm; Apr–Jun and Sep 10am–6pm; Oct–Mar certain days 10am–5pm.* ○*Closed Jan and 25 Dec.* ☞*5€.* ♪*04 68 77 56 02.*
The ruins of four castles stand out in this rugged rocky landscape between the Orbiel and Grésillou valleys. The **Cabaret**, Tour Régine, Fleur d'Espine

and Quertinheux castles comprised the Cabaret fortress in the 12C. Cathar refugees sought protection at Cabaret, which resisted every attack. For an exquisite **view** of the Châteaux de Lastours ruins, drive up to the viewpoint on the opposite side of Grésillou valley.

▶ Follow D 701 to Salsigne.

Salsigne

Mining has given a livelihood to this area long before Roman and Saracen invaders extracted iron, copper, lead and silver here. After gold was discovered in 1892, mining concessions grew up at Salsigne, Lastours and Villanière. 92t of gold, 240t of silver and 30,000t of copper has been extracted since 1924.

▶ From Salsigne, follow the signs to the Grotte de Limousis.

Grotte de Limousis

○♣♟♛*Guided tours Jul–Aug 10am–6pm; Apr–Jun and Sep 10.30am–6.30pm; Mar and Oct 2.30–5.30pm; Nov Sun and public holidays 10am–6pm.* ○*Closed rest of year.* ☞*8.80€ (children 5.60€).* ♪*04 68 77 50 26.*
Discovered in 1811, this cave is set in an arid, bare limestone countryside of vines and olive trees. The cave's chambers extend for 663m/2 179ft with curiously shaped concretions alternating with mirrors of limpid water. An enormous **chandelier★** of white aragonite crystals is the main feature of the cave.

▶ Return on D 511 to D 111 and there, follow the signs to **Villeneuve-Minervois**. Go through the village, which earns a living mainly from wine-growing, and take D 112 towards Cabrespine.

Gorges de la Clamoux

These gorges show the striking contrast between the two slopes of Montagne Noire. The road traverses the floor of the valley and its orchards and vineyards as far as Cabrespine.

▶ Take the road on the left which climbs to the Gouffre de Cabrespine.

Gouffre de Cabrespine

♿🧗‍♂️🗣️📷*Guided tours: Jul–Aug 10am–6pm; Apr–Jun and Sep–Oct 10am–noon, 2–5.30pm; rest of year: request opening hours.* 🕐*Closed 10 Dec–10 Feb.* 💿*9.20€ (children aged 5–12, 5.90€).* 📞*04 68 26 14 22.*

The upper part of this gigantic chasm is a huge network of subterranean galleries drained by the River Clamoux. The 'Salle des Éboulis' (chamber of fallen earth) is 250m/820ft high.

Follow the balconied walkway through stalactites and stalagmites, dazzling curtains of aragonite crystals, the 'Salles Rouges' (red galleries) and the 'Salle aux Cristaux' (crystal gallery).

▶ Return to D 112. The road reaches **Cabrespine**, overlooked by Roc de l'Aigle, then winds up bends between chestnut groves. At Pradelles-Cabardès, take D 87 to the right towards the Pic de Nore.

Pic de Nore★

Montagne Noire's highest point, the Pic de Nore (*1,211m/3,973ft*), towers over the undulating heath-covered countryside. The **panorama★** stretches from the Lacaune, Espinouse and Corbières mountains, to Canigou, the Carlit massif and Midi de Bigorre.

▶ Return to Pradelles-Cabardès and turn left onto D 89 then right onto D 620 towards Caunes-Minervois.

Lespinassière

Built on an isolated peak inside a mountain cirque, Lespinassière has a castle with a 15C square tower.

Gorges de l'Argent-Double

The river Argent-Double, which springs up near Col de la Salette, flows through a deep and sinuous gorge.

Caunes-Minervois

The village is known for its grey and white-veined red marble quarried

nearby. This marble was used to decorate the Grand Trianon in Versailles, the Palais Garnier in Paris and the St-Sernin Basilica in Toulouse.

Fine mansions dominate the town hall square: Hôtel Sicard (14C) and **Hôtel d'Alibert** (16C). The former Benedictine **abbey church** (♿🕐*open Jul–Aug 10am–7pm; Apr–Jun, Sep–Oct 10am–noon, 2–6pm; Nov–Mar 10am–noon, 2–5pm;* 🕐*closed Jan;* 💿*5€;* 📞*04 68 78 09 44; www.caunesminervois.com*) has retained its 11C Romanesque east end.

▶ Drive SW along D 620. Beyond Villegly, turn right onto D 35.

Conques-sur-Orbiel

This pretty village has traces of its earlier fortifications, including the 16C south gateway and the church belfry-porch.

ADDRESSES

🛏️ STAY

👛🍴 **Hôtel Espace Cité** – *132 r. Trivalle.* 📞*04 68 25 24 24. www.hotelespacecite.fr. Apr. 48 rms. 80/93€* 🍽️*8.50€. Free wifi* Modern hotel at the foot of the citadel, with bright and functional rooms.

👛🍴 **Chambre d'hôte La Maison sur la Colline** – *Lieu-dit Ste-Croix.* 📞*04 68 47 57 94. www.lamaisonsurlacolline.com. Closed end Dec–mid Feb.* 🅿️🍽️*. 5 rms. 85/95€. Restaurant, table d'hôte 30€.* This restored farm has a view of the Cité from its garden. Rooms are spacious and colourful.

👛🍴🍽️ **Hôtel Montmorency** – *2 r. Camille-St-Saëns.* 📞*04 68 11 96 70. www. lemontmorency.com.* 🅿️ *30 rms. 80/300€.* 🍽️*12€. Free wifi.* Close to La Cité. Very smart rooms, well furnished, but simple.

👛🍴🍽️ **Hôtel Aragon** – *15 montée Combéléran.* 📞*04 68 47 16 31. www. hotelaragon.fr.* 🅿️🍽️*. 29 rms. 85/120€ (according to season and view).* 🍽️*9€.* An attractive hotel close to the Porte Narbonnaise. Comfortable rooms and warm welcome.

👛🍴🍽️🍽️ **Hôtel Best Western Le Donjon** – *2 r. du Comte-Roger.* 📞*04 68 11 23 00. www.hotel-donjon.fr.* ♿*. 61 rms. 245/390€* 🍽️*12€. Restaurant from 19€. Free*

wifi. This hotel combining old stonework and renovated décor occupies part of a 15C orphanage at the heart of the Cité.

NEARBY

⊝ **Camping Le Martinet Rouge Birdie** – *11390 Brousses-et-Villaret.* ℘04 68 26 51 98. *www.camping-lemartinetrouge.com. Open Mar–Nov.* ♿⛽. *63 places. 28/30€.* In a fabulous setting in the Montagne Noire.

⊝⊝ **Chambre d'hôte Le Relais St-Dominique** – *11270 Prouille (3km/2mi northeast of Fanjeaux on D 802, D 623, D 4 and D 119).* ℘04 68 24 68 17. *www. lerelaisdesaintdominique.com.* ⛽. *5 rms. 70€*⛽. This rural house, a short way from the medieval village, has a rustic interior which is at once simple and charming. The rooms are comfortable and well-maintained. Breakfast is served on the patio. Beautiful swimming pool and shop selling regional products.

⊝⊝ **Chambre d'hôte L'Olivette** – *R. Pierre-Duhem, 11160 Cabrespine.* ℘04 68 26 19 25. *http://olivette-cabrespine.com.* P⛽. *3 rms. 58/62€.* ⛽. *Evening meal 18€ by reservation only.* A family home charming in its simplicity, situated not far from the Gouffre de Cabrespine. Three comforable and well maintained rooms furnished with antiques. The table d'hôte dinner (available by reservation) is prepared with great enthusiasm and enlivened by local aromatic herbs. Full information about walks in the local region is available.

⊝⊝ **Chambre d'hôte Les Anges au Plafond** – *R. de la Mairie, 11170 Montolieu.* ℘04 68 24 97 19. *www.lesangesauplafond. com. 3 rms. 70€*⛽. Let your gaze wander upwards and you will understand the name of the establishment, "The Angels on the Ceiling". Above the cafe are three light, bright rooms, each with its own colour scheme down to the painted floorboards. Tea rooms and restaurant open at lunchtime; dinner is available for guests by reservation.

⊝⊝ **Chambre d'hôte de l'abbaye de Villelongue** – *À l'abbaye, 11170 St-Martin-le-Vieil.* ℘04 68 76 92 58 (after 7.30pm). *www.abbaye-de-villelongue.com. 4 rms. 68€*⛽. Accommodation at the heart of the abbey, with modern comforts replacing Cistercian austerity. The bedrooms are charming and all open onto the flowery cloister.

⊝⊝⊝ **Auberge du Château** – *Château de Cavanac, 11570 Cavanac.* ℘04 68 79 61 04. *www.chateau-de-cavanac.fr.* P♿. *29 rms. 75/185€.* ⛽*12€. Restaurant 45€.* Beautiful rooms with view over vineyard; fine restaurant.

⊝⊝⊝ **Hostellerie St-Martin** – *11000 Montredon (4km/2.5mi northeast).* ℘04 68 47 44 41. *www.chateausaintmartin.net. Closed 12 Nov-19 Mar.* ♿⛽. *15 rms 85/ 110€.* ⛽*10€. Free wifi.* This modern building in regional style stands in peaceful grounds. It is surrounded by countryside and has views of the Cité. Pleasant bedrooms.

⊝⊝⊝ **Hôtel La Bergerie** – *Allée Pech-Marie, 11600 Aragon.* ℘04 68 26 10 65. *www.labergeriearagon.com. Closed three weeks in Feb and two in Oct.* ♿ *8 rms. 100/130€.* ⛽*10€. Restaurant 27/75€.* In a lovely village; rooms have views over vineyard. Cuisine and wines of the region.

⊝⊝⊝ **Chambre d'hôte La Rougeanne** – *8 allée du Parc. 11170 Moussoulens,* ℘04 68 24 46 30 / 06 61 94 69 99. *www.la rougeanne.com.* P⛽. *5 rms. 90/110€* ⛽. Enjoy the peace and quiet of this old wine estate house. The rooms (equipped with internet), are lovingly decorated in pastel tones and look onto the tree-filled grounds. Beyond is a view of the Pyrénées. Two rooms on the ground floor, "Verveine" and "Tomette", have mezzanines, making them ideal family accommodation.

♈/EAT

⊝ **Le Bar à Vins** – *6 r. du Plo.* ℘04 68 47 38 38. *www.lebaravins.fr. Closed two weeks in Jan or Feb.* ♿. *5/12.50€.* In the heart of the medieval Cité, this wine bar's shady garden has a view of the St-Nazaire basilica. Tapas and fast food.

⊝ **La Vinothèque (Comptoir des Vins et Terroirs)** – *3 r. du Comte-Roger.* ℘04 68 26 44 76. *www.comptoir-vins.fr. 11/80€ per bottle.* As its name suggests, this is above all a wine bar where you can taste excellent local vintages, accompanied by toasts, salads and foie gras. Bottles of wine and other regional produce can also be bought here..

⊝⊝ **Auberge de Dame Carcas** – *3 pl. du Château.* ℘04 68 71 23 23. *www.dame carcas.com. Closed 24–26 Dec. 16/26.50€.* On the restaurant's logo, Dame Carcas, wife of king Sarrasin, carries a small pig.

According to legend, she persuaded Charlemagne to lift his siege of Carcassonne by throwing a fattened suckling pig over the battlements to prove that the inhabitants still had plenty of food. The auberge is renowned for its original dishes.

☞☞ **La Marquière** – *13 r. St-Jean ℰ04 68 71 52 00. Closed Wed and Thu and 10 Jan– 10 Feb. 26/36€.* Roughcast building near northern ramparts. Serves traditional cuisine.

☞☞ **Brasserie Le Donjon** – *4 r. Porte-d'Aude. ℰ04 68 25 95 72. www.hotel-donjon.fr. Closed Sun evening and Nov–Mar. Menus 16/29,50€.* A master-restaurateur offers the choice of a brasserie menu or a more complete meal combining, among other things, foie gras and cassoulet.

☞☞☞ **Au Comte Roger** – *14 r. St-Louis. ℰ04 68 11 93 40. www.comteroger.com. Closed 8 Feb–3 Mar, Sun and Mon (except in season) and holidays. Set menu lunch 19/27€. 42/61€.* A stroll around the Cité can be happily punctuated with a meal at this restaurant on a lively little street which has a modern décor and a shady terrace. The menu is inspired by market availability.

☞☞☞☞ **Le Parc Franck Putelat** – *80 ch. des Anglais (south of the Cité). ℰ04 68 71 80 80. www.restaurantleparc franckputelat.fr.* 🅿 *Open Tue–Sat. Set menu lunch 35€. 60/125€.* A restaurant of high standing, set in exceptional surroundings, with exquisite décor. Here you can enjoy cuisine that unites tradition with unexpected innovations such as bouillabaisse de foie gras. No gourmet misses this place under any circumstances.

NEARBY

☞ **Aux Deux Acacias** – *D 6113, 11150 Villepinte (14km northeast of Fanjeaux by D 4 then D 6113). ℰ04 68 94 24 67. www. les-deux-acacias.com. 13/26€. 10 rms. 50/65€.* ⚏*6.50€. Free wifi.* The simplicity of the décor is quickly forgotten once you see what is on your plate. You have to realize that the star here is the famous homemade cassoulet, expertly prepared with fresh ingredients. Warm welcome. Rooms are available, all air-conditioned.

☞ **Le Marque-Page** – *Pl. de la Liberté, 11170 Montolieu. ℰ04 68 24 76 72. Closed Sun evening, Mon, Wed evening. Set menu lunch 14.50€. 25€.* A pleasant menu (including homemade cassoulet) to enjoy in the shade of the plane trees.

SHOPPING

MARKETS
Flower, vegetable and fruit market – *Pl. Carnot. ℰ04 68 10 24 30. 7am–12.30pm. Tue, Thur and Sat.*

Spiritueux Cabanel – *72 allée d'Iéna. ℰ04 68 25 02 58. 8am–noon, 2–7pm. Closed Sun and hols.* This wine merchant's has been selling a wide variety of original spirits since 1868. They include l'Or-Kina, made with plants and spices; Micheline, whose origin dates back to the Middle Ages; Audoise, known as the liqueur of the Cathars, and the house grog. These are complemented by a small range of regional wines.

CRAFTS
Le Vieux Lavoir – *R. du Plô. ℰ04 68 71 00 04. Open 10.30am-6pm (winter), 10am-7pm (spring, autumn), 10am–11pm (summer). Closed Jan.* This craft co-operative is a chance to discover the work of the region's artisans. It sells pottery, marquetry, leather goods, jewellery and textiles, all at workshop prices.

Abbaye de Villelongue – *11170 St-Martin-le-Viel. ℰ04 68 24 90 38. www.abbaye-de-villelongue.com. Easter–Jun, Sep and Oct Tue–Sun 10am–noon 2–6.30pm (4pm Sat); Jul–Aug Tue–Sun 10am–noon 2–7pm (4pm Sat). Closed Nov–Mar.* The abbey's gift shop sells a curious local speciality: decorated gourds. Also on sale are models of sculptures in the abbey, made with resin and stone dust.

EVENTS

Knights in Armour – *Jul and Aug.*
Festival des 2 Cités – *Jul. www.festivaldecarcassonne.com.*
Antiquarian Book Fair– *Information from GLM, Yann Lartisien, pl. des Tilleuls, 11170 Montolieu. ℰ04 68 24 82 70.*
Feria – *End Aug–beginning Sept. (novilladas and animations).*
Fête des courges – *Abbaye de Villelongue (Sept).*

Castelnaudary

The town famous for its thick *cassoulet* stew makes an excellent stop-over for anyone cruising the Canal du Midi. The Grand Bassin offers plenty of mooring space. The restored 17C Moulin de Cugarel testifies to Castelnaudary's once important flour-milling activity.

- ▶ **Population:** 11,575.
- **Michelin Map:** 344: C3.
- **Info:** Pl. de Verdun, 11400 Castelnaudary. ℰ04 68 23 05 73. www.castelnaudary-tourisme.com.
- ▶ **Location:** 63km/39mi SE of Toulouse, and 39km/24mi W of Carcassonne.
- **Timing:** Half a day.
- **Don't Miss:** Le musée archéologique du Présidial.

WALKING TOUR

THE TOWN

The **bell tower** of Église St-Michel is impressive, as are the Gothic and Renaissance **gates** in the north façade.

Go into rue du Collège, then right into rue Goufferand. Cross rue de Dunkerque to reach the **Grand Bassin**. The basin forms part of the Canal du Midi as a reservoir for the locks at St-Roch.

Go a short way up ave. des Pyrénées and turn right into rue de la Haute-Baffe, then rue des Batailleries. Turn left towards the **Musée archéologique du Présidial** (open Jul–mid Sep daily except Mon 2.45–7pm; ℰ04 38 23 00 42), which traces the early history of the country from Gallo-Roman to modern times. One room is dedicated to regional products and ceramics. Go back into the rue des Batailleries to visit the **chapel**, which has a fine display of gilded woodwork. Return along rue de l'Hôpital.

VISIT
Moulin de Cugarel

N of the town along the rue des Moulins. At the start of the 20C, a dozen mills were still operating on the heights above Castelnaudary. The 17C Cugarel mill commands a fine **view** of the Lauragais plain. It was restored in 1962.

HIKES

A forest road stretches from the Prise d'eau d'Alzeau to the Bassin du Lampy (15km/9.3mi). The GR 7 long-distance footpath traverses woodland, skirting the Rigole de la Montagne from the Bassin du Lampy to the Cammazes dam (11km/6.8mi).

The GR 653 long-distance footpath, the 'Pierre-Paul Riquet' variation of GR 7, starts from the Bassin de St-Ferréol, links with the Rigole de la Plaine in Revel, skirtings it as far as the Poste des Thommasses (9km/5.6mi) before running on to the Seuil de Naurouze (another 24km/15mi).

EXCURSION
Abbaye de St-Papoul

▶ *5km/3mi NE on the D 103.* Open Jul–Aug 10am–6.30pm; Apr–Jun and Sep–Oct 10–11.30am, 2–5.30pm (Oct 4.30pm); Nov–Mar weekend and hols 10–11.30am, 2–4.30pm. 3.50€. ℰ04 68 94 97 75. www.saintpapoul.free.fr. Founded in 768 by Pepin the Short, the abbey became a cathedral in 1317 before becoming a simple parish church.

ADDRESSES

STAY

Hôtel du Centre et du Lauragais – *31 cours de la République.* ℰ04 68 23 25 95. www.hotel-centre-lauragais.com. *Closed 5–27 Jan. 16rms. 50/70€.* 8€. *Restaurant (closed Sun evening) 19/53€. Free wifi.* A town house offering functional rooms with modern furnishings. Traditional cuisine including cassoulet as a speciality.

Hôtel du Canal – *88 av. Arnaut-Vidal.* ℰ04 68 94 05 05. www.hotelducanal. com. *38 rms. 58/75€.* 5.50€. *Free wifi.* A beautiful ochre building, once a lime factory on the canal du Midi. Practical and peaceful rooms.

La Montagne Noire★

The Montagne Noire, or Black Mountain, forms the south-western tip of the Massif Central and is separated from the Agout massif (Sidobre and the Lacaune and Espinouse ranges) by the furrow formed by the Thoré.

A BIT OF GEOGRAPHY

The mountain's densely forested northern slope rises sharply over the Thoré and culminates in the Pic de Nore. Its more Mediterranean southern slope drops gently down to the Lauragais and Minervois plains. The rainy northern slopes shelter oak, beech, fir, spruce forests, and the rugged southern slopes are scattered with *garrigue*, gorse, sweet chestnut trees, vines and olive trees. The Montagne Noire's greatest wealth lies in its abundant reserves of water and its beautiful countryside. Only a meagre income can be made by raising stock or growing crops here, but the Salsigne gold mines still operate and marble is mined at Caunes-Minervois.

🚗 DRIVING TOURS

CABARDÈS REGION★
🐾 *See region map. Round tour from Carcassonne –* 🐾 *See p103.*

HARNESSED WATER★
From the Prise d'Alzeau to the Seuil de Naurouze. 114km/71mi. Allow 5hr.
🐾 *See regional map p74.*

This itinerary follows the water-supply system of the Canal du Midi first devised in the 17C by Pierre-Paul Riquet and improved upon over the centuries.

▶ From Saissac, follow D 408 towards Lacombe then a forest road on the right.

🐾 **Michelin Map:**
344: E-2 to F-2.

📋 **Info:** Office du tourisme de Revel Saint-Ferréol Montagne Noire, Pl Phillippe-VI-de-Valois-Beffroi, 31250 Revel.
📞 05 34 66 67 68.
www.revel-lauragais.com.

▶ **Location:** La Montagne Noire comprises the extreme SW of the central Massif.

👁 **Don't Miss:** Saint-Ferréol basin and the Abbey-école of Sorrèze.

👫 **Kids:** Sylvea à Revel; Explorarôme à Montégut-Lauragais.

Prise d'Alzeau

A monument commemorating Pierre-Paul Riquet, designer and builder of the Canal du Midi, retraces the various stages of canal construction.

▶ Turn back and continue to Lacombe. Turn left towards Lampy along forest roads.

Forêt domaniale de la Montagne noire

This 3,650ha/9,000-acre forest of beech and fir trees includes the Ramondes and Hautaniboul forests. The road crosses the Alzeau in a lovely woodland setting at La Galaube.

Bassin du Lampy

This reservoir on the Lampy was built between 1776 to 1780 to supply the Canal du Midi. It flows into the Montagne Noire channel where a pleasant footpath runs for 23km/14.5mi to the village of Les Cammazes. Magnificent beech groves and shady paths make the Bassin du Lampy a popular place for a stroll.

▶ Follow D 4 towards Saissac then turn right onto D 629. Just before Les Cammazes, turn right onto a road leading to the dam.

St-Ferréol reservoir

© Jean-Paul Azam / hemis.fr

Barrage des Cammazes

The reservoir retained by this dam feeds the Canal du Midi, supplies 116 towns and villages with drinking water and irrigates the Lauragais plain. Footpaths lead down to the edge of the Sor.

▷ Return to D 629 and turn right. Continue along the Rigole de la Montagne.

Voûte de Vauban

Outside Cammazes, the Rigole de la Montagne runs through the Voûte de Vauban, a 122m/133yd-long tunnel.

Bassin and barrage de St-Ferréol★

The water channel joins the Laudot river and flows towards the Bassin de St-Ferréol, the principal reservoir for the canal du Midi on the Atlantic side of the watershed. Before reaching the reservoir the waters are divided by a sluicegate: part enters the lake, the other part is directed into a bypass channel (the "rigole de ceinture", which rejoins the Laudot downstream from the dam. The sluicegate serves to divert the waters of the upper Laudot during maintenance work on the reservoir, which takes place every ten years or so.

Framed by wooded hills, the 🏖🚣bassin covers 67ha/166acres. A footpath leads around the lake and there is a **beach** on the north shore. In summer it is an ideal location for swimming and sailing.

The dam (barrage) was built between 1667 and 1672 by a workforce of thousands of men, women and children. It is composed of three parallel walls: the upstream wall, submerged beneath the water, the "great wall" (35m/115ft high) and the downstream wall. Two tunnels run between the upstream wall and the great wall: the *voûte d'enfer* and above it the *voûte du tambour*. Two other tunnels, the *voûte du vidange* and *voûte des robinets*, pass through the structure on the downstream side of the great wall. The spaces between the three walls are filled with earthworks up to 120m/394ft thick.

Musée et jardins du Canal du Midi★ – 🕿05 61 80 57 57. *www.museecanal dumidi.fr*. The house where Pierre-Paul Riquet himself once lived is now a museum that retraces the incredible history of the canal from its inception (🕮*see Canal du Midi p83*). The displays explain the context of the achievement and how the technical and geographical challenges were overcome by a massive construction operation that employed up to 12,000 workers. The finished work was not only a technical achievement. The supporting structures of the canal are perfectly integrated into the natural environment, merging human economic activity into the landscapes. Exhibits in the museum include interactive models, plans, documents and portraits. There are also photographs of the protagonists of this epic and of the works of art that Riquet visualised in order to surmount the difficulties of the terrain. The changing function of the canal is also explained, from its inauguration to its successful latter-day conversion for the purposes of tourism.

Below the museum, the **jardin des Illustres** is a romantic park punctuated by **portraits** of celebrated people (Colbert, Riquet, Vauban…). It also has a superb fountain. As well as appreciating the beauty of the place, a walk in these gardens is an opportunity to better understand the hydraulic methods that control the supply of water to the canal. The *voûte des robinets* leads into the heart of the dam and to a system of regulation installed in 1829.

Revel

On the edge of the Montagne Noire and the Lauragais region, Revel's economy is based on cabinet-making, marquetry, bronze work, gold-plating and lacquer work. This bastide has a geometric street layout around a main square surrounded by covered arcades or *garlandes*. The 14C **covered market** features its timber roof and belfry, renovated in the 19C.

Sylvea (*13 r Jean-Moulin*) is a **museum** providing an overview of the wood trade, and the skills of cartwrights, clog-makers, coopers and violin-makers (*℘05 61 27 65 50; www.sylvea.com*).

▶ Follow D 85 E to Pont-Crouzet.

Pont-Crouzet

The Rigole de la Plaine starts here. This canal collects water from the Sor and takes it to the Poste des Thommasses.

▶ Return to Revel and follow D 622 S then D 624 towards Castelnaudary.

Poste des Thommasses

This catches the water of the Laudot from St-Ferréol and that of the Sor, diverted from Pont-Crouzet via the Rigole de la Plaine. This water is then sent onto the Seuil de Naurouze.

▶ Turn right onto D 217.

Seuil de Naurouze★

◔ *See p85*
◔ *Also see Castelnaudary (p108).*

ADDRESSES

🛏 STAY

⌂🍴 **Hôtel Le Pavillon des Hôtes** – *18 r. Lacordaire, 81540 Sorèze. ℘05 63 74 44 80. www.hotelfp-soreze.com. 20 rms. 59/75€. ⌷12€, plus tourist tax 0.70€/ pers and "historic monument tax" 4,06€/ room. Restaurant 21/42€.* This annexe to the Hotel Abbaye École occupies the old girls' dormitories. The rooms, simple and tasteful, are arranged around a pleasing patio and look on to either the garden or the village of Sorèze. There is a programme of cultural activities.

⌂🍴 **La Comtadine** – *Lieu-dit L'Hermitage, 31250 St-Ferréol. ℘05 61 81 73 03. www.lacomtadine.com. 🅿🍴♿. 9 rms. 55/80€. ⌷9€. Restaurant 15/18€, or à la carte. Free wifi.* A short way from the lake is this peaceful, little hotel. Bright contemporary-style rooms are adorned with pieces of old furniture. Regional cuisine is served in the restaurant.

⌂🍴 **Hôtel Abbaye École Logis des Pères** – *18 r. Lacordaire, 81540 Sorèze. ℘05 63 74 44 80. www.hotelfp-soreze.com. 🍴♿. 72rms. 72/159€. ⌷12€. Restaurant 21/50€. Free wifi.* Hotel housed in a wing of the famous Benedictine Abbey School (17C), founded in 754 by Pepin the Short. Sober and tasteful decoration is complemented with 6ha of gardens. Traditional meals are served in the refectory or in the shade of trees. The atmosphere is hardly monastic, especially as guests enjoy a relaxation area with spa, heated pool, fitness centre, sauna and massage room.

🍴 EAT

⌂🍴 **Hôtel-Restaurant Du Midi** – *34 bd Gambetta, 31250 Revel. ℘05 61 83 50 50. Set lunch 14€, 23/48€. 17rms. 50/72€. ⌷8€. Free wifi.* Situated on a popular Revel boulevard, this 19C coach house offers individually styled rooms, which are quieter to the rear of the property.

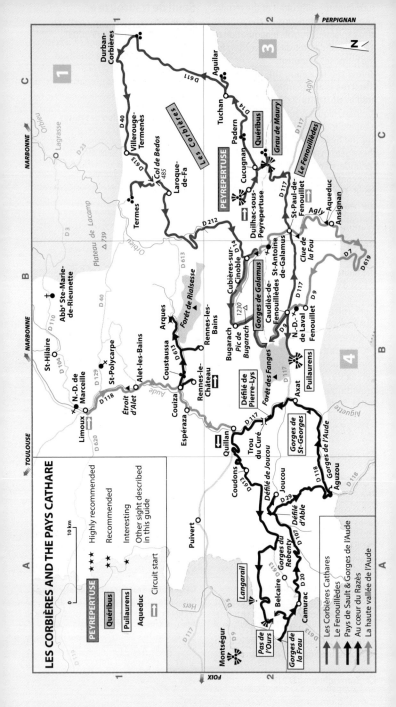

LES CORBIÈRES AND THE PAYS CATHARE

0   10 km

PEYREPERTUSE ✹✹✹	Highly recommended
Quéribus ✹✹	Recommended
Puilaurens ✹	Interesting
Aqueduc	Other sight described in this guide
○	Circuit start

Les Corbières Cathares
Le Fenouillèdes
Pays de Sault & Gorges de l'Aude
Au cœur du Razès
La haute vallée de l'Aude

Between Limoux and the Pyrénées stretches a rugged land of wild countryside carved into hills, deep valleys and gorges. This is the Pays Cathare – Cathar Country – named after the Christian heresy that flourished here briefly in the 12C, before it was brutally quashed by an army of knights from northern France. The persecuted Cathars took refuge in seemingly impregnable castles, especially Quéribus and Montségur. These strongholds are today in ruins but are still atmospheric places to visit, offering spectacular views from their hilltop locations. In between these and other spectacularly-sited castles, which didn't play a part in the Cathar wars, are expanses of the wild garrigue countryside and vineyards of the Corbières and the Fenouillèdes, two lesser known regions of France worth exploring. Mystery hunters love this area not only for its unending supply of Cathar legends, but also because of the mystery surrounding the career of the priest Béranger Saunière of Rennes-le-Château.

The First 'Champagne'

Blanquette de Limoux, a sparkling white wine, was 'invented' more than a century before champagne. The first reference to *blanquette* – the Occitan word for white – appears in papers written by Benedictine monks in 1531 at the abbey of St-Hilaire. They write of the production and distribution of St-Hilaire's blanquette in cork-stoppered flasks. Local folklore asserts that Dom Pérignon invented sparkling white wine while serving in the abbey, before leaving for the Champagne region and popularising the drink there.

The Cathar conundrum

The rise and persecution to death of the Cathars was all over within the space of less than a hundred years – and that eight centuries years ago. Catharism, you would have thought, would be long forgotten by now: a footnote to history of interest to medievalists only. Not a bit of it. The Cathars today are the engine driving the local tourist industry. Because of the extreme violence of the crusade against them, and the apparently overwhelming unfairness of the odds, the Cathars have acquired an irresistible mystique. They are universally portrayed as non-conformist rebels and free-thinkers representing the Languedoc against the imposition of orthodoxy from northern France. This, together with austere but beautiful landscapes and atmospherically ruined castles, has turned them into a legend. The Aude department markets its sights under the

Highlights

1 **Blanquette de Limoux** claims to predate Champagne (p114, 119)

2 Visit the mountain-top Cathar castles of **Montségur** and **Quéribus** (p130 and p124)

3 Explore the wild **Corbières** and taste its red wines (p119)

4 Go down into the **Gorges de Galamus** (p129)

5 Climb up to the sprawling ruined fortress of **Peyrepertuse** (p126)

Pays Cathare (Cathar Country) brand and there are endless books on the subject, fiction and nonfiction, relaying stories of conspiracy, mystery, legend, speculation and buried Cathar treasure.

Blanquette de Limoux

© Irene Alastruey / Author's Image / Photononstop

Limoux

Limoux is the production centre of sparkling **blanquette**, made from the Mauzac, Chenin and Chardonnay grapes using the *méthode champenoise*. The town's skyline features the Gothic spire of St Martin's Church and its lively narrow streets are still partly enclosed within a 14C fortified wall.

SIGHTS

It is a pleasure to stroll around old Limoux. The streets converge on the place de la République, bordered by arcades.

Musée du Piano

Pl. de 22 Septembre. ⊙*Open mid-Jun–Sept daily except Sun 10am–noon, 2–5pm.* ⊙*Closed Oct–May and hols in Jun.* ✆*3.50€.* ✆*09 6368 34 54.*
An interesting exhibit of French pianos from late 18C to today, presenting the evolution of the instrument.

Musée Petiet

Prom. du Tivoli. ⊙*Open Jul–Aug 9am–12pm, 2–6pm; Sep–Jun Wed–Fri 9am–noon, 2–6pm, Sat 10am–noon, 2–5pm.* ⊙*Closed 1 Jan, 1 May and 25 Dec.* ✆*3.50€.* ✆*09 63 68 34 54.*
This museum in the former workshop of the Petiet family, displays local paintings such as *The Ironers* by Marie Petiet (1854–93), battle scenes from the 1870 Franco-Prussian War by Étienne Dujardin-Beaumetz, and works by Henri Lebasque (*Reading*) and Achille Laugé (*Notre-Dame de Paris*).

EXCURSIONS
Jardin aux Plantes parfumées

▶ *Leave Limoux on the road for Carcassonne then turn right under the railway line as far as the commerical centre. Turn right at the first roundabout and follow signs for ' R. Dewoitine - domaine de Flassian.* ⊙*Open mid-Jul–mid-Aug 10am–6pm; May–mid-Jul and end Aug–Sep 1–6pm.* ⊙*Closed Mon and Tue.* ✆*6.90€.* ✆*04 68 31 49 94. www.labouichere.com.*

◔ **Michelin Map:** Region map B1.
▣ **Info:** 7 av. du Pont-de-France, 11300 Limoux. ✆04 68 31 11 82. www.limoux.fr.
▶ **Location:** 26km/16mi S of Carcassonne and 28km/17.5mi N of Quillan via D 118.
◷ **Timing:** If possible, come during carnival. At other times of year, allow a half day for Limoux and its surroundings.
⌖ **Don't Miss:** A tasting of blanquette de Limoux, and Limoux's carnival (January to April) with streets full of costumed dancers and musicians.
⚇ **Kids:** The Arques dungeon, and nautical activities. Musée des Dinosaurs.

A garden of a thousand-and-one scents: a perfumed rose garden, dry garden, medieval garden with plants for the Cathar centuries. Simply an enchanting place spread over 2ha, with more than 2,500 plants… and donkeys?

Notre-Dame-de-Marceille

▶ *2km/1mi N of Limoux on the D 104.*
This 14C pilgrimage church is built in the Gothic style.

St-Hilaire

▶ *12km/7.5mi N of Limoux on the D 104.*
It was the Benedictine monks of St-Hilaire who are traditionally credited with the discovery of the techniques for making the *blanquette de Limoux*.

Abbaye Ste-Marie-de-Rieunette

▶ *19km/12mi to the NW. After St-Hilaire turn right onto the D 110 and continue for 6km/4mi after Ladern-sur-Laquet.*
In 1994, Ste-Marie-de-Rieunette came back to life thanks to a community of five Cistercian nuns for the Boulaur abbey in Gers.

St-Polycarpe

▷ *8km/5mi SE along D 129.*

The **fortified church** here was part of a Benedictine abbey which was dissolved in 1771. On display are the 14C head reliquary (bare head) of St Polycarp, St Benedict and of the Holy Thorn, as well as 8C fabrics. The walls and vault feature the restored remains of 14C frescoes.

🚗 DRIVING TOUR

LA HAUTE VALLÉE DE L'AUDE

120km/75mi round tour from Limoux – Allow one day. &See region map.

▷ Leave Limoux south along D 118.

Castles along this route had quite efficient defences during the Albigensian Crusade. The Aude valley cuts across a fold in the Corbières mountain massif, before narrowing into the **Étroit d'Alet** gorge.

Alet-les-Bains

Surrounded by 12C ramparts Alet's **old town** has many interesting house on **place de la République**. Picturesque narrow streets branch off from the square to the city gates: Porte Calvière and Porte Cadène. Not far from D 118 are the **ruins** of the 11C abbey church, raised to the status of cathedral from 1318.

▷ Turn left off D 118 onto D 70 then right onto a minor road towards Arques.

Couiza

& *See p116. From Couiza, you can go off in search of the secrets of Father Béranger Saunière at Rennes-le-Château, or the Donjon d'Arques on the D 613 (see p118).*

▷ Leaving Couiza, turn left on the D 12.

Espéraza

This small town on the banks of the Aude was an important hat-making centre, whose past is commemorated in the

Musée de la Chapellerie (&🕙*open Jul–Aug 10am–7pm; Feb–Jun and Sep–Dec 10.30am–12.30pm, 1.30–5.30pm; 🕙Closed Jan, 25 Dec; ℘04 68 74 00 75; www.museedelachapellerie.fr).* Organised like a factory, the museum shows the stages of making of a felt hat and displays various headdress.

The 👥**Musée des Dinosaures★** reconstructs a local 19C dinosaur dig and displays bone fragments, semi-fossilised eggs and the skeleton of an enormous sauropod. (&🕙*open Jul and Aug: 10am–7pm last admission 45min before closing, Feb–Jun and Sep–mid-Nov 10.30am–12.30pm, 1.30–5.30pm; 🕙closed Jan, 25 Dec; ⊜8€; ℘04 68 74 26 88; www.dinosauria.org).*

Quillan &*See QUILLAN.*

ADDRESSES

🛏 STAY

🛌 **Camping Val d'Aleth** – *Chemin de la Paoulette, 11580 Alet-les-Bains. ℘04 68 69 90 40. www.valdaleth.com.* & *Reservations advised, 37 places.* Close to the village centre, pleasantly shaded along the river.

🍴 EAT

Good to know – If you're feeling hungry, then you will be spoiled for choice in the place de la République where there are many places to buy tapas, gargantuan salads and grills including the **Café Gourmand**.

SHOPPING

Blanquette de Limoux – For details of the producers who accept visitors to their cellars contact the tourist office or the Union of Limoux AOC (*20 av. du Pont-de-France; ℘04 68 31 12 83).* **Les Vignerons du Sieur d'Arques** (*av. du Mauzac; ℘04 68 74 63 45)* are responsible for booking visits.

Rennes-le-Château

Rennes-le-Château stands on a plateau over the Aude valley. Rumour still abounds about the fortune of the enigmatic Father Béranger Saunière, parish priest from 1885 to his death in 1917. How from 1891 onwards was he able to fund the complete restoration of his ruined church, build a sumptuous mansion (the Villa Bétania), a bizarre, semi-fortified library-tower (the Tour Magdala) and a tropical greenhouse, and lead a life fit for a prince? The abbot must have discovered some hidden treasure – of the Knights Templar, the Cathars, or treasure brought back from the Holy City by the Visigoths, perhaps?

- **Michelin Map:** Region map B1. 344: E5.
- **Info:** 11190 Rennes-le-Château. ℘04 68 74 05 84. www.rennes-le-chateau.fr.
- **Location:** 16km/10mi N of Quillan.
- **Parking:** The village is closed to traffic during Jul–Aug, but 3 car parks are available at the bottom of the village.
- **Timing:** Allow at least 1 hr.
- **Kids:** Le donjon d'Arques.

SIGHTS
Église Ste-Marie-Madeleine

The church is decorated with 19C neo-Gothic murals and polychrome statues. At the entrance to the church is a font supported by the Devil.

Domaine de l'abbé Saunière

The **Espace Bérenger Saunière** in the presbytery includes a local history **museum** displaying the Visigothic pillar said to have contained Father Saunière's treasure.

In the Domaine de l'abbé Saunière, is the priest's garden, private chapel, Villa Bétania and the curious crenelated Magdala tower (*open Jul–mid-Sep 10am–7.15pm; May–Jun and Sep 10am–6.15pm; 1–mid-Oct 10am–5.45pm; mid-end Oct 10am–5.15pm; Nov–Apr 10am–1pm, 2–5.15pm;*4.50€; ℘04 04 68 74 72 68; www.rennes-le-chateau.fr).

Return to Couiza and follow D 118 towards Quillan.

DRIVING TOUR

AU CŒUR DU RAZÈS
See region map. 24km/14.9mi.

First a Roman then a Visigoth city, in the 12C, Rennes (Rhedae) became the seat of the powerful but short-lived county of Razès, which for a time drew much envy before being united in the county of Carcassonne in 835. The county had feudal jurisdiction in Occitania, and was founded in 781 after the creation of the kingdom of Aquitania.

3.5km/2mi from Rennes-le-Château.

Couiza

Couiza, in the foothills of the Pyrénées on the Aude river and at the foot of the hill leading to Rennes-le-Château, is an industrious place, mainly manufacturing shows and hats. The old **castle** of the Dukes of Joyeuse is mid 16C, flanked by round towers and quite well preserved; today it houses a hotel with a Renaissance courtyard.

Take the D 613 towards Villerouge-Termenès.

The road passes **Coustaussa** and the ruins of its castle (inaccessible and dangerous). Constructed in the 12C by Raimond-Roger Trencavel, it was attacked by Simon de Montfort in 1210 and 1211 as a stronghold of Cathars. Members of the breakaway religious sect were still present in the village in the 14C.

Magdala tower,
Rennes-le-Château

© Jean-Paul Garcin / Photononstop / Tips Images

Conspiracies of Rennes-le-Château

As you move south from Carcassonne into the beautiful but complex folds of the mountains that were the Cathar stronghold, so you delve deeper into a world of mystery. Until recent times, the tiny and largely obscure village of Rennes-le-Château was virtually unknown. But then rumours started to surface, originating in the mid-1950s, concerning a local 19C priest. Father Bérenger Saunière arrived in the village in 1885, and acquired large sums of money during his tenure by selling masses and receiving donations. This was not uncommon, but the source of the wealth became a topic of conversation, and stories circulating within the village ranged from the priest having found hidden treasure to espionage for the Germans during World War I. During the 1950s, these

Devil supporting the
stoup in Rennes-le-
Château church

© D. Pazery / MICHELIN

rumours, in true entrepreneurial fashion, were given wide local circulation by a local man who opened a restaurant in Saunière's former estate (L'Hotel de la Tour), and hoped to use the stories to attract business.

From then on Rennes-le-Château became the centre of conspiracy theories claiming that Saunière had discovered hidden treasure and/or secrets about the history of the Church that could threaten the foundations of Roman Catholicism. Suddenly, the area became the focus of increasingly outland-ish claims involving the Knights Templar, the Priory of Sion, the Rex Deus, the Holy Grail, the treasures

of the Temple of Solomon, the Ark of the Covenant, ley lines and sacred geometry alignments. Saunière's story, true or false, found its way into contemporary novels, notably *Sepulchre*, by Kate Mosse, who had previously penned a novel set in the times of the Cathars, *Labyrinth*.

This is all grist to the mill of speculation. Is there treasure here? Or is it wishful thinking?

Donjon d'Arques

© Eurasia Press / Photononstop

▶ 8.5km/5mi from Couiza by the D 613 then the D 14 on the right.

Rennes-les-Bains

Crossed by a stream this small community is a source of treatment for rheumatological problems.

▶ Return to the D 613. 9km/5.5mi from Rennes-les-Bains.

Donjon d'Arques

🕐 *Open Jul–Aug 10am–7pm; Apr–Jun and Sep 10am–1pm, 2–5pm; Mar and Oct–Nov 10am–1pm, 2–6pm.* ⊚5€ *(children 2€).* 📞*04 68 69 82 87. www.chateau-arques.fr.*
👥 Used as living quarters since the late 13C, this keep of beautiful gold-coloured sandstone has three rooms open to the public. **Maison Déodat Roché** presents an audio-visual exhibition on the Cathar doctrine compiled by the eponymous Déodat Roché (1877–1978), a specialist in Catharism, and, some might say, something of a Cathar himself.

▶ Slightly farther on to the left, a forest track leads through the Rialsesse Forest.

Forêt de Rialsesse

The forest is well established, mainly in Austrian pine, and today is popular with walkers and cyclists alike.

ADDRESSES

🛏 STAY

🛏 **Camping La Bernède** – *11190 Rennes-les-Bains.* 📞*04 68 69 86 49.* 🕐*12 May–Sep. 34 sites. 16€.* A haven of peace and well-being. Mobile homes for hire.

🛏🛏 **Chambre d'hôte M. et Mme Pons** – *Pailhères, 11260 Espéraza.* 📞*04 68 74 19 23. www.domaine-de-pailheres.fr.* 🅿️🗗. *5 rms. 46€* 🖵. *Restaurant 18€.* Come and discover the calm of this family-run farm set apart from the village. The rooms, created in the beautifully converted outbuildings, give on to a panoramic terrace that has superb views of the surrounding countryside. Renowned table d'hôte meals made with the produce of the farm.

🛏🛏 **Chambres d'hôte Au Coeur de Rennes** – *R. de l'Église, 11190 Rennes-les-Bains.* 📞*04 68 69 59 68. www.aucoeurde rennes.com. 5 rms.* Comfortable rooms, sometimes decorated a little quirkily. Friendly atmosphere.

🛏🛏 **Hostellerie de Rennes-les-Bains** – *1 r. des Bains-Forts, 11190 Rennes-les-Bains.* 📞*04 68 68 88 49. www.hotel-renneslesbains. com. 7 rms. 65/80€* 🖵. *Free wifi.* Literally built over the water, a little hotel in which some of the rooms have balconies. Comfortable and pleasant place despite an over-colourful décor.

🛏🛏🛏 **Château des Ducs de Joyeuse** – *11190 Couiza (5km/3mi north of Rennes-le-Château on a minor road).* 📞*04 68 74 23 50. www.chateau-des-ducs.com. Closed 15 Nov–31 Mar. 35 rms. 94/230€.* 🖵*14€. Restaurant 35/59€. Free wifi.* Magnificent 16C château set back from the main road, standing on the bank of the river Aude. It is entered by a beautiful cobbled courtyard. Stone dominates the décor of the sitting rooms, dining rooms and some bedrooms.

ACTIVITIES

Thermes de Rennes-les-Bains – 📞*04 68 74 71 00. www.renneslesbains.org.* Fitness area, spa (open Apr 4–Nov 5) and accommodation (open Apr 2–Nov 6).

Les Corbières★★

Corbières is best known for its ruined castles and its wine, and a massif landscape showered with luminous Mediterranean light. The spiny sweet-smelling *garrigue* covers much of the countryside.

A BIT OF HISTORY

Vines have overgrown the area east of the Orbieu and around Limoux, the region producing sparkling white *blanquette*. The **Corbières** has been awarded the *Appellation d'Origine Contrôlée* for its fruity, full-bodied wines (mainly red, some white and rosé) with bouquets evocative of local flora.

The region's widely differing soil types produce a variety of grapes – Carignan, Cinsaut and Grenache, making any *dégustation* tour a real voyage of discovery. The red wines of neighbouring **Fitou**, also an *Appellation d'Origine Contrôlée*, are dark and robust with a hint of spiciness.

Many local villages have their own wine cooperatives (*cave coopérative*) and encourage customers to taste their wares, but private producers often require reservations, which makes having a wine guide listing telephone numbers quite useful.

🚗 DRIVING TOURS

LES CORBIÈRES CATHARES★★

ROUND-TRIP FROM DUILHAC-SOUS-PEYREPERTUSE

117km/73mi. Allow an overnight stopover. See Les Corbières map.

Magnificent castles and castle ruins, including the 'Five Sons of Carcassonne,' dot the Corbières landscape. These vertiginous feudal fortresses sheltered Cathars fleeing from the Inquisition.

Duilhac-sous-Peyrepertuse

Leaving the upper town to the north, note the village fountain fed by a bursting spring.

Michelin Map: Region map C1-2.

Info: Chemin de Padern, 11350 Cucugnan. ✆04 68 45 69 40. www.corbières-sauvages.com.

Location: Bounded on the S by the D 117 between Perpignan and Quillan, on the W by the D118 between Quillan and Carcassonne, to the N by the A61 between Carcassonne and Narbonne, and to the E by the A9 linking Perpignan.

Timing: Beware of the sun in summer: wear a hat and apply sun cream. Carry drinking water in the car, especially when visiting out-of-the-way châteaux. A pair of good walking shoes is recommended. Binoculars can be useful for looking at the landscapes and watching birds of prey. Don't forget to fill the fuel tank before setting off because filling stations can be scarce. Allow two days. Take your time when following the minor roads that wind through the garrigue countryside, often twisting and climbing.

Don't Miss: The chateaux de Peyrepertuse, Quéribus and Puilaurens.

Kids: Cathar castles and Cucugnan's 'Pocket' Theatre de poche.

Château de Peyrepertuse★★★

See p126.

Return to Duilhac; drive to Cucugnan and continue on the D 14.

Château de Padern

20min on foot round-trip. Be careful; the ruins are dangerous in places. To reach the castle, follow the yellow-marked 'Sentier Cathare.'

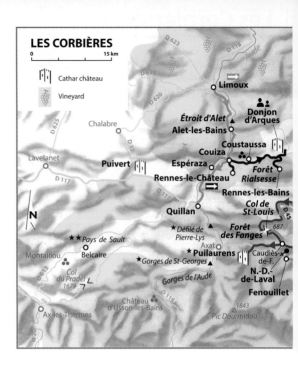

LES CORBIÈRES

0 — 15 km

[||] Cathar château

🍇 Vineyard

🏃 The Château de Padern, owned by the abbots of Lagrasse until 1579, was completely rebuilt in the 17C. You can see the remains of a round tower, leading to the upper part of the keep (now in ruins) and fine views of the village and the river Verdouble.

▷ At end of D 14, turn left onto D 611.

Tuchan
This town is a production centre for Fitou wines (AOC). The picturesque D 39 winds through the Tuchan valley.

▷ East of Tuchan, a surfaced path going through vineyards branches off D 39 to the left and leads to Aguilar Castle.

Château d'Aguilar
10min on foot from the parking area. Enter the enclosure from the SW.
On the orders of the king of France the Château d'Aguilar fortress was reinforced in the 13C, with a hexagonal curtain wall flanked by six reinforced round towers. The wall and a Romanesque chapel remain intact.

▷ Return to Tuchan and turn right onto D 611 to Durban.

Durban-Corbières
The castle overlooking the village includes a crenellated rectangular two-storey building with 13C twin bays and 16C mullioned windows, as well as remains of curtain walls and towers.

▷ Drive W out of Durban along D 40.

A charming **Mediterranean botanic garden** has been laid out on the side of the hill on the road to Albas. A winding footpath leads through 8 000 m²/2 acres planted with a variety of species.

👥 Villerouge-Termenès
At the heart of the medieval village stands the (12C–14C) **castle** flanked by four towers which was owned by the

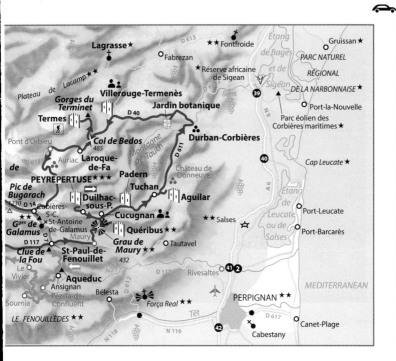

bishops of Narbonne and in 1321 witnessed the burning at the stake of the last Cathar Parfait, Guilhem Bélibaste. Audio-visual exhibits describe Bélibaste's life and works and the daily life of medieval Villerouge and its inhabitants. Enjoy views of the village and its surroundings from the sentry walk.

Every summer Villerouge re-enacts medieval banquets and various activities evocative of life in medieval Languedoc (🕐 open daily Jul–Aug 10am–7.30pm; Apr–Jun and Sep–mid-Oct 10am–1pm, 2–6pm; mid-Oct–Mar ask for opening times; 🕐 closed Sat morning out of season, Jan; ∞6€; ℘04 68 70 09 11).

▷ Follow D 613 SW of Villerouge to Col de Bedos then turn right onto D 40.

Col de Bedos

Bedos Pass is located on D 40, a **ridge road★** winding through wooded ravines. From the dip formed by the lower gorge of the Sou, see the ruins of the Château de Termes.

Château de Termes

The ticket office for the château is at the bottom of the hill, after the village bridge. 🕐 Open Jul–Aug 9.30am–7.30pm; Apr–Jun and Sep–Oct 10am–6pm; Mar and Nov–Dec Sat–Sun, public and school holidays, 10am–5pm. 🕐 Closed Jan–Feb. ∞3€. ℘04 68 70 09 20. www.chateau-termes.com. Leave the car at the foot of the hill, beyond the bridge. 🚶 30min on foot roundtrip; follow a steep track up then climb a succession of tiers that mark the curtain walls.

The castle held by Cathar Raymond de Termes succumbed to Simon de Montfort after a four month siege (August to November 1210) during the first stage of the Albigensian Crusade. The site on the promontory defended by the natural trench of the Sou valley (Terminet gorge) is more interesting than the fortress ruins, offering good views of the **Terminet gorge** from near the northwest postern (⚠ *dangerous slopes*) and top of the rock.

Les Corbières

© B. Gardel / hemis.fr

▶ Return to Col de Bedos and turn right onto D 613.

Laroque-de-Fa

This picturesque village is built on a rock outcrop above the river Sou, which plunges down to join the Orbieu.

▶ After Mouthoumet, at Pont d'Orbieu, turn left on D 212, passing the ruins of the château d'Auriac. At Soulatgé, take D 14 to the right towards Cubières-sur-Cinoble. From here it is possible to make a detour to visit the Gorges de Galamus.

Gorges de Galamus★★

♿ See p129.

▶ Follow the D14. Just before Bugarach, turn left onto D 45.

Pic de Bugarach

The rugged Bugarach summit is visible from the virtually deserted valleys surrounding it. The ascent to the Col du Linas, winding through the upper Agly valley, is particularly impressive.

▶ Bear left on D 46 to col de St-Louis.

Forêt domaniale des Fanges

This forest massif covers 1,184ha/2,924 acres and shelters exceptional Aude firs. The **Col de St-Louis** (*alt 687m/2,253ft*) is a good departure point for ramblers (rocky, often very uneven ground).

▶ Turn left at the Col de St-Louis on D 9 heading southeast to Caudiès-de-Fenouillèdes. Turn right onto D 117 to Lapradelle.

Château de Puilaurens★

Just south of Lapradelle, on D 22. ♦*Open Jul–Aug 10am–8pm; Jun and Sep 10am–7pm; May 10am–6pm; Feb–Apr and Oct–mid-Nov 10am–5pm.* ♦*Closed mid-Nov–Jan.* ♦*4€.* ♦*04 68 20 65 26.* ⚡*Leave the car and continue on foot; 30min round-trip. Closed in bad weather.*

High above the upper Aude valley, this castle with its crenellated curtain wall, four towers and projecting battlements, is impregnable from the north and remains more or less intact.

▶ Rejoin D 117 and turn right back through Caudiès-de-Fenouillèdes. Continue through St-Paul-de-Fenouillet (see p128) to Maury. Turn left on D 19.

Grau de Maury★★

From this little pass, the southern gateway to the Corbières, is a fine panorama of mountain chains and the jagged ridge overlooking the dip formed by the Fenouillèdes to the south.

▶ A steep narrow road to the right leads up from the Grau de Maury to the ruined fortress of Quéribus.

Château de Quéribus★★

See p124.

▶ Head back to Cucugnan and turn left onto D 14 to return to Duilhac.

ADDRESSES

STAY

Also see accommodation and places to eat in Cucugnan, p125.

Chambre d'hôte Le Fitoun – *1 Le Mas, 11350 Paziols (4km/2.5mi south of Tuchan). ℘04 68 45 43 49. www.lefitoun. com. 5 rms. 52€.* This charming village house surrounded by vines and olive trees manages to be both simple and highly agreeable. The rooms are bright and well maintained. Warm welcome to a peaceful spot where the prices are reasonable.

Les gîtes La Capelle – *R. La Capelle, 11540 Roquefort-des-Corbières. ℘04 68 48 82 80. www.gitelacapelle.com. 27 rms. 55/75€.* Arranged around the swimming pool and solarium are twelve very comfortable modern cottages: perfect for a leisurely stay beneath the palm trees. Various activities are available.

Chambre d'hôte du Domaine Grand Guilhem – *1 chemin du Col-de-la-Serre, 11360 Cascastel (6km/4mi southwest of Durban). ℘04 68 45 86 67. www.grand guilhem.com. 4 rms. 90€.* A superb wine estate house dating from the 19C standing in grounds planted with ancient trees. The interior is decorated with great taste in warm colours and incorporates beautiful family furniture and old tiles. "Wine and music" evenings are held as well as themed weekends (introductions to wine tasting, vine-cultivation etc).

Chambre d'hôte du Château de Haut Gléon – *11360 Villesèque-des-Corbières (4km/2.5mi northeast of Durban). ℘04 68 48 85 95. www.hautgleon.com. 6 rms. 65/70€. Free wifi in public areas.* The old houses of this wine estate were once used by farmhands; grape-pickers have been converted into rooms decorated in individual and unusual styles. You can taste the property's wines in the cellar.

⚑EAT

La Cave d'Agnès – *29 r. Gilbert-Salamo, 11510 Fitou. ℘04 68 45 75 91. Closed 13 Nov–31 Mar, Wed. 23,50/31,50€.* An old building in the upper part of the village, which has preserved its rustic charm: old fireplace, beams, exposed wood and stone. Regional cuisine. Exhibition and sale of paintings.

Le Clos de Cascastel – *Quai de la Berre, 11360 Cascastel-des-Corbières. ℘04 68 45 06 22. Closed mid-Jan– early Feb., mid-Nov– mid-Dec, Mon. Set menu lunch 17€ – 19/32€.* Typical regional dishes and a choice of Corbières wines can be enjoyed in the cosy dining room or on the shady terrace, with its teak furniture, next to plane and olive trees.

SHOPPING

The Aude department awards appropriate products with its "Pays Cathare" quality-control label, which is intended to uphold strict standards, providing a guarantee of authenticity and value for the consumer.

Cave des Vignerons de Fitou – *Les Cabanes, D 6009, 11510 Fitou. ℘04 68 45 71 41.* Created in 1933, this winemakers' co-operative produces vins de table, sparkling wines, the famous muscat de Rivesaltes, and various highly-praised vintages of Fitou.

Château de Québirus★★

Perched on a narrow, rocky peak at 729m, and beaten by the winds, Québirus was the last refuge of the Cathars, a real eagle's nest overlooking Corbières and Fenouillèdes on the edge of the Pyrénées-Orientales.

A BIT OF HISTORY

The end of the Cathars – Mentioned for the first time in 1020 in the will of the Catalan count of Besalú, Québirus castle lived its finest moment in the era of the Cathars. In fact, it is within the château's stone walls that the bloody epic of the Albigensian crusade came to an end. After the fall of Montségur in 1244, Chabert de Barbaira, the seigneur of the château, offered the Cathars their last refuge. Amongst them was the deacon of Razès, Benoît de Termes, who lived here until his death. Eleven years later, in 1255, Chabert de Barbaira, protector of the Cathars, was taken prisoner by Olivier de Termes, formerly his companions in arms in the service of Louis XI. He was forced to surrender the castle in exchange for his freedom. The Cathars who escaped the torturers and butchers fled to Catalonia or Lombardy, or feigned submission. After its fall, this last Cathar stronghold passed to the crown

- **Michelin Map:** Region map C2. 344: G5.
- **Info:** Office du tourisme de Cucugnan, Chemin de Padern, 11350 Cucugnan. ℘04 68 45 69 40. www.corbieres-sauvages.com.
- **Location:** 40km/25mi NW of Perpignan, and 50km/31mi E of Quillan.
- **Don't Miss:** The Gothic room in the keep and the views from the ramparts.
- **Kids:** Take them to see *Le Sermon du curé de Cucugnan*.
- **Timing:** Allow a minimum of 30min, but it can take longer.

of France. In 1258, the Treaty of Corbeil, which fixed the Franco-Aragonese frontier south of the Corbières, made Québirus a royal fortress. The castle, which became one of the "Five Sons of Carcassonne", continued to be of strategic importance until the signature of the **Treaty of the Pyrénées** in 1659.

VISIT
Château★

⚠ *20min. Stout walking shoes recommended. Audio guides available. Jul–Aug 9am–8pm; Apr–Jun and Sep 9.30am–7pm; Oct 9am–6.30pm; Nov–*

Château de Québirus

© Eric Teissedre / Photononstop

Jan 10am–5pm; Feb 10am–5.30pm; Mar 10am–6pm. ⏱*Closed 1 Jan.* |*5.50€ (children, 6–15, 3€) ticket combined with the Théâtre de poche Achille-Mir de Cucugnan.* ✆*04 68 45 03 69. www.queribuscucugnan.fr.*

Three successive enclosures protect the main tower, placed at the very summit of the rock. Polygonal in shape, it has two floors: a lower hall, and a high, vaulted **gothic room★**. The simplicity of its design has given rise to speculation that it has some astronomical or solar symbolism, similar to Montségur. But speculation is all it is for nothing remains of the pre-Crusade castle. What you see today was built in the late-13C, and remodelled in the 16C to accommodate advances in artillery. Even so, it is a moving experience to climb to the top for the panoramic **views★★**.

EXCURSION
Cucugnan

This pretty village is well known from the tale of *Le Sermon du curé de Cucugnan* adapted into French by Alphonse Daudet in the second half of the 19C. The **Achille-Mir theatre** on place du Platane hosts a virtual theatre performance on this theme. (&⏱*open Mar–Oct 10am–7.30pm; Nov–Feb 1.30–6pm;* ⏱*closed in Jan, 25 Dec;* ᴥ*5€ (ticket combined with the château de Quéribus);* ✆*04 68 45 03 69).*

ADDRESSES

🛌 STAY

ᴥ **Chambre d'hôte Les Santolines** – *11 r. Alphonse-Daudet, 11350 Cucugnan.* ✆*04 68 45 00 04 / 06 89 99 02 55. www. les-santolines.fr. 3 rms. 50€* ⌑. If you are looking for a simple bed and breakfast, this unpretentious rustic village house is just the ticket. The three well-maintained guest rooms combine practicality and comfort. The charming owners can advise on visits and activities in the local area.

ᴥᴥ **Chambre d'hôte et gîte L'Écurie de Cucugnan** – *10 r. Achille-Mir, 11350 Cucugnan (in the upper part of the village).* ✆*04 68 33 37 42 / 06 76 86 38 52. www.*

Cucugnan and its vineyards

© E. Larribère / MICHELIN

queribus.fr. ⛷🏊. *5 rms. 60/65€* ⌑. Located in the upper part of the village, this old stable has five well-equipped, individual rooms. In addition there is a self-catering gîte rented by the week. Beautiful bathrooms, impeccable beds and numerous little details transform a stay into a delight. In summer there are lively wine tastings.

ᴥᴥᴥ **Chambre d'hôte La Tourette** – *4 passage de la Vierge, 11350 Cucugnan.* ✆*04 68 45 07 39. www.latourette.eu.* &⛷. *3 rms. 100/120€.* ⌑ *10€.* The owner of this house has decorated it with a confident sense of taste. The rooms – Prune (Plum), Turquoise and Indigo– are unusual but delightful. Jacuzzi under an olive tree on the patio.

🍴 EAT

ᴥᴥ **Auberge de Cucugnan** – *2 pl. de la Fontaine, 11350 Cucugnan.* ✆*04 68 45 40 84. www.auberge-de-cucugnan.com. Closed Jan–Feb.* 🅿. *18/46€. 9 rms. 50€.* ⌑*7€. Free wifi.* A country atmosphere reigns in this converted barn, which is reached via a maze of little streets. Generous, appetizing cuisine. Well maintained rooms.

ᴥᴥ **Auberge du Vigneron** – *2 R. Achille-Mir, 11350 Cucugnan.* ✆*04 68 45 03 00. Closed 13 Nov–28 Feb, Mon noon in Jul–Aug; Sun eve and Mon.* This village house offers guests the delights of simple cooking, Corbières wine and cosy little rooms. The restaurant occupies an old wine shop, opening onto a fine summer terrace with mountain views.

Château de Peyrepertuse★★★

The craggy outline of the ruined fortress of Peyrepertuse only properly comes into view when seen from the outskirts of Rouffiac, to the north. The largest of the 'Five sons of Carcassonne', it sits on a crest in the Corbières, standing boldly atop its rocky base. The château is one of the finest examples of a medieval fortress in the Corbières.

A BIT OF HISTORY

The pierced rock – Peyrepertuse owes its name to the crag on which it perches: pèira, "rock" in Occitan and " trouée" (pierced). The discovery of amphoras and coins on the site provides evidence of human occupation here since the 1C BC. The first documented mention of the château is in 1070. Owned by the Catalan counts of Besalú until the beginning of the 12C, the castle became part of the domain of the counts of Barcelona, then a fief of the counts of Narbonne. Contrary to legend, Peyrepertuse did not play a part in the crusade against the Cathars, even if it is true that its seigneur, Guilhem de Peyrepertuse, was sympathetic to their cause. He surrendered without a fight to **Simon de Montfort** in 1217. Excommunicated seven years later for his enduring links to Catharism, he joined the revolt of **Raimond Trencavel** and tried to recover his possessions in 1240, but ended by submitting definitively on 16 November of the same year, again before the chateau could be besieged.

- **Michelin Map:** Region map C2.
- **Info:** Office du tourisme de Cucugnan, Chemin de Padern – 11350. ℰ04 68 4569 40. www.chateau-peyrepertuse.com.
- **Location:** Get here from Duilhac: 3.5km/2mi up a steep, narrow road. Visitors should have a good head for heights and take great care while exploring the castle, particularly if there is a strong wind. During the summer, bring water, sunhats and suncream.
- **Timing:** Allow 20min of walking up a steep path to reach the château and 1h for the visit.
- **Don't Miss:** The view over the surrounding valley from east of the castle.

A frontier fortress – Having become a royal fortress, Peyrepertuse was transformed into a formidable stronghold by Louis XI (Saint Louis), who was keen to take advantage of this defensive position. In 1242, he ordered the construction of a flight of steps to reach the highest parts of the rock and had the keep, the château de San Jordi (or St-Georges) erected in the 1250s. In this same period he recommended the restoration of the old keep below and the church. In 1258,

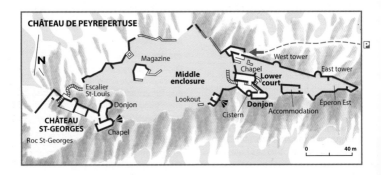

CHÂTEAU DE PEYREPERTUSE

N

Magazine

Middle enclosure

West tower

East tower

Chapel

Escalier St-Louis

Lookout

Lower court

Donjon

Donjon

Accommodation

Éperon Est

CHÂTEAU ST-GEORGES

Cistern

Chapel

Roc St-Georges

0   40 m

the treaty of Corbeil made Peyrepertuse one of the "Five Sons of Carcassonne", along with the fortresses of Aguilar, Quéribus, Termes and Puilaurens. The impressive line of defence formed by these five fortresses protected the frontier with Aragon (and later Spain) until 1659, when the Treaty of the Pyrénées allocated Roussillon to France. Peyrepertuse then lost all strategic significance. The château, however, was occupied by a small garrison until the outbreak of the French Revolution in 1789.

VISIT

From the car park, follow a path along the north face, leading up to the castle entrance. Sturdy footwear advised. Allow 2hr. There is very little shade within the castle. Be sure to take adequate protection as well as water. Open Jul–Aug 9am–8.30pm; Jun and Sep 9am–7pm; Apr–May and Oct 10am–6.30pm; Nov–Mar 10am–5pm. Closed Jan. No visits during stormy weather. 7.50€. 06 71 58 63 36. www.chateau-peyrepertuse.com.

Peyrepertuse consists of two structures separated by an esplanade or middle ward: the Château Vieux at the eastern end of the promontory and the **Château de San Jordi** or St-Georges at the western extremity, also the highest point. The whole castle measures 300m/984ft at its longest point.

Lower Court

The triangular shape of the oldest part of the castle is dictated by the form of the promontory, which tapers like the prow of a ship. The fortifications here are only complete on the north side, being protected by a strong curtain wall and two semicircular towers open on the inner side. The southern defences consist of a simple parapet that has been rebuilt. The largest and best preserved buildings are the Château or Donjon Vieux which formed the heart of the complex. The eastern wall, looking over the large courtyard, was remodelled in the 13C. It is composed of two semi circular towers connected by a crenellated wall. The **keep** *(enter by the high door)*, is

flanked by a round tower (cistern). The building was completed between the 12 and 13C with a fortified church.

Middle Enclosure

The northern wall connecting the two ends of the castle runs along the edge of the cliff. A polygonal building, in ruins, is thought to have served as a storehouse, stable for donkeys or as a magazine. On the southern side of the ward, an isolated lookout post gives good views of the castle of Quéribus.

Château St-Georges

This part of the castle was not accessible by horse or even by mule. It is connected to the middle ward by a steep, narrow staircase, the **escalier St-Louis**, built on the orders of Louis XI around 1242 (*the steps may be slippery; take care especially in high winds*).

At an altitude of 796m/2611ft, this royal fortress is around 60m/200ft higher than the Chateau Vieux. It was built in one operation on the highest point of the hill after the incorporation of the Languedoc into the royal domaine. It has high walls, a keep and an chapel, but much of the interest is in the site, which serves as a magnificent vantage point. There are impressive **views**★★ from here over the rest of the castle, of the Verdouble basin, the château de Quéribus and, on the horizon, the Mediterranean.

Château de Peyrepertuse

© Pixelmania / Fotolia.com

Le Fenouillèdes★★

The Fenouillèdes region between the southern Corbières and Conflent evokes the aromatic plant known as fennel, and surprises you with its wild beauty; a delight to explore by car. The region links the furrow hollowed out between the Col Campérié and the more populated Estagel area (including the Maury vineyards and 'Côtes du Roussillon') and a rugged mountain range that becomes quite arid between Sournia and Prades.

🚗 DRIVING TOUR

ROUND TRIP FROM ST-PAUL-DE-FENOUILLET
60km/37mi. About 4hrs.
🦽*See region map.*

- 🦽 **Michelin Map:** Region map C2.
- **Info:** Office du tourisme de St-Paul-de-Fenouillet, 26 bd de l'Agly. 📞04 68 59 07 57. www.st-paul66.com
- ▶ **Location:** Estagel marks the start of the region, 24km/15mi west of Perpignan on the D117.
- 🕐 **Timing:** Allow a good half day with a lunchstop at St-Paul-de-Fenouillet, or Cubières for a picnic.
- **Don't Miss:** Ansignan Roman; Gothic church of the hermitage Notre-Dame-de-Laval; the view of Canigou from the terrace at the hermitage of St-Antoine-de-Galamus.

St-Paul-de-Fenouillet
This town stand on the left bank of the river Agly just before its confluence with the Boulzane. Its abbey was founded in the 9C, became a collegiate church in the 14C and was crowned with a dome during the baroque period. The chapterhouse is used for art exhibitions and also houses a small museum of crafts and traditions.

▶ Leave St-Paul heading south on D 619.

Clue de la Fou
Strong winds blow through this valley gouged out by the Agly. Cross the river and follow D 619 as it bends around the Fenouillèdes furrow and its vineyards. See the ruined Quéribus castle on its rocky pinnacle and Canigou peak in the distance. The road skirts the still-used Roman aqueduct at **Ansignan** before reaching Sournia via Pézilla-de-Conflent.

▶ Turn right onto D 7 towards St-Prats-de-Sournia.

The road offers a fine view of the Corbières and the Mediterranean Sea through the **Agly valley**.

Ermitage St-Antoine-de-Galamus

© D. Hée / MICHELIN

◗ Beyond Le Vivier, turn left onto D 9 towards Caudiès.

On the way up to **Fenouillet**, a village dominated by two ruins and which has given its name to the region, there are good views of the hermitage of Notre-Dame-de-Laval and, on the horizon, the pic de Bugarach.

Notre-Dame-de-Laval

The Gothic church of this ancient hermitage stands on an esplanade planted with olive trees. The nave, topped by a tiled roof, is flanked by an octagonal tower crowned by a brick spire. At the bottom of the slope, the lower door is in the form of an oratory housing a 15C statue of the Saint Parenté (Saint Anne). The upper door is dedicated to Our Lady "of our Daily Bread" (Virgin and Child, also 15C) and incorporates reused Romanesque columns and capitals. The church is just outside **Caudiès-de-Fenouillèdes**, western gateway to the Fenouillèdes.

◗ Continue N along D 9 to Col de St-Louis then turn right onto D 46 and right again onto D 45.

Pic de Bugarach

See p122.

◗ Turn right onto D 14.

Cubières-sur-Cinoble

A rest area near the old mill has picnic tables on the shady banks of the Agly.

◗ Turn right onto D 10 which runs alongside the Cubières stream then the river Agly.

Gorges de Galamus★★

Watch out for traffic jams in summer… if you have time it is better to visit the gorge on foot.

The spectacular rock-carved road and the hermitage clinging to the hillside create a fantasy world bathed in Catalan sunlight. The narrow gorge offers glimpses of the mountain stream below.

Ermitage St-Antoine-de-Galamus – *Leave the car in the car park at the hermitage before the tunnel.* ⊠ *30min on foot round-trip.* The path runs down from the hermitage terrace (**view** of Canigou). The hermitage building conceals the chapel in the dim depths of a natural cave.

◗ The D 7 follows a sinuous course through vineyards enroute to St-Paul-de-Fenouillet.

ADDRESSES

⌂ STAY

Domaine de Coussères – *66220 Prugnanes – 5km/3mi NW of St-Paul-de-Fenouillet by D 117 and D 20. ℘04 68 59 23 55. www.cousseres.com. Closed 15 Oct–1 Apr. 5 rms. 83€. ⊠10€. Restaurant 25€.* Perched on a small hill amid the vines, this superb *bastide* dominates a majestic landscape of mountains and *garrigues*. Large, tastefully decorated rooms, and a warm welcome in the dining room.

⌂ EAT

Le Relais des Corbières – *10 Ave. Jean-Moulin, 66220 St-Paul-de-Fenouillet. ℘04 68 59 23 89. www.relaisdescorbieres. com. Closed 2–28 Jan, Sun eve and Mon except Jul–Aug and public holidays.* Enjoy a warm welcome and simple honest fare in a dining room with rustic décor or terrace.

Pascal Borrell – *La Maison du Terroir, av. Jean-Jaurès, 66460 Maury (8km/5mi east of St-Paul-de-Fenouillet on D 117, towards Perpignan). ℘04 68 86 28 28. www.maison-du-terroir.com. Closed 2 weeks in Feb, Sun eve, Mon and Wed (Sep–Jun). 25/65€.* Catalan cuisine is brought up to date in this restaurant, which also has a stock of local wines and regional products for sale.

ACTIVITIES

Train touristique du Pays cathare et du Fenouillèdes – *℘04 68 59 99 02. www. tpcf.fr.* The train runs daily during July and August, but at other times according to demand, providing a 60km/37.5mi journey from Rivesaltes to Axat.

Quillan

This town is a major tourist centre for the upper Aude valley and one of the best points of departure for forays into the forests of the Pyrénéan foothills. Until the Second World War, hat-making was big business in the area; these days local industry other than tourism, which plays a major part in the area's economy, includes the production of laminates (Formica), luxury and garden furniture, trousers and shoes.

VISIT

On the esplanade in front of the station there is a quaint little monument to Abbot Armand (*see Défilé de Pierre-Lys p133*). On the east bank of the Aude stand the ruins, sadly being left to fall into disrepair, of a 13C fortress with a square ground plan – most unusual in this region.

EXCURSIONS
Puivert

▶ *16km/10mi east. Leave Quillan on D 117 and after the col du Portel continue towards Lavelanet.*

In the undulating and wooded landscapes of the plateau de Sault, the gentle pastures of Puivert (from the Latin *podii viridis*, green hill) come as a welcome surprise. Its little lake is a melancholy replica of a natural lake that was brusquely drained in the 13C. If the stone silhouette of the keep no longer echoes to the sound of troubadours it still adds a romantic note to the landscape.

All that remains of **Puivert Castle** *(from the hamlet of Camp-Ferrier, before reaching the village of Puivert, 500 m/550 yds by a steep and narrow track;* ⏱ *open May–mid-Nov 9am–7pm; mid-Dec–Apr 10am–5pm;* ⏱ *closed mid-Nov–mid-Dec, 1 Jan, 25 Dec;* 🎫 *5€;* 📞 *04 68 20 81 52; www.chateau-de-puivert.com) dating* from before the siege of 1210, are sections of wall to the west. Of the partly destroyed 14C castle, a keep and a tower-gate decorated with the Bruyères lion are still standing. Visit the keep, chapel and 'Minstrels' room evoking

▶ **Population:** 3,445.
🚗 **Michelin Map:** 344: E5.
ℹ️ **Info:** Square André-Tricoire, 11500 Quillan. 📞 04 68 20 07 78. www.aude-en-pyrenees.fr.
▶ **Location:** 28km/17.5m S of Limoux by the D118 and 76km/47.5m W of Perpignan by the N9 then the D117.
👀 **Don't Miss:** The view from the Langarail pastures, the Pas de l'Ours viewpoint and the walk through the Gorges de la Frau, in the Pays de Sault; the scenery of the Défilé de Pierre-Lys… and the château de Puivert.
🕐 **Timing:** Quillan is the departure point for day-trips to the pays de Sault and the Aude gorges.
👪 **Kids:** Quercorb Museum and the visit of the grottes de l'Aguzou (only for children over 10); winter skiing in the little resort of Camurac.

Puivert court life during the age of the troubadours. The **Musée du Quercorb** (⏱ *open mid-Jul–Aug 10.30am–7pm; Apr–mid Jul and Sep 10am–12.30pm, 2–6pm; Oct 2–5pm;* ⏱ *closed Nov–Mar;* 🎫 *4€, children ages 6–15 1.60€;* 📞 *04 68 20 80 98; www.quercorb.com/musee)* on local history, traditions and livelihoods displays casts of medieval musical instruments which once ornamented the castle.

Montségur★★

⏱ *Open Jul–Aug daily 9am–7.30pm; Apr–Jun 10am–6.30pm; Sep 9.30am–6.30am, Oct 10am–6pm, Nov 10.30am–5pm; Feb and Dec 11am–4.30pm, Mar 10.30–5.30pm (except Mon).* ⏱ *Closed Jan, 25 Dec.* 👥 *Guided visits available. Can be closed in bad weather conditions.* 🎫 *4.50€ (children 2€).* 📞 *05 61 01 10 27/ 06 94. www.montsegur.fr.* 👀 *It's worth bringing good walking shoes. Allow*

Puivert Castle

© B. Rieger / hemis.fr

at least an hour for the steep ascent to the château on foot and the return to the car park. The path to the chateau begins outside the village on the D9 to Lavalanet and Foix.

It would be hard to imagine a better **site★★** for a castle than that of Montségur which is built on a rock, the 'Pog', at an altitude of 1,207m/4,000ft. This is not just another spectacular fortress. What draws visitors here is the story of its downfall and its consequences.

A Bit of History

By 1243, the Albigensian crusades were over and the Inquisition was at work rounding up the remaining heretics. The last **Cathars** were reduced to a few remote enclaves, of which the castle of Montségur was the main one. It was inhabited by a community of Cathar faithful protected by a garrison of soldiers. While Catharism was still practised, the Inquisition had unfinished business. Siege was laid to Montségur by Hugh d'Arcis, seneschal of Carcassonne, and for some time success was not assured.

Then the east tower was damaged by a projectile from trebuchet and subsequently overrun by intrepid Basque volunteers after they had scaled the impossible slopes.

On 2 March 1244 the castle capitulated but on favourable terms. The soldiers, most of whom were not Cathars, would be allowed to depart in return for a light penance. Everyone else was given 15 days grace before they faced their fate, a delay which has never been satisfactorily explained. On 16 March over 200 unrepentant Cathars were marched down the mountainside in chains and burnt alive on pyres. Catharism lingered on for a few years but it never recovered from after the fall of Montségur.

Fortress★

The fortress as seen today, a stretched pentagon following the contours of the platform on top of the rock is not quite the same as the one that existed in 1244 – but is still impressive. The views over the valley and over the surrounding hills and towards the Pyrénées are superb.

The **village** of Montségur is in the Lasset valley below the château. An **archaeological museum** (*◐opening times vary; ◐2€, children 1€; ✆05 61 01 10 27*) in the town hall (*mairie*) contains information on Cathar philosophy and displays objects from the excavations.

🚗 DRIVING TOUR

PAYS DE SAULT AND GORGES DE L'AUDE★★

144km/90mi round tour. Allow one day.
🕓 See region map. ▷ Leave Quillan West along D 117.

This trip includes a large stretch of the **Route du Sapin de l'Aude**, a drive through woodland where there are conifers over 50m/160ft tall.

▷ Turn left onto D 613 which runs across the Sault plateau.

Deeply scored by the valley of the Rebenty, the plateau de Sault, reached via **Coudons**, is an agreeable place to tour, at least in summer when the sun illuminates the fields of wheat.

▷ Beyond Espèzel, watch out for a crossroads marked with a cross and turn right onto D 29 towards Bélesta. Take the left turn past the forest lodge, drive along the forest road to a left bend and park the car by the Langarail drinking troughs.

Langarail pastures★

🥾 *45min on foot there and back.*
As its name suggests, this is a rural site. Follow the stony track until the bumpy stretch from which there is a **view** to the north, beyond the Bélesta Forest as far as the foothills of the chain towards the Lauragais.

River Aude runs through the gorges

© A. Thuillier / MICHELIN

▷ Return to the forest road and continue west.

Pas de l'Ours★

The road runs along a rocky cliff above the Gorges de la Frau.

▷ At Col de la Gargante, take the steep road to the left which is signposted 'Belvédère 600m'.

Belvédère du Pas de l'Ours★★

15min on foot there and back.
🥾 From the look-out point, there is a magnificent view of the **Gorges de la Frau**; 700m/2 296ft lower down are the Montségur outcrop and the Tabe mountain; beyond these, and much higher up, the white patches of the Trimouns quarry can be seen.

▷ Beyond Col de la Gargante, follow the road to Comus and turn right.

Gorges de la Frau★

1hr 30min on foot there and back.
🥾 Park the car at the entrance to a wide forest track climbing a tributary valley. The path runs along the base of yellow-tinged limestone cliffs. After a 45min walk, turn back at the point where the valley makes a sharp bend.

▷ Return to Comus and take the road to the right towards Camurac.

🎿 Camurac ski area

Alt 1,400–1,800m/4,593–5,906ft.
Camurac is a family resort equipped with 16 Alpine ski runs suitable for all levels of proficiency, a country-skiing loop and a marked track for snowshoeing.

▷ Turn left on D 613 in the direction of Belcaire.

Belcaire – The "capital" of the Pays de Sault is dominated by the "casteillas", the remains of an ancient castle. Otherwise, the village is an agreeable stopover with an artificial lake providing a chance to freshen up in summer.

▷ Shortly after leaving Camurac, turn

right on D 20 and continue to Niort-de-Sault. In Niort, turn left.

Drive down the **Rebenty gorge**, passing beneath the impressive overhangs of the **Défilé d'Able** and through the **Défilé de Joucou**, where the road follows a series of tunnels and overhangs, to reach **Joucou**, a sheltered village gathered around an old abbey.

▶ Turn back. After driving through a couple of tunnels, turn left onto D 29 which runs through Rodome, Aunat and Bessède-de-Sault before joining D 118 where you turn left towards Axat.

This pretty stretch of road runs along the edge of the Sault plateau.

▲▲ Grottes de l'Aguzou
Potholing outings by appointment (3 days in advance); departure at 9am. ☜1 day (7hrs): 50€; ½ day (2hrs): 30€. Take plimsolls, light walking boots or shoes and a cold meal. ℘04 68 20 45 38. www.grotte-aguzou.com.
This complex network of caves was discovered in 1965. On the tour, visitors can see a large number of crystals and some wonderful examples of aragonite.

Gorges de St-Georges★
This river gorge, cutting straight down through bare rock, is the narrowest in the upper Aude Valley.
In the **Aude gorge**, a reach of some 10km/6mi, the river surges along between high cliffs thickly covered with plant life.

▶ Drive on to **Axat**, a white-water sports resort, left onto D 177 to Quillan.

Défilé de Pierre-Lys★
This is an impressive stretch of road between the ravine's sheer cliff walls, to which the odd bush clings tenaciously. The final tunnel is known as the **Trou du Curé** ('priest's hole') in memory of Abbot **Félix Armand** (1742–1823), parish priest of St-Martin-Lys, who had the passage cut through the rock with pickaxes.

ADDRESSES

🍽 STAY

☺ **Résidence de tourisme l'Espinet** – *1km/half a mile north on D 118. ℘04 68 20 88 88. www.lespinet.com. &. 111 villas and 24 studios 65/127€/per night for 5 pers.* As well as being a holiday centre, this beautiful building is also a fitness and health centre. Open air sports, tennis and a covered swimming pool.

☺☺ **Hôtel-Restaurant Bayle** – *38 av. d'Ax-les-Thermes, 11340 Belcaire. ℘04 68 20 31 05. www.hotel-bayle.com. 10 rms. 45/48€. ☐6€. Restaurant 18/30€.* An institution of the Pays de Sault, this simple hotel will give you a warm welcome. Regional cuisine is served in the restaurant, which expands onto a terrace with a mountain view in good weather.

☺☺ **Chambre d'hôte La Cocagnière** – *3 pl. du Pijol, hameau de Camp-Sylvestre (6km/4mi east of Puivert on D 117, then a minor road on right). ℘04 68 20 81 90. www.lacocagniere.com. Closed 15 Nov-15 Mar. 4 rms. 53/63€. ☐. Evening meal 20€.* This lovingly renovated farmhouse on the edge of the hamlet of Camp-Sylvestre is a charming combination of high-quality accommodation, warm welcome from the young owners, an excellent table d'hôte and a natural setting.

☺☺☺ **Hôtel La Chaumière** – *25 bd Charles-de-Gaulle. ℘04 68 20 02 00. www.pyren.fr. ▣. 26 rms. 75/100€. ☐11€. Restaurant 24/55€.* A great rounded facade in mountain style gives access to this comfortable hotel, which makes an ideal base in Quillan for exploring the region. Regional cuisine.

ACTIVITIES
MULTISPORTS
▲▲ **La Forge** – *Rte de Perpignan (D 117), ℘04 68 20 23 79. Closed Jan–Mar and mid-Sep–mid-Dec but open all year round for groups. 40€.* A youth hostel, campsite and outdoor sports centre all in one, offering a variety of activities including watersports, hiking and climbing.

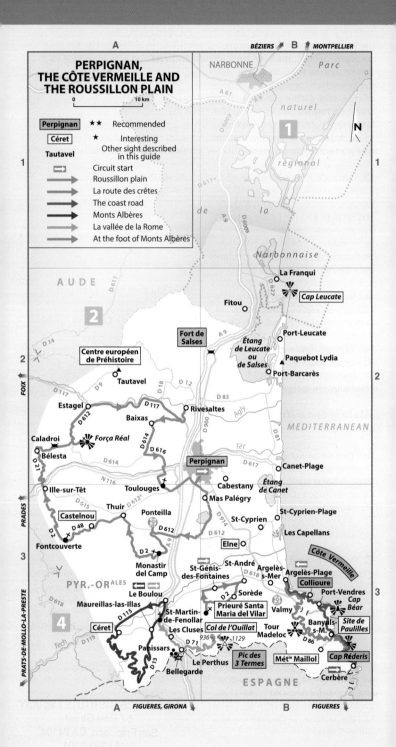

PERPIGNAN, THE CÔTE VERMEILLE AND THE ROUSSILLON PLAIN

0 ——————— 10 km

Perpignan	★★ Recommended
Céret	★ Interesting
Tautavel	Other sight described in this guide
⇨	Circuit start
→	Roussillon plain
→	La route des crêtes
→	The coast road
➤	Monts Albères
→	La vallée de la Rome
➤	At the foot of Monts Albères

N

BÉZIERS B MONTPELLIER

NARBONNE

Parc

naturel

régional

de la

Narbonnaise

La Franqui

Cap Leucate

Fitou

Fort de Salses

Étang de Leucate ou de Salses

Port-Leucate

Paquebot Lydia

Port-Barcarès

AUDE

Centre européen de Préhistoire

Tautavel

MEDITERRANEAN

Estagel

Baixas

Rivesaltes

Agly

Caladroi

Força Réal

Bélesta

Tét

Perpignan

Canet-Plage

Ille-sur-Têt

Toulouges

Cabestany

Étang de Canet

Mas Palégry

St-Cyprien-Plage

Thuir

Ponteilla

St-Cyprien

Les Capellans

Castelnou

Fontcouverte

Monastir del Camp

Elne

Côte Vermeille

St-Génis-des-Fontaines

St-André

Argelès-s-Mer

Argelès-Plage

Collioure

PYR.-OR ALES

Le Boulou

D 2

Sorède

Valmy

Port-Vendres

Cap Béar

Maureillas-las-Illas

Céret

St-Martin-de-Fenollar

Les Cluses

Prieuré Santa Maria del Vilar

Col de l'Ouillat

Tour Madeloc

Banyuls-s-M.

Site de Paulilles

Panissars

Le Perthus

Bellegarde

Pic des 3 Termes

Mét.le Maillol

Cap Réderis

Cerbère

ESPAGNE

A FIGUERES, GIRONA B FIGUERES

PRATS-DE-MOLLO-LA-PRESTE

PRADES

FOIX

The Vermilion Coast, the undiscovered Spanish facet of France, has been the source of inspiration for many of the world's leading artists, and led to its own style of painting. Bathed in a magical light, the waves dash against rocky shores, craggy mountains do battle against the sea, and steeply sloping vineyards cling to the hillsides. The area has been settled since prehistoric times, as the remains of Tautavel Man testify, but the principal town of Perpignan seems to have been founded only in the 10C. This is France of course, but above all else it is Catalonia, as evidenced by the mix of languages used across the Franco-Spanish border. In this frontierland, the buildings speak of past times, of the counts of Roussillon, the kings of Majorca, the Catalans and Aragonese, and then the French. Inevitably, over centuries of cultural co-habitation, a unique identity has formed.

Tautavel Man

Tautavel man is the name of an extinct hominid that lived about 300,000–450,000 years ago. He is named after fossils found in an ancient karst cave on the site known as *Caune de l'Arago*, very close to the village of Tautavel. Although excavations had been going on for some years, the skull of this early ancestor of man was only found there in 1971. Tautavel Man has a flat and receding forehead and a well-developed arch of the eyebrows; he has a large face and rectangular eye sockets.

Highlights

1 Enjoy a town walk in ancient **Perpignan** (p137)

2 Check out the half-buried **Fort de Salses** (p144)

3 Spend some time in the artists' paradise that is **Collioure** (p151)

4 Try Banyul's distinctive fortified **wine** (p154)

5 Explore the cliffs and coves of the **Vermilion Coast** (p156)

Littorally Speaking

This lovely stretch of coastline – the littoral, in French – has numerous enchanting border villages, where the influence of Spain is plain to see. Castle ruins pepper the landscape, and peaceful, hidden villages are found at every turn. This is the best of both worlds: a launch pad from which to explore the Mediterranean, yet only a few minutes from the Spanish Costa Brava. This, the Côte Vermeille, is the last stretch of French coast before Spain, and extends from Argelès-sur-Mer, a superb stop for families, to the border village of Cerbère in the secluded valley of Cervera.

Collioure, Côte Vermeille

© Walter Bibikow / age fotostock

Perpignan★★

Perpignan, once the capital city of the counts of Roussillon and the kings of Majorca, is an outlying post of Catalan civilisation north of the Pyrénées, and a lively commercial city, with shaded walks lined with pavement cafés. The economy is largely based on tourism, wine and olive oil, and the production of cork, wool and leather.

A BIT OF HISTORY

During the 13C, the city profited from the great upsurge in trade between the south of France, and the Levant stimulated by the crusades. In 1276, Perpignan became the capital of Roussillon as part of the kingdom of Majorca.

The second Catalan city – After the kingdom of Majorca had ceased to be in 1344, Roussillon and Cerdagne were integrated into the princedom of Catalonia which, in the 14C and 15C, constituted a kind of autonomous federation in the heart of the State of Aragón. Catalan 'Corts' sat at Barcelona, but delegated a 'Deputation' to Perpignan. Between the two slopes of the Pyrénées, a commercial, cultural and linguistic community came into being.

French or Spanish? – In 1463, Louis XI helped King John II of Aragón to defeat the Catalans and took possession of Perpignan and Roussillon. However, hostilities with France broke out once more and French armies besieged the city. The people of Perpignan put up fierce resistance and surrendered only when ordered to do so by the king of Aragón, who gave the city the title of 'Fidelissima' (most faithful).

In 1493, Charles VIII gave the province of Roussillon back to the Spanish. Later, however, Cardinal Richelieu seized the opportunity offered by a Catalan rebellion against Spain, forming an alliance with rebels and, in 1641, Louis XIII became count of Barcelona.

The final siege of Perpignan – As a Spanish garrison was holding Perpignan, the city was laid to siege. Louis XIII arrived with the elite of the French army

Region Map: AB2.

Info: Palais des Congrès, pl. A.-Lanoux, 66000 Perpignan. ✆04 68 66 30 30. www.perpignan tourisme.com. Guided tour of the town: www.vpah.culture.fr.

Location: The A 9 (exit 42) and the N 9 both lead to Perpignan; access to the centre by Boulevard Edmond Michelet (west), Avenue des Baléares (south) or Pont Arago (north, over the Têt River).

Parking: Parking in the centre of Perpignan isn't easy. You may find a place on the promenade des Platanes: access by bd Wilson and cours F.-Palmarole.

Don't Miss: The Palais des Rois de Majorque; the Gothic arcades in the patio of Maison Julia; the Musée des Beaux-Arts Hyacinthe-Rigaud

Timing: Allow a day. Take advantage of the coolness of the morning to walk around town and spend the afternoon in the museums.

Kids: The palais des Rois de Majorque, the Musée Numismatique Joseph-Puig, the Romanesque tympanum at Cabestany, Le Centre Européen de Préhistoire and the Musée de la Préhistoire Européenne at Tautavel and the Jardin Exotique de Ponteilla.

and Perpignan finally surrendered on 9 September 1642.

The Treaty of the Pyrénées ratified the final reunification of Roussillon with the French crown.

La Sardane, a traditional Catalonian dance

© S. Grandadam / age fotostock

🐾 WALKING TOUR

HISTORIC PERPIGNAN
🐾 *See town map.*

Le Castillet★
This monument, an emblem of Perpignan dominates place de la Victoire. Its two towers are crowned with exceptionally tall crenellations and machicolations.

Promenade des Platanes
This wide avenue is lined with plane trees and adorned with fountains. Palm trees grow along the side avenues.

La Miranda
This is a small public park behind the church of St-Jacques. It is given over to the plant life of the *garrigue* and shrubs which are either native or have been introduced to the region.

Église St-Jacques
At the west end of the nave, a vast chapel added in the 18C was reserved for the brotherhood of La Sanch ('of the precious Blood'). From 1416, this penitents' brotherhood performed a solemn procession on Maundy Thursday (now Good Friday), carrying its *misteris* to the singing of hymns.

Cathédrale St-Jean★
The church was begun in 1324 by Sancho, second king of Majorca, and was consecrated in 1509. The oblong façade of the basilica is constructed from pebbles alternating with bricks. It is flanked on the right by a square tower with an 18C wrought-iron campanile housing a 15C bell.

Campo Santo
♿ 🕐 *Open daily except Mon: Apr–Sep noon–7pm; Oct–Mar 11am–5.30pm.* 🕐 *Closed 1 Jan, 25 Dec.* 📞 *04 68 66 30 30. www.perpignan tourisme.com.*
South of the cathedral, the Campo Santo is a vast square graveyard and one of the few medieval graveyards remaining in France. Pointed funeral alcoves and marble recesses are set into walls adorned with pebbles and courses of brick.

Castillet with the Catalan flag

© Bertrand Rieger / Hemis / Photoshot

WHERE TO STAY

Alexander (Hôtel)......................①

Domaine du Mas Boluix
(Chambre d'hôte)..................③

Domaine du Moulin
(Chambre d'hôte)..................⑤

France (Hôtel de)......................⑮

Kyriad (Hôtel)............................⑨

Loge (Hôtel de la)......................⑰

Mas des Arcades (Hôtel Le)...⑪

New Christina (Hôtel)..............⑬

WHERE TO EAT

Antiquaires (Les)......................①

Barathym (Le)............................⑱

Galinette (La)............................⑦

Passerelle (La)............................⑨

Rencontre (La)............................⑲

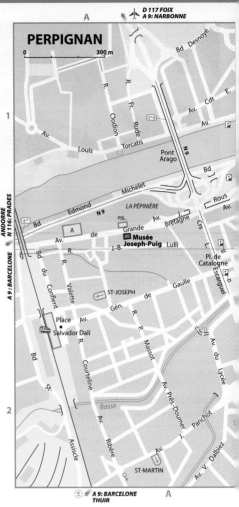

Place de la Loge

This square and the pedestrianised rue de la Loge, paved in pink marble, form the lively centre of town life. Here, in summer, the *sardana* is danced several times a week.

Loge de Mer★

This fine Gothic building, dating from 1397 and refurbished and extended in the 16C, once housed a commercial tribunal in charge of ruling on claims relating to maritime trade.

Hôtel de Ville★

🕐*Daily except Sun 8am–noon, 2–6pm.*

In the arcaded courtyard stands a bronze by Maillol: *The Mediterranean*. On the façade of the building, three bronze arms, which are said to symbolise the 'hands' or estates of the population required to elect the five consuls, were in fact originally designed to hold torches.

Palais de la Députation

During the reign of the kings of Aragón this 15C palace was the seat of the permanent commission or *députation* representing the Catalan 'Corts'.

▶ Follow the rue d'Alsace-Lorraine. On the right, the rue Mailly gives access to the musée des Beaux-Arts.

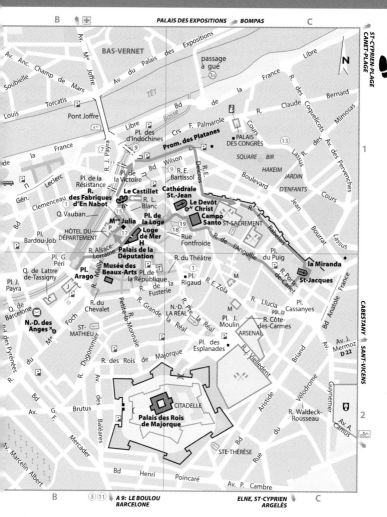

Musée des Beaux-Arts Hyacinthe-Rigaud

Hôtel de Lazerme. &⟳*Open daily except Mon: 10.30am–6pm.* ⟳*Closed 1 Jan, 1 May, 14 Jul, 25 Dec.* ⊚*4€.* ✆*04 68 35 43 40.*

Hyacinthe-Rigaud (1659–1743) was a French baroque painter of Catalan origin whose career was largely based in Paris. He is renowned for his portrait paintings of Louis XIV, the royalty and nobility of Europe, and members of their courts, and was considered one of the most notable French portraitists of the Classical period.

▷ Return along the rue d'Alsace-Lorraine.

Place Arago

This lively, pleasant square, adorned with palm trees, magnolias and cafés, attracts crowds of people. In the centre stands the statue of the famous physician, astronomer and politician **François Arago** (1786–1853).

▷ Return to the Palais de la Députation.

Opposite the Palais de la Députation, take a little detour down the small rue des Fabriques d'En Nabot, The **Maison**

Julia★ at No. 2 is one of the few well-preserved *hôtels* of Perpignan, possessing a patio with 14C Gothic arcades.

▷ Return to Le Castillet.

ADDITIONAL SIGHTS
♿ Palais des Rois de Majorque★

🕐☛Open Jun–Sep 10am–6pm; Oct–May 9am–5pm. 🕐Closed 1 Jan, 1 May, 1 Nov, 25 Dec. ✆4€. 📞04 68 34 48 29.
When the kings of Majorca came to the throne in 1276, they built their palace on the hill of Puig del Rey.
A vaulted slope leads across the red-brick ramparts to a pleasant Mediterranean garden. Pass beneath a tower to the west, the **tour de l'Homage**, to get to the square-shaped main courtyard. This is open on the east and west sides with two storeys of arcades.
On the first floor of the south wing, the **great hall of Majorca** has a chimney-piece with three fireplaces. Beyond it, the Queen's suite has a superb ceiling painted with the Catalan colours (green and red). The most splendid part of the building is the **chapel-keep** of Ste-Croix rising above the east wing. It comprises two sanctuaries built one above the other in the 14C by Jaime II of Majorca.

Chapelle N.-D.-des-Anges
32 r. du Mar.-Foch.
This old Gothic chapter house (13C) of the monastery was turned into a military hospital in the 19C; it stages temporary exhibitions.

Musée Numismatique Joseph-Puig★
42 Ave. de Grande-Bretagne.
🕐Visit by prior reservation, one day in advance 🕐Closed Sat pm–Mon. ✆4€. 📞04 68 66 24 86.
Part of the Villa 'Les Tilleuls' (1907) has been converted into a museum, at the donor's request, to display the numismatic collection bequeathed by Joseph Puig to his native city of Perpignan.

EXCURSIONS
Cabestany
▷ *5km/3mi on D 22 to the SE.*
Inside the church of **Notre-Dame-des-Anges**, on the wall of the chapel on the right is a famous Romanesque **tympanum★** by the 12C travelling sculptor, the master of Cabestany.

Tautavel
▷ *27.7km/17.2mi NW, D 117 and D59.*
This little village of 800 inhabitants, on the banks of the Verdouble, is an important centre of prehistory following the discovery here of objects of vital significance in the study of the origins of human life. Tautavel is in a wine growing area in the Catalan, the Corbières, between the sea and the mountains, at the bottom of the foothills of the high Pyrénées. In spite of its prehistoric notoriety, the village is equally renowned, in rather different circles, for the quality of its wine which uses grenache, syrah and carignane grapes. The remains of the village's castle are nearby, and while Tautavel is close to the mountain areas occupied by the Cathars, the village and surrounding area seem to have escaped the attention of the Crusading army.

♿ Centre Européen de Préhistoire★ – *Route de Vingrau.*
♿🕐Open Jul–Aug 10am–7pm; Apr–Jun and Sep 10am–12.30pm, 2–6pm; Jan–Mar and Oct–Dec 10am–12.30pm, 2–5pm. 🕐Closed 1 Jan, 25 Dec. ✆8€. 📞04 68 29 07 76. www.tautavel.com.
Devoted to the evolution of man and his environment (based on the significant discoveries made in the Caune de l'Arago and surrounding area).

♿ Musée de la Préhistoire européenne - Préhistorama – ♿🕐Open Jul–Aug 10am–7pm, Apr–Jun and Sept 10am–12.30pm 2–6pm, Jan–Mar and Oct–Dec 10am–12.30, 2–5pm. 🕐Closed 1 Jan, 25 Dec. ✆8€. 📞04 68 29 07 76. www.450000ans.com. Europe before time began! Five "virtual theatres" present the daily life of the first inhabitants of Europe in 3D as seen through their tools, hunting practices and living spaces. Prepared by professor **Henry de Lumley**, the displays here give an

Palais des Rois de Majorque

© J.-P. Azam / hemis.fr

understanding of our most distant ancestors. Complements a visit to the Centre Européen de Préhistoire (&see p140).

🚗 DRIVING TOUR

ROUSSILLON PLAIN

128km/80mi. Allow one day.
&See region map. ▷ *Leave Perpignan S, turn left onto N 114 then take a little road on the right towards Villeneuve-de-la-Raho.*

Situated among vineyards, **Mas Palégry** is the setting for an **Aviation museum**. (&◐visit by arrangement; ⊚5€; ℘06 18 92 64 14; www.musee-aviation.com).

▷ Follow D 612 towards Thuir, and then turn right to Ponteilla.

The **Jardin Exotique de Ponteilla** (&◐open Jun–Aug Mon–Fri 10.30am–6.30pm, Sat, Sun 2–6.30pm, May and Sep 2–6.30pm; ◐closed rest of year; ⊚5€; ℘04 68 53 22 44) has a signposted botanical trail.

Turn back, cross D 612 and drive on to Trouillas, turn right onto D 37 to Villemolaque and continue along D 40 towards Passa, where the **Prieuré du Monastir del Camp** is an imposing building with an elegant fortified front

(&◐⌐guided tours daily, except Thu; ⊚4€; ℘04 68 38 80 71).

Drive along D 2 to Fourques, then turn right to D 615 to **Thuir**, known mainly for its wine cellars (&◐⌐Jul–Aug guided tours daily; ⊚2€; ℘04 68 53 05 42; www.byrrh.com). Continue along the D 48. The road climbs the slopes of the Aspre. Suddenly the medieval, fortified village of **Castelnou★** comes into sight with Mont Canigou rising in the background, making a wonderful **view★**. Continue to the **Église de Fontcouverte**, an isolated church shaded by oak trees. This is a beautiful, solitary site.

Take the D 2 north to **Ille-sur-Têt** (&see Ille-sur-Têt). The D 21 leads to **Bélesta**, a remarkable village built on a rocky nose rising from the vineyards. The village has long been known to archaeologists for its wealth of prehistoric remains. The **Chateau-musée** (◐open mid-Jun–mid-Sep 2–7pm; rest of year daily except Tue and Sat 2–5.30pm; ⊚4.50€; ℘04 68 84 55 55) gives an insight into the prehistoric finds.

Drive in the direction of the col de la Bataille (D 38). **Castle Caladroi** soon appears in the middle of a park planted with exotic species. From the col you reach the **ermitage de Força Réal**, which offers a superb **panorama★★**.

Go back to the col, and from there reach **Estagel**, and continue on the D 117 to **Rivesaltes**, one of the wine capitals of Roussillon.

Head SW on the D 614 to **Baixas**, an agreeable medieval village dominated by the silhouette of its **church★**.

Continue on the D 614, then turn left at the D 616. At **Baho**, take the road south, passing over **la Têt** and the D 116. Turn right, then left to reach **Toulouges** (church). Return to Perpignan on the D 900.

ADDRESSES

🛏 STAY

🛏 **Hôtel de la Loge** – *1 r. des Fabriques-d'En-Nabot.* ☎04 68 34 41 02. www.hotel delaloge.fr. 22 rms. 55/70€. ☐8/10€. Perpignan's most centrally located hotel occupies a beautiful 16C mansion, which has been decorated and furnished with taste. There is a warm welcome to this charming and romantic place in which the facilities are being gradually renovated.

🛏 **Hôtel de France** – *Quai Sadi-Carnot.* ☎04 68 84 80 35. www.hoteldefrance-perpignan.fr. 24 rms. 59/81€. ☐9€. *Free wifi.* An historic mansion that first opened its doors in 1833 and has since accommodated many famous people, including Salvador Dalí. Largely renovated (the last work being done in 2010), its rooms are often a little small but are well sound-proofed and comfortably furnished. Its best feature is its central location.

🛏🛏 **Hôtel Alexander** – *15 Bd. Clemenceau.* ☎04 68 35 41 41. www.hotel-alexander.fr. 23 rms. 36/95€. ☐7.50€. This little downtown hotel has balconied, air-conditioned guestrooms on three levels (with elevator). Enthusiastic welcome.

🛏🛏🛏 **Hôtel New Christina** – *51 cours Lassus.* ☎04 68 35 12 21. www.hotelnew christina.com. 25 rms. ☐9.95€. *Restaurant (dinner only) 23€ menu, 15€ dish of the day.* 🛏🛏. A small, modern hotel, near the city centre, with a rooftop swimming pool.

🛏🛏🛏 **Hôtel Kyriad** – *8 bd. Wilson.* ☎04 68 59 25 94. www.kyriad.fr. 49 rms. 89/180€. ☐12€. *Free wifi.* Recently renovated hotel; functional furnishings, integral courtyard with fountain.

NEARBY

🛏🛏🛏 **Chambre d'hôte du Domaine du Moulin** – *66300 Caixas, 6km/4mi S of Fontcouverte (direction Fourques).* ☎04 68 38 87 84. www.domaine-du-moulin-caixas.fr. Closed end Nov–Mar. Reservation advised. 3 rms. 120/160€. ☐8€. Rest. 29€. In the mountains, a former miller's house, now a B&B with an excellent restaurant.

🛏🛏🛏 **Chambre d'hôte Domaine du Mas Boluix** – *Chemin du Pou de les Colobres. 5km/3mi S of Perpignan towards Argelès.* ☎04 68 08 17 70. 🛏🛏. www.domaine-de-boluix.com. 5 rms. 91€. ☐. Removed from the bustle of Perpignan, this nicely restored 18C **mas** is a peaceful place in the middle of Cabestany grapevines. Each guest room is named after a local artist.

🛏🛏🛏🛏 **Le Mas des Arcades** – *840 av. d'Espagne 2km/1mi on the D 9.* ☎04 68 85 11 11. www.hotel-mas-des-arcades.fr. 62 rms. 95/180€. ☐11€. *Restaurant set menu lunch 20€. 24/48€. Free wifi.* Tidy rooms, half with balconies; fine restaurant.

🍴 EAT

🍴 **Le Barathym** – *7 r. des Cardeurs.* ☎04 68 50 98 14. Set menu lunch 14/18€. This restaurant in a little street near the place de la Loge serves an inspired cuisine and enjoys a certain popularity among the people of Perpignan who come for the smart dining room and the culinary innovations of the chef. It could adapt its prices to the clientele better, even if the lunch-time menus are reasonable.

🍴🍴 **Les Antiquaires** – *Pl. Desprès.* ☎04 68 34 06 58. www.lesantiquaires perpignan.fr. Closed Sun eve and Mon. 25/44€. This family restaurant is decorated with antique china; the chef serves a traditional cuisine.

🍴🍴 **La Rencontre** – *18 r. des Cardeurs.* ☎04 68 34 42 73. www.restaurant-larencontre.fr. Closed lunch Sat–Mon. Set menus lunch 9.50/14/17€. 27€. More classic than its neighbour across the road, this is a well-run restaurant that has a menu based on regional and seasonable produce, sourced from the sea and the mountains.

La Passerelle – *1 cours Palmarole. ℘04 68 51 30 65. Closed Mon lunch, and Sun. 22€.* A cosy restaurant where seafood stars and reminds you that the sea is not far away.

La Galinette – *23 R. Jean-Payra. ℘04 68 35 00 90. Closed Sun and Mon, mid-Jul–mid-Aug, 22 Dec–5 Jan. Set menu lunch 19€. 62€.* Contemporary furnishings, beautifully set tables and southern-style dishes created with market-fresh ingredients.

DRINK
Espi – *43 bis quai Vauban. ℘04 68 35 19 91. Winter: daily 7.30am–7.30pm; summer: 7.30am–12.30am.* Immense store where each type of product (sweets, pastries, etc) features specialities original to the house.

ON THE TOWN
A number of bars in the old part of the city have live music in the evenings, such as O'Shannons Irish pub, le Corto Maltese and le Tio Pepe or le Mediator.

SHOPPING
STREETS
Clothes shops can be found in the pedestrianised city centre (Rue Mailly). The avenue du Gén.-de-Gaulle, in a lively part of town, is full of shops. The rue de l'Adjudant-Pilote-Paratilla, also called la rue des Olives by locals, is known for its two grocery shops and delicatessen.

MARKETS
Fruit and vegetable markets are held daily except Mon on the pl. de la République and every morning on place Cassanyes. Flea market Av. du Palais-des-Expositions on Sun morning. Organic market on pl. Rigaud Wed and Sat mornings. **Flea Market,** avenue du Palais-des-Expositions, Sunday morning.

GOURMET TREATS
Au Paradis des Desserts – *13 Ave. du Gén.-de-Gaulle. ℘04 68 34 89 69. Tue–Sun 8am–12.10pm, 4–7.30pm. Closed public holiday afternoons and 3 wks in Aug.* Here a talented patissier devotes himself to the creation of a wide range of truly individualised taste sensations.

Maison Sala – *1 r. Adjudant-Pilote-Paratilla. ℘04 68 51 03 75. 8.15am–7pm. Closed Sun, Mon and early Jul.* The Sala family has been running this grocery since 1913. Their reputation is built on two specialities; Collioure anchovies, either salted or as *boquerones*, and wild Icelandic cod. They also sell spices, olives, dried fruits, nuts and vegetables by weight, as well as Catalan souvenirs.

Lor – *12 r. Becquerel, mas Guérido, Cabestany. ℘04 68 85 65 05. 9.30am–noon, 2–7pm. Closed Sun and hols. Free.* A video presentation of the great Perpignan factory that makes sweets such as tourons, rousquilles and croquants. All these can be tasted at the end of the visit.

PERPIGNAN GARNETS
Bijouterie Gourgot – *13 r. Louis-Blanc. ℘04 68 34 27 46. Tue–Sat. 9.30am–noon, 2–6.45pm, Mon 2.30–7pm. Closed hols.* Shop and workshop specialising in Perpignan garnets.

Jacques et Maxime Creuzet-Romeu – *9 r. Fontfroide. ℘04 68 34 16 94. 9am–noon, 2–7pm. Closed weekends, public hols, first two weeks of Aug.* This craft jeweller makes jewellery using Perpignan garnets. The workshop can be visited by prior appointment.

ARTISANAT
Centre d'artisanat d'art Sant Vicens – *R. Sant-Vicens. ℘04 68 50 02 18. www. santvicens.fr.* Exhibitions and sales of works of art by Roussillon artists, as well as antiques, paintings, local wines etc. Also on show are Sant Vicens ceramics, decorated according to the designs of Lurçat and Picart le Doux.

EVENTS
Procession de la Sanch – Good Friday. To the sound of *goigs* (traditional chants), penitents dressed in *caparutxa* (capes de ») go in procession through the city from the cathedral to the Eglise St-Jacques, carrying representations of the Passion.

Jazzèbre – Open air concerts, and in bars. End of Sept. *www.jazzebre.com.*
Festival Visa pour l'Image – *2 weeks in Sep. www.visapourlimage.com.* Gathering of press photographers.

Fort de Salses★★

Rising above the surrounding vineyards, this half-buried fortress is surprisingly big. The colour of the brickwork, bronzed by the sun, blends harmoniously with the golden sheen of the stonework, mainly of pink sandstone. Built in the 15C, on a site with a source of spring water, the fort is a unique example of the medieval military architecture of Spain, adapted by Vauban in 1691 to the needs of the military of the time. The Treaty of the Pyrénées of 1659 redrew the border with Spain, and Salses then lost its strategic importance.

- **Michelin Map:** Region Map B2.
- **Info:** ℘04 68 38 60 13. www.salses.monuments-nationaux.fr.
- **Location:** 16km/10mi N of Perpignan by the N 9 (direction Sigean).
- **Don't Miss:** The rounded crests of the walls, the polygonal form of the moat and its embankment, and the keep.
- **Kids:** A clue-hunting game gives kids an activity to do while exploring the fortress.

A BIT OF HISTORY

Hannibal's passage – In 218 BC, Hannibal made plans to cross Gaul and invade Italy. Rome immediately sent emissaries, to ask the Gauls to resist the Carthaginians' advance. The Gauls declined and Hannibal was allowed through as a 'guest'. When the Romans, who remembered the episode with bitterness, occupied Gaul, they built a camp at Salses. After Roussillon had been restored to Spain in 1493, Ferdinand of Aragón had this fortress built. Designed to house a garrison of 1,500 men, it could also withstand attack by newly evolving artillery. French troops reconquered Roussillon in mid-17C.

A Nobel in the vines – **Claude Simon**, winner of the 1985 Nobel Prize for literature, was born in Madagascar in 1913 but grew up in and around Perpignan. On his mother's side he belonged to an old Roussillon family descended from Jean-Pierre Lacombe-Saint-Michel, a general and politician during the Revolution and Empire. A writer of memories somewhat in the tradition of Proust, Simon evokes scenes from his childhood in a very full, sensual and "visual" way, repeatedly

Fort de Salses

© L. Campion / MICHELIN

coming back to them in books such as L'Acacia (The Acacia, 1989), and espeically his last work, Le Tramway (The Trolley 2001). He died in Paris in July 2005.

VISIT

🕐☀️Jun–Sep 9.30am–7pm; Oct–May 10am–noon, 2–5pm. 🕐Closed 1 Jan, 1 May, 1 and 11 Nov, 25 Dec. ⊛7€.

The fortress illustrates the significant transition from that of medieval castle to a modern fortress. With walls from 6–10m/20–33ft thick, the construction has three wholly independent parts running from east to west. The various levels are connected by a labyrinth of passages with a zigzagging complex network of internal underground defences. The fortress today houses rotating exhibitions of contemporary art.

The best place to start a visit is at the top of the walls to get an overview of the fortress. Here it is worth noting how upper parts of the walls are rounded, a rare feature in the 15C, intended to make cannoballs richochet off and to discourage attempts to scale the walls with ladders. The polygonal shape of the counterscarp or outer moat embankment can be clearly seen: this allowed the besieged garrison to make their shots ricochet in the corners. The walls of the fortress (the scarp) are an average 9m/30 ft thick. The various buildings within them served as barracks, casemates and all necessary facilities in the event of a siege, including cowshed and bakery. The vaulted basement around the central courtyard served as stables (for around 100 horses and 1500 men). Above these are large chambers, which were safe from fire and bombardment. One of these, on the east side of the courtyard, is a chapel.

The keep is separated from the courtyard by its own moat and protecting wall. The keep is divided into seven levels, alternately vaulted or with ceilings. Built as accommodation for the commander of the fortress, it served as a powder store until the 19C. Zigzagging passageways and drawbridges for footsoldiers provided the last lines of defence.

EXCURSION
Vineyards of Fitou
▶️ To the N on the D 900.

Here, separated from the sea by the lake of Leucate, lie the vineyards of Corbières Maritime, whose centre is at Fitou, which gave its name to a robust AOC.
🕐See p20, 47, 119.

ADDRESSES

&️ See also addresses in Perpignan (p142) and Port-Barcarès (p146).

🛏️ STAY

🍽️🛏️ **Chambre d'hôte La Salsepareille** – 4 av. Xavier-Llobères 66600 Salses-le-Château. ☎️04 68 38 61 70. www.salsepareille.com. 🍴 4 rms. 60€⊡ ("weekend Escapade" 2 nights with meals, 150€), meal 23€. Townhouse offering unpretentious rooms. It is hard to resist the delicious table d'hôte served by the proprietor who is passionate about cooking. Excellent regional cuisine served in the enormous dining room. Drinks and smiles included!

🍽️🛏️ **Chambre d'hôte Casa Clara** – 21 r. des Commerçants 66510 St-Hippolyte (10km/6mi on D 11 towards Le Barcarès). ☎️04 68 28 48 14 / 06 78 13 14 53. www.casaclara66.com. 🍴 3 rms. 60/68€. ⊡. Three beautiful room are concealed behind the lavender-coloured shutters – "Marocaine ", "Africaine" and " Bord de mer " – in which the exotic and luxurious décor invites you to go on a journey… Don't forget to enjoy the soothing Jacuzzi, surrounded by bougainvilleas in the inner courtyard.

🍴 EAT

🍽️🛏️ **Le Commerce** – 2 bd de la Révolution, 66250 St-Laurent-de-la-Salanque (12km/7.5mi southeast via St-Hippolyte). ☎️04 68 28 02 21. www.lecommerce66.com. Closed Sun eve except in Jul and Aug, Mon, 1–21 Mar, 30 Oct–21 Nov. 16.50/39€. 11 rms. 52/56€. ⊡8.50€. Free wifi. A regional cuisine is served with a smile in the yellow-toned dining room of this restaurant in the centre of the village. The small rooms are equipped with Catalan furniture.

Port-Barcarés

The urban planners of this resort developed this site to satisfy tourists, providing for easy access to swimming and other outdoor activities and building self-catering accommodation, family camps and conventional hotel facilities. Residential areas have been grouped together, saving the seafront from overbearing blocks of buildings that would stifle the horizon.

VISIT
Le Lydia

This ship, which was deliberately run aground in 1967, is the main attraction of the new Roussillon shoreline (disco and casino). Just by the *Lydia*, along an esplanade by the sea, the **Allée des Arts** (*signposted*) hosts a small display of contemporary sculpture including the 'Soleillonautes', totem poles sculpted from the trunks of trees from Gabon.

Port Leucate

▶ *9km/5.5mi north of Port-Barcarès by the coast road.*

This resort was created at the same time as its coastal neighbours and is similarly popular in the summer months. The new harbour complex of **Port-Leucate** and **Port-Barcarès** constitutes the largest marina of all on the French Mediterranean coast.

▶ **Population:** 3,514.
♿ **Michelin Map:** Region map B2. 344: J6.
🛈 **Info:** Pl. de la République, 66420 Port-Barcarès. ℘04 68 86 16 56. www.portbarcares.com.
▶ **Location:** 25km/15.5mi N of Perpignan and 50km/31m SW of Narbonne by the A9.
🅿 **Parking:** Along the beaches or near the Tourist Office.
👪 **Kids:** Aquamagic.
🕐 **Timing:** Allow 30 minutes for sightseeing.

👪 **Aquamagic** – *In Port-Leucate.* ⏰*Open 18 Jun–4 Sep 10am–7pm.* ∞20€. ℘04 68 21 49 49. *www.aqualand.fr.* This seaside leisure park (water chutes, swimming pool) is particularly suitable for young children.

HIKE
Cap Leucate★

🚶*2hrs via a footpath running along the cliffs. Start from the Sémaphore du cap, at Leucate-Plage (10km/6mi N of Port-Barcarès along D 627).*

From the look-out point by the signal station on the cape, there is a fantastic **view★** from the Languedoc to the Albères mountains.

Le Lydia

© L. Campion / MICHELIN

Canet-Plage

This seaside resort has beautiful, long stretches of find sand and lots of activities for kids. Named after the nearby Étang de Canet and only 13km/8mi from Perpignan, this is a favourite resort with locals who head here from the city at the first sight of the sun. It's population can swell eightfold in summer.

SIGHTS

The classic resort of the Perpignanais because of its liveliness, yacht marina, sport facilities and casino.

Beaches

Plage Sardinal is ideal for camping. Shady family-friendly beaches and minigolf, volleyball and sailing schools.

♣♣ Aquarium

Boulevard de la Jetée, at the harbour.
Open Jul–Aug 10am–11pm; Jan–Jun: 10am–noon, 2–6pm. 6.50€ (children, 4.50€). 04 68 80 49 64.
Children will enjoy the colourful display of local and tropical species.

♣♣ Étang de Canet

W of Canet-Plage along D 81 towards St-Cyprien. Accessible by car (parking area), on foot or by bus. 04 68 80 89 78 and 06 10 75 70 41.
This lagoon, covering 956ha/3.7sq mi, is classified as a protected natural site. A village of ten fishing cabins made of sanils (reeds used because of their solidity and impermeability) have been reconstructed on the shore. Only one of them can be visited, the nine others being hired out to professional fishermen who keep their equipment here out of season (eels are caught in the lagon between March and May, and between October and December). A 2.5km/1.5mi footpath provides a chance to discover the wildlife (including 300 species of bird) and the flora of the lagoon. The Etang de Canet, and especially the reeds that grow in it, reveal the meaning of the resort's name: Canet comes from the Latin *canna*, meaning "reed".

▶ **Population:** 11,702.

Michelin Map: Region map B2. 344: J6.

Info: Pl. de la Méditerranée, 66140 Canet-en-Roussillon. *04 68 86 72 00.* www.ot-canet.fr.

Location: 13km/8mi east of Perpignan by the D 617. Go through Canet-en-Roussillon to get to the resort (head for the port or the sea front).

Parking: Several car parks in the port (Barcelone, Bastia and Ajaccio) and along the sea front (Espace Méditerranée, Côte Vermeille). In summer, the road to St-Cyprien is likely to be congested: stress is guaranteed.

Timing: Choose the morning for the beach if you want to avoid the crowds. The afternoon is a good time to visit the Centre d'Art Contemporain in St-Cyprien, or go for a walk around the village or along the shore of the lagoon.

Don't Miss: The fishing cabins on the Etang de Canet and the Centre d'Art Contemporain in St-Cyprien.

♣♣ **Kids:** The beach, the aquarium, the trail along the Étang du Canet.

EXCURSIONS
St-Cyprien

▶ *9km/5.6mi S.*
This small elegant residential town with palm tree-lined streets has preserved its historic Catalan village.
Centre d'art contemporain – *Pl. de la République. 04 68 21 32 07. Open daily except Tue 10am–noon, 2–6pm. 5€ (under 12 free).* A renowned arts

TRANSPORT

Beaches – In July and August the beaches are served by buses running between Cerbère and Barcarès, and by tram and road train in Canet. *Information from the tourist information office. Bus n° 1 (CTP, ℘04 68 61 01 13).*

centre holding exhibitions of contemporary work. There is a programme of activities for children.

Collections de St-Cyprien – *4 rue Émile-Zola, near the town hall.* ⏰*Open Jul–Aug 10am–noon, 3–7pm; Sep–Jun daily except Tue 10am–noon, 2–6pm.* ⏰*Closed 1 Jan, 1 May, 11 Nov, 24–25 and 31 Dec.* 🎫*4€.* ℘*04 68 21 06 96. www.collections desaintcyprien.com.* This museum contains works of local painter **François Desnoyer** (1894–1972), as well as his collection of works by Gleizes, Picasso, Pierre Ambroggiani etc.

St-Cyprien-Plage

The seaside resort has a residential district, harbour and 3km/1.8mi of sandy beaches. Its lively marina is the second-largest in Mediterranean France.
The life of the resort is mostly concentrated around the marina, the second most important on the Mediterranean, and at Capellans where 5–10 storey high buildings and marinas were constructed in the 1960s. The sandy beaches (3km/1.5mi) offer all the pleasures of swimming and water sports.

🧒**Jardin des plantes des Capellans** – *Follow the signs for "ZA du Port", and then for "Jardin des Plantes". ℘04 68 37 32 00.* ⏰*Open daily (except Mon in winter) 2am–7pm (5pm in winter).* A pleasant place to visit and linger, this garden is a chance to get to know some of the treasures of the Mediterranean region's flora.

ADDRESSES

🛏 STAY

🍴🛏🛏 **Hôtel La Lagune** – *28 av. Armand-Lanoux 66750 St-Cyprien, 9km/6mi S of Canet on D 81A. ℘04 68 21 24 24. www. hotel-lalagune.com.* 🅿. *Closed 11 Nov–2 Apr. 49 rms. 94/164€.* 🍽*13€. Restaurant 29/34€. Free wifi.* Two swimming pools and a beach make this hotel, between land and sea, a pleasure. Rooms are functional.

🍴🛏🛏 **Chambre d'hôte La Vieille Demeure** – *4 r. de Llobet, 66440 Torreilles. ℘04 68 28 45 71. www.la-vieille-demeure. com.* 🍴. *5 rms. 75/120€.* 🍽*7€. Free wifi.* This house located in the heart of the village has lots of character: Andalusian-style patio, orchard of citrus fruits, and elegant rooms.

🍴 EAT

🍴🛏 **Le Don Quichotte** – *22 av. de Catalogne. ℘04 68 80 35 17. Closed mid-Jan–mid-Feb, Mon and Tue (except hols). 18/48€.* The vibrant dining room serves up classical cuisine.

ACTIVITIES

FLYING

Aéro Service Littoral - base ULM – *Rte de Ste-Marie, 66440 Torreilles. ℘04 68 28 13 73. www.ulm66.fr. 8am–12.30pm, 2–7pm.* This company runs courses in piloting microlights (hangliders, powered paragliders, light aircraft) and helicopters. It also offers taster flights for first timers and tourist trips.

WATER SPORTS

🧒 **Club nautique Canet-Perpignan** – *Zone technique, Le Port, Canet-Plage. ℘04 68 73 33 95. www.asso.ffv.fr/cn-canet. Summer, 9am–7pm; rest of the year Sat and Sun 9am–5pm.* Sailing school authorised by the French Federation of Sailing.

WATER PARK

🧒 **Aqualand** – *Av. des Champs-de-Neptune, St-Cyprien-Plage. ℘04 68 21 49 49. www.aqualand.fr.* 🅿 *Jul and Aug 10am–7pm; 20 Jun–6 Jul and first week Sept 10am–6pm. 25€ (under 12 18.50€).* Wave pools, bubble baths, curving slides.

Elne★

Set among apricot and peach orchards by the coast, Elne was named after the Empress Helen, Constantine's mother, and Iberians knew it as 'Illiberis'. At the end of the Roman Empire, it was the true capital of the Roussillon area and is a major stopping point on the road to Spain. The superb cathedral cloisters testify to Elne's former splendour.

SIGHTS
Cathédrale Ste-Eulalie-et-Ste-Julie★

Building of the cathedral began in the 11C. The ribbed vaulting of the six chapels in the south aisle, built from the 14C to the mid-15C, reflects the three stages in the evolution of Gothic architecture.

Cloisters★★ – *To enter the cloisters, walk round to the left.* ⏰*Open daily May–Sep 10am–7pm; Apr and Oct daily except Mon 10am–6pm; Nov–Mar daily except Mon 10am–noon, 2–6pm.* ⏰*Closed 1st week Jan, 1 May, 25 Dec.* ✆*4.50€ (children, 2€).* ✆*04 68 22 70 90.*

The south cloisters were built in the 12C; the other three date from the 13C and 14C. The superb **capitals** on the twin columns are decorated with imaginary animals, biblical and evangelical figures, and plants, but the most remarkable work is Capital 12, depicting Adam and Eve, in the Romanesque south gallery.

Cloisters of Cathédrale Ste-Eulalie-et-Ste-Julie

© Peter Holmes / age fotostock

> **Population:** 7,325.

🕒 **Michelin Map:** Region map B3. 344: I7.

ℹ **Info:** Office du tourisme d'Elne, Pl. Sant-Jordi. ✆04 68 22 05 07. www.ot-elne.fr

📍 **Location:** 14km/8.75mi S of Perpignan on the N114.

🕐 **Timing:** Allow 2h for the cathedral and museums.

Don't Miss: Adam and Eve column in the Cathédrale Ste-Eulalie-et-Ste-Julie.

Kids: Cathedral; Tropique du Papillon.

Musée d'Archéologie – *Entrance up the staircase at the end of the east cloisters.* The archaeological museum in the old chapel of St-Laurent exhibits 15C to 17C earthenware, Attic ceramics (4C BC) and sigillated ceramic ware from Illiberis (Elne under Roman rule) and reconstructions of Véraza culture huts of wood and reeds.

Musée d'Histoire – *Entrance via the west cloisters.* The history museum contains archives, literature and town seals, along with statues of the Virgin Mary, the Vierge des Tres Portalets (13C) and the Vierge du Portail de Perpignan (14C).

Musée Terrus

♿⏰*Open May–Sep 10am–7pm; Oct–Apr (except Mon) 10am–noon, 2–6pm.* ⏰*Closed 1 Jan, 1 May, 25 Dec.* ✆2.50€. ✆*04 68 22 88 88.*

This museum named after Étienne Terrus (1857–1922) displays works by him and other artists he knew, such as Luce, Maillol and G de Monfreid.

Le Tropique du Papillon

Entrance via avenue Paul-Reig, at the intersection with the Argelès-Perpignan road (N 114). ♿⏰*Open Apr–Sep. Ask for opening hours.* ⏰*Closed the rest of the year.* ✆7€. ✆*04 68 37 83 77. www.tropique-du-papillon.com.*

Night and day, butterflies and moths flutter freely around this tropical hothouse; there is a nursery and an educational area.

Argelès-Plage

Argelès-Plage, with its beautiful sandy beaches, is the camping capital of Europe, with tens of thousands of holidaymakers descending on 60 parks contained within a 5km/3mi radius. Argelès-Plage is the 'Kid Station' resort par excellence with 5km/3mi of supervised golden sand beaches (June to September) and a 2km/1.2mi-long seafront promenade with umbrella pine trees and aloe, mimosa, olive and oleander.

SIGHTS

The name Argelès comes from the Latin argilla meaning "clay". The town may be built on clay soils but is best known for its beaches which, although popular with tourists today, harbour a dark souvenir from the Retirada, the tragic end of the Spanish Civil War. In 1939, after the fall of Barcelone to Franco's forces, an estimated 100,000 republican refugees, soldiers and civilans, were interned here in a makeshift camp.

The Beaches

The Plage Nord, Plage des Pins and Plage Sud (where a lifeguard is on duty from June to September): 7km/4.5mi of white sand. Le Racou (south of the port): 3km/2mi of coves. A 2km/1mile long promenade beside the sea, planted with maritime pines, mimosas, olives, aloes, and oleanders…

Argelès-sur-Mer

2.5km/1.5mi W along D 618.
In the heart of the old town, the **Casa de les Albères** (*4 Pl des Castellans;* ◷*open Jun–Sep Tue–Fri 10am–6pm, Sat and Sun 10am–1pm, 2–6pm, Oct–May Tue–Sat 10am–noon, 2–5pm;* ◓*3€;* ✆*04 68 81 42 74*) is a Catalan museum of folk art and traditions such as wine making, manufacturing barrels, espadrilles (rope-soled sandals) and wooden toys.

👪 Parc de Valmy

♿◷*Open mid-Jun–mid-Sep 10am–7pm; 1–15 Jun and 15–30 Sep 1–7pm; May 2–7pm.* ◓*2€.* ✆*04 68 81 25 70.*

◔ **Region Map:** B3.
🛈 **Info:** Pl. de l'Europe, 66700. ✆04 68 81 15 85. www.argeles-sur-mer.com.
▶ **Location:** 28km/17.5mi S of Perpignan. A bus service operates from Jun–Sep from Argelès-sur-Mer (the town) to the beach.
👁 **Don't Miss:** The large sandy beaches; the secluded coves, walks along the sea shore.
🕐 **Timing:** In summer, allow for traffic jams: sunbathe in the morning and leave the beach when the crowds arrive.
👪 **Kids:** Argelès-Plage has been awarded the Famille Plus mark, which denotes a resort with facilities and activities for children. The eagle displays in the grounds of the Parc de Valmy make for a good excursion.

www.chateau-valmy.com. In the grounds of the Château de Valmy are a discovery trail and falconry featuring **eagles**, kites, vultures and other birds of prey.

ADDRESSES

🍽 EAT

◒◔ **L'Amadeus** – *Av. des Platanes.* ✆*04 68 81 12 38. www.lamadeus.com. Closed Tue, Wed and Thu in Feb–Mar and Mon except Jul–Aug.* This restaurant has a light and airy dining room, a terrace and patio. Well-cooked regional cuisine.

ACTIVITIES

Antares Sub – *Quai Marco-Polo .* ✆*04 68 81 46 30 / 06 14 98 31 37. www.antares-sub.com. Jul–Aug daily 8am–noon, 2pm–8pm; Sep–Jun daily 8am–noon, 2pm–6pm.* The oldest scuba diving school in Argelès offers courses from levels 1–4.

Collioure★★

This colourful little fortress town on the Côte Vermeille attracts huge crowds of tourists. Its lovely setting amidst the Albères foothills has been immortalised on canvas by painters like Derain, Braque, Othon, Friesz, Matisse, Picasso and Foujita. Its many attractions include a fortified church, royal castle, seaside promenade, brightly coloured Catalan boats, old streets with flower-bedecked balconies, outdoor cafés and inviting boutiques.

A BIT OF HISTORY

When Catalan naval forces ruled the Mediterranean as far as the Levant, medieval Collioure was the trading port for Roussillon. In 1463 Louis XI's invading troops marked the beginning of a turbulent period in which the castle was built on the rocky spur separating the port into two coves. After the Peace Treaty of the Pyrénées, the enclosed town was razed to the ground in 1670 and the lower town became the main town.

☞WALKING TOUR

Walk to the old port or 'Port d'Amont' via quai de l'Amirauté on the banks of the 'Ravin du Douy.'

Chemin du Fauvisme

A marked route through the streets of Collioure passes 20 stages celebrating city views painted by Henri Matisse and André Derain. (☞*Guided tours available In Jul–Aug; contact the tourist office for details, or l'Espace Fauve ℘04 68 98 07 16*).

Église Notre-Dame-des-Anges

Built between 1684 and 1691 this church's distinctive bell-tower was once the lighthouse for the old port. Inside are nine ornately carved and gilded **altarpieces★** including the 1698 high altar work of Catalan artist Joseph Sunyer. An immense three-sto-

▸ **Population:** 2,937.
ё **Michelin Map:** Region map B3. 344: J7.
▤ **Info:** Collioure Tourism Office, Pl du 18 Juin. ℘04 68 82 15 47. www.collioure.com.
▶ **Location:** 31km/19.3mi S of Perpignan via the N114, then D114.
◷ **Timing:** Allow 1h to explore the town, longer if possible to get the most out of it.
✿ **Don't Miss:** Boramar beach; anchovy tastings; the Old Port; Museum of Modern Art.
▲▪ **Kids:** A diving orientation with Centre International de Plongee (CIP).

rey triptych completely hides the apse. The sacristy houses a beautiful Louis XIII vestment cupboard, 15C paintings, a 16C reliquary and 17C Madonna.

Ancien îlot St-Vincent

The former island is connected to the church by two beaches. Behind the little chapel, a panorama takes in the Côte Vermeille and a sea wall leads to the lighthouse.

Old district of Mouré

Enjoy pleasant strolls through the steep flower-filled back streets of this old district near the church.

▶ Cross the Douy, at the end of the marina.

Château Royal

◷*Open Jun–Sep 10am–6pm; Oct–May 9am–5pm.* ◷*Closed 1 Jan, 1 May, 15–16 Aug, 25 & 31 Dec.* ⬡*4€ (children under 15 free).* ℘*04 68 82 06 43. www.cg66.fr.*
This imposing castle built on a Roman site juts into the sea between the Port d'Amont and the Port d'Avall. It was the

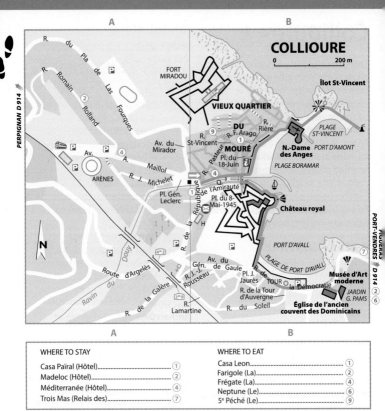

WHERE TO STAY	
Casa Païral (Hôtel)	①
Madeloc (Hôtel)	②
Méditerranée (Hôtel)	④
Trois Mas (Relais des)	⑦

WHERE TO EAT	
Casa Leon	①
Farigole (La)	②
Frégate (La)	④
Neptune (Le)	⑥
5ᵉ Péché (Le)	⑨

summer residence of Majorcan kings from 1276 to 1344 until it was taken over by the kings of Aragón. Tour the underground passages and main courtyard, parade ground, 16C prison, 13C chapel, Queen's bedchamber and upper rooms and ramparts. The 17C barracks house exhibitions on grape vines, cork, Sorède whips, *espadrilles* (rope-soled sandals) and Catalan boats.

▶ Continue to the Port d'Avall beach called the 'Faubourg'

Église de l'ancien couvent des Dominicains

This old church now houses the local wine co-operative.

Musée d'Art moderne

🕐Open Jul–Aug 10am–noon, 2–6pm; Sept–Jun daily except Tue 10am–noon, 2–6pm. 🕐Closed 1 Jan, 1 May, 1 Nov and 25 Dec. ♿2€. 📞04 68 82 10 19.

The artistic success of Collioure is well deserved, and it is down to one man, Jean Peské (1870–1949), who was the inspiration and driving force. Collections are housed in the villa Pams at the foot of a terraced garden abundant in olive trees. The collection, enriched by regular donations, is regular put on display in exhibitions.

ADDRESSES

🏨 STAY

◯◯◯ **Hôtel Méditerranée –** *Av. Aristide-Maillol.* 📞*04 68 82 08 60.* *www.mediterranee-hotel.com. 23 rms.* *65/105€.* ⬚*10€. Free wifi.* Retro building; rooms with balconies. Garden; solarium.

◯◯◯ **Hôtel Madeloc –** *R. Romain-Rolland.* 📞*04 68 82 07 56. www.madeloc.* *com.* 🅿. *22 rms. 65/114€.* ⬚*11€.* Rooms furnished in rattan; some with terraces. Garden.

Casa Païral – *Imp. des Palmiers.*
℘04 68 82 05 81. www.hotel-casa-pairal.com.
P. Closed 11 Nov–Easter. 27 rms. 89/269€.
14€. Free wifi. This noble old house rests
within a beautiful Mediterranean garden.
The rooms have lots of personality.

Relais des Trois Mas –
Rte Port-Vendres. ℘04 68 82 05 07. www.
relaisdestroismas.com. P. Closed Dec–Jan.
23 rms. 100/340€ low season; 165/465€
high season. 18€. Lovely rooms; garden,
pool, jacuzzi.

♈EAT

La Frégate – *24 quai Camille-*
Pelletan. ℘04 68 82 06 05. www.fregate-
collioure.com. Closed Jan. Rooms: €50/150.
This hotel-restaurant in front of the
château has been given a makeover. The
dining room has been decorated with ceramics,
providing a setting for simple and tasty
regional cuisine. Small, well maintained
rooms.

Le 5e Péché – *18 r. de la Fraternité.*
℘04 68 98 09 76. Closed Mon–Tue (except
Jul–Aug), Jan, 23 Nov–26 Dec. 18/24€. The
'fifth sin' here is that of gourmet eating!
Here we willingly give into astonishing
Japanese-Catalan fusion cuisine.
Absolution isnt guaranteed, but it doesnt
matter. Gourmet sins are rarely repented.

La Farigole – *Rte de Port-Vendres.*
℘04 68 98 09 59. P. www.arapede.com.
Closed Jan and Dec. 27/36€. Rooms 65/110€
. 11€. A modern hotel-restaurant built
on the side of a hill. The dining room is
decorated with old photos of Collioure
and has a terrace looking onto the sea.
Regional dishes are served. Harmonious
Catalan style furniture in the large
bedrooms, which look on to the sea and
the infinity swimming pool.

Casa Leon – *2 r. Rière Collioure.*
℘04 658 82 10 74. 26.50/33€. Very popular
among Colliourencs, this little restaurant
offers excellent fish and seafood. You are
sure to enjoy the grilled tuna and other
fish or the fried prawns. Everything is
very fresh.

Le Neptune – *Rte de Port-Vendres.*
℘04 68 82 02 27. www.leneptune-collioure.
com. Closed Mon Jul–Sep and Wed Oct–Jun.
38/79€. Seafood dishes and regional
specialities. The décor uses the colours of
the south of France and is enlivened with
paintings. There is an unobstructed view
of the Old Port from the terraces.

ON THE TOWN
HOTEL BARS
Bar des Templiers – *12 quai de l'Amirauté.*
℘04 68 98 31 10. www.hotel-templiers.com.
Closed 8–20 Nov. The Hotel des Templiers
is the most prestigious establishment
in Collioure: some great artists (Derain,
Picasso, Matisse) have passed through
its doors. The canvases that cover its
walls are testament to this period. An
authentic place full of poetry where
regulars and visitors mix.

SHOPPING
WINE
Le Dominicain Cave – *Rte de*
Port-Vendres. ℘04 68 82 05 63. www.
dominicain.com. Open 8am–noon, 2–6pm.
P. Closed Sun Sep–Apr. Occupying a 13C
Dominican convent, this co-operative
sells wines from Banyuls and Collioure.
Warm welcome. Wine tastings.

ANCHOVIES
Anchois Desclaux – *3–5 rte dép. 914.*
℘04 68 82 05 25. www.anchoixdesclaux.
com. P. Open 9am–noon, 2–7pm,
Sun and hols 9.30am–12.30pm, 2–7pm.
For over a century the skills of anchovy
processing have been handed down
from generation to generation in this
family-run business. Guided tour of the
curing and conserving workshop. Free
tastings. The factory shop sells Catalan
products.

Anchois Roque Collioure – *17 rte*
d'Argelès. ℘04 68 82 22 30. Open Mon–
Sat 8am–6.30pm, Sun and hols 9.30am–
noon, 2–6.30pm. Tours with tasting
(weekdays only) 9am–noon, 2–5pm.
Since 1870 Roque has been keeping
alive the traditional method of preparing
anchovies. There is a shop on the ground
floor and a workshop on the first floor
where you can watch as expert hands
process the little fish.

ACTIVITIES
CIP – *15 r. de la Tour d'Auvergne, 66190*
Collioure. www.cip-collioure.com. Excursions
from 27€; courses from 400€. Children must
be over 8 years old to partake. This diving
centre in the heart of the village offers
diving and snorkelling excursions and
courses of different levels.

EVENTS
Feria – *Around 15 August.* Bullfighting
(novillada) in the bullring.

Banyuls-sur-Mer

Set on a promontory, Banyuls is France's most southerly seaside resort, known for its lovely bay, yacht harbour, vineyards and seawater therapy centre. Sheltered from the *tramontane*'s harsh northwesterly gusts, tropical flora like carob, eucalyptus and palms thrive along this Mediterranean coast all the way to the Riviera.

- **Region Map:** B3
- **Info:** Av. de la République, 66650 Banyuls-sur-Mer. ℘04 68 88 31 58. www.banyuls-sur-mer.com.
- **Location:** 38km/23.75mi S of Perpignan on the N114.
- **Don't Miss:** The view from Cap Réderis.

THE RESORT
The Beach
The main beach is sheltered by a cove and two islands, Île Petite and Île Grosse. The Côte Vermeille's coastal waters are deep, clear and teeming with fish.

👥 Aquarium du Lab. Arago
⊙*Open daily Jul–Aug; ask for opening times.* ⊙*Closed Jan.* ✆*4.80€ (children under 6 free).* ℘*04 68 88 73 39. www.biodiversarium.fr.*
This **Aquarium** displays Mediterranean fauna in a recreated environment.

Écrin bleu: Underwater Trail
Part of the Banyuls-Cerbère Marine Nature Reserve. ⊙*Open Jul–Aug noon–6pm. Equipment rental from noon to 5pm. Meeting point on the Peyrefite beach and information area on the yachting harbour.* ✆*No charge.* ℘*04 68 88 56 87.*

Observe red mullets, bass, rainbow wrasse, and on a lucky day, dolphins, loggerhead turtles and spotted sea horses. This 250m/820ft supervised underwater trail has five observation stations (at depths up to 5m/16ft) marked by buoys. Underwater information plaques guide you along.

Réserve naturelle marine de Banyuls-Cerbère
Created in 1974 to protect marine species endangered by intensive fishing, tourism activities and waste water pollution this conservation area covers 650ha/1,606 acres and 6.5km/4mi of rocky Languedoc-Roussillon coastline.

EXCURSION
Métairie Maillol★
▶*5km/3mi SW.* ⊙*Open May–Sep 10am–noon, 4–7pm; Oct–Apr 10am–noon, 2–5pm.* ⊙*Closed Mon and public holidays.* ✆*5€.* ℘*04 68 88 57 11.*

Cellier des Templiers–cave du Mas Reig

© Nicolas Thibaut / Photononstop

Aristide Maillol (1861–1944) was born in Banyuls. At 20 he 'went up' to Paris to learn painting and became interested pottery and tapestry. After the age of 40 he gained renown for his sculptures of nude figures, remarkable for their grace and power. Maillol enjoyed his little country retreat, which now as the Musée Maillol, displays many of his sculptures, terracotta, paintings and drawings.

Banyuls wine

The famous **Banyuls wine** complements the best of tables, served as an apéritif, with dessert, or foie gras and strongly flavoured cheeses and game. Several cellars (**caves**) welcome the public, including two on the vertiginous Route des Crêtes. At the **Grande Cave** (🕐 ☕ *open Apr–Oct guided tours (1hr) 10am–7.30pm; Nov–Mar daily except Sun 10am–1pm, 2.30–6.30pm;* 🕐 *closed 1 Jan and 25 Dec;* ☎ *no charge;* 📞 *04 68 98 36 92; www.banyuls.com*) see a video on the history of Banyuls and enjoy a guided tour of the oak barrel storage rooms, wines maturing in the sun and cellars containing antique casks.

The **Cellier des Templiers-cave du Mas Reig** (♿ 🕐 ☕ *Jul–Aug guided tours 10am–7.30pm;* ☎ *no charge;* 📞 *04 68 98 36 70)* dates from the days of the (13C) Knights Templar, whose feudal castle and sub-commandery (Mas Reig) are next door.

ADDRESSES

🏠 STAY

🛏 **Hôtel Les Elmes** – *Plage des Elmes.* 📞 *04 68 88 03 12. www.hotel.des.elmes.com. 31 rms. 48/159€.* ⫿ *10€. Restaurant 28/48€. Free wifi.* Welcoming hotel situated on the beach. Rooms have been renovated in a maritime style (2nd floor). Fish and seafood are the pride of the menu in the restaurant (**Littorine**) which has a terrace beside the sea.

🍴 EAT

🍽🍽🍽 **Al Fanal** – *18 av. du Fontaulé.* 📞 *04 68 88 00 31. 19/58€. 13 rms: 52/60€.* 🅿. Flavourful fish cuisine and a good

selection of regional wines to enjoy in a dining room looking onto the sea. Hotel (**El Llagut**) without pretensions.

DRINK

TEAROOM

La Paillote – *14 r. St-Pierre.* 📞 *04 68 88 30 30. www.lapaillote.com. Jul & Aug and school holidays: noon-1.30, 8pm–2am- except Sun. Rest of the year open at lunchtime except Wed and Sun and Thu–Sat evening.* Small tearooms on one of the little streets of old Banyuls. Good list of fresh fruit juice cocktails and ice creams. You can also choose the ambiance via a "menu" of world music. Internet cafe.

SHOPPING

MARKETS

Bric à Brac Fair – *Allées Maillol.* 📞 *04 68 88 78 10. Jul–Aug Fri 7am-1pm.*
Crafts Market – *Av. de la République.* 📞 *04 68 88 00 62. www.banyuls-sur-mer. com. Jul–Aug daily on the seafront 6pm– midnight.* This noctural market of local crafts in all their varieties brings life to Banyuls during the summer months.

VIN DE BANYULS

Cave L'Étoile – *26 av. du Puig-del-Mas.* 📞 *04 68 88 00 10. Mid-Jun–mid-Sept 8am–12.30pm, 2–7pm, Sat & Sun 10am–12.30pm, 3–6.30pm; rest of the year 8am–noon, 2–6pm, Sat, Sun and hols 9.30–noon, 3–6.30pm.* The oldest wine co-operative in town (founded 1921), specialises in aged wines. A dozen vintages that have earned the confidence of some great restaurants. L'Étoile also makes Collioures AOC, reds and rosés.

Cave St-Jacques – *25 av. du Puig-del-Mas.* 📞 *04 68 88 00 10. www.cave-saintjacques. com. Jul–Aug 9am–8pm; rest of the year 9am–12.30pm, 2–7pm, Sun 9am-12.30pm. Closed 1 Jan, 25 Dec.* Large choice of regional wines – AOC Collioure, Côtes-du-Roussillon, Banyuls – chosen by tastings at small wineries.

ACTIVITIES

THALASSOTHERAPY

Thalacap Catalogne – *Av. de la Côte-Vermeille.* 📞 *04 68 98 36 66. www. thalacap.com. Closed Jan (except Jan 1).* Sea water spa in the upper part of Banyuls, looking out on the Mediterranean. Accommodation and restaurant.

Côte Vermeille★★

The resorts along this rocky stretch of coast, tucked into little bays, were once small maritime fortresses. The 'vermilion' coast is named after the local landscape, whose colour is enhanced by the clear light of this region. Explore the Côte Vermeille via the Route des crêtes (N 114) mountain road, and Route du littoral, the coast road, via Collioure and Port-Vendres (heavy summer traffic).

🚗 DRIVING TOURS

LA ROUTE DES CRÊTES

See Côte Vermeille map. 37km/23mi from Argelès-Plage to Cerbère. About 2hr 30min.

Beyond Argelès and the stretch of beach to the north, the coast becomes much more dramatic as the (D 114) climbs into the Albères foothills and cuts across rocky headlands lapped by the Mediterranean.

▶ At the roundabout just before Collioure, take D 86 left. The road

- **Michelin Map:** Region map B3. 344: J7– K8.
- **Info:** Office du Tourisme de Collioure, Pl du 18 Juin. ℘04 68 82 15 47. www.collioure.com.
- **Location:** 30km/18.75mi SW of Perpignan by D 914. Argelès Plage is the gateway to the Vermeille Coast.
- **Don't Miss:** The picturesque port of Collioure and the Spanish ambience of Cerbère.
- **Kids:** Swimming off the beaches along the coast!

heads uphill, through the Collioure vineyards.Turn left again at the first intersection, onto a downhill road.

Notre-Dame-de-Consolation

This hermitage is well known throughout Roussillon. Its chapel contains votive offerings from sailors.

▶ Turn back to D 86 and turn left (Note: this stretch of mountain road has no safety barriers or other protection).

Cap Réderis

© Franck Guiziou / Hemis / Photoshot

Cork-oaks appear between patches of exposed black rock schist.

▷ Follow the signs for the 'Circuit du vignoble' wine route through the vineyards towards Banyuls.

This spectacular road leads to a viewing table and ruins of an 1885 barracks.

▷ Take the steep, narrow track to the right leading up to Tour Madeloc (⚠Note: extreme caution required: gradient of 1:4, with tight hairpin bends and no space for passing).

The road passes two more fortified constructions before reaching a small level plateau.

Tour Madeloc

Alt 652m/2 138ft. 15min on foot return.
This old round signal tower was part of a network of lookout posts during the reign of the kings of Aragón and Mallorca. Tour de la Massane surveyed the Roussillon plain and Tour Madeloc kept watch out to sea. Enjoy a splendid **panorama★★** of the Albères mountains, the Vermeille and Roussillon coasts. The track back down to D 86 gives breathtaking **views★** of the sea and Banyuls.

▷ Turn right onto D 86.

The road leads to Banyuls, passing the Mas Reig underground wine cellar situated in the oldest vineyard in the Banyuls area, as well as the modern cellar in which wines from the Cave des Templiers are aged.

Banyuls-sur-Mer
See p154.

Cap Réderis★★
Where the road edges the cliff, you'll have a magnificent **panorama** of the Languedoc and Catalonia coasts as far south as the Cabo de Creus. Farther along you'll see the bay of Banyuls, spectacular at high tide.

Cerbère
This charming seaside resort is the last French town before Spain and the Costa Brava. Set in a little cove with a pebble beach, it has white houses, outdoor cafés and narrow pedestrian streets.

THE COAST ROAD
33km/21mi from Cerbère to Argelès-Plage. About 2hr.

Beyond Cerbère, the road winds through vineyards overlooking a vast seascape.

Cap Réderis★★
See p157.

Catalan boats, Collioure

© J. Puig / age fotostock

Site de Paulilles★

Opened in 2008 this is a free ecological recreational park which was once the site of a dynamite factory. The coast itself is protected, as it cultivates a rare breed of seagrass. Visitors enjoy diving, bike riding and hiking here.

Banyuls-sur-Mer

See BANYULS-SUR-MER.
Leaving Banyuls, the road passes a seaside spa for heliotherapy. Before Port-Vendres is an excellent view of the port.

▶ Turn right towards Cap Béar then, after the Hôtel des Tamarins, cross the railway line and drive to the S of the bay.

Cap Béar

From the lighthouse on the headland, you can see down the coast from Cap Leucate to Cabo de Creus.

Port-Vendres (Port of Venus)

This town developed as a naval port and became a major port for trade.

Collioure★★

See p151.

▶ The road leaves the foothills of the Albères before reaching Argelès.

ADDRESSES

🍴 STAY

🛏🛏🛏 **Chambre d'hôte Domaine de Valcros** – *Paulilles 66660 Port-Vendres.* ℘*04 68 82 04 27. www.domainedevalcros.com.* 🅿 🛁. *3 rms. 75/89€* 🍽. *1 apartment (450/980€/week). Free wifi.* Situated between the sea and the mountain at the heart of the Banyuls vineyards is this old Catalan farmhouse. Recently renovated, it offers spacious and elegant air-conditionded rooms. There is a private path to the beach (300 m/350 yds). A beautiful terrace overlooks the bay.

🍴 EAT

🛏🛏🛏 **La Côte Vermeille** – *Quai Fanal, Port-Vendres (towards the fish market).* ℘*04 68 82 05 71. Closed 5 Jan–2 Feb, first week Jul, Sun & Mon (except Jul and Aug). 29€/58€.* This restaurant is anchored in the port: the chef only has to take a couple of steps from the door and shout out to find the best of the day's fishing catch. Mediterranean flavours.

🛏🛏🛏 **Ferme-auberge Les Clos de Paulilles** – *Baie de Paulilles Port-Vendres.* ℘*04 68 98 07 58. www.clos-de-paulilles.com. Closed at lunchtime except Sun (Jun–Sep).* 🅿. *39€.* At the heart of a wine estate, this restaurant serves country cuisine, each dish washed down with a different wine from the property. Shady terrace where a refereshing breeze blows from the sea.

Le Boulou

This spa resort at the foot of the Albères mountains makes an ideal base for exploring the Roussillon. On the fringe of an exotic cork-oak wood, Le Boulou has two cork-making factories.

VISIT

The town's medieval past is reflected in remnants of its 14C curtain wall and early 15C chapel of St-Antoine.

Église Notre-Dame d'El Voló

Of the original 12C Romanesque church, the white-marble **portal** by the Master of Cabestany has survived.

🚗 DRIVING TOURS

MONTS ALBÈRES

49km/30mi round tour. Half a day.

The Albères mountain range is the last outcrop of crystalline rocks on the eastern flank of the Pyrénées. Its highest peak, Pic Neulos, towers 1,256m/4,120ft above sea level.

▶ Leave Le Boulou W on D 115.

Céret★ See p164.

▶ Leave Céret heading SW on D 13F towards Fontfrède.

This road climbs through chestnut groves, offering many pretty views. Turn right off the Las Illas road at the Col de la Brousse into a very winding road to the **Col de Fontfrède** (June 1940–June 1944).

▶ Return to the Col de la Brousse and turn right towards Las Illas.

The road winds through dense vegetation, terraced gardens and scattered farmhouses. The Case Nove mas (farmhouse) and the Mas Liansou are traditional Albères dwellings. After Las Illas,

▶ **Population:** 5,066.
▶ **Michelin Map:** Region map A3. 344: I7.
▶ **Info:** 1 r. du Château, 66160 Le Boulou. ☎04 68 87 50 95. www.ot-leboulou.fr. Guided tours *(1hr 30min)* leave at 3pm on Thu from the tourist office.
▶ **Location:** 27km/17mi S of Perpignan by D 900.
▶ **Timing:** Allow 30min for a tour of Le Boulou.
▶ **Don't Miss:** Céret Museum of Modern Art, the panorama from Fort de Bellegarde and Pic des Trois Termes.
▶ **Kids:** Musée du Liège at Maureillas-las-Illas; the Fort de Bellegarde; the vallée des Tortues; the Abbaye de St-André.

the road follows the river, clinging to the rock face and affording excellent views of the river gorge.

Maureillas-las-Illas

In this holiday village amidst cork-oak groves and orchards, cork-cutters have created a cork museum, **Musée du Liège** (*open Jul–Aug 10.30am–noon, 3.30–7pm; Sept–Jun daily except Tue 2–5pm; closed Jan, public hols; 3€; ☎04 68 83 15 41*). Learn about cork and see astonishing cork sculptures and magnificent oak casks showcasing local handicrafts.

Chapelle St-Martin-de-Fenollar

Guided tours Jul–Aug 10.30am–noon, 3.30–7pm; rest of the year daily except Tue 2–5pm. Closed Jan and public hols. 3€. ☎04 68 87 73 82.
This modest 9C chapel founded by Benedictines from Arles-sur-Tech contains interesting 12C **mural paintings★**.

▶ D 900 leads back to Le Boulou.

LA VALLÉE DE LA ROME

53km/33mi from Le Boulou to Pic des Trois Termes – allow half a day.
From Boulou guided tours of the Rome valley are organised by the Association pour le patrimoine de la vallée de la Rome (Information and reservations: Mairie du Boulou ℘04 68 87 51 58 and Le Boulou tourist office. ℘04 68 87 50 95).

The **Vallée de la Rome** is an essential communication route between France and Spain, traversed for two millennia since the Via Domitia's construction in c.120 BC. Leave the 'Catalane' motorway to discover awesome megalithic, Gallo-Roman and medieval sites in a superb landscape.

▶ Leave Le Boulou on D 900, S towards Le Perthus, until you reach Chapelle St-Martin-de-Fenollar (&see left). Go back to D 900.

Les Cluses

These hamlets on either side of the gorge between the Via Domitia and the Rome valley contain 3C–4C Roman remains: the **Château des Maures** or 'Castell d els Moros' and **Fort de la Cluse Haute**. Next to the fort, the **church of St-Nazaire** is a pre-Romanesque construction with three naves and traces of frescoes attributed to the Master of Fenollar.

Le Perthus

Since prehistory, Le Perthus has seen the comings and goings of nomadic hordes, armies, refugees and tourists. The hamlet became a town in the late 19C.

▶ From the centre of Le Perthus, turn left towards the Fort de Bellegarde.

Fort de Bellegarde

Open May–Sep 10.30am–6.30pm; rest of the year ask for opening times. 3.50€. ℘04 68 83 60 15.
This fortress overlooking Le Perthus was rebuilt by Saint Hilaire, and then by Vauban between 1679 and 1688. The terrace offers a **panorama★★** of the Canigou and Fontfrède peaks, the Rome valley, Le Perthus, the Panissars site and in Spain, the Rio Llobregat valley.

Panissars

During the Roman occupation, the Panissars Pass was the main Pyrénées route. In 1984, foundations of a huge Roman monument were discovered and thought to be the remains of the Trophy of Pompey.

▶ Turn back and, N of Le Perthus, turn right onto D 71 to the Col de l'Ouillat.

This road passes by groves of chestnut trees and the magnificent oaks of St-Martin-de-l'Albères, with views of the Canigou and the southern Albères slopes and St-Christophe summit.
From a right-hand bend catch a view of Trois Termes Peak.

Col de l'Ouillat★

A cool stopping place with a viewing terrace on the edge of the Laroque-des-Albères Forest. The road winds through beeches and pines to the rocky outcrop of Trois Termes.

Pic des Trois Termes★★

Enjoy a **panorama** of the Albères mountains, Roussillon plain and coastal lagoons, the Confluent and Vallespir valleys, and the Spanish Costa Brava.

▶ Turn back.

The unsurfaced road between the Pic des Trois Termes and Sorède is accessible only by four-wheel-drive.

AT THE FOOT OF MONTS ALBÈRES

32km/20mi. Allow 3hrs. ▶ Tour begins from Saint-Génis-des-Fontaines 10km/6mi E of Le Boulou. Drive W of Argelès-Plage along D 2 to Sorède.

Saint-Génis-des-Fontaines

Open Jul–Aug 9.30am–12.30pm, 3–7pm; Apr–Jun and Sep 9.30am–

12.30pm, 2–6pm; rest of year 9.30am–
noon, 2–5pm. ⊙Closed 1 Jan, 1 May,
25 Dec.

The decorations in the parish church
and cloisters, namely the white-marble
sculpted lintel from 1020, show the importance of this former Benedictine abbey.

▷ Continue E along D 618.

Saint-André

*Leave the car in the shaded square to the
right of the village high street. Reach the
church by walking through an archway.*
This 12C church's exterior has pre-
Romanesque fishbone features, a marble lintel and foiled altar table.
Wind up your visit at the **Maison trans-
frontalière d'art roman** (⊙open mid-
Jun–mid-Sep daily except Mon 10–12pm;
2.30–7pm; mid-Mar–mid-Jun and mid-
Sep–mid-Nov daily except Sun and Mon
3–6pm; ⊙closed mid-Nov–mid-Mar;
⊛2€; ℘04 68 89 04 85; www.saint-
andre66.fr/musee.htm).

Sorède

This village is a centre for the breeding
and study of tortoises.
🐢 **Vallée des tortues** – ⊙Open mid-
May–mid-Aug 9am–7pm; mid-Aug–Sep
10am–6pm; rest of the year ask about
opening hours. ⊛10€ (children aged
2–10, 8€). ℘04 68 95 50 50. www.laval-
leedestortues.com. The 2ha/5-acre park
houses some 25 species of land and
international water tortoises.

▷ Return to Sorède and continue
left along D 2 to Laroque-des-Albères,
then follow D 11 to Villelongue-dels-
Monts. In the village, take Cami del
Vilar to the priory 2km/1.2mi away.

Prieuré Santa Maria del Vilar★

⊙Open Apr–Oct 3–6pm (Jul–Aug
6.30pm); Nov–Mar 2.30–5.30pm.
⊛4€. ℘04 68 89 64 61.
The 11C priory is shaded by olive trees,
holm oaks and cypresses.

▷ Return to Villelongue-dels-Monts,
turn left onto D 61A then right onto
D 618 to Génis-des-Fontaines.

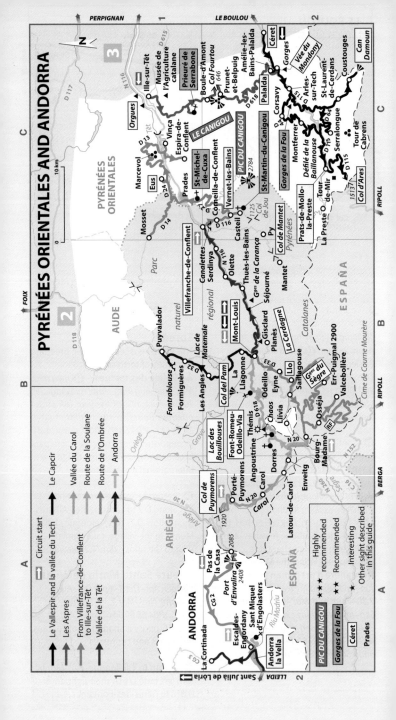

PYRÉNÉES ORIENTALES AND ANDORRA

Circuit start

▲ Circuit start		

↑ Le Vallespir and la vallée du Tech

↑ Les Aspres

↑ From Villefranche-de-Conflent to Ille-sur-Têt

↑ Vallée de la Têt

↑ Le Capcir

↑ Vallée du Carol

↑ Route de la Soulane

↑ Route de l'Ombrée

↑ Andorra

Highly recommended ★★★

Recommended ★★

Interesting ★

PIC DU CANIGOU	★★★
Gorges de la Fou	★★
Céret	★
Prades	★

Highly recommended ★★★

Recommended ★★

Interesting ★

Other sight described in this guide

PERPIGNAN

LE BOULOU

N 116

D 615

D 117

N 117

FOIX

AUDE

D 118

PYRÉNÉES ORIENTALES

ARIÈGE

ANDORRA

La Cortinada
Escaldes-Engordany
Sant Miquel d'Engolasters
Andorra la Vella
Port d'Envalira 2408
Pas de la Casa 2085
CG 2
CG 3

ESPAÑA

Sant Julia de Loria
LLEIDA

Latour-de-Carol
Enveitg
Carol
Porté-Puymorens
Col de Puymorens 1920

Bourg-Madame
Dorres
Angoustrine
Col del Pam
Font-Romeu-Odeillo-Via
Chaos Thémis
Dorres
N 20
RF
N 152
BERGA
C 16
N 260

Lac des Bouillouses

Les Angles
Fontrabiouse
Formiguères
Puyvalador

Lac de Matemale

Mont-Louis
La Llagonne
Col del Pam

La Cerdagne
Giscard
Planès
Odeillo
Eyne
Llo
Saillagouse
Osséja
Valcebollère
Err-Puigmal 2900
G^nes du Segre
Cime de Coume Mourère

RIPOLL

ESPAÑA

Puyvalador
Mosset
D 14
Eus
Marcevol
Orgues
Ille-sur-Têt
Musée de l'Agriculture catalane
Prieuré de Serrabone
Boule-d'Amont
Col Fourtou 646
Prunet-et-Belpuig
D 618

Vinça
Espira-de-Conflent
Prades
St-Michel-de-Cuxa
LE CANIGOU
D 13
D 24

Villefranche-de-Conflent
Canalettes
Serdinya
Olette
Thuès-les-Bains
G^nes de la Carança
Séjourné
Mantet
Col de Mantet

Corneilla-de-Conflent
Vernet-les-Bains
PIC DU CANIGOU 2784
St-Martin-du-Canigou
Gorges de la Fou
Casteil
Py
Prats-de-Mollo-la-Preste
La Preste
Col de Jou 1125
Tour de Mir 1513
Col d'Ares

N 116
D 116
N 118
N 116

Céret
Gorges
Vée du Mondony
Amélie-les-Bains-Palalda
Palalda
Corsavy
Montferrer
Défilé de la Baillanouse
Serralongue
Tour de Cabrens
D 618
D 115
D 44

Arles-sur-Tech
St-Laurent-de-Cerdans
Coustouges

Can Damoun

RIPOLL

Z

0   10 km

Parc naturel régional Pyrénées Catalanes

ESPAÑA

Orgue
Têt
Agly
Grave
Carol
Ariège
Oriège
Riù Madriù

There is a certain mellow softness about the long valley north of Canigou, like the downy skin on the peaches and apricots that grow here in abundance. The whole setting is relaxed, gentle, pleasing. The local economy is founded these days on tourism, and much of this is geared towards exploring the mountains, which provide dazzling walking potential at all standards, as well as plentiful opportunity for those who enjoy messing about in snow. The absence of heavy industry makes this the most attractive of places, set against a stupendous backdrop of high mountains. The old province of Roussillon is an historical and cultural region, comprising what is now the southern French department of Pyrénées-Orientales lying between the eastern extremities of the mountains and the Mediterranean coastal lowlands.

Pablo Casals

Prades was chosen by the world-renowned cellist **Pablo Casals** (1876–1973) as his exiled home, one that while not in his homeland of Spain nevertheless remained in his beloved Catalonia. He is generally regarded as the pre-eminent cellist of the first half of the 20C, and one of the greatest cellists of all time. He made many recordings throughout his career, of solo, chamber, and orchestral music, also as conductor. Not surprisingly, many of the surrounding villages and their fine buildings are embraced in an annual Pablo Casals Festival from mid-July to mid-August, which the maestro founded in 1950. The main venue is the Abbaye Saint Michel-de-Cuxa (&see p171).

Andorra

Set among the eastern Pyrénées, the principality of Andorra is no mere tax-free shopping haven. This tiny Catalan-speaking nation is also a wild, scenic land of lofty plateaux and precipitous valleys.

Highlights

1. Marvel at the Romanesque wonders of the **Prieuré de Serrabone** and the abbey of **St-Michel-de–Cuxa** (p169, 171)

2. The annual **Pablo Casals Music Festival** (p171, 174)

3. Discover the magnificent medieval abbey of **St-Martin-de-Canigou** (p175)

4. Climb **Mount Canigou** for a magnificent view (p176)

5. Spend time in **Andorra** (p190)

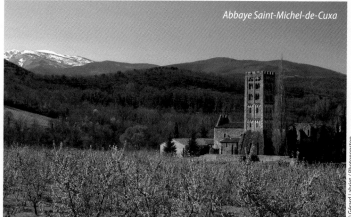

Abbaye Saint-Michel-de-Cuxa

© Gérard Labriet / Photononstop

Céret★

Céret in the Vallespir region is the lively hub of Catalan tradition in the northern Pyrénées, with bullfights and *sardana* dancing. This major fruit-growing area is becoming a popular arts and crafts centre.

SIGHTS
Old Céret

Majestic plane trees shade strollers between place de la République and place de la Liberté. Remnants of the original ramparts include the Porte de France in place de la République and the Porte d'Espagne in place Pablo-Picasso. The wrought iron and stainless steel monument to Picasso – *Sardane de la Paix* (1973) is based on a Picasso drawing, and the town's World War I Memorial is by Aristide Maillol.

Old Bridge★ (Vieux pont)

The 14C 'Devil's Leap' bridge spans the Tech in a single arch. Enjoy lovely views of the Canigou massif and the Albères range.

Musée d'Art Moderne★★

8 bd Mar. Joffre. &. ⊙*Open Jul–mid-Sept 10am–7pm; May–Jun, mid-Sept–end Sept and Jan–Apr 10am–6pm.* ⊙*Closed Tue Jan–Apr; 1 Jan, 1 May, 1 Nov, 25 Dec.* ⊛*8€.* ℘*04 68 87 27 76. www.musee-ceret.com.*

▶ **Population:** 7,500.

⚲ **Michelin Map:** Region map C2. 344: H8
⚲*also see Le Boulou, p159.*

ⓘ **Info:** 1 av G-Clemenceau. ℘04 68 87 00 53. www.ot-ceret.fr. Amélie-les-Bains Tourism Office; 22 av de Vallespir; ℘04 68 39 01 98. www.amelie-les-bains.com.

▶ **Location:** 33km/20.65mi SW of Perpignan.

⊙ **Timing:** Comptez 1h pour la ville (plus le samedi, jour de marché) et autant pour le musée.

⊛ **Don't Miss:** The views from the Old Bridge and the Musée d'Art Moderne; in July, the feria and folk festival. Nearby: the Gorges de la Fou and the view from Can Damoun.

▲▲ **Kids:** Visit the Musée d'Art Moderne and Ceret and the Musée Médiéval in Serralongue.

This modern museum features ceramics by Picasso, works from the Céret period (1909–50) and contemporary works from 1960 to 1970.

Vieux pont, Céret

© Claudio Giovanni Colombo / Bigstockphoto.com

🚗 DRIVING TOUR

LE VALLESPIR AND LA VALLÉE DU TECH★

130km/81mi. Allow 6hrs.
🕭 *See region map.*
▶ *Leave Céret on the D115.*

Leading towards Spain, the Vallespir is criss-crossed by the meandering Tech river. Steep slopes rise from the gentle terrain on the valley floor, while cherry and mimosa trees add to the variety of the palette. Anyone who loves authenticity and tradition will enjoy a visit to the villages here, which are the most southerly communes in France.

Amélie-les-Bains (℘04 68 39 01 98; *www.amelie-les-bains.com*) is a town named after the wife of Louis-Philippe, Queen Marie-Amélie. who made France's **southernmost spa** fashionable in the 19C. The inhabitants are called the Améliens.

Mediterranean flora like mimosas, oleanders and palm trees reflect the mild climate and abundance of sunshine.

From here it is possible to make a cool and pleasant walk around the **Gorges and vallée du Mondony** (🚶*30min round-trip on foot*).

▶ 6km/3.5mi on D 115 to Mas Pagris.

The road to Montalba climbs the rocky spur of Fort-les-Bains and skirts the cliff-tops overlooking the **Vallée du Mondony**★ gorge. It then crosses a series of stepped terraces.

▶ 3km/2mi on the D 618.

The medieval town of **Palalda**★ is a fine Catalan village. The **Palalda Museum** (🕒 *open by prior request 7 days in advance, mid-Feb–mid-Dec Tue–Fri 10am–noon, 2.30–5.30pm (Mon, Sat and public holidays 2.30–5.30pm);* 🕒*closed Sun, mid-Dec–mid-Feb;* ∞*2.50€;* ℘*04 68 39 34 90*) is divided into two sections: **Museum of Folk Arts and Traditions** – antique tools and a reconstruction of an early 20C kitchen, wherein local dishes

like *cargolade* (grilled snails with *aïoli* – garlic mayonnaise) were enjoyed.

Roussillon Postal Museum – This reconstruction of a late 19C post office presents the history of the local postal service and the Roussillon lighthouse system.

Go back to Amélie and follow the D 115 to **Arles-sur-Tech**, a place dealing with traditional Catalan fabrics, originally built around an abbey, c.900.

Stay on the D 115 as you leave Arles for the **Gorges de la Fou**★★; a walk here is something you won't forget!

Continue on the D 115 for 3km/2mi, then turn left on the D 3, and after 10km/6mi reach **St-Laurent-de-Cerdans**, the most populous town of the southern part of Vallespir (small **museum**).

Only 4km/2.5mi further on, **Coustouges** is a small mountain village occupying the site of a Roman guard. **Can Damoun**★ is a panoramic site above the valleys.

Turn round and drive to La Forge-del-Mitg, and left onto the D 64, then head for **Serralongue**, where there is a Romanesque **church** and medieval **museum**.

Turn round again and take the D 64, and then the D 115 towards Le Tech. The **Défilé de la Baillanouse** is renowned for a huge landslide in 1940 that completely blocked the road to a depth of 40m/131ft. In the climb to the **Col d'Ares**, on the frontier with Spain, you pass **Prats-de-Mollo**★ (🕭*see p167*) the **Tour de Mir**, one of the highest signal towers in Roussillon.

Go back to Le Tech, and turn left onto the D 44, passing through **Montferrer** (chateau ruins).

ADDRESSES

🛏 STAY

🍴🍴 **Hôtel Les Glycines** – *R. du Jeu-de-Paume 66150 Arles-sur-Tech.* ℘*04 68 39 10 09. Closed mid-Nov–mid-Feb.* 🅿. *49/52€.* ☕*7.50€. Set menu lunch 13€. 16/27€.* The ochre facade of this building close to the town centre conceals an agreeable hotel-restaurant. The rooms are functional. The dining room is contemporary in style and has a terrace shaded by an ancient wisteria; a good place to sit and enjoy a traditional dish or a Catalan speciality.

🍴🛏🛏 **Le Rousillon** – *Av. Beau-Soleil, Amélie-les-Bains-Palalda.* 𝄡*04 68 39 34 39.* 🅿. *30 rms. 73€.* ⬜*10€. Restaurant 16.50/ 23€.* Situated on the way into town; bright and spacious rooms.

🍴🛏🛏 **Chambre d'hôte Sanglier Lodge** – *6 r. Route-Royale, 66230 Le Tech.* 𝄡*04 68 39 62 51. www.sanglierlodge.com. Closed Nov–Apr.* 🍴 *4 rms. 68€* ⬜. *Restaurant 25€.* Of the four guest rooms in this house in the middle of the village, the most unusual is the former bakery, which still has a bread oven. The bathrooms have been created through an ingenious use of space. Regional cuisine and grills with South African influences.

🍴/EAT

🍴🍴 **Le Chat qui Rit** – *1 r. de Céret, 66400 Reynès (La Cabanasse, 1.5km/1mi on the road to Amélie).* 𝄡*04 68 87 02 22. www.restaurant-le-chat-qui-rit.fr.* Closed *Christmas week, 4–31 Jan, first fortnight Mar, Tue evening, Wed (except Jul and Aug).* 🅿. *Set menu lunch 14€. 24/40€.* This house built in 1884 beside the road is now a restaurant serving a seasonal cuisine based on locally-sourced ingredients in surroundings that nourish pleasant thoughts. Generous buffets of hors-d'œuvres and desserts. Good service and friendly atmosphere.

DRINK

TEAROOMS
La Rosquilla Fondante Séguéla (Pâtisserie Pérez-Aubert) – *12 r. des Thermes, Amélie-les-Bains-Palalda.* 𝄡*04 68 39 00 16. Open 8am-12.30pm, 3–7pm. Closed Wed, 2 weeks in Feb, 3 weeks in Jul.* In 1810, Robert Séguéla, pâtissier by nature, invented the rousquille, a biscuit perfumed with lemon and wrapped in a sugar icing. His bakery is now a bright and peaceful tearooms offering a choice of 50 teas, fruit teas, home made ice creams etc.

SHOPPING

MARKET
Fruit and vegetable market – *Pl. de la République.* Daily 7am–noon.

ESPADRILLES
Création catalane – *Chemin du Baynat- d'En-Pouly, St-Laurent-de-Cerdans.* 𝄡*04 68 54 08 68. www.espadrille-catalane.com. Open May–Sept Mon–Sat 10am–noon, 2–7pm, Sun (mid-Jun–mid-Sep) 3–7pm; rest of the year Mon–Fri 3–5pm.* Since 2008, this company has been carrying the torch for the manufacture of espadrilles (rope-soled shoes) and *vigatanes* (traditional Catalan espadrilles worn by sardana dancers, with plaited ribbons that are tied around the ankles). The collections on sale offer a wide choice of styles and colours.

WINE
Les Caves du Roussillon – *10 r. des Thermes.* 𝄡*04 68 39 00 29. Open daily 9am–12.30pm, 4–7.30pm.* Tastings of local vintages, plus more than 300 Roussillon wines.

ACTIVITIES

SPAS
Thermes– *Pl. du Mar.-Joffre, Amélie- les-Bains-Palalda.* 𝄡*0825 826 366. www.chainethermale.fr. High season 7am–4pm; rest of the year, ask about opening times. Closed Sun, 21 Dec–25 Jan.* The mimosas, oleanders, palms and agaves are evidence of the gentle climate of Amélie-les-Bains (alt. 230 m/755 ft). The spa is fed by sulphur-rich waters that gush out of the ground at 63 °C/145.4 °F. They are said to be good for the treatment of rheumatism and respiratory conditions. The facilities are in two parts: the Thermes du Mondony, and the Roman spa, which includes a restored Roman swimming pool. The Thermes (open Sat) offers special half-day "Aqua" treatments starting from 55€; or access to a swimming pool with underwater jets and a mud bath for 25€.

Prats-de-Mollo★

Prats-de-Mollo lies in the broad
upper Tech valley overlooked by
the close-cropped slopes of the
Costabonne massif and Mont
Canigou. It combines the character
of a walled fortress town designed
by Vauban with the charm of a lively
Catalan mountain town.
A picturesque Fête de l'Ours (Bear
festival) takes place in February.

⫻ WALKING TOUR

*Enter the town through Porte de France
and follow the shopping street of the
same name.*
Opposite place d'Armes, climb the
steps up rue de la Croix-de-Mission,
overlooked by a Cross and Instruments
of the Passion.

Église

A Romanesque church, of which only the
crenellated bell tower remains, predated
the present building which has a Gothic
structure, despite dating from the 17C.

▶ Follow the south side of the
church and take a fortified rampart
walk round the chevet. Leave the
precinct and walk uphill for about
100m towards Fort Lagarde. Turn
round for a good view of the church.

▶ **Population:** 1,141.
⚬ **Michelin Map:** Region
map C2. 344: F-8.
🛈 **Info:** Pl. du Foiral, 66230
Prats-de-Mollo-la-Preste.
☎ 04 68 39 70 83.
www.pratsdemollo
lapreste.com.
◗ **Location:** 63km/39.5m
SW of Perpignan by the
A9 then the D115.
◔ **Timing:** Allow 2 hours
for the town.
👪 **Kids:** Fort Lagarde.

👪 Fort Lagarde

◔ *Open Jul–Aug 10.30am–1pm,
2–6.30pm; Apr–Jun and Sep–Oct daily
except Mon 2–6pm.* ⫻ *Possibility
of guided tours (1.30 hr) on request.*
☞ *3.50€ (children under 12 2.50€).*
☎ 04 68 39 70 83.
The fortress was built in 1692 on a
rocky spur overlooking the town, and
at the centre of the site there are now
the remains of the old castle. Take the
steps up the side of the curtain wall to
get to the fort.

▶ Return to the church and take
the street to the right.

In sight of the **almshouse**, go down the
steps on the left and follow the street
as it runs along below the almshouse
gardens. Cross the torrent over the forti-

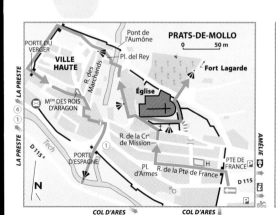

Prats-de-Mollo-la-Preste

© Claudio Giovanni Colombo / iStockphoto

fied bridge, just downstream of the old humpback bridge of La Guilhème, to get to the upper town.

Ville haute (Ville d'Amoun)★

Place del Rey, where an old house once belonging to the military engineers stands, used to be the site of one of the residences of the counts of Besalù, who, in the 12C, reigned over one of the pieces of land that formed part of the patchwork of Catalan territory. Where rue des Marchands leads off to the left, take a carved stairway up to the right.

◐ Continue along the curtain wall. Leave the town through a modern gateway, and return to it through the next one round (a gatehouse), the 'Porte du Verger'.

The street leads to a crossroads, overlooked by a house in the shape of a ship's prow; some people think this was once a palace of the kings of Aragón, and others think that it once housed the trade union of the weavers' guild. An alleyway leads downhill to the exit from the upper town. Go through Porte d'Espagne onto the footbridge over the Tech, from where there is a good view of the south side of the town.

EXCURSION
La Preste

◐ *8km/5mi NW along D 115A.*
This spa town has five springs (temperature 44°C/111°F) recommended for the cure of infections of the colon. Napoléon III had this road up to the spa built. He had intended to follow a course of hydrotherapy at the spa, but the war of 1870 intervened, and he was forced to abandon the idea.

Ripoll★

◐ *55km/34mi southwest, in Spanish Catalonia.* ♨ *see p221.*

ADDRESSES

🛏 STAY

◗◐ **Hotel Bellevue** – *Pl. du Forail.* ☏*04 68 39 72 48. www.hotel-le-bellevue.fr. Closed Tue and Wed from 30 Oct–30 Mar. 17 rms. 50/70€.* ⊐*10€ Restaurant 23/50€.* Spa guests and tourists alike are attentively looked after in this guest house whose young owner cooks the Catalan dishes served in the restaurant. Fresh, well-kept rooms with wood furniture. Terrace and small garden.

◗◐ **Hôtel Le Val du Tech** – *La Preste, 66230 Prats-de-Mollo-La-Preste.* ☏*04 68 39 71 12. www.hotel-levaldutech. com. Closed 1 Nov–7 Apr. 25 rms. 50/56€.* ⊐*7€. Restaurant 16/26€.* This hotel-restaurant clings to the hillside a short distance from the thermal baths. Walkers will enjoy the rustic dining room, and the delicious traditional dishes. The rooms look out over the valley.

🍴 EAT

◗◐ **Ribes** – *La Preste, 66230 Prats-de-Mollo-La-Preste.* ☏*04 68 39 71 04. www.hotel-ribes.com. Closed 23 Oct–17 Apr. 17/29€.* Secluded in the middle of meadows, with a relaxing and beautiful view of the Pyrénées and the valley of the Tech, this lovely restaurant has a convivial family atmosphere, and generous regional dishes at the table. This place exudes authenticity, and the rooms are clean and well equipped.

ACTIVITIES

👥 Guided tours of the fort *(mid-Jul–mid-Aug daily except Sat show at 3.30pm; 9.50€ (children: 6.50€);* ☏*04 68 39 70 83)* with a military theme: costumed horsemen give demonstrations of 18C French military training.

Prieuré de Serrabone★★

The steep, winding road up to Serrabone in the rather bleak part of Roussillon known as Les Aspres, does not at any stage give so much as a glimpse of the splendid Romanesque priory that lies at the end of it. Built of schist and standing in a fragrant botanic garden in the middle of a green sea of countryside, this is one of the wonders of Romanesque art.

Region Map: C1.

Location: 41km/25.5mi W of Perpigan by the N116. After Ille-sur-Têt, turn left on the D618.

Don't Miss: The pink marble tribune in the church.

Timing: Allow 45 minutes.

VISIT

Entrance to the church is through the south gallery. Open 10am–6pm (last admission 30min before closing). Closed 1 Jan, 1 May, 1 Nov, 25 Dec. 3€ (children: 2€). 04 68 84 09 30. www.cg66.fr.

Serrabone simply means "the good mountain"; a reminder that the land around were once dedicated to fields and pastures. During a visit in 1834, **Prosper Mérimée** vigorously deplored that "The monastery buildings are falling into ruin and the church itself is in a very bad state". Soon after, restoration began, thanks to the financial aid of **Henri Jonquères d'Oriola**.

The exterior of the priory has an impressive, if somewhat forbidding, appearance with its rugged architectural style and dark schist stonework.

The priory was founded in 1082, on the site of a pre-existing that church was enlarged and reconsecrated in 1151. Once a prosperous and flourishing priory, it saw the first signs of decline towards the end of the 13C.

South gallery★ – *12C*. Overlooking the ravine, the gallery was used as a covered walkway by Augustinian canons. It is imbued with serenity and harmony, and decorated with capitals reflecting oriental themes, typical of the romantic sculptors of Roussillon.

Church – The nave dates from the 11C; the chancel, transept and the north side aisle are 12C. The church contains a pink-marble **tribune★★** with impressively rich ornamentation. The most remarkable feature is the delicate ornamentation of three archivolts – an ornamental moulding or band following the curve of the underside of an arch.

Romanesque gallery of pink marble, Serrabone priory

© T. Balaguer / age fotostock

ADDRESSES

SHOPPING

Relais de Serrabone – *66130 Boule-d'Amont. 04 68 84 26 24. At the foot of the road which leads to the priory. Open Mar–Oct 10am–7pm, closed Nov–Feb.* Run by local producers, this shop presents a mouth-watering selection of honeys, aromatic herbs, charcuterie, preserved ducks and other tasty treats.

Ille-sur-Têt

This little town in the Roussillon plain between the Têt and the Boulès is an important fruit and vegetable market.

SIGHTS

Follow the green line traced on the ground, which will allow you to walk around the town without missing any of its splendours.

Église des Carmes – Built in the 17C, the Eglise des Carmes houses a collection of paintings from the workshop of the Guerra, a dynasty of Baroque artists in Perpignan.

Hospici d'Illa – *Opening times vary. Closed Dec, Jan, 1 May. 3.70€. 04 68 84 83 96.* The former Hospice St-Jacques (16C and 18C) houses Romanesque and Baroque paintings, sculpture and gold and silver plate, and runs cooking workshops.

Les Orgues d'Ille-sur-Têt★

North of Ille-sur-Têt; 15min on foot. Opening times vary. 3.70€ (under-10 free). 04 68 84 13 13. www.ille-sur-tet.com.
Earth pillars known as the 'Organ Pipes'. Towards Montalba, look for deep ochre formations to the left of the road.

DRIVING TOUR

LES ASPRES★

56km/35mi from Ille-sur-Têt to Amélie-les-Bains. Allow 3hrs. See region map.
In this rugged sparsely inhabited region, the beautiful Mediterranean landscape is covered by olive groves and cork oaks. Les Aspres own their name to their aridity: the "âpreté" (harshness) of their rocky landscapes covered with garrigue scrub.

Leave Ille-sur-Têt S on D 2, then turn right onto D 16 to Bouleternère.

D 618 (*turn left in Bouleternère*) leaves the orchards in the Têt Valley for the garrigues along the Boulès gorge.

- **Michelin Map:** Region Map: C1.
- **Info:** Sq. de la Poste, 66130 Ille-sur-Têt. 04 68 84 02 62. www.ille-sur-tet.com.
- **Location:** On the N116, 26km/16.25mi W of Perpignan and 21km/13mi E of Prades.
- **Timing:** 1hr for the town, 1hr for Les Orgues and 3hr for Les Aspres.
- **Don't Miss:** The Hospici d'Illa sculptures and fairy landscapes of Orgues d'Ille.
- **Kids:** The silver pieces of Hospici d'Ille and landscapes of the Orgues d'Ille.

After 7.5km/4.5mi turn right to Serrabone. TSee p169.

Boule d'Amont

A winding and narrow road leads to this small village, and then up to the Col Fourtou, for a view of the highest Corbières summits.

Col Fourtou

Alt. 646 m/ 2,120 ft.
View looking back at the Pic de Bugarach, the highest point of the Corbières (alt. 1 230 m/4,036 ft). In front are the mountains of the Spanish frontier above Vallespir: Roc de France and the right, Pilon de Belmatx, with its jagged silhouette. To the right is Mt Canigou.

Prunet-et-Belpuig

The **Chapelle de la Trinité** has a door with scrolled hinges. Brooding **castle ruins** on a rocky spur overlook Mont Canigou, the Albères, the Roussillon and Languedoc coasts and the Corbières.

After the col Xatard, the road descends to Amelie-les-Bains, punctuated by the villages of Saint-Marsal and Taulis, and bypassing the upper basin of the Ample, on slopes rich with oaks and chestnuts.

Abbaye Saint-Michel-de-Cuxa★★

The success of this Romanesque abbey is celebrated in its rich ornamentation and the impressive number of relics that it sheltered in the Middle Ages – 90, plus the graves of two martyrs – when it was the largest pilgrimage church in Catalonia. Despite the effects of history, the floral decorations are the most beautiful in Roussillon.

Michelin Map: Region map C1. 344 F7.

Info: ℰ04 68 96 15 35.

Location: The abbey is located 45km/28mi W of Perpignan along the D 116, then from Prades on the D 127 (direction Taurinya).

Timing: 1hr is sufficient.

Parking: Nearby car park.

Don't Miss: The oriental influences displayed in the capitals of the cloister.

VISIT

One of the finest gems of the Pyrénées, the abbey's sturdy, crenellated bell tower is visible from afar. The 10C pre-Romanesque church is the biggest in France, and a superb aesthetic and acoustical venue for the summer cello concerts. The six-voice Gregorian vespers service held (rather sporadically) at 7pm in the monastery next door is hauntingly simple and medieval in tone and texture.

The abbey is the main venue for the annual **Pablo Casals Music Festival**, founded in 1950. Some concerts are held in St Pierre in Prades (*Festival Pablo Casals, 33 rue de l'Hospice, 66502 Prades; ℰ04 68 96 33 07; www.prades-festival. casals.com*). Pablo Casals himself participated up to the age of 90.

In the year 878 the River Têt flooded, forcing the monks of Eixalada monastery to look for a new home. The counts of Cerdagne offered them money and protection in their endeavour and five years later they were able to found a new monastery, that of Cuxa (pronounced "coutcha"). Due to its extraordinary number of relics, it became an important focus of pilgrimage and this influenced its architecture.

After passing through a chamber in which various documents relating to the history of the abbey are displayed, you reach the remains of the cloister.

Cloister★ – This structure is far from complete but it has been partially reassembled using arches and capitals recovered in Prades and from private houses. The arches of the gallery adjoining the church, a large section of the western gallery and the first part of the eastern gallery have been reconstructed, together constituting almost half of the cloister. The sculpture of the capitals (12C) is characterised by an absence of religious subjects. The whole thing, pink in tone, is dominated by the the church and is a marvel of lightness. Various unusual influences can be found.

Abbey church – This is entered from the cloister by a portal adorned with an arch, the remains of an ancient tribune (12C, dismantled in the 16C) which, as at Serrabone (&see p169), stood in the centre of the nave.

The **nave** is one of the very few surviving examples of pre-Romanesque architecture in France, distinguished by the use of the horseshoe or "Visigothic" arch.

The central nave, which ends in a rectangular apse, is covered by a timber framed roof. The architecture is typical of pilgrimage churches: two side aisles lead to the apse where the relics would have been displayed. Originally, pilgrims would have climbed a monumental staircase over the crypt to pass through the atrium and enter the church.

Crypt – *Under the atrium and the chapel of the Trinity.* In the centre of this elegant 11C sanctuary, the circular chapel of the Virgin of the Crib is covered by a **vaulted ceiling★**. Go around the buildings to see the Romanesque **bell-tower★**.

Villefranche-de-Conflent★

Villefranche-de-Conflent, founded in 1090 by Guillaume Raymond, Count of Cerdagne, occupies a remarkable site on the confluence of the Cady and the Têt, closely surrounded by rock cliffs. Villefranche was a fortified town from the start. Its fortifications were improved over the centuries and finally completed in the 17C by Vauban.

THE FORTIFIED TOWN★

As its name indicates, Villefranche ("free town") benefitted from fiscal privileges from its origin in the 11C. Because of this it served as the administrative and economic capital of the Conflent until the 18C.

There is great pleasure to be had in a stroll around the lively little streets of the town, in which there is variable mix of craft ateliers and shops selling typical Catalan products (espadrilles and *vigatanes*, crème brûlée salamanders, sweets such as rousquilles…).

Enter the walled area through the Porte de France, built by Louis XVI (to the left of the old gateway) and go up rue St-Jacques.

Rue St-Jean

© arenysam / Fotolia.com

Michelin Map: Region map C1-2.

Info: Pl d l'Eglise, 66500 Villefranche-de-Conflent. ☎04 68 96 22 96. www.villefranchedeconflent.fr.

Location: 42km/25mi E of Font-Romeu by the N116 and 8km/5mi SW of Prades.

Parking: Laissez la voiture à l'extérieur des remparts (plusieurs parkings aménagés, mais y trouver une place peut se révéler chose ardue en pleine saison).

Don't Miss: Guided tour of the town, or a trip on the **Train Jaune** linking Villfranche-de-Conflent and Latour-de-Carol (see p180).

Timing: Allow two hours, and stay for lunch.

Ramparts★

Entrance at No 32 bis, rue St-Jacques. Open Jul–Aug 10am–8pm; Jun and Sep 10am–7pm; Mar–May 10.30am–12.30pm, 2–6pm. Rest of year 10.30am–noon, 2–5pm (Dec 2–5pm). Closed Jan and 25 Dec. 4€. ☎04 68 96 22 96. The tour of the ramparts takes in two storeys of galleries, one above the other: the lower watch-path, dating from the construction of the fortress in the 11C, and the upper gallery, dating from the 17C.

Église St-Jacques

The church, which dates from the 12C and 13C, comprises two parallel naves. Enter the church through the doorway with four columns and a cabled archivolt; the capitals are by the St-Michel-de-Cuxa School.

Porte d'Espagne

This gateway, like the Porte de France, was refurbished as a monumental entrance in 1791.

Rue St-Jean

After returning to the Porte de France, walk through the village along rue St-Jean with its 13C and 14C houses, many of which still feature their original porches with rounded or pointed arches.

Fort Liberia★

Access via the staircase of a 'Thousand steps', via a footpath or by means of a 4-wheel-drive vehicle. Departure from within the ramparts, to the right of Porte de France. ⏰*Open Jul–Aug 9am–8pm; May–Jun 10am–7pm. Rest of the year 10am–6pm.* 💶*6€ (children 5–11, 3.50€).* 📞*04 68 96 34 01.*

Overlooked as it is by Mont Belloc, the town was rather too exposed to attack from any enemy encamped above it. Therefore, from 1679 when he was in charge of the project to fortify the town, Vauban planned to protect it by building a fort.

This fort, equipped with a cistern and powder magazines, clearly illustrates some of Vauban's strategic defensive designs. The 'Stairway of a Thousand Steps' (there are in fact 734) was built from pink Conflent marble to link the fort to the town by the little fortified St-Pierre bridge over the Têt.

From the fort, there are **wonderful views★★** of the valleys below and Mont Canigou. 👁*We recommend taking the 'Stairway of a Thousand Steps' back down into the village.*

3 GROTTES CAVES

Les Grandes Canalettes, Cova Bastera. ⏰*Open Jul–Aug 11am–7pm, Jun & Sep 2–5pm.* 💶*7€. Les Canalettes* 🚶*Guided visits Jul–Aug, hourly 11.30am–5.30pm.* 💶*9€.* ⏰*Open Apr–Jun 10am–6pm, Jul & Aug 10am–7.30pm, Sep–Oct 10am–5.30pm, Nov–Mar Sat, Sun, hols 11am–5pm.* 💶*10€. (combined ticket for all three caves 19€ adult, 9€ child).* 📞*04 68 05 20 20 or 06 07 27 11 31. www.3grottes.com.*

Cova Bastera

This cave, situated on the Andorra road opposite the ramparts, is at the far end of the Canalettes network. It reveals Vauban's underground fortifi-

cation system and the various phases of occupation of the site, portrayed in life-size tableaux.

Grotte des Canalettes

Parking 700 m to the south, below the road to Vernet.

The concretions in this cave take on an amazing variety of shapes: petrified calcite torrents and eccentrics. Some of the finest include the Table, a natural hollow *(gour)* that gradually filled up with calcite, and some dazzling white draperies.

Grotte des Grandes Canalettes

This cave forms part of the same network as the Canalettes cave.

🚗 DRIVING TOUR

FROM VILLEFRANCE-DE-CONFLENT TO ILLE-SUR-TÊT

68km/42.2mi. Allow about 6hrs. 🧭*See region map.* ▷ *Leave Villefranche-de-Conflent to the south on the D 116.*

Corneilla-de-Conflent

The beautiful Romanesque **church** belonged to a former Priory of Canons Regular of St. Augustine. Flanked by a square tower built of granite, the short façade is pierced by a gate of six marble columns of the 12C.

▷ The road climbs the valley of the Cady, domain of shepherds, and fruit growers.

Vernet-les-Bains★

At the foot of the wooded foothills of Canigou, the village is both refreshing and peaceful, and a spa resort of some importance (📞*04 68 05 55 35; www.vernet-les-bains.fr).* The weekly market here is small but comprehensive.

▷ In Vernet, take the narrow route du Canigou, and drive 2.5km/1.5mi.

Casteil

👥 **Parc animalier de Casteil** (📞*04 68 05 67 54; www.zoodecasteil.com)* has a number of trails for you to follow in search of bears, wolves, lions and more peaceful herbivores.

▶ Go back to Vernet, and take the D 27 towards Taurinya.

Abbaye St-Michel-de-Cuxa★★
ᵔSee p171.

Prades

The main town hereabouts, Prades is a lively, brightly coloured market town set among orchards, and renowned both for its bustling Tuesday street market and its buildings and pavements, many of which are constructed from the soft-hued, variegated pink Conflent marble quarried locally. In 1939, Prades was chosen by the world-renowned cellist **Pablo Casals** (1876–1973) as his exiled home, and the **Musée Pablo-Casals** enables you to discover much about the man and his music.

▶ Follow the D 619 NW for 12km/7.5mi, then take the D 14.

Mosset

Mosset is a delightful little place of narrow streets, the remains of a chateau, and a **perfumed garden** (𝓟04 68 05 38 32; www.mosset.fr) wherein the aromas of mountain flowers – lavender, valerian, rosemary, chamomile, cat mint – assault the senses and brings a new dimension to the silence of the mountains.

▶ Continue on the D 14, and go as far as Catlar on the D 619. There, turn left onto the D 24.

Eus★

This pyramidal pile – not unlike a child's sand castle or a precarious tower of playing cards – originally built for defensive reasons, has repelled both French and Spanish attempts at possession by force. Eus is an unmissable location, perched on a hillside just a short way to the east of Prades.

▶ Follow the D 35, leaving to the right the pont de Marquixanes.

Prieuré de Marcevol

Below a tiny village, home to shepherds and winemakers, is a 12C priory founded by the canons of the Holy Sepulchre.

▶ Turn right onto the D 116, then left onto the D 25, and finally the D 55.

Espira-de-Conflent

The furniture inside the Romanesque church of Espira (1165) illustrates the heyday of Baroque sculpture between 1650 and 1730.

Vinça

Another fortified village, this with a church displaying fine Baroque features and rich decoration.

ADDRESSES

⌂ STAY

◓◓ **Mas Lluganas** 66500 Mosset. 𝓟04 68 05 04 84. www.maslluganas. com. 8 rms. 55€ for two people. ⌑ Free wifi. An unusual undertaking belonging to four partners, this farm operates as a ferme-auberge at weekends from April to October and daily in July and August. Rooms are simple but comfortable. Five are in the farmhouse (the mas) and three are in a separate property, La Forge. there are also two gîtes for rent. A regional cuisine is served in a rustic dining room.

⌇/EAT

◓◓ **Auberge St-Paul** – 7 pl. de l'Église 66500 Villefranche-de-Conflent. 𝓟04 68 96 30 95. http://perso.wanadoo.fr/auberge. stpaul. Closed 5–29 Jan, 15–20 Jun, 23 Nov–3 Dec, Mar (out of season), Sun night, Mon. Menus from 20€. This 13C chapel houses a delightful rustic restaurant. The menu is renewed each season and there is a good choice of Burgundy and Roussillon wines. Shady terrace.

Abbaye de Saint-Martin-du-Canigou★★

This abbey perched in its eagle's eyrie 1,055m/3,460ft above sea level is one of the prime sights to be seen in the area around Vernet-les-Bains. Guifred, Count of Cerdagne, great-grandson of Wilfred le Velu, founder of the Catalonian dynasty, chose Mont Canigou, a solitary place venerated by his people, to found a Benedictine monastery in 1001.

- **Region Map:** C2.
- **Info:** 66820 Casteil. ✆04 68 05 50 03. http://stmartinducanigou.org.
- **Location:** 14km/8.75mi S of Prades by N 116. The abbey can be reached from Vernet-les-Bains. Alternatively, park the car in Casteil and continue on foot (1hr).
- **Don't Miss:** The view of the abbey from the woods above.
- **Timing:** Allow two hours.

VISIT

Guided visits only (1hr) Jun–Sep 10am, 11am, noon, 2pm, 3pm, 4pm, 5pm (Sun and public holidays 10am, 12.30pm, 2pm, 3pm, 4pm, 5pm); Oct–May (except Mon) 10am, 11am, 2pm, 3pm, 4pm (Sun and public holidays 10am, 12.30pm, 2pm, 3pm, 4pm). Closed Jan. ⊚5€. ✆04 68 05 50 03. http://stmartinducanigou.org.

Cloisters – At the beginning of the 20C, all that remained of the cloisters were three galleries with somewhat crude semicircular arcades. Restoration work included rebuilding a south gallery overlooking the ravine, using the marble capitals from an upper storey which was no longer extant.

Churches – The lower church (10C), dedicated to 'Notre-Dame-sous-Terre' in accordance with an old Christian tradition, forms the crypt of the upper church (11C).

Walk to the **viewpoint** (*after reaching the abbey, take a stairway to the left which climbs into the woods. Just past the water outlet turn right; 30min on foot there and back*) to appreciate the originality of St-Martin's site. From here, there is an impressive view of the abbey. Its **site★★** dominating the Casteil and Vernet valleys is most striking.

EXCURSION
Col de Mantet★

20km/12.5mi to the SW – about 1hr. The cliff road is very steep and narrow upstream of Py.

After leaving Vernet to the west, from Sahorre on, the road (D 27) climbs the Rotja valley, first amid apple trees then along a gorge sunk into the granite rock. Above Py, a pretty village 1,023m/3,356ft above sea level, the road scales steep slopes with granite outcrops bristling here and there. After 3.5km/2mi, in a wide bend in the road, a **look-out point★** gives a good view of the village with its red roofs and Mont Canigou. The Mantet Pass opens up at an altitude of 1,761m/5,777ft, near the evergreen forest of La Ville. On the opposite slope is the site of **Mantet**, an almost deserted village, huddled in a dip.

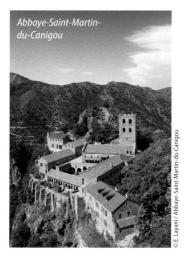

Abbaye-Saint-Martin-du-Canigou

© E. Layani / Abbaye-Saint-Martin-du-Canigou

Le Canigou★★★

Towering above the Roussillon orchards, Canigou mountain is revered by Catalonians from France and Spain, who still light the first of their Midsummer Eve bonfires on its summit. The best season for **climbing** is autumn, with mild temperatures and perfect visibility. Patches of snow cover northern slopes in Spring and early summer. Mid-summer brings heat and crowds.

A BIT OF HISTORY

A geographer's mistake recorded Canigou as the highest peak in the Pyrénées for quite some time. Ever since the first ascent, reputedly by King Peter of Aragon in 1285, Catalonian sportsmen have vied to conquer this peak: by bicycle in 1901, on skis and on board a Gladiator 10 cc automobile in 1903, and by horseback in 1907. Vernet-les-Bains and Prats-de-Mollo are linked only by forest roads.

The Sacred Mountain – In the same way that Mount Fuji symbolises Japan, Canigou is linked to Catalan identity. *"Canigou is a giant magnolia flower, That blooms out of the Pyrénées, Bees and fairies fly around it, Butterflies and swans and eagles, Its jagged forms create a chalice, Silver in winter, in summer gold"* …wrote the poet **Jacint Verdaguer** (1845–1902). Catalans come here to light the first fires of Midsummer's Day and at dawn on 24 June to gather wildflowers for "good luck": everlasting, stonecrop, St John's wort and walnut leaves are shaped into a cross and placed on the doors of houses to ensure happiness and safety from harm.

🚶 HIKES
FROM VERNET-LES-BAINS VIA MARIAILLES

12km/7.5mi – 45min by car and 10hr on foot for the return trip. 🚶 *See Le Canigou map. Experienced hikers only. From Vernet-les-Bains (* 🚶 *see p173) take D 116 to the Col de Jou via Casteil and park the car at the pass. Follow the GR*

- 🚌 **Michelin Map:** Region map C2. 344: F7.
- ▶ **Location:** 69km/43mi west of Perpignan by the N 116 then the D 27; 24km/15mi south of Prades by the D 27. The summit of Canigou can only be reached on foot or by 4x4 because there is no surfaced road. The restricted access at least offers some protection to the mountain's wild beauty.
- 👁 **Don't Miss:** The climb to the summit; the view from the top; also the views from le Ras del Prat Cabrera.
- 🕐 **Timing:** In early summer some patches of snow persist on the northern slopes and rhodedendrons flower on the heights. Autumn is pleasant for its mild weather and for the visibilty from the summit. Summer is to be avoided due to the heat and the numbers of visitors. Allow a day for the routes that pass the chalet des Cortalets.
- 👪 **Kids:** Make sure of the time, distance and difficulty of these hikes before taking your children.

10 footpath via Mariailles, to the refuge at the summit. Continue to the Canigou peak along the Haute Randonnée Pyrénéenne.

Pic du Canigou★★★
Alt 2,784m/9,131ft.

🚶 On the Canigou summit are a cross and remains of a stone hut used in the 18C and 19C for scientific observations. Listen for the tinkling of bells from grazing animals in the Cady valley below. The **panorama** is vast: to the north-east, the east and the southwest, towards the plain of Roussillon and the Mediterranean coast. Although the hills of

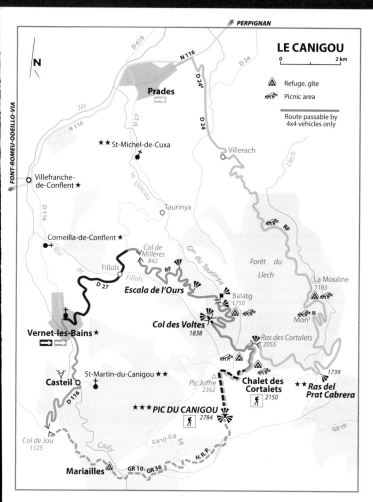

LE CANIGOU

the Albères form a barrier in the fore-ground they don't interrupt the view, which reaches far into Spanish Catalonia and along the Costa Brava. To the northwest and the west the eastern Pyrénées appear in crystalline layers (Madrès, Carlit etc.), contrasting with the more rugged limestone formations of the Corbières (Bugarach). Sometimes you can see Canigou all the way from Marseille's church of Notre-Dame-de-la-Garde, 253km/157mi as the crow flies.

FROM VERNET-LES-BAINS VIA THE CHALET-HÔTEL DES CORTALETS

23km/14.5mi – about 1hr30min by car and 3hr30min on foot there and back.

🐚 *See Le Canigou map.* ⏳ *The track starting from Fillols is closed on the way up from 1 to 6pm and on the way down from 8am to 3pm. The old Cortalets road built for the Club Alpin in 1899 is a picturesque but rough mountain road, accessible only in July and August, in dry weather, in a four-wheel drive or Jeep. Beware of the road's poor condition, and a very narrow 21 percent gradient (protected by a parapet) and 31 harrowing hairpin bends.*

Start your tour from Vernet-les-Bains (🐚 *see p173*) and take D 27 in the direction of Prades. After Fillols, turn right. After leaving Vernet-les-Bains, beyond Col de Millères, alt 842m/2,762ft, the road corkscrews along the rocky crest rocks leads to the summit (3hr30min there and back).

Pic du Canigou★★★
See p176.

FROM PRADES VIA THE CHALET-HÔTEL DES CORTALETS

20km/12.5mi – allow 2hr by car and 3hr30min on foot there and back. See Le Canigou map. Accessible only in dry summer weather, the road is very rough along the Llech gorge; a 10km/6mi stretch cuts into the rock face. Excursions by Jeep or four-wheel drive are organised from Prades. This tour leaves Prades on N 116, towards Perpignan, then turn right onto D 24B.

After leaving Prades, beyond Villerach, the D 24 traverses the Conflent orchards and overlooks the Llech gorge 200–300m/700–1,000ft below, before pushing up to the La Mouline forest hut *(alt 1,183m/3,880ft; picnic area).*

between the Fillols and Taurinya valleys, with views of Prades and St-Michel-de-Cuxa. You'll wind through larch trees and rocky outcrops to a stunning view of the Cerdagne and Fenouillèdes regions.

Escala de l'Ours

This vertiginous cliff road is the trip's most spectacular. It cuts a narrow tunnel through the rock itself, over the Taurinya gorges far below, with viewpoints along the way. Arolla pines thin out beyond the Baltag forest hut, and the countryside becomes a pastoral with open meadows.

Col des Voltes

From the pass is a view of the northern slopes of Canigou and the Cady basin.

▷ At the Ras dels Cortalets (picnic area), turn right.

Chalet des Cortalets
Alt 2,150m/7,050ft.
Hotel-chalet at the mouth of the cirque formed by the Canigou, Joffre and Barbet peaks.

West of the hotel-chalet, follow the path waymarked by red and white flashes along the lakeshore, then up the eastern face of Joffre peak. Leave the path as it descends to Vernet and continue the ascent on the left, below the ridge. A zigzag path between the

Ras del Prat Cabrera★★
Alt 1,739m/5,704ft.
This delightful rest stop overlooking the La Lentilla valley offers a panorama of the Roussillon plain, Albères mountains and the Mediterranean. The road opens out in the upper cirque of the Llech Valley with stupendous **views★★★** of the Corbières southern border and the Galamus gorge.

▷ Follow the 'Balcon du Canigou' road W to the **Chalet des Cortalets** (p178) and then continue on foot to the **Pic du Canigou★★★** (see p176).

ADDRESSES

Also see the addresses in Conflent (p172).

 STAY

MOUNTAIN LODGING

If you are thinking of making the ascent on foot you might want to stop either for a midday meal or to spend the night in a mountain refuge. Reservation in advance is advised.

TRANSPORT
GETTING TO CANIGOU BY CAR
A few rules to respect – Access to Canigou from the Col de Jou and Col de Vernet (1st and 2nd routes) and from Prades (3rd route) is not recommended for "city cars": tracks are often rutted and passing is difficult. These routes are, however, passable by four-wheel drive vehicles. Note however that the track taken by the 2nd route is only open to traffic between 8am and 6pm in summer. Parking is prohibited except in equipped and designated areas. The movement of vehicles away from the marked tracks is strictly controlled. For information about using a vehicle in other parts of the Canigou massif contact Canigou Grand – *☎04 68 96 45 86. For other enquiries, contact the tourist information office at Vernet: ☎04 68 05 55 35.*

THE SOLUTION?
Several companies will take you to Canigou from Vernet, Corneilla-de-Conflent and Prades:

From Vernet-les-Bains: *Garage Villacèque ☎04 68 05 51 14; JPB Transport ☎04 68 05 99 89; Tourisme Excursions-Taurigna ☎04 68 05 63 06.*

From Corneilla-de-Conflent :
Transports Circuits Touristiques – *☎04 68 05 64 61 (M. Cullell), mid-Jun–Sept: departures in 4x4 vehicles 8–11am from Corneilla-de-Conflent and Vernet-les-Bains. 16€ return.*

From Prades : **Excursions La Castellane** – *Rte Nationale, 66500 Ria-Sirach. ☎06 14 35 70 64, M. Colas, or 04 68 05 27 08. Jul–Sept departures 8–11am; second fortnight of Jun and Sep–mid-Oct departures 9am. 25€/pers. for 1–4 people (the price is cheaper the greater the number of passengers).* Ask at the tourist information office for other options.

Refuge de Mariailles – *66820 Casteil – ☎04 68 05 57 99. http://refugedemariailles.fr. Restaurant 6/12€.* Rooms and dormitory (55 places).

Refuge du chalet des Cortalets – *2 r. San-Juan-de-Porto-Rico, 66500 Prades. ☎04 68 96 36 19. Restaurant 13/22€.* Rooms and dormitory (85 places).

Refuge pastoral de Mariailles – *66000 Perpignan. bernard.latour@onf.fr.* A refuge without a warden. Access by vehicle is impossible in winter (from beginning of Dec to end May).
Refuge de Balatg – *66000 Perpignan. ☎04 68 35 21 63.*

🍽 🍽 **Chambre d'hôte Les Fenêtres du Soleil** – *R. de la Fontaine 66320 Arboussols. ☎04 68 05 56 25 / 06 11 08 60 41. www.lesfenetresdusoleil.com. 4 rms. 69/79€* 🛏. This village house is built into the hillside as evidenced by the blocks of stone in the dining room. The four rooms are magnificent and equipped with all comforts. Superb view of Canigou from the flowery garden. Exhibition and sale of paintings by local artists.

🍽 🍽 **Chambre d'hôte Las Astrillas** – *12 Carrer-d'Avall, 66500 Taurinya. ☎04 68 96 17 01. Closed mid-Nov–early Mar.* 🅿 🛏. *5 rms. 49/68€.* 🛏. *Restaurant 19€.* Once known as a poor hamlet, this old farm has been so well renovated that it almost feels like a museum dedicated to rural heritage. It has five rooms and one suite, all with great personality. Table d'hôte inspired by Catalan and Mediterranean cuisine.

🍴/EAT
🍴 There are numerous picnic areas provided for the convenience of hikers.

Mont-Louis★

Mont-Louis was originally a fortified town founded in 1679 by Vauban to defend the new borders laid down in the **Treaty of the Pyrénées**. Mont-Louis became an excellent border stronghold. A statue in the church square of this austere fortress town pays tribute to General Dagobert, who drove the Spaniards out of the Cerdagne in 1793, during the invasion of Roussillon.

VISIT

The Louis honoured by this town built by Vauban is, of course, **Louis XIV**, the Sun King. It was a wise move for the town to place itself under the protection of the Sun King because today, as one of the works of Vauban, it is classed as a UNESCO World Heritage Site, but it is also well known for its solar furnace.

Fortified town

Guided tours (1hr) Jul–Aug 10.30am–4pm; Jun 11.30am–2pm; rest of year 11am-2pm. ○*Closed Sun.* ☞*4.50€ (children, 2.50€).* ℰ*04 68 04 21 97.*

This consists of a citadel and a lower town, built entirely within the ramparts. The citadel has a square layout, with cut-off corners extended by bastions. Three demilunes protect the curtain walls. As the town was never besieged, the ramparts, the main gatehouse (Porte de France), the bastions and the watch-towers have remained intact.
Note the **Puits des Forçats**, an 18C well designed to supply the garrison with water in the event of a siege.

Train Jaune

The 'Canary' (ℰ*08 92 35 35 35*), painted in Catalonia's yellow and red, has been running between Villfranche-de-Conflent and Latour-de-Carol (62km/38.5mi) since 1910. The Mont-Louis to Olette section crosses the Giscard Bridge and Séjourné Viaduct.

▶ **Population:** 292.
⌚ **Michelin Map:** region map B2. 344: D7.
ℹ **Info:** 3 r Lt-Pruneta, 66210. ℰ04 68 04 21 97. www.mont-louis.net.
▷ **Location:** 36km/22.5mi SW of Prades, and 9km/5.6mi E of Font-Romeu-Odeillo-Via.
⊘ **Timing:** Allow 1h for a tour of the town.
⊚ **Don't Miss:** The Forçats artesian wells.
👥 **Kids:** The solar oven. In the Capcir, the animal park and ski slopes at Les Angles. The Train Jaune.

👥 Solar Furnace

Guided tours (45mins): summer 9.30am–12.30pm, 2–7pm; autumn 9.30am–12.30am, 2–6pm; rest of the year 9.30am–12.30am, 2–5pm. ○*Closed 1 Jan, 25 Dec.* ☞*6€ (children ages 7–17, 4.50€).* ℰ*04 68 04 14 89. www.four-solaire.fr.*

The solar furnace was installed in 1953. The concentrating panel refurbished in 1980, consists of 860 parabolic mirrors and the heliostat of 546 flat mirrors. The structure focuses the sun's rays into its centre where temperatures reach up to 3,000–3,500°C/5,400–6,300°F. Since July 1993 it has been used for commercial rather than research purposes.

EXCURSIONS
Planès

▷*6.5km/4mi S on the road to Cabanasse and St-Pierre-dels-Forçats. Leave the car in front of the Mairie-École in Planès and take the path on the right to the church.*

A small cemetery around the church offers a beautiful **view**★ of the Carlit massif. The tiny **church** has a curious ground plan in the shape of a sort of five-pointed star, the 'rays' of which are formed by alternately pointed or blunted semicircular chapels. The central dome rests on three semi-domes.

The origins of this monument have given rise to intense speculation over the years, as its structure was extremely rare in the medieval western world. Local tradition attributes it to the Saracens, hence the church was known locally as *la mesquita* or mosque. It is probably a Romanesque building inspired by the symbol of the Holy Trinity.

Lac des Bouillouses★

◗ *14km/9mi NW of Mont-Louis on the D 118; 300m after a bridge over the Têt, turn left onto the D 60.*

A dam has transformed the lake into an impressive reservoir. The walk to Pic Carlit starts at the lake (🚶*3hr*).

🚗 DRIVING TOURS

VALLÉE DE LA TÊT

30km/18/6mi. ◖ See region map. Allow about 4hr. ◗ Leave Mont-Louis on the D 116 (direction Prades).

The road runs across a cliff between Mont-Louis and Olette. During the descent, at every turn, high peaks appear on the bank of the Têt.

Pont Gisclard

This railway bridge is named after the engineer who built it, but who was accidentally killed during testing. The road becomes more tortuous as it descends to pass Fontpédrouse.

Viaduc Séjourné

An elegant and robust viaduct, named after its builder, Paul Séjourné (1851–1939).

◗ Follow the road to Thuès-Entre-Valls.

Gorges de la Carança

🚶 *Leave Thuès-Entre-Valls by a path running along the Carança or use the car parks. Start of the walking route is above the parking, after the railway bridge.* ◌*Good walking shoes recommended; no pets allowed.*

A small loop of about 1hr30min runs along the gorges, past a waterfall and a bridge. The road climbs steeply on the

other side to a junction where you turn right (signposted *'Parc auto par chambre d'eau'*). After a fairly narrow ridge, the path descends to the parking.

A larger loop (3hr) is available to strong walkers. This, too, starts along the river to the first bridge, but instead of crossing the bridge, go forward along an ascending path. The main difficulty is the return on the other side of the river.

Thuès-les-Bains

A modest location that has established itself as a spa resort.

The road passes through **Olette**, where many of the houses back against the cliff face. Quite soon the ruins of **château de la Bastide** come into view.

LE CAPCIR

◖*See region map. Allow half a day.*
◗ *Leave Mont-Louis and head N on the D 118.*

Rising gently, the road offers a view of the citadel rising above the wood, before the massif of Cambras d'Azé. The mountains of Capcir are covered in a thick cloak of pine dotted with lakes. At any time of year, this is a paradise for walkers, and in winter for cross-country skiing.

La Llagonne

The name of this village means 'The Lagoon', and, indeed, before the construction of the Bouillouses dam, the land was often marshy, especially after the resurgence of water in springtime.

◗ At the col de la Quillane which marks the entry into the Capcir mountains, turn left onto the D 32F.

Les Angles

12 av. de l'Aude, 66210 Les Angles.
🕐*Open Jul–Aug 9am–12.30pm, 2–7pm; rest of year 9am–12.30pm, 2–6pm.*
📞*04 68 04 32 76. www.lesangles.com.*
Overlooking the Capcir plateau, this important resort was established in 1964 around an old village. Areas of **Alpine and Nordic skiing** extend

over 40km/25mi of tracks. The station is equipped for **extreme sports** like ice diving or ice surfing.

Parc animalier des Angles – ◷*Open 9am–5pm.* ◉*11€ (children 4–14, 9€).* ☎*04 68 04 17 20.* At the S entrance to the village, branch left on the path to Pla del Mir to visit wild animals living in the Pyrénéan landscape.

Lac de Matemale
Reservoir covering 240 ha/1 sq mi – popular for watersports, hiking, horseriding and fishing (in designated areas).

Formiguères
This small resort has 18 ski runs, and cross-country trails.

▷ Turn left on the D 32B and follow the signs for 'Grotte de Fontrabiouse'.

👬 Grotte de Fontrabiouse
☞*Guided visits (1hr) Jul–Aug 10am–6pm; rest of year 10am–noon, 2–5pm.* ◷*Closed 15 Nov–5 Dec, 25 Dec, 1 Jan.* ◉*8.80€ (children, 5.60€).* ☎*04 68 30 95 55. www.fontrabiouse.fr.* This cave was discovered in 1962, when quarrying for onyx used in the Palais de Chaillot in Paris and the Palace of the Majorcan kings in Perpignan.

Puyvalador
The name of this station means 'Mountain Sentinel', and rightly so. It has 16 ski runs, facing the Puyvalador lake, much loved by windsurfers.

▷ Continue beyond the D 118 to reach Quillan (&See p130) via Axat.

ADDRESSES

🛌 STAY

🛏 **Chambre d'hôte Cal Simunot** – *23bis r. de la Mouline, 66210 Matemale.* ☎*04 68 04 43 17. www.calsimunot.fr.* 🍽 *4 rms. 48€.* 🍴*. Meals 20€.* Each of the four rooms in this farm, situated a short way from the Lac de Matemale, bears

the name of a season in Catalan. They are simply furnished but comfortable. On the ground floor there is a sitting room and small kitchen. Breakfast can be eaten on the terrace. Goat's milk cheeses are made on the farm.

🛏🛏 **Chambre d'Hôte Lou Rouballou** – *R. des Écoles-Laïques, 66210 Mont-Louis.* ☎*04 68 04 23 26 / 06 98 84 49 98. www. mont-louis.net/rouballou.html.* 🍽 *Closed May, Oct & Nov. 5 rms. 65€.* 🍴*.* With its flowery balconies, this house located among the fortifications of the upper part of the village will please anyone looking for authentic rural charm.

🛏🛏 **Hôtel Corrieu** – *66210 La Llagonne.* ☎*04 68 04 22 04. www.hotel-corrieu.com.* 🅿🚻*. Open 11 Jun–19 Sept, 22 Dec–5 Jan and 12 Jan–15 Mar; restaurant closed Thu lunch except school holidays. 24 rms. 62/65€ (plus one "loft" room for 4 people 160€).* 🍴*10€. Set menu lunch 20€, menu 27/42€. Free wifi.* The same family has been welcoming guests to this ancient coaching inn since 1882. The rooms are peaceful and soberly furnished and have the Pyrénées as a backdrop. New tennis court. A simple traditional cuisine is served in the refurbished dining room.

🍴 EAT

🍽 **Crêperie La Grange** – *Pl. du Coq-d'Or, 66210 Les Angles.* ☎*04 68 30 90 98. http:// lagrange-lesangles.com. Closed Mon, Jun, Nov. Reservation advised. 12.70/25.40€.* An attractive wooden terrace distinguishes this beautiful mountain house, which faces the town hall. This is an unusual restaurant in which diners can watch the chefs at work. The menu offers a variety of pancakes, both savoury and sweet. Other choice dishes include the homemade raclette and camembert rôti (a salad served with melted cheese).

🍽🍽 **Le Coq d'Or** – *2 pl. du Coq-d'Or, 66210 Les Angles.* ☎*04 68 04 42 17. www.hotel.lecoqdor.com. Reservation advised. 18/31€. 36 rms. 56/69€.* 🍴*8€.* On the main square of the village, this hôtel-restaurant is a veritable institution in the region. Large rustic dining room with coloured table cloths.

Font-Romeu-Odeillo-Via★

Font-Romeu is a health resort on the sunny side of the French Cerdagne, higher than any other mountain village. It is protected from northerly winds and offers a superb valley panorama. Its impressive sports facilities (swimming pool, ice rink and stables) attract international athletes for altitude training.

FONT-ROMEU/ PYRÉNÉES 2000 SKI AREAS

Accessible by road or by gondola from Font-Romeu (2.5km/1.5mi via the route des pistes leading off from the calvary). Forty downhill slopes accommodate skiers of all levels. The Pyrénées 2000 resort specialises in ski techniques for people with physical disabilities. Font-Romeu's **Centre Européen d'Entraînement Canin en Altitude** offers dog-sledding instruction year-round.

LA FONTAINE DU PÈLERIN

This hermitage bears witness to the famous Catalan pilgrimage that gave Font-Romeu its name (*Fontaine du Pèlerin* or 'Pilgrim's fountain').

- **Region Map:** B2.
- **Info:** Office du tourisme de Font-Romeu-Odeillo-Via 82 av Emmanuel-Brousse-66120. ℘04 68 30 68 30. www.font-romeu.com.
- **Location:** 89km/55mi W of Perpignan and 9km/6mi W of Mont-Louis via the D618.
- **Timing:** Allow half a day to discover Font-Romeu and the Spanish enclave of Llívia.
- **Don't Miss:** The panorama from the Calvary.
- **Kids:** In winter, the ski slopes of Font-Romeu and Pyrénées 2000. Numerous outdoor activities are available in the region (see addresses) in summer.

The **hermitage**★ is known for its statue of the Blessed Virgin Mary called the 'Vierge de l'Invention'. The **chapel**★ dates from the 17C and 18C. Its magnificent **altarpiece**★★ by Joseph Sunyer dates from 1707. The staircase to the left of the high altar leads to the **camaril**★★★, the Virgin Mary's small

Detail of the camaril by Josep Sunyer at the chapel

© J. Frumm / hemis.fr

'reception room', Sunyer's masterpiece *(For guided tours contact the tourist office)*. Some 300m/984ft from the hermitage on the road to Mont-Louis, turn right onto a path lined with stations of the cross. The calvary affords a **panorama★★** over Cerdagne.

EXCURSIONS
Col del Pam★
🏃 *15min round-trip.* The observation platform over the Têt valley affords a **view** of the Carlit range, Bouillouses plateau, Capcir and Canigou summit.

Llivia
▶ *9km/5.6mi S along D 33E.*
This is Spanish enclave on French territory with picturesque lanes and the remains of a medieval castle and old towers.

ADDRESSES

🏠 STAY

🛏 **Camping L'Enclave** – *66800 Estavar (south of Font-Romeu, near Llívia).* ☎*04 68 04 72 27.www.camping.lenclave.com. Closed 26 Sep–end Nov. Reservation advised. 175 sites. 27.50€.* This campsite, close to the Spanish enclave of Llivia, has well maintained sites, as well as a fully-equipped selection of mobile homes. The shower and toilet blocks are up to date. Enclosed swimming pool, playground and tennis court.

🛏🛏 **Hôtel de la Poste** – *2 av. Emmanuel-Brousse.* ☎*04 68 30 01 88. http://hoteldelaposte.free.fr. 23 rms. 49/59€.* ☕*8.50€. Free wifi.* The façade of this family-run hotel is decorated with paintings of mountain animals. The refurbished rooms are well-maintained and offer both peace and comfort. In the restaurant, the cuisine is generous and inspired by the region. The staff ensure that there is a friendly and welcoming atmosphere.

🛏🛏🛏 **Sun Valley** – *3 av. d'Espagne.* ☎*04 68 30 21 21. www.hotelsunvalley.fr. Closed 31 Oct–4 4 Dec.* 🅿 *41 rms. 71/119€.* ☕*9€. Restaurant 22€ (guests only). Free wifi.* The rooms, being renovated in turn in chalet-style, catch the sun on their balconies. Well being and relaxation facilities on the top floor. Meals are simple and generous.

🍴 EAT

🍽 **Complexe Casino** – *46 av. Emmanuel-Brousse.* ☎*04 68 30 01 11. Restaurant closed Mon and Tue (out of season). 10/36€.* A casino, cinema, discothèque and restaurant are waiting for you in this modern house in the town centre. A carefully-prepared traditional cuisine is served in the pleasant dining room. Set menu lunches at reasonable prices.

ACTIVITIES
MOUNTAIN SPORTS
Bureau des Guides-École de la Montagne – *9 r. Maillol.* ☎*04 68 30 23 08. nosaumasson@hotmail.com. Closed Nov.* The local association of mountain guides offers to teach or accompany you on a wide range of outdoor activities: hiking, rafting, canyoning, caving, riverboarding, rock climbing and negotiating an aerial adventure park. In winter, there are excursions on snow shoes and canyoning in warm-water waterfalls.

MULTI SPORT
Ozone 3 Montagne et Loisirs – *38 av. Emmanuel-Brousse.* ☎*04 68 30 36 09. www.ozone3.fr. Open 9am–noon, 4–7.30pm.* Mountain bike tours, hikes, snow shoe walking, cross-country skiing, via ferrata and rock climbing. White water sports (rafting, riverboarding…) in the Aude and balloon flights. Also organises courses and workshops.

Drakkar Traîneau Aventure – *Les Airelles* – ☎*06 08 62 87 45.* After a guided tour of the kennels *(1 hour),* you can try your hand at driving a team of dogs pulling a sledge.

L'Aventurine rando – *9 av. Cambred'Aze* – *66210 Bolquère.* ☎*06 14 31 79 72. www.aventurine-rando.com. Jul–Apr, ask for opening hours; rest of the year, reservations by phone.* Activities available: hiking, rock climbing, via ferrata, aerial adventure park, canyoning, rafting, riverboarding etc.

EVENTS
La Transpyrénéenne – *February.* Cross-country skiing competition, open to all.

La Cerdagne★

The half-French, half-Spanish Cerdagne region in the eastern Pyrénées lies in the upper valley of the Sègre, between St-Martin gorge (alt 1,000m/3,300ft) and La Perche Pass (alt 1,579m/5,179ft). This peaceful sunlit valley framed by majestic mountains is a rural idyll of fields, pastures and streams lined with alders and willows. To the north the granite massif of Le Carlit towers at 2,921m/9,581ft and to the south lies the Puigmal range (alt 2,910m/9,545ft) with its forests and ravines.

- **Michelin Map:** Region map AB2. 344: C7/D8.
- **Info:** Porté-Puymorens. ✆04 68 04 82 41. www.porte-puymorens.net
- **Location:** SW of Perpignan, 1hr from Spanish border.
- **Timing:** Allow at least a day to visit the region.
- **Don't Miss:** The panorama from col Puymorens and col de l'Ombrée.
- **Kids:** The solar furnace at Odeillo and the Cerdagne Museum at Ste-Léocadie.

TRANSPORT

Le Train jaune – See Villefranche-de-Conflent (p172) and Mont-Louis (p180).

SKI AREAS

Espace Cambre d'Aze at Eyne 🎿

Alt 1,600–2,400m/5,249–7874ft.
The resorts of Eyne and St-Pierre-del-Forçats comprise 27 Alpine ski runs for all levels of skiers.

Err-Puigmal 2900 🎿🎿

Alt 1,850–2,520m/6,070–8,268ft.
18 Alpine runs and 10km/6mi of cross-country trails on Mont Puigmal.

Porté-Puymorens 🎿

Alt 1,615–2,500m/5,298–8,202ft.

In March the Grand Prix Porté-Puymorens is held at this ski resort with 16 downhill slopes, 25km/15mi of cross-country trails, snowboarding and ski-biking.

🚗 DRIVING TOURS

VALLÉE DU CAROL★★

27km/16.5mi from Col de Puymorens. Allow 1hr. 🛈 See La Cerdagne map.
After leaving gentle slopes of the Ariège's upper valley, the road descends deeper into the valley.

Col de Puymorens★

Alt 1,920m/6,300ft.
The pass lies on the Atlantic-Mediterranean watershed between the Ariège and the Sègre. The road crosses a bridge

Col du Puymorens

©gRaNdLeMuRleN/Fotolia.com

and leads down into the **Carol valley**, with views of **Porté-Puymorens** and the glacial threshold beneath the Tour Cerdane's ruins.

Beyond Porté, the road traverses a narrow ravine, the Défilé de la Faou, before squeezing between sheer valley walls on the way to Enveitg. Before Bourg-Madame, look for the Grand Hôtel de Fort-Romeu on the left, with the Spanish enclave of Llivia in the foreground. To the right, on the Spanish side, see Puigcerdà on the hilltop.

Bourg-Madame

In 1815 the duke of Angoulême named this village on the River Rahur to honour his wife Madame Royale.

ROUTE DE LA SOULANE★

36km/22.5mi. Allow 2hr. 🐾 *See La Cerdagne map.* ◗ *Start at Bourg-Madame (see above); leave north on N 20.*

Ur

Note the church's Lombardy banding surmounted by a cogged frieze, and the altarpiece by Sunyer.

◗ At Ur, turn right onto D 618 and at Villeneuve-des-Escaldes take D 10 to the left.

Dorres

The **church's** north side altar Our Lady of Sorrows typifies the Catalans' penchant for dressing up their statues. The south chapel has an impressive Black Madonna *(contact the town hall; ℘04 68 04 60 69)*. The path from the hôtel Marty in Dorres leads to a **sulphur spring** used for open-air thermalism (🕐*open 8.30am–8pm, Jul and Aug 8am–9pm; ℘04 68 04 66 87; 30min round-trip on foot).*

◗ Go back to D 618.

Angoustrine

The Romanesque **church** offers guided tours (🕐 🐾 *guided tours available 2–5pm, reserve 7 days in advance; ℘04 68 30 08 00).*

Chaos de Targasonne

This gigantic heap of contorted granite boulders dates from the Quaternary Era. A short distance *(2km/1.2mi)* away, view the border mountains from Canigou to Puigmal and the jagged Sierra del Cadi.

Thémis

Many experiments on solar energy have been conducted in the region, as evidenced by this prototype solar tower plant closed in 1986. It remains an imposing building with 100m/328ft high tower dominating the Catalan landscape.

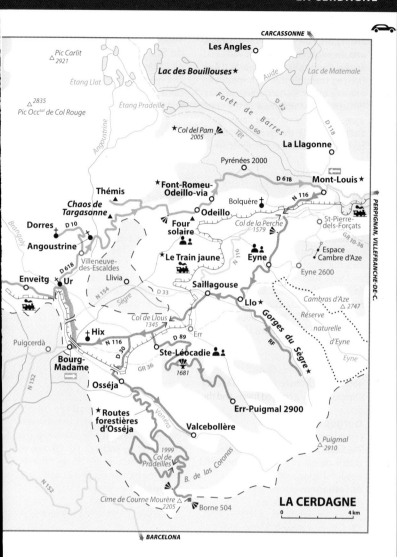

LA CERDAGNE

Odeillo

Near the village stands the huge **solar furnace** inaugurated in 1969 (♟♟ ♿ ◷open Jul–Aug 10am–7.30pm; Sep–Jun 10am–12.30; 2–6pm; ◷closed 1 Jan, mid-Nov–early Dec and 25 Dec; ◎6€, children 8–18 years; 3.50€; ✆04 68 30 77 86). This valley's sunny slopes are reflected in the enormous parabolic surface covered with over 9,000 mirrors, whose temperatures can exceed 3,500°C/6,300°F.

Font-Romeu-Odeillo-Via★
See p183.

The road runs through the pine forest above the picturesque village of **Bolquère** to the Mont-Louis plateau and Aude valley and Conflent region.

Mont-Louis★
See p180.

ROUTE DE L'OMBRÉE
112km/70mi. Allow half a day.
See La Cerdagne map.

From Mont-Louis, D 116 climbs steadily to the La Perche Pass (*alt 1,579m/5,179ft*) linking the valleys of the Têt (Conflent) and the Sègre (Cerdagne).

To the south rises the Cambras d'Azé. Driving through the high moorland enroute to Eyne, you'll enjoy an ever-broadening **panorama★** of the Cerdagne: the ragged outline of the Sierra del Cadi, Puigcerdà, the mountains on the border with Andorra and the Carlit massif.

▷ Turn left onto D 29.

Eyne

At the entrance to this attractive terraced village is an annex of the 👥 **Musée de Cerdagne**, the casa de la Vall d'Eina all about water, and a botanical garden of endemic plants (🕐🌡🌿 *open mid-Jun–mid-Sep 9.30am–6pm; rest of the year call for information; 👛3€ (children under 12 free); 📞04 68 04 97 05).*

▷ Follow D 33 S towards Llo.

Llo★

This steeply sloped village has an interesting watchtower and Romanesque church.

Gorges du Sègre★

Leave from the church in Llo.

The Sègre flows down from the Puigmal massif, creating torrents and a beautiful needle-shaped rock.

At **Saillagouse**, look for the famous Cerdagne charcuterie.

▷ Continue along D 116 towards Puigcerdà.

👥 Ste-Léocadie

Cal Mateau farm houses the **Musée de Cerdagne** (🕐 *open daily except Sat mid-Jul–mid-Sep 2–8.30pm; rest of year call for information; 3.50€; 📞04 68 04 08 05).* This fine 17C–18C building houses exhibitions on shepherds, horse-breeding and traditional flask-making.

▷ Turn left onto D 89 leading to the Puigmal ski resort; at the edge of the forest, take the surfaced forest road to the right just after a hairpin bend.

Table d'Orientation de Ste-Léocadie

Alt 1,681m/5,513ft.

The viewing table here offers a **panorama★** of the Cerdagne, the Carol valley and Fontfrède summit.

▷ Go back to D 89 and turn right. The mountain road leads up the Err valley. Go back to D 116, turn left and a little further on left again (D 30).

Routes forestières d'Osséja★

Just above Osséja, leave the Valcebollère road to follow the route forestière to the edge of one of the Pyrénées largest forests. Take the right fork to boundary post 504 (Courne Mourère summit, 2,205m/7,232ft above sea level). Enjoy **views★** of the Cerdagne, the mountains on the Andorra border and Catalonia sierras.

▷ Descend to Osséja by a branching forest road, and then turn right onto the D 30.

Valcebollère

Lost at the end of a road in a cul-de-sac, Valcebollère is the southernmost village of Catalonia. Nicely restored, it is dominated by ancient ruins clinging to an austere mountain of shale. Athletes enjoy the locality which is a good starting point for walking and skiing.

▷ Go back to the D 116 and turn left.

Hix

🌡🌿*Off season, guided tours by request at the Bourg-Madame tourist office. 📞04 68 04 55 35.*

Hix was the residence of the counts of Cerdagne and the commercial capital of the region until the 12C. The little Romanesque **church** contains an early 16C altarpiece dedicated to St Martin, a 13C seated Madonna and Romanesque Christ.

ADDRESSES

🛏 STAY

⊜⊜ **Hôtel Planes (La Vieille Maison Cerdane)** – *6 pl. de Cerdagne, 66800 Saillagouse. ✆04 68 04 72 08. www. planotel.fr. Closed 10 days in Mar and mid-Nov–mid-Dec. 19 rms. 58/73€. ⊐7€. Rest 22/43€.* Old coaching inn with refurbished rooms. Restaurant offers 'mountain' cuisine in a rustic décor – Catalan dishes, omelettes and salads.

⊜⊜ **Auberge Catalane** – *10, av. du Puymorens, 66760 Latour-de-Carol. ✆04 68 04 80 66. www.auberge-catalane.fr. Closed one week in Apr, 9–25 Dec, Sun evening and Mon. 10 rms. 54/58€. ⊐7.50€. Rest. 17/20€. Free wifi.* At 1,200m/3,936ft, a cosy inn with charming, renovated rooms. Rustic dining room with a Catalan ambiance and cuisine.

⊜⊜ **Hotel Marty** – *3 carrer Major-66760 Dorres. ✆04 68 30 07 52. www.hotelmarty. com. Closed 15 Oct–20 Dec. 🅿. 21 rms. 48€. ⊐7€. rest. 15/30€.* This popular family-run guest house has a large dining room serving hearty regional meals; a terrace, and some rooms with verandas.

⊜⊜⊜ **Planotel** – *6 pl. de Cerdagne, 66800 Saillagouse. ✆04 68 04 72 08. www.planotel.fr. Closed Oct–May except school holidays. 20 rms. 65/75€. ⊐8€.* Built in the 1970s, this hotel is ideal for a relaxing and calm break. All the rooms have been refurbished, and all but two have balconies. Swimming pool with sliding roof. Generous country cuisine.

⊜⊜⊜ **Clair Soleil** – *29 av. François-Arago, rte d'Odeillo. ✆04 68 30 13 65. www. hotel-clair-soleil.com. Closed 13 Apr–16 May and 2 Nov–18 Dec. 🅿. 29 rms. 69/76€. Rest. 22/38€.* This family guest house faces the Odeillo solar furnace. Modest rooms with balcony or terrace. Regional cuisine served in a small dining room.

⊜⊜⊜ **Auberge les Écureuils** – *Carrer de la Coma, 66340 Valcebollère. ✆04 68 04 52 03. www.aubergeecureuils. com. Closed 5 Nov–5 Dec. 16 rms. 90/110€. ⊐11€. Rest. Set menu lunch 19€, menu 24/50€.* This old barn has been converted into a cosy country inn. Nicely decorated rooms. Garden at the edge of the stream. Organised walks, skis and snowshoes available. Restaurant of character, classical menu and Catalan dishes. Small crêperie.

🍴 EAT

⊜⊜ **Brasserie de la Vielle Maison Cerdagne** – *6 pl. de Cerdagne, Saillagouse. ✆04 68 04 72 08. www.planotel.fr. Closed 2 Nov–19 Dec. Set menu lunch 11/15€ ♿. 19 rms. 58/73€. ⊐7€.* At the Hôtel Planes, an old coaching stop in Saillagouse village, enjoy a range of family cuisine.

SHOPPING

Charcuterie Bonzom – *Rte d'Estavar, Saillagouse. ✆04 68 04 71 53. www.bernard-bonzom.com. Open 8am–12.30pm, 3–7.30pm. Closed Mon and Wed (out of season).* Here, at the heart of one of the centres for the renowned Catalan sausage, is a shop where you will have no trouble filling your bags with sausages or dried hams, with over 1,500 to choose from!

ACTIVITIES

SPA RESORTS

Les Bains de Llo – *Rte des Gorges de Llo, 66800 Llo. ✆04 68 04 74 55. http:// lesbainsde.llo.free.fr. Open 10am–7.30pm.* Bathe in sulphurous springs at 35°–37°C/95°–99°F. Snack bar with freshly squeezed fruit juice, pancakes and waffles.

Bains chauds de Dorres – *66760 Dorres. ✆04 68 04 66 87. www.bains-de-dorres. com. Open 8.30am–8pm.* Down the concrete road, below the hôtel Marty at Dorres, you reach (30min on foot, there and back) a sulphur source (41°C/105.8°F) where Cerdan and summer visitors come to enjoy the outdoor spa.

FLYING

École de parapente Vol'Aime – *92 r. Creu-de-Fé, 66120 Targassonne. ✆04 68 30 10 10. www.volaime.com. 8am–5pm for paragliding. Closed Nov–Mar.* Discovery courses, lessons, or just flights.

EVENTS

Grand Prix Porté-Puymorens – *March.* Alpine skiing competition.

Andorra★

This small independent state has a total area of 468sq km/180sq mi (about one and a third times the area of the Isle of Wight). Andorra lies at the heart of the Pyrénées and has remained curiously apart from its neighbours, France and Spain. Visitors are attracted by its rugged scenery and picturesque villages.

▶ **Population:** 82,000.
⏱ **Michelin Map:** Region map A1-2. 343 G9.
🗊 **Info:** Pl. de la Rotonda, AD 500 Andorra la Vella. ℘00 376 827 117. www.andorralavella.ad.
▶ **Location:** From France, there is only one road, the N 22 which passes through the border post Pas de la Casa.
🕐 **Timing:** At least a day.
👁 **Don't Miss:** The panorama from the port d'Envalira.
👥 **Kids:** Le musée de la Microminiature ; le musée national de l'Automobile ; le centre Caldea.

A BIT OF HISTORY

'Charlemagne the great, my father, delivered me from the Arabs' begins the Andorran national anthem, which then continues, 'I alone remain the only daughter of Charlemagne. Christian and free for 11 centuries, Christian and free I shall carry on between my two valiant guardians, my two protecting princes.'

From co-principality to independent sovereignty

Until 1993, Andorra was a co-principality under a regime of dual allegiance, a legacy from the medieval feudal system. Under such a contract, two neighbouring lords would define the limits of their respective rights and authority over a territory that they held in common fief. Andorra was unusual, however, in that its two lords came to be of different nationality, but left the status of the territory as it was under feudal law, with the result that neither of them could claim posses-

sion of the land. This dual allegiance to two co-princes was established in 1278 by the Bishop of Urgell and Roger Bernard III, Count of Foix. However, while the bishops of Urgell remained co-princes, the counts of Foix passed their lordship on to France (when Henri IV, Count of Foix and Béarn, became king in 1589) and thus eventually to the President of the French Republic. On 14 March 1993 the Andorrans voted in a referendum to adopt a new democratic constitution making the principality a fully independent state. The official

Andorra

© B. Gardel / hemis.fr

ANDORRA

0   4 km

AX-LES-THERMES

COL DE PUYMORENS

FRANCE

Sant Joan
de Caselles

La Cortinada

Canillo †

Ordino

La Massana

† Nostra-Senyora-
de-Meritxell

Port
d'Envalira
2408

Encamp

Grau Roig

Pas de la
Casa
2085

Garg. de Sant Antoni

Estany d'Engolasters
1616

Cirque de
Font-Nègre

Andorra la Vella

†

Sant Miquel
d'Engolasters

GR 7

Escaldes-
Engordany

Circuit start

Vallée du Valira d'Orient

Sant Julià
de Lòria

Vallées de Gran Valira et
Valira del Nord

Estany d'Engolasters

ESPAÑA

LA SEU D'URGELL / SEO D'URGEL

language of the country is Catalan. The principality has signed a treaty of cooperation with France and Spain, the first countries to officially recognise its independence. It has also become a member of the United Nations.

A taste for liberty

Andorrans pride themselves above all on seeking and fiercely defending their liberty and independence. A long-standing system of representative government and 11 centuries of peace have given them little incentive to alter the country's administration. The country is governed by a General Council, which holds its sessions at the 'Casa de la Vall' (⟲ see p308) and ensures the proportional representation of the various elements of the Andorran population and the seven parishes. Andorrans do not pay any direct taxes, nor do they have to do military service. They also have free postal services within their country. Most of the

Pas de la Casa

©bysinka/Fotolia.com

191

land is communally owned, so there are very few private landowners.

Work and play

Until recently this essentially patriarchal society traditionally made a living from stock rearing and crop cultivation. In between the high summer pastures and the hamlets you can still see the old cortals, groups of barns or farmhouses, which are gradually becoming more accessible as the tracks leading up to them are made suitable for vehicles. The mountain slopes exposed to the sun are cultivated in terraces. Tobacco, the main crop in the Sant Juliá de Lòria Valley, is grown up to an altitude of 1,600m/5,200ft. The first roads suitable for vehicles linking it with the outside world were not opened until 1913, on the Spanish side, and 1931, on the French. The population of Andorra numbered 82,000 in 2009, most of whom speak Catalan.

🚗 DRIVING TOURS

VALLÉE DU VALIRA D'ORIENT★

From Pas de la Casa to Andorre la Vella. 30km/18.6mi – Allow half to a full day. See Andorra map.

Pas de la Casa

A simple border crossing, this village, the highest in the Principality, became an important ski centre. The town consists mainly of large hotel complexes and duty-free shops: there is throughout the year an intense animation, accompanied, especially in the summer, with impressive congestion!

Undulating and winding, the road winds through the mountains before reaching the port of Envalira. The climb offers beautiful views of the pond and the Circus Font-Negro.

Port d'Envalira★★

The port d'Envalira can be obstructed by snow but is usually re-opened within 24 hours. Even so, you can avoid this pass by a tunnel. The highest pass in

the Pyrénées, marking the watershed between the Mediterranean (Valira) and the Atlantic (Ariège) has a good road. Its **panorama** includes the Andorra mountains (2,942m/9,653ft) stretching away to Coma Pedrosa. The road descends to Pas de la Casa, offering spectacular views of the **Font-Nègre** cirque and lake.

Saint Joan de Caselles

This Romanesque church dominates the surroundings at one of the highest points in the area.

Canillo

This village church has the tallest belltower in Andorra (27m/88ft). Nearby is Andorra's national shrine, the **chapel of Our Lady of Meritxell**.

Encamp

In addition to two churches of note, the village contains the **Casa Cristo**★ (ℰ*00 376 833 551*), which has retained its original furniture and is now a museum; the 👥**Musée national de l'Automobile**★ is also of interest (ℰ*00 376 839 760*), it invites you to explore the history of the automobile.

Escaldes-Engordany

Here you will find the **Musée des Maquettes**, displaying models that illustrate the architecture of the region. And nearby, the **Musée du Parfum**, which explores the many facets of perfume.

Andorre la Vella

Andorra's capital, 1,409m/4,620ft above the Gran Valira valley, is a bustling commercial town, but hidden away from the busy main axis you'll find traditional quiet old streets. This is the highest capital city in Europe, and also, at 3 hours driving time, the furthest from the nearest airports at Toulouse, Girona, Perpignan and Barcelona.

Casa de la Vall – The Casa houses Andorra's Parliament building and its Law Courts in a massive 16C stone building (ℰ*00 376 829 129*).

Port d'Envalira

© Claudio Giovanni Colombo / Bigstockphoto.com

VALLÉES DE GRAN VALIRA & VALIRA DEL NORD★

Allow half to a full day.
See map opposite

Sant Julià de Lòria

This village houses the **Museu del Tabac★**, displayed in a former tobacco factory (*℘00 376 741 545*).

Gargantas de Sant Antoni

From a bridge across the Valira del Nord you can see the old humpback bridge used by muleteers. The Coma Pedrosa peaks loom in the distance beyond the Arinsal valley.

▷ Before La Massana, turn left towards Sispony.

La Massana

The **Casa Rull de Sispony★** (*℘00 376 839760; www.museus.ad*) was one of the finest and richest houses in the parish of Massana.

Ordino

This village's picturesque streets are worth exploring. Old Catalan forges produced attractive wrought-iron works like the balcony of 'Don Guillem's' house, the gates of the church and (1676) **Casa Areny-Plandolit★** (*guided tours daily except Mon, reservation recommended 9.30am–1.30pm, 3–6.30pm (Sun 10am–2pm); 3€; ℘00 376 83 97 60*).

Musée de la Microminiature

In a small space, in keeping with its subject, the museum houses miniatures by Ukranian artist Nikolai Siadristy.

Musée iconographique et du Christianisme

The museum contains about 80 religious icons from 17C–19C, mainly from Russia.

La Cortinada

Village highlights are its pleasant setting, a splendid house with galleries and dovecot, and the Romanesque frescoes and Baroque altarpieces in the **church of Sant Marti** (*open Jul–Aug; guided tours 10am–1pm, 3–7pm; rest of the year by request; ℘00 376 84 41 41*).

ESTANY D'ENGOLASTERS

9km/5.5mi, then 30min round-trip on foot. See map p308.

▷ Leave Escaldes E of Andorra, on the road to France, and at the outskirts of the village turn right, doubling back slightly, to follow the Engolasters mountain road.

The outstanding landmark on the Engolasters plateau is the lovely Romanesque bell-tower of **Sant Miguel**. Enjoy a walk to the dam, and lake reflections of the dark forest lining its shores.

Andorran Influences

Until the 1950s, Andorra's population, almost entirely Andorran-born, barely exceeded 6,000. These days only about 25 percent of the population – almost two-thirds of whom live in Andorra la Vella and around – are Andorran nationals. The remainder are largely Spanish, French and Portuguese.

The official language is Catalan (Català), a Romance language closely related to Provençal, but with roots in Castilian and French. Local spin has it that everyone in Andorra speaks Catalan, Spanish and French, but there are plenty of people who can't understand more than a few words of French; hardly anyone speaks English.

Andorran cuisine is mainly Catalan, with significant French and, perhaps surprisingly, Italian influences. Sauces are typically served with meat and fish. Pasta is also common. Local dishes include *cunillo* (rabbit cooked in tomato sauce), *xai* (roast lamb), *trinxat* (bacon, potatoes and cabbage) and *escudella* (a stew of chicken, sausage and meatballs).

Given the fondness of the Catalans for music, it is no surprise that Andorra has a Chamber Orchestra, and that it also stages a famous international singing contest. In 2004, Andorra participated in the Eurovision Song Contest for the first time. This attracted media attention from Catalonia, since it was the first song to be sung in Catalan.

But the single most important event in Andorra cultural life is the Escaldes-Engordany international jazz festival, which has featured such international stars such as Miles Davis, Fats Domino and B.B. King.

Typical dances, such as the marratxa and the contrapàs, are especially popular at feasts, at which exuberant Andorran people tend to celebrate enthusiastically and loudly.

ADDRESSES

🛏 STAY

🍴🛏 **Hôtel Florida** – R. Llacuna 15, Andorre-la-Vieille. ✆00 376 820 105. www.hotelflorida.ad. 🌐. 27 rms. 62.40/104€. ☕ Free wifi. Family run hotel; small gym and sauna.

🍴🛏 **Hôtel Coray** – Caballers 38, Encamp. ✆00 376 831 513. Closed Nov. 85 rms. 50/64€. ☕ Rest. 10.50€. Free wifi. Good location in the hills above the town; large and bright dining room.

🍴🛏 **Hôtel Coma Bella** – Sant Julià de Lòria. 7km/4mi au SW of Andorra la Vella. ✆00 376 84 12 20. www.hotelcomabella.com. Closed 15–25 Apr and 4–22 Nov. 🅿. 30 rms. 56/96€. Rest. 13€. Free wifi. This hotel in the peaceful La Rabassa forest features rooms decorated with contemporary Andorran furnishings.

🍴🛏 **Hôtel Guillem** – C/ dels Arinsols 10, Encamp. ✆00 376 733 900. www.hotelguillem.net. 42 rms. 55/86€. ☕. Rest. 15€. Free wfi. This hotel is peaceful, and offers every comfort.

🍴🛏 **Hôtel Coma** – Ctra Gral d'Ordino, Ordino. ✆00 376 736 100. www.hotelcoma.com. 48 rms. 45/91€. ☕. Rest. 20€. Conveniently located, this welcoming hotel offers comfortable rooms with private terraces.

🍴🛏🛏 **Hôtel Univers** – R. René-Baulard, Encamp. ✆00 376 731 105. www.hoteluniversandorra.com. ♿🅿. 31 rms. 72/83€. Rest. 13€. Free wifi. Located on the banks of the East Valira and close to the futuristic city hall; friendly hotel with comfortable rooms.

🍴🛏🛏 **Hôtel de la Espel** – Pl. Creu Blanca 1, Escaldes-Engordany. ✆00 376 820 855. www.hotelespel.com. Closed May. ♿. 84 rms. 64/106€. ☕. Rest. 16€. Rooms with wooden floors and functional furnishings.

🍴 EAT

🍴🛏🛏 **Borda Estevet** – Rte de La Comella 2, Andorra la Vella. ✆00 376 86 40 26. www.bordaestevetandorra.com. 33/55€. This old stone-walled house welcomes its clients with rustic décor, local Pyrénéan cooking and a wow of a dessert trolley.

🍷🍴🛏 **Can Benet** – *Antic carrer Major 9, Andorra la Vella.* ℘*00 376 828 922. www. restaurant-canbenet.com. Closed 15–30 Jun and Mon.* ♿🐾. *30/50€.* Small ground floor bar; main dining room is upstairs.

🍷🍴🛏 **La Borda Pairal 1630** – *R. Dr-Vilanova 7, Andorra la Vella.* ℘*00 376 869 999. Closed Sun evening and Mon. 33/48€.* Old Andorran stone farm, retaining its rustic décor.

🍷🍴🛏 **Taberna Angel Belmonte** – *R. Ciutat-de-Consuegra 3, Andorra la Vella.* ℘*00 376 822 460. www.tabernaangel belmonte.com. 35/55€.* A pleasant tavern-style restaurant serving seafood.

🍷🍴🛏 **El Rusc** – *La Massana. t00 376 838 200. Closed 15 Jun–15 Jul. Sun evening and Mon.* 🅿. *40/62€.* Beautiful local house with an attractive rustic dining room. Traditional dishes, Basque specialities and good cellar.

SHOPPING

🅰*Normal opening hours are 9am-1pm, 4–8pm (9pm in school holidays).* Andorra is renowned for its shopping. A wide range of products is available (food, luxury items, clothes, electronic equipment etc.) often at competitive prices. Note that on returning to France customs officials check the quantity and value of duty-free goods that have been purchased. Allowable limits per person, for example, include: 1.5ltr of alcohol (over 22°) – or 3ltr (under 22°) – 300 cigarettes, 75g of perfume, 375ml of eau de toilette etc. Vehicles are systematically stopped and searched on roads out of the principality, both those going into Spain and into France. You can even be stopped further on by "flying" customs patrols.

ACTIVITIES

SKIING

Andorra has two areas of downhill skiing and one resort specialising in cross-country. Other activities include snowmobile driving, snowshoe hiking, dog-sledding, ski-biking, speedriding and panoramic flights,

Domaine skiable Grandvalira – *www.grandvalira.com.* This vast area of slopes and lifts combines two resorts: **Soldeu El Tarter** and **Pas de la Casa-Grau Roig**. Alt. 1,710–2,640 m/ 5,610–8,662 ft. 110 runs (193km/ 120mi), all levels, over 1,150 ha/4.5 sq mi, served by 67 lifts.

Domaine skiable Vallnord – *www. vallnord.com.* Again, this ski area is formed by two resorts: **Pal-Arinsal** and **Ordino-Arcalís**. Alt. 1,550–2,560 m/ 5,085–8,399 ft. 66 runs (89km/55mi) and 41 lifts spread out over 1,149 ha/4.4 sq mi.

Domaine skiable La Rabassa Naturlandia – *Sant Julià de Lòria. www.naturlandia.ad.* Alt. 1,960– 2 160 m/6,430–7,086 ft. Cross-country ski resort with 15km/9mi of runs. In summer it is dedicated to seasonal sports such as **tobotronc**, a toboggan run of 5.2km/3.2mi.

THERMAL

👥♨ **Caldea.** *Open Aug and Easter school holidays 10am–midnight, rest of the year 9.30am–11pm (Sat midnight). 34.50€ (3h), 69€ (3 days/3 hours per day), 103.50€ (5 days/3 hours per day).* ℘*00 376 800 999. www.caldea.com.* At an altitude of 1,000m, and fed by the thermal waters of Escaldes-Engordany which come out of the ground at 68 °C/154.4 °F, Caldea is a vast aquatic (or "thermoludique") leisure centre, in which everything is intended for well-being and pleasure. Designed by Français Jean-Michel Ruols, the complex looks like a giant futuristic cathedral built of glass. Facilities include Indo-Roman baths, hammam, Jacuzzi, water beds, sauna, vaporisation showers etc. There are also two restaurants, a shopping centre, and a panoramic bar reached by lift.

HIKING

Andorra has numerous hiking paths through the mountains with refuges for overnight stays. Good places to go walking are the **vallée glaciaire du Madriu**, **the Parc naturel de Sorteny** and the **Parc naturel des Vallées du Comapedrosa**.

EVENTS

La fête nationale – The feast of the Virgin of Meritxell, held on September 8, is evidence of the depth of faith among Andorrans. Mass is held in the presence of the clergy and authorities, followed by picnics, in the manner of any Aplec (pilgrim) Catalan.

Lloret de Mar
© J. Arnold / hemis.fr

5. EXCURSIONS
in Spanish Catalonia

The formidable barrier of the Pyrénées separates the French and Spanish parts of Catalonia. For 160km/100mi there are only six main roads through the mountains and most of these are a slow procession of hairpin bends. Once across, however, the contrast between the two countries is striking and there is much to discover. This chapter visits places easily accessible on short excursions over the border from France. It focuses particularly on the beautiful Costa Brava and its hinterland but also extends inland, into the mountains to visit the valleys and mountains around the historic cities of La Seu d'Urgell (south of Andorra) and Ripoll.

Dalí and the Costa Brava

Costa Brava means "the wild coast" and despite the development of several large resorts (notably Lloret de Mar), overall it is still one of Spain's most attractive shorelines, with cliffs and secluded coves interspersed between its long sandy beaches. There are several good spots for snorkelling and diving. Meanwhile, within reach of the coast are several attractive medieval towns, including Pals and Peralada. The coast's most beautiful town, Cadaqués, sited on a headland protruding into the Mediterranean, is associated with the Surrealist painter, Salvador Dalí who left behind an extraordinary "theatre-museum" in the inland town of Figueres, where he was born and later died. A self-declared genius, shameless self-publicist, brilliant draughtsman and disturbingly obsessive character: Dalí inspires love and loathing in equal measure. Even if you don't like it, there is something mesmerizing about his work which is inseparable from the man and his singular life.

The Catalan Pyrénées

The mountains drop gradually in height as they descend towards the coast but the eastern Pyrénées still reach over 2,900m/9,500 ft in places. This is a good area for touring by car, although the contours make the going slow and sometimes you have no choice but to return down the road you have just driven up. Attractions include innumerable viewpoints, a piece of Spanish territory stranded in France and a singular rack railway climbing to a shrine and ski resort in the Vall de Nuria. The Catalan Pyrénées also have an important cultural legacy to impart. Between the 10C

Highlights

1 Explore the beautiful coast line of the **Costa Brava** (p198)

2 The Benedictine monastery of **Sant Pere de Rodes** (p205)

3 Seafood anywhere on the coast but especially in the charming, village of **Cadaqués** (p207)

4 Dalí's extraordinary "theatre-museum" in **Figueres** is a place of wonders (p209)

5 Get some insights into ancient history from the Greco-Roman ruins at **Empúries** (p214)

and 12C Romanesque architecture and art flourished in the foothills, as Catalonia emerged as a nation. The portal of the monastery in Ripoll is considered a masterpiece, but there is great satisfaction to be had in seeking out lesser known village churches, which are gems in their own right.

Sant Pere de Rodes

© D. Chapuis / MICHELIN

Costa Brava★★★

Spain's Costa Brava (literally "Wild Coast") is a twisted, rocky shoreline where hills fall away into the sea as dramatic cliffs. Beautiful inlets, clear waters, picturesque harbours, and leisure and sporting activities draw tourists to these shores. Inland there are delightful medieval towns and villages.

DISCOVER
👥 The Beaches

The coast is at its most rugged in the comarca (region) of La Selva, around **Blanes**, **Lloret de Mar** et **Tossa**. The cliffs, which in places reach almost 100m/330ft high, plunge vertically into the sea, forming small coves that are ideal for family holidays.

The coast of Baix Empordà, which takes in the bay of Palamós, is also extremely beautiful. The pine-woods here spread everywhere and the transparent waters sparkle in tones of blue and green. **Begur**, **Palafrugell**, **Platja d'Aro** – one of the busiest resorts of the Costa Brava – and **Sant Feliu de Guíxols** have plenty of watersport to offer but also make good places for excursions inland. The northernmost part of the coast is the Alt Empordà where **Roses** sits on a gulf of the same name, a shining 15km/9mi curve of sandy beaches. To the northeast, the great headland of Cap de Creus is punctuated by the picturesque **Cadaqués** and the smaller **El Port de la Selva**.

The Ports

The image of moored boats bobbing in the water is one of the Costa Brava's trademarks. Marinas, serving both for leisure sailing and yachting competitions, alternate with working harbours that come alive when the day's fishing catch is auctioned off at the quayside. The best known marinas in the area are **Empuriabrava** (5,000 berths), **Roses** (1,100 berths), **Palamós** and **Platja d'Aro** (almost 900 berths) and **L'Estartit** (738 berths). Other towns, such as L'Escala, Blanes, Llancà and

Michelin Map: 574 E 39, F 39, G 38-39 – Catalunya (Girona).

Info: Girona: Joan Maragall 2. ☎872 975 975; Blanes: Plaça Catalunya 21. ☎972 33 03 48; Cadaqués: Des Cotxe 2 A. ☎972 25 83 15. www.costabrava.org.

Location: The Costa Brava is the coastline from Blanes up to Portbou on the border with France. Lloret de Mar, Tossa de Mar and Platja d'Aro are major tourist centres; towns to the north are more low key.

Don't Miss: The beauty spots of the coast, notably the Cap de Creus. The villages and towns that have retained some traditional Catalan character, especially Cadaqués and Tossa de Mar. The treasures inland which are relatively unvisited, such as Peratallada.

Timing: A car is the best way to get around the various villages and towns of the Costa Brava. Avoid July and August when resorts and roads along beaches can be grid-locked and other roads congested. To find the best fish and seafood, or the delicious dishes made inland, look for the smaller family-run restaurants that still serve succulent home-cooking.

Kids: The beaches, especially the sandy ones around Roses; a boat trip to the Medes islands; the Aqua Brava waterpark at Roses; larger resorts have fun-fair type amusements aimed especially at children (see "addresses" at end of the chapter).

El Port de la Selva also have good facilities for visiting craft.

The various resorts are connected by **boat services** running between them. Tossa de Mar, Lloret de Mar, Blanes and San Feliu de Guíxols are linked by regular ferries in summer, which also provide a chance to see the wild scenery of the coast from the sea.

The Villages and Towns

The villages and towns of the Costa Brava are very varied; each has its own source of interest. Don't miss the famous **Cadaqués**, sometime haunt of artists and bohemians, which is a delightful place to stroll around. **Peratallada**, perched on the living rock, is also a picturesque place, as is **Begur**, both the town itself with its little white houses, and the coves of its coastline. The old town of **Pals** (El Pedró), an ensemble of medieval buildings with views of the coast, is also worth visiting. **Tossa de Mar**, as well as being a popular resort, has a remarkable set of ramparts that draws thousands of visitors.

The Gardens

Gardens are another special attraction of the Costa Brava. Between **Lloret de Mar** and **Blanes** there are three major botanic gardens: Marimurtra (6,000 species of plant from around the world), Pinya de Rosa (the largest cactus garden in the world) and Santa Clotilde (in Italian Renaissance style).

Some gardens offer exceptional views over protected parts of the coast that otherwise cannot be seen. Such is the case of the Cap Roig botanic garden, at **Calella de Palafrugell**, laid out on a panoramic terrace and overhanging the sea.

Nightlife

The nightlife of the Costa Brava is one of its biggest attractions; there is a lot of choice from sedate cocktail bars beside the beach to great open-air clubs. The nightlife is at its liveliest in the bigger resorts, especially **Lloret de Mar** and **Platja d'Aro**. There are also plenty of bars in Tossa de Mar, Roses, Blanes and Calella de Palafrugell. In smaller towns such as Palamós, Sant Feliu de Guixols and Cadaqués there are quieter and more elegant bars. Any tourist information office will provide details of events including traditional fiestas.

🚗 DRIVING TOURS

FROM BLANES TO PALAMÓS
51km/31mi. Allow one day.

The route follows two narrow coastal roads, GI 682 from Blanes to Sant Feliu and C 253 from Sant Feliu to Palamós, providing excellent views of the coast.

Blanes★
www.visitblanes.cat

Blanes, known to the Romans as *Blandæ*, was founded close to the mouth of the river Tordera. Now an important tourist resort focussing on the main street, Carrer Anselm Clavé.

The **Passeig Marítim★** offers a lovely panorama of Blanes and its beach. The remains of the Castillo de Sant Joan are to the east, above the 14C Gothic Església de Santa Maria.

To the southeast is the **Jardí Botànic Marimurtra★** *(Pg. Carles Faust;* ⏱*open daily Apr–May and Oct 9am–6pm; Jun–Sept 9am–8pm; Nov–Mar 10am–5pm;* ⏱*closed 1 and 6 Jan, 24–26 Dec.* €6; 📞*972 33 08 26, www.marimurtra.cat)*, a botanical park with 5,000 plant species including many rare exotic varieties. At each bend the twisting paths reveal wonderful **views★** of Cala Forcadera and the coast.

Jardí Botànic Pinya de Rosa★ *(Platja Santa Cristina, above Marimurtra);* ⏱*open 9am–6pm;* ⏱*closed 1 and 6 Jan, 24–26 Dec;* €4; 📞*972 355 290)*. Created in 1945, Pinya de Rosa has became the largest cactus garden in the world, with over 7,000 varieties.

Its founder, Fernando Riviere de Caralt, was an engineer who spent several decades on its development. Trails through the garden meander over the side of a steep cove, leading to a small pool surrounded by palm trees.

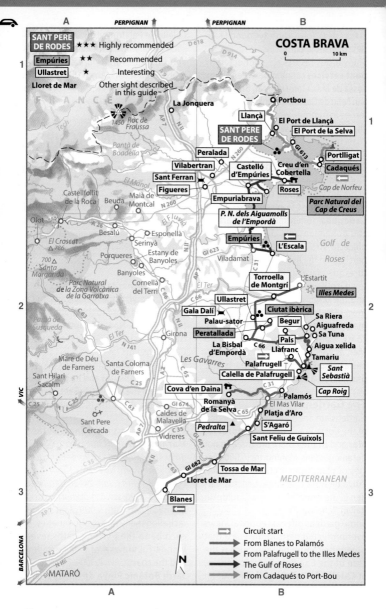

COSTA BRAVA

SANT PERE DE RODES ★★★ Highly recommended
Empúries ★★ Recommended
Ullastret ★ Interesting
Lloret de Mar Other sight described in this guide

Circuit start
From Blanes to Palamós
From Palafrugell to the Illes Medes
The Gulf of Roses
From Cadaqués to Port-Bou

N

▶ 5km/3mi from Blanes.

Lloret de Mar

www.lloretdemar.cat.

Lloret de Mar has become the epicenter of bucket and spade tourism on the Costa Brava, replacing its original maritime ambiance with one of high rise hotels, outdoor discos, water parks and pleasure beaches.

Jardins de Santa Clothilde★★ – *South of the road in from Blanes.* ⊙*Open Apr–Sept 10am–8pm; Oct–Mar Tue–Sun 10am –5pm.* ⊛€4. ✆972 370 471. This rare oasis of tranquillity in Lloret de Mar was created in 1919 by architect and landscape designer Nicolau Maria Rubió i Tudurí (1891–1981). The proprietor asked him to draw inspiration from the Italian Renaissance; terraced gardens are crossed by

*Golfet beach,
Calella de Palafrugell*

© Ingolf Pompe / hemis.fr

paths and stairs lined with ivy. Pines and cypresses abound and jazz concerts are held here in summer.

▷ 11km/7mi from Lloret de Mar.

Between Tossa and **Lloret de Mar**, the road follows a spectacular **clifftop route★★**.

Tossa de Mar★
www.infotossa.com.
This sandy beach curves around to Punta del Faro, the promontory on which stand the lighthouse and the 13C walls of the **Vila Vella★** (old town).
The **Museu Municipal★** *(Roig i Soler;* ◷*open Tue–Sat 10am–2pm, 4–6pm, Sun 10am–2pm;* ◈*€3;* ℘*972 34 07 09)* contains artefacts from an ancient Roman villa nearby, and works by artists who stayed in the 1930s including Chagall, Masson and Benet.

▷ 20km/12mi from Tossa de Mar.

Sant Feliu de Guíxols★
www.guixols.cat.
Sheltered from the last spurs of the Serra de les Gavarres, this is a popular location on this coast, alongside bigger draws like Lloret, Tossa, Platja d'Aro and Blanes. Its seaside boulevard, Passeig de la Mar, is lined with pavement cafés.
The **Església-Monastir de Sant Feliu★** is part of a former Benedictine monastery. Its remains tower over the small municipality. It has retained its Romanesque façade, known as the **Porta Ferrada★★**, with horseshoe arches dating to pre-Romanesque times. The interior (14C) is Gothic in style.
The lookout by the chapel of Sant Elm commands beautiful **views★★**.
Sant Feliu de Guixol has an exciting new venue; the **Centre d'art de Pintura Catalana Carmen Thyssen-Bornemisza**. An immense 19C cork factory, situated in front of the monastery, is being converted for the museum, to house over 350 works from 19C and 20C Catalan painters, as well as an auditorium.
Located on the edge of the town of Vila d'Aro, the **Roca de Pedralta★**, one of the largest rocking or "logan" stones in Europe, is a wonderful vantage point on the bay.

▷ 3km/1.8mi north of San Feliu, along the coast.

S'Agaro★
An elegant resort with chalets and luxury villas surrounded by tidy gardens and pine forests. The Camino de Ronda offers fine **views★** of the sheer cliffs.

▷ 3.3km/3mi from S'agaro via the C 253.

Platja d'Aro
www.platjadaro.com.
This coastal resort was built for the sole purpose of holidays. It comes alive during the summer when the streets become cosmopolitan and noisy and its fine stretch of sand packed with holiday makers.

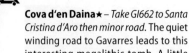

Cova d'en Daina★ – *Take Gl662 to Santa Cristina d'Aro then minor road.* The quiet winding road to Gavarres leads to this interesting megalithic tomb. A little further along, the medieval village of Romanyà de la Selva is worth a look.

▶ 5.5km/3.5mi from Platja d'Aro.

Palamós
www.palamos.cat.
This fishing port has a vibrant marina offering a range of leisure services.
Museu de la Pesca – ◷*Open mid-Jun–mid-Sept 10am–9pm; rest of the year Tue–Sat 10am–1.30pm, 3–7pm; Sun and hols 10am–2pm, 2–7pm.* ◷*Closed 1 and 6 Jan, 1 May, 24 and 31 Dec.* ◉€3. ℘*972 600 424. www.museudelapesca.org.* This museum takes you on a journey into the world of fishing and its traditions, particularly those inherent to the Costa Brava. The traditional boats are a highlight.

FROM PALAFRUGELL TO THE ILLES MEDES
59km/36.5mi. Allow half a day.
This stretch of the Costa Brava is where the scenery is at its most spectacular, particularly around the Cap de Begur.

Palafrugell
www.visitpalafrugell.cat.
The town centre is set back a short way from the coastline, on which a number of small resorts have developed. In the early 20C, the production of cork made it extremely prosperous.
It is also the birthplace of the prolific writer Josep Pla (1897–1981). Palafrugell is very popular with visitors, especially in summer when they come for its festive atmosphere. *Suquet* – a fish stew – is a local speciality.
Museu del Suro (Cork Museum) – *Calle Tarongeta 31.* ℘*972 307 825. www.museudelsuro.cat.* This museum explains the different processes involved in the manufacture of cork. Most interesting are the old utensils used for to wash and cut the substance.

▶ 4.5km/2.7mi S on the GIV 6546.

Calella de Palafrugell★
This fishing harbour is known for its **Festival de Habaneras** on the first Saturday in July. Visitors enjoy Afro-Cuban songs and dances while sipping *cremat*, flambéed coffee with rum.
The **Jardí Botànic del Cap Roig** (◷*open Apr–Sept daily 9am–8pm; rest of the year daily 9am–6pm;* ◉€6; ℘*972 61 45 82)* is built on terraces carved out of the rock, overlooking the Mediterranean. It is planted with more than 1,200 species laid out along shaded avenues. The gardens offer wonderful **views★★** of the coast.

▶ 2km/1.2mi from Calella de Palafrugell by the small coastal road leading to Cap de Sant Sebastià or walk by the GR 12 footpath, which runs along the coast (15min).

Llafranc
As is the case of Calella de Palafrugell, traditional fishermen's houses are juxtaposed with modern summer residences in Llafranc. The marina, which has 140 moorings, is the main attraction along with a small beach offering a host of summer activities.

Phare de Sant Sebastià★
Built in 1857, the lighthouse stands on a tiny isthmus surrounded by steep cliffs. The nearby hermitage commands a lovely **view★**.

Tamariu
The coves of Aigua-Xelida (Gelida), Llarga and Marquesa are all extremely beautiful and in some cases relatively unspoilt thanks to careful planning.

Begur★
www.visitbegur.cat.
The town stands back from the sea at an altitude of 200m/656ft. The castle ruins (16C–17C) offer a nice view of the Cap de Begur. Its short coastline includes pretty coves notably Aiguablava and Sa Tuna.

▶ Leave the coast road and go towards Pals on the GI 653.

Pals★★

The Barri Vell of Pals (Old Quarter also called **El Pedró★**) has preserved its medieval atmosphere intact. A Romanesque tower, the Torre de les Hores, stands proud of a cluster of handsome stone houses standing on narrow streets. The Platja de Pals, a long broad stretch of sand, is at some distance from the town.

Take the GI 652 through Torrent, then turn right on the C 66. 12km/7.5mi from Pals.

La Bisbal d'Emporda

The capital of the Baix Empordá region has been famous for its ceramics and pottery for centuries and around this a vibrant crafts community has evolved. Along its main streets you will find dozens of shops selling the distinctive yellow, green and clay-coloured pots, vases and cookware of the Costa Brava. **Castell★** – *Pl. del Castell.* ○*Open winter Tue–Sun 10am–1pm; summer daily 11am –2pm, 5–8pm.* ✆*€2.* 🖉 *972 645 166.* The former residence of the Bishops of Girona is the most remarkable building in La Bisbal, combining Romanesque and Gothic elements. Part of the building houses archives of the region.

Back on the C 66, turn left on the C 252, then right on the GI 651.

Peratallada★★

This fortified **village** is considered one of the finest medieval ensembles in the Empordà.
Winding old streets lead to the Plaça Major (main square) where a grand castle-fortress sits, now a luxury hotel. Also seek out the **Plaça de les Voltes**, with charming porticoes and ancient dwellings, one of the most characteristic snapshots of the village.
The church of **Sant Esteve**, an austere 13C building situated outside the village, has a bell perforated with a pattern common to the region.

Continue on the GI 651.

Sant Julià de Boada

This Pre-Romanesque church (10C) stands in the municipal area of Palau-sator. It has been well restored.

Return for Peratallada, then right.

Palau-sator

At weekends and in holiday periods, people descend on the restaurants of this peaceful little village, which is laid out on a well-preserved medieval plan.

Minor road to Ullastret.

Ullastret★

This is one of the most picturesque villages in Empordà's hinterland. Its old medieval streets exude bags of character and it's a great place to buy regional products. The Church of Sant Pere – located in the centre of the village – is a fine example of Romanesque architecture. Notice the curious Gothic ossuary with its carvings of characters and animals.
Ciutat Ibérica★★ – *1km/half a mile E of Ullastret.* ○*Open Oct–May daily except Mon 10am–2pm, 3–6pm, Jun–Sept daily except Tues 10am–8pm.* ○*Closed 1 Jan, 25 and 26 Dec.* ✆*€2.30 (no charge under 16 years).* 🖉 *972 179 058. www.mac.cat.* One of Catalonia's most extensive Iberian discoveries is situated near Ullastret on the crest of Mont de Sant Andreu. Here you can see the remains of a settlement built by the Indiket tribe in the 5C, who constructed canals, a reservoir and a main square. Artefacts such as scripts can be viewed in the Archaeological Museum on the same site.

Take the GI 644 north and then turn right on the GI 643.

Torroella de Montgrí★

Despite a Baroque front, the 14C **Església de Sant Genís** *(Pas. de l'Església)* is a fine example of Gothic Catalan art.
The **castle** on Montaña de Montgrì (🚶 *1hr on a signposted path among the rocks)* is an extraordinary **belvedere★★** with a view to the sea and the Gavarres mountain range.

▶ GI641 to L'Estartit on the coast.

👤👤 Illes Medes★★

Boat trips around the islands leave from l'Estartit. 🛈*For information contact the tourist office.* 📞*972 75 17 49 . www.visitestartit.com.*

These seven islets and coral reefs are the extension of the calcareous massif of Montgrí. They are interesting to ecologists for their marine species and ecosystems. The islets are popular for snorkelling and scuba diving.

③ THE GULF OF ROSES

36km/22mi. ▶ *Leave from L'Escala, 15.5km/9.5mi north of Torroella de Montgrí, on the C 31 and the GI 632.*

The vast majority of this stretch of coastline forms part of the Parc Natural dels Aiguamolls de l'Empordà.

L'Escala★

This resort has sandy beaches and a long fishing tradition (anchovies are salted). Two inlets protect its harbour.

Empúries★★

👣*See p214.*

▶ Leaving Empúries, take the C 31 and join the C 260 towards Roses, via Castelló d'Empúries.

Castelló d'Empúries★

The former capital of the principality of Empúries (11C–14C) is on a promontory near the coast. The 14C–15C **Basílica de Santa Maria**★ (🕐*open daily noon–2pm, 4–8pm;* 📞*972 25 05 19)* is flanked by a typical Catalan belfry. The **portal**★★ is a unique example of Gothic art in Catalonia: the tympanum illustrates the Adoration of the Magi while the Apostles are shown on the jambs. The large central nave is lined by fine cylindrical pillars. The alabaster **retable**★ in the high altar (15C) depicts the Passion.
The village retains buildings from its golden age: the **Ajuntament** (Maritime Commodities Exchange), combining Romanesque and Gothic elements, and the **Casa Gran**, of Gothic inspiration.

▶ Take the C 260 heading east.

Empuriabrava★

The luxury marina-residential development alternates roads with canals and offers the unusual spectacular of yachts moored at the doors of houses.

▶ Take the C 260 heading east.

Roses★

www.roses.cat.
Sailors from the Greek island of Rhodes founded a colony on this splendid natural harbour in the 4th century BC. Its 16C Renaissance **citadel**★ *(Av. de Roses;* 🕐*open Jul–Aug 10am-9pm Apr & Sept Tue–Sun, 10am–8pm; Oct–Mar Tue–Sun 10am–6pm;* 🕐*closed 25 Dec, 1, 6 Jan;* 🎫*€5;* 📞*972 15 14 66; www.rosesfhn.org)*, a pentagon with many bastions, was commissioned by Charles V. The Benedictine monastery inside was destroyed by the French during the War of Independence. The town is both resort and fishing port.

FROM CADAQUÉS TO PORT-BOU

52km/32mi. Allow half a day.

This route traverses the northernmost stretch of the Catalan coast, from the beautiful peninsula of Cap de Creus (👣 *see p208)* reaching Port-Bou at the French border. Begin the drive at Cadaqués (👣*see p207.*

Cadaqués★★

👣*See p207.*

Portlligat★

👣*See p207.*

Parc naturel du Cap de Creus★★

Cabo de Creus. 👣*See p208.*

▶ Return to Cadaqués and take the little roads heading inland (the GI 614 and the GI 613).

Illes Medes

© Toni Leon / Torroella de Montgri–Estartit

El Port de la Selva★

This bay is bathed in golden sunlight at dusk. Traditional white houses stand beside numerous flats and hotels. Fishing is still one of the main activities.

▷ Leave the town heading towards Llançà and turn left on the little road that heads up to the monastery.

Monestir de Sant Pere de Rodes★★★

Leave your car in the car park and proceed on foot for 10min. *Open Tue–Sun Oct–May 10am–5pm; Jun–Sept 10am–8pm.* *Closed 1 Jan, 25 Dec.* *€4.50; no charge Tue.* *972 38 75 59.*
This imposing Benedictine monastery stands in a beautiful **setting**★★ overlooking the Gulf of León and the Cap de Creus peninsula. Begun in the 10C, it was pillaged, and abandoned in the 18C. The remarkable **church**★★★, showing pre-Romanesque influence, is an unusual example of architectural harmony. The nave roof is formed by barrel vaulting, while the narrow side aisles are covered by segmental vaults. They are separated by huge pillars, reinforced with columns on raised bases. Splendid **capitals**★ carved with intricate tracery and acanthus leaves evoke the tradition of Córdoba and Byzantium. The left arm of the transept leads to an upper ambulatory offering a sweeping view of the nave.
The 12C **bell tower**★★ is a magnificent example of Lombardy Gothic.

The coast between El Port de la Selva and Cadaqués has many irregular coves with crystal-clear waters, accessible only by sea.

▷ Go back down to the GI 612 and continue heading northwest.

El Port de Llançà★

Plaça de la Estación.
A pleasant tourist resort sited on a bay, sheltered from winds like the *tramontana* and sudden Mediterranean storms. The shallow waters are ideal for swimming.

▷ Take the N 260 or the GI 612.

Portbou★

Bordering French Roussillon, this popular holiday spot is also one of Catalonia's main border crossings, especially for rail traffic. The nucleus of Portbou is in fact situated next to the railway station. Nevertheless, Portbou does offer some amazing coastal scenery. Whether you come in via the N 260 or by the magnificent GI 612 coastal route, you can admire some of the steepest cliffs on the Catalan coast and countless pristine coves.

ADDRESSES

🛏 STAY

Accommodation on the **Costa Brava** can be expensive, and it is often difficult to find a room during high season without having booked well in advance. For more reasonable prices and better availability search inland as well.

Hotel La Goleta – *Pintor Terruella 22, El Port de LLançà.* 972 38 01 25. *www.hotellagoleta.com. 30rms. 78/105€.* Close to the port, the La Goleta offers comfort and an interesting décor of paintings and other furnishings. A friendly atmosphere and good value for money.

Hotel Diana – *Plaça de Espanya 6, Tossa de Mar.* 972 34 18 86. *www.hotelesdante.com. 21rms. 135/180€.* The interior of this splendid Modernist building by the sea is exquisite, with high ceilings, cool rooms and a patio adorned with a marble fountain. The rooms are comfortable and furnished in style.

Hotel Plaça – *Pl. Mercat 22, Sant Feliu de Guíxols.* 972 32 51 55. *www.hotelplaza.org. 19rms. 89.50/123€.* A practical choice for location and functional character. Pleasant, bright rooms – some overlook a square that's lively on market days. Outdoor jacuzzi and solarium on the top floor.

Hotel Sant Roc – *Pl. Atlàntic 2 (Sant Roc district), Calella de Palafrugell.* 972 61 42 50. *www.santroc.com. 45rms. 90/154€. Rest. 30/40€.* This charming building crowned by a small tower enjoys a peaceful, relaxing setting amid pine groves overlooking the Mediterranean. The rooms are spacious and elegant, while the restaurant terrace enjoys fine views of neighbouring coves. Half-board compulsory in summer.

⌾/EAT

Snackmar Las Golondrinas – *Sant Sebastià 63, Roses.* 972 153 705. *Closed Mon and Nov–Dec. 6/15€.* This small tapas bar, run by a former alumnus of El Bulli (Ferran Adrià's restaurant), is where many of the chefs who worked there ate in their down time. Well above the average tourist haunts in Roses.

La Brasa– *Pl. de Catalunya, 6 El Port de Llançà.* 972 38 02 02. *Closed Tue except in summer, mid-Dec–late Feb. 25/44€.* Low-key restaurant serving excellent grilled meat and fish on its shady terrace.

L Ca l'Herminda– *L'Illa, 7, El Port de la Selva.* 972 38 02 02. *Closed Mon and Tue eves Apr–Jun. 35/40€.* Housed in a former fisherman's cottage this is a perfect restaurant for eating fresh fish at reasonable prices. Rustic in décor, the dining rooms are spread over several levels.

NIGHTLIFE

Moxo – *Empuriabrava.* The Moxo is the focal point for nightlife in this modern tourist resort, which has about 20 bars, nightclubs and restaurants. The Saloon specialises in country music and the Glass in techno.

Café Latino – *Rbla Roma, 10, Lloret de Mar.* 972 366 153. A lively dance bar where Latin music and cocktails are king.

Cala Banys – *Cami Cala Banys, Lloret de Mar.* 972 366 515 3. One of the most romantic bars in the Costa Brava. This little paradise is as enchanting by day as it is by night with a shady terrace overlooking the water.

ACTIVITIES

Nautilus – *Pg Marítim 23, L'Estartit.* 972 751 489. *www.nautilus.es.* Tours of the Medes Islands on board glass-bottom boats (90min, €18 per person); Jul–Sep three sailings a week to Sant Martí to Empúries (2.30hr, €22pp), and twice a week to Cadaqués and Cap de Creus (5hr, €27pp).

International Diving Center – *At the far end of the port, L'Escala.* 972 770 077 and 610 015 920. *www.internationaldiving.com.* Authorised dives around the Cap de Creus. (€24–65pp depending on options chosen).

Creuers Mare Nostrum – *Maranges 3, L'Escala.* 972 773 797. *www.creuers-marenostrum.com.* A fleet of 10 glass-bottom boats (including 2 catamarans) that tour the Medes Islands.

Parc Aquàtic Aqua Brava – *Ctra de Cadaqués. 1km/0.5mi from Roses. Jun–mid-Sept 10am–7pm.* 972 254 344. *www.aqua brava.com.* Water park known for its huge wave pool, sandy beach and tropical vegetation. €25 day (children up to 1.20m/3ft6 €15) or €18 half a day (€10).

SHOPPING

Carrer de l'Aigüeta – *La Bisbal d'Empordà.* Ceramics are a centuries-old tradition, and you'll find all sorts of objects in the shops on this street. Try El Risser.

Cadaqués★★

This beautiful fishing village is one of the most charming in Catalonia. Located on the southern coast of Cap de Creus, its picturesque streets and bohemian atmosphere fascinated many famous artists in the first half of the 20C, including Picasso, Man Ray, Buñuel and Thomas Mann. Salvador Dalí spent much of his life in nearby Port Ligat. Cap de Creus became a recurring theme in his work.

THE TOWN TODAY

In high summer, Cadaqués has remained a fashionable retreat for Catalans and a large number of French visitors, so at times it can feel more like a resort on the French Riviera than a remote village in Northern Spain. Chic galleries and cafés line the waterfront and the local fleet of fishing boats is joined by pleasure yachts. Such is the town's cachet that a seaside development in China will reproduce the whitewashed and bougainvillea-covered houses in a project that aims to replicate this archetypal Catalan seaside resort.

SIGHTS
Església de Santa Maria

Pl. Dr Callis 15. ⚬━ Open Mass only: Sat 7pm, Sun 11am (altarpiece can be viewed from the exterior via window). Overlooking the *casco antiguo* and indeed the focal point of the village, white-washed houses with picturesque porticoes cluster around the Església de Santa Maria, whose sober exterior contrasts with its interior: note the lovely **Baroque altarpiece★★** in gilded wood by Joan Torres. The town hosts an annual international music festival *(late Jul–early Aug; www.festival cadaques.cat).*

EXCURSIONS
Portlligat★

2km/1.2mi to the north.
The **Casa-Museu Salvador Dalí★** (⏱ *open mid-Jun–mid-Sept daily 10.30am–8pm; mid-Sep–Dec and mid-*

▶ **Population:** 3 000
⚙ **Michelin Map:** 574 F 39.
🔲 **Info:** Des Cotxe 2-A. ℘972 258 315. www.cadaques.cat.
◑ **Location:** 36km/21mi S of the French border and 39km/24mi E of Figueres.
◷ **Timing:** If Cadaqués becomes a quiet, out-of-the-way place in winter, in summer it is just the opposite. The road from Roses is converted into one long traffic jam and the town centre is blocked with vehicles, making it difficult to park. Nevertheless, a car is essential you want to get to the less frequented beaches. Whatever the season, make reservations well in advance.
🚫 **Don't Miss:** A boat trip to see the Cap de Creus nature reserve.
👨‍👦 **Kids:** The Surrealist décor of the Casa-Museu Salvador Dalí, in particular the gardens; the natural splendour of the Cap de Creus.

View of Cadaqués

© Calle Montes / Photononstop

Mar–mid-Jun Tue–Sun 10.30am–6pm; ⏰closed Jan–mid-Mar, 25 Dec; ⬤€11; ☎972 25 10 15; www.salvador-dali.org) is a cluster of fishermen's houses converted by Dalí and his wife Gala into a studio, library and other rooms, all now open to the public. The garden is particularly interesting.

👥 Parque Natural de Cap de Creus★★

4km/2.4mi to the north.

Steep roads and paths wind between cliffs and hidden bays to Cap de Creus, Spain's most easterly point. Many people come to enjoy a spectacular **view at sunset★★★**, which can be experienced from the terrace of the Restaurant Cap de Creus, next to the lighthouse at the highest point (☎972 19 90 05).

ADDRESSES

♿*See also* addresses of accommodation and restaurants under **Costa Brava** (p206).

📇 STAY

🛏 Cadaqués has around ten hotels of two or three stars, without having disfigured the seafront. In the streets of the old town there are several comfortable pensions in which the price varies according to the season. Half a dozen estate agents can arrange apartment rentals *(ask for a list in the tourist information office).*

⬤🛏 **Hostal Vehi** – *Pl. de l'Església 6. ☎972 258 470. www.hostalvehi.com. Closed Nov–Mar. 11 rms. 35/75€. ⬛6€.* Long-established, family-run hotel offering a warm welcome, situated in a peaceful corner of the old town, near the church. Comfortable bedrooms and well-maintained shared bathrooms. Charming place to stay.

⬤🛏 **Hotel Ubaldo** – *Unió 13. ☎972 258 125. www.hotelubaldo.com. 26 rms. 60/80€.* Behind its white façade, this hotel hides an elegant décor illuminated by indirect light. The rooms look onto the little streets of old Cadaqués.

⬤🛏🛏🛏 **Hotel Port Lligat** – *Avenida Salvador Dalí 1, Port Lligat. ☎972 25 81 62. www.port-lligat.net/hotel. 30 rms. 79/141€. ⬛€10.* The creature comforts in this attractive blue and white building, in a cove full of fishing boats near Dalí's house, are particularly popular with guests. Every room is different, and if you don't mind paying a bit extra, ask for one with a sea view.

🍴 EAT

🍽 All along the Passeig, as far as the Punta des Baluard, there are various types of restaurant to choose from. Set lunch menus are affordable (around 15€).

⬤🍽 **Casa Anita** – *Miquel Rosset 16. ☎972 258 471. www.cbrava.com/anita/anita.fr.htm. Open daily except Mon 1.30–3pm, 8.30–10.30 pm. Closed Nov. 20/40€.* "Here all customers are equal and the king himself is treated like all the rest." That's the philosophy of this little tavern, which is an institution in the region and is not to be missed. The menu is devised with seasonal produce from the market and is presented by Joan, who can also advise on wines and *cavas*. Reserve or you will have to queue in the street!

⬤🍽🍽 **Compartir** – *Unió 14 . ☎952 258 483. fr.compartircadaques.com. Open lunch 1–3.45pm; dinner 8–11pm Jul–Sept: Tue–Sun lunch and dinner; May–Jun and Oct Tue–Sat lunch and dinner, Sun lunch only; Dec: Wed–Sat lunch and dinner, Sun lunch only seult. Closed 30 May, 3, 12, 17 and 28 Sep, Jan–Apr, 5 Nov–2 Dec and 25–27 Dec. 30/60€.* "Compartir" means to share and that is what three of Ferran Adrià's former associates intend you to do. They have pooled their talents to create this restaurant where the recommended dishes are shared among all diners. Two apartments and two guest rooms.

ON THE TOWN

La Habana – *Doctor Bartomeus –* ☎*972 258 689. 9pm–2.30am.* A bar for romantics: the ideal place to round off an evening with a cocktail.

ACTIVITIES

Sotamar Diving Center – *Av. Caritat Serinyana, 17. ☎972 258 876. www.sotamar.com.* Hire of diving equipment, trips out to sea, trial dives.

SHOPPING

Market – Every Monday at the entrance to town, carrer Riera de Sant Vincenç.

Figueres★

Figueres, capital of Alt Empordà,
the birthplace of Surrealist artist
Salvador Dalí (1904–89), is one of
Catalonia's premier destinations.
Dalí spent his last years here,
building his extravagant museum.

A BIT OF HISTORY
The end of the Spanish Civil War – The
last meeting of the Republican Cortes
was held here on 1 February 1939. Three
days later, Girona fell to the Nationalists.
Two days after, the Republican leaders
crossed into France.

SIGHTS
Figueres has a pleasant historical centre
with attractive squares and alleys. The
Rambla is a pleasant street full of outdoor bars and restaurants.

Museu de l'Empordà
Rambla 2. ◷*Open Tue–Sat 11am–7pm,
Sun and public holidays 11am–2pm.*
◷*Closed 1, 6 Jan and 25–26 Dec.* ◉*€4;
no charge with Museu Dalí ticket.* ℘*972
50 23 05. www.museuemporda.org.*
This building houses collections devoted
to the art, history and archaeology of
the region. Of note is the exhibition of
works by 19C and 20C painters (Nonell,
Sorolla, Dalí and Tàpies).

Església de Sant Pere
Pl. de l'Església. ◷*Open Tue–Fri 9am–
1pm, 4.30–8pm (9pm Sat); Sun 8.30am–
1pm, 6–9pm.* ◷*Closed 25–26 Dec, 1, 6
Jan.* ◉*€2; no charge 18 May.*
℘*972 50 03 25.*
Built in the late 13C, this church has a
single nave of Gothic influence. Most of
the church was rebuilt after the Spanish
Civil War.

Teatre-Museu Dalí★★
Pl. de Dalí i Gala. ◷*Open Jun–Sep
daily 9am–8pm; Oct–May Tue–Sun
10.30am–6pm.* ◷*Closed 1 Jan, 25 Dec.*
◉*€13.* ℘*972 67 75 24. www.salvador-
dali.org.*
The theatre-museum, a world of folly
and caprice, may charm or exasperate

- **Population:** 44 255
- **Michelin Map:** 574 F 38 –
  map 122 Costa Brava.
  See local map under Costa
  Brava p347.
- **Info:** Plaça del Sol. ℘972
  50 31 55. www.figueres
  ciutat.com
- **Location:** Figueres is
  located 20km/12.4mi
  inland, at the heart of the
  comarca of Alt Empordà,
  and at the crossroads of
  routes leading to the Costa
  Brava and the French city of
  Perpignan, 58km/36mi N.
  ▭Plaça de La Estació.
- **Don't Miss:** Everything
  Dalí: the Museum and
  Tower.
- **Timing:** Take a half-day
  at least, or longer if Dalí is
  your thing.
- **Kids:** As a change from
  Surrealism, take your
  children to the Museu del
  Joguet (Toy Museum),
  which has a collection of
  4,000 exhibits.

but never fails to impress. The artist himself said: "The museum cannot be considered as such; it is a gigantic surrealist
object, where everything is coherent,
where nothing has eluded my design."
To a restored 1850 theatre Dalí added
an immense glass dome (beneath which
he is buried) and patio, and decorated
everything with fantasy objects: giant
eggs, bread rolls, basins and gilt dum-
mies. He gave his eccentricity full rein in
the squares around the museum where
figures perch on columns of tyres, as
well as inside. Some of his canvases are
exhibited as well as works by Pitxot and
Duchamp.

Torre Galatea★
The decoration of this tower by Dalí used
vivid colours and fantasy objects.

Museu del Joguet★

Hotel París, Sant Pere 1. ○*Open Jun–Sept Mon–Sat 10am–7pm, Sun and public holidays 11am–6pm; Oct–May Tue–Sat 10am–6pm, Sun and public holidays 11am–2pm.* ○*Closed 25 Dec, 1 Jan.* ∞*€5.* ☏*972 50 45 85. www.mjc.cat.*

The museum displays toys and stuffed animals from different countries.

EXCURSIONS
Castell de Sant Ferran★

⟜⟜*Guided tours (2hr) daily Jul–mid-Sept 10.30am–8pm; Oct–Jun 10.30am–3pm. mornings only* ○*Closed 1 Jan, 25 Dec.* ∞*€3.* ☏*972 51 45 85. www.castillosanfernando.org.*

This mid-18C fortress, with star-shaped perimeter, defended the border with France. The castle was the second largest of its kind in Europe, with a parade ground alone that covered 12 000sq m/14 340sq yd. The **stables★** are worthy of particular note. The **views★** from the walls take in the Empordà plain.

Vilabertran★

⊙ *2km/1.5mi north via a turning off the N II.*

This unusual village grew up around a monastery. It has a picturesque centre with straight narrow streets lined with old houses. Some of these have beautiful Gothic doorways.

Canònica de Santa Maria★★ – ☏*972 508 787.* ∞*3€ (under 18 2€).* The monastery was founded in the 11C as a community of Augustinian canons and despite subsequent changes is still a remarkable assembly of Romanesque buildings. In 1295 it was the setting for the marriage of James II of Aragon and Blanche of Anjou. Each year in September it becomes the venue for the **Schubertíada Music Festival**, an event of great prestige.

Built in the 11 and 12C, the **church★** is basilical in plan, with a nave and two aisles. It's a simple building but one of great beauty, the columns and pilasters giving it a sense of lightness in contrast with the solidity of the walls. Three apses open from the transept. The nave is covered by a barrel vault, while the aisles are roofed with vaults of segmental arches and the apses with semi-domes. To the right of the church stands the **belltower**, rising through three storeys, each bearing paired windows and decorated with Lombard bands.

The Romanesque **cloister★** (12C), trapezoid in plan, is surrounded by monastic outbuildings (12–14C). Built according to the norms of Cistercian architecture, the cloister is austere in character. The arcades, constructed with segmental arches, open onto the quadrangle through semi-circular arches supported on unadorned capitals.

The **abbot's house★** was built by abbot Antonio Girgós (1410–1424). A remarkable example of the Gothic style, its sober appearance, in perfect harmony with the other buildings, emphasises the solemnity of the monastery. The **façade** is pierced by a portal and delicate Gothic windows.

Peralada★

⊙ *7km/4.5mi northeast of Figueres by the N 260.* ▯ *Pl. Peixateria 6.* ☏*972 538 840. www.peralada.org. Jul–Aug : 10am–8pm ; Sep–Jun : daily except Mon 10am–2pm, 4–7pm, Sun and hols 10am–2pm.*

This little town is perched on a hill in the middle of an extraordinary landscape of vines, north of Figueres. Contained within the medieval walls is an interesting nucleus of small, irregular squares and narrow streets on which stand many antique shops. The **castle★** serves as a setting for a prestigious international music festival.

La Jonquera

⊙ *16km/10mi north by the N II or the A 7 motorway.*

This town has become one vast supermarket serving French day-trippers in search of bargains, due to its location just a few kilometres from the border.

Teatre-Museu Dalí, Figueres

© Teatre-Museu Dalí/ Spanish Tourist Office

The World of Dalí

Born in 1904, Dalí was to become one of the most famous Surrealist artists. His "paranoid-critical" method, based on an ironic vision of reality, resulted in his expulsion from the Surrealist ranks by its founder, André Breton. In his most famous paintings, *The Great Masturbator*, *The Persistence of Memory*, *Atomic Leda and Premonition of the Civil War*, Dalí expresses his personal world through bland forms loaded with sensuality and sexual connotations.

The Dalían attractions in Figueres are both located around the lively Plaça de Dalí i Gala. Further examples of Dalí's creativity can be seen in two museums within a short distance of Figueres: the first, the **Casa-Museu Salvador Dalí**, is situated in the charming fishing village of **Portlligat★★** (*see p207*), 31km/19.2mi E of Figueres on the C 260 and GI 614; the second, the **Casa-Museu Castell Gala Dalí** in Púbol, 16km/10mi E of Girona on the C 66, is housed in the castle that Dalí gave to his wife, Gala, as a gift in 1970. Together they are known as the Dalían Triangle.

ADDRESSES

🍽 STAY

IN FIGUERES

🛏🛏 **Hotel Los Ángeles** – *Barceloneta 10.* 𝄐*972 510 661. www.hotelangeles.com.* 🅿. *40 rms from 60€.* 🍽*5€.* Beautiful hotel in a small, peaceful street. Some rooms on the top floor have a view of the town. Half-board and full-board packages are available, in partnership with the El Gallo Rojo restaurant.

🛏🛏 **Hotel Rambla** – *Rambla 33.* 𝄐*972 676 020. www.hotelrambla.net. 24 rms 55/75€.* 🍽*6€.* Giving onto the Rambla, this little hotel is simple and comfortable with well-equipped rooms.

🛏🛏 **Hotel Travé** – *Balmes 70.* 𝄐*972 500 591. www.hoteltrave.com.* 🅿🏊. *76 rms. 66/96€.* 🍽*8€. Restaurant 17€.* Although a little far from the centre, this discreet family hotel offers rooms that are both classic and comfortable, even if the décor is a little plain. Good restaurant.

🛏🛏🛏 **Duràn Hotel** – *Lasauca 5.* 𝄐*972 50 12 50. www.hotelduran.com. 65rms. 69/119€.* 🍽 *€11. Rest. 20/45€.* This hotel is in the town centre near the Dalí Museum. It has large, comfortable rooms. The restaurant, specialising in Catalan dishes, is where Dalí himself used to dine.

🛏🛏🛏🛏 **Hotel Rural Mas Falgarona** – *Avinyonet de Puigventós. 5.4km/3.3mi SW of Figueres on the N 260.* 𝄐*972 54 66 28. www.masfalgarona.com. 11 rms. 160/198€.* 🍽. *Restaurant 40/65€.* This luxury hotel is housed in an old farmhouse. The minimalist décor, enhanced by various works of modern art, brings out the natural beauty of the stone, brick and wood. Delightful garden with pool.

IN PERALADA

🛏🛏 **Hostal de la Font** – *Font 15–19.* 𝄐*972 538 508. www.hostaldelafont.es. 12 rms. 75/122€.* 🍽. Pleasant rooms with wood floors, rustic style furniture and up-to-date bathrooms. The charming sitting room looks onto a beautiful inner patio full of plants.

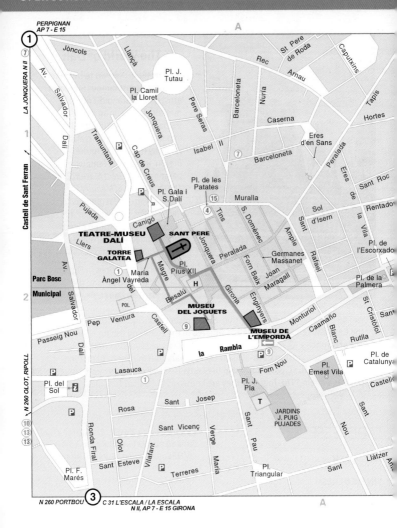

⍲/EAT

IN FIGUERES AND NEARBY

⌓ **Restaurador** – *Muralla, 1 (near the pl. de les Patates). Menu 12€.* This little restaurant away from the crowds serves an excellent seasonal cuisine in a modern setting.

⌓ **El Café del Barri Vell** – *Pl. de les Patates 7. ☏972 505 776. Open daily except Mon 5pm–2am. Around 15€.* Vegetable dishes, salads and toasts are served in this cafe, which stands on a very agreeable little square. Performances of dance and music are held in summer.

⌓ **Gastrobar Sentits** – *Rambla 12. ☏972 677 546. Menu 12€.* The perfect place for a light lunch, away from the crowds visiting the Theatre-Museum.

⌓⊜⊜ **Antaviana** – *Llers 5. ☏972 510 377. www.restaurantantaviana.cat. Closed Mon and Tue. 35/40€.* A place to relax after visiting the museums. A creative cuisine, accompanied by regional wines, is served in a beautiful dining room decorated with the works of local artists.

⌓⊜⊜ **El Molí** – *Pont de Molins. 6km/4mi northwest of Figueres on the N 11 and 2km/ 1mi west of Pont de Molins. ☏972 529 271. Closed Tue evening, Wed and mid-Dec–mid-Jan. Around 45€.* Welcoming restaurant in a converted mill. Rustic decoration with attention to detail. The menu includes dishes typical

WHERE TO STAY

Duràn Hotel .... ①

Hotel Los Ángeles .... ⑦

Hotel Rambla...................... ⑨

Hotel Rural
Mas Falgarona .... ⑩

Hotel Travé .... ⑬

WHERE TO EAT

Antaviana .... ①

El Café del
Barri Vell .... ④

El Molí .... ⑦

Gastrobar Sentits................ ⑨

Mas Pau .... ⑬

Restaurador....................... ⑮

FIGUERES

of the Empordà. Also a hotel with 15 comfortable rooms.

⊜⊜⊜⊜ **Mas Pau Hotel and Restaurant** – *Avinyonet de Puigventós. 5km/3mi SW of Figueres on the N 260. ℘972 54 61 54. www.maspau.com. Closed Sun evening, Mon and Tue lunch except in summer, and Jan–mid-Mar. 53/72€. Rooms 100/115€.* This 16C farmhouse has been sympathetically restored and decorated in exquisite taste. The restaurant serves creative Catalan cuisine. Also a hotel.

IN PERALADA

⊕ Today the name of Peralada is assoociated with some excellent wines and *cavas*.

⊜⊜⊜ **Cal Sagristà** – *Rodona 2. ℘972 538 301. Closed Mon evening and Tue (except Jul–Aug and public holidays), 2 weeks in Feb and 2 weeks in Nov. Around 35€.* A restaurant installed in an old house in the centre of Peralada. Rustic decoration, attentive service and traditional cuisine.

⊜⊜⊜ **Ca la Maria** – *Mollet de Peralada. 4km/2.5mi north of Peralada. ℘972 563 382. www.restaurantcalamaria.net. Reservation advised. Around 35€.* Spacious restaurant in the countryside, which gets busy at weekends. Catalan cuisine.

Empúries★★

The history of the Mediterranean is written into the ruins of this archaeological site which, from its beautiful emplacement on the coast, looks over the blue waters from which its founders emerged. From the Greek colony of Emporion (meaning "market") and the Roman city of Emporiæ that replaced it, classical culture spread throughout the Iberian peninsula.

A BIT OF HISTORY

Empúries is divided into three parts tracing the settlement's historical development. In the mid-6C BC, Greek settlers founded the old town, known as the **Palaia Polis**, on an offshore island. The site, now joined to the mainland, is occupied by the village of Sant Marti d'Empúries which stands apart from the rest of the archaeological remains.

A new town, the **Neapolis,** gradually eveloved on the shore opposite the Palaia Polis. Together, the two parts of the town made up Emporion.

- **Michelin Map:** 574 F 39.
- **Location:** Empúries is 2km/1mi from L'Escala (see p204), a fishing town on the south coast of the Gulf of Roses. The archaeological site is in the comarca (region) of l'Empordà, to which it gives its name.
- **Timing:** Allow 2hr. Vist in the late afternoon to enjoy the sunset over the charming village of Sant Martí d'Empúries.

As a Roman ally during the Punic Wars, Emporion saw the arrival of an expedition led by Scipio Africanus Major in 218 BC. In 100 BC the Roman town was established to the west. The two centres became one when Augustus bestowed Roman citizenship upon the Greeks. The further evolution of Emporiæ, however, was slowed during the first century BC by the growth of the nearby towns of Barcino (Barcelona),

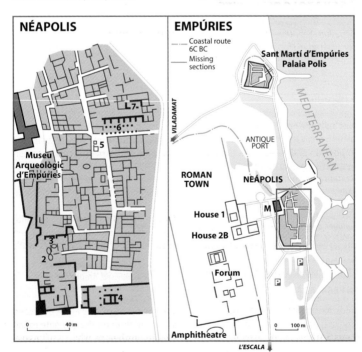

Archaeological Museum of Catalonia-Empúries

© Fons MAC-Empúries photo S. Font

Gerunda (Girona) and, above all, Tarraco (Tarragona). In the third century AD, the town declined and parts of it were abandoned, although it still served as an episcopal see, as testified by the remains of a 4C Palaeo-Christian basilica.

Later, after the expulsion of the Moors by the Franks in the 8C, the town became the capital of the medieval county of Empúries until it was replaced in this role by Castelló d'Empúries to the north.

ARCHAEOLOGICAL SITE

Puig i Cadafalch. ⏰*Oct–May 10am–6pm; Jun–Sep 10am–8pm.* ⏰*Closed 1 Jan, 25 and 26 Dec.* ⊕*€3; no charge last Sun in month, 23 Apr, 18 May and 11 Sep.* ✆*972 77 02 08. www.mac.cat.*

Neapolis

Unlike Palaia Polis, over which a village was built, the new town has been completely excavated. However, the superimposition of different structures over hundreds of years has complicated the work of archaeologists and made interpretation of the ruins more difficult. The site occupies an area of 26ha/64 acres and was fortified on three sides (to the southwest a large section of wall is preserved). It was entered by a single gateway protected by towers.

The **Templo de Asclepio** (Aesculapius – god of healing) and a sacred precinct contained altars and statues of the gods. Nearby stood a **watchtower** and drinking water cisterns. The **Templo de Zeus Serapis** (a god associated with the weather and with healing) was surrounded by a colonnade. The **Agora** was the centre of town life; three statues remain. A street from the agora to the sea was bordered on one side by the **stoa** or covered market. Behind it are the ruins of a 6C **palaeo-Christian basilica** with a rounded apse.

Museu Arqueológic

A section of Neapolis is displayed along with models of temples and finds from the excavations.

Roman Town

This was built across the road from Neapolis, on a hill overlooking the Greek town. The rectangular town covers 20ha/50 acres. Its curtain walls have been partially restored but the town has not been completely excavated.

House no. 1 (entrance at the back) has an atrium (inner courtyard) with six columns. Around this are residential apartments, the peristyle, or colonnaded court, and the impluvium, or rainwater catchment. The reception rooms are paved with mosaic.

House no. 2B has rooms paved with their original mosaic. One has been reconstituted in clay with its walls resting on stone foundations.

The **forum**, a large square lined by porticoes and, to the north and south respectively, by temples and shops, was the centre of civic life. A porticoed street led through the city gate to the oval **amphitheatre**, which is still visible.

La Seu d'Urgell★

Capital of the comarca (region) of Urgell, La Seu stands at the confluence of the Segre and Valira rivers, at the heart of an agreeable landscape of pastures, springs and high summits. The historic centre, with its narrow streets and arcades, is dominated by its magnificent cathedral and the whole thing is imbued with medieval charm. As if to create a contrast with the old quarter, two parks have been laid out and named after the rivers that flow through the town.

TOWN
Cathedrale de Santa Maria★★

Santa Maria. ◷*Open Mon–Sat 10am–1pm, 4–6pm (Jun–Sept to 7pm); Sun and public holidays 10am–1pm.* ◷*Closed 1 Jan, 1 May, 7 Jul, 15 Aug, 1 Nov, 25 Dec.* ⬤€3 (with museum). ℘*973 35 32 42.*

The cathedral, started in the 12C, shows a strong Lombard influence. The central section of the west face, crowned by a small campanile, is typically Italian.

◷ **Michelin Map:** 574 E 34.

▯ **Info:** Av. Valls d'Andorra, 33. ℘973 351 511. www.turismemseu.com. Closed Sun and holidays.

◖ **Location:** La Seu is 9.5km/5.5mi south of Andorra (p. 291). It stands at the crossroads of the N 145 and the N 260 (heading east, towards Puigcerdà), which the C 14 extends south towards LLeida. Within 30km/18mi of the town there are a few cross-country ski resorts, including Sant Joan de l'Erm.

▣ **Parking:** There is a large car park close to the historic centre.

◷ **Timing:** La Seu makes a perfect base for excursions to Andorra, to Cadí-Moixeró and the Cerdanya.

▲▲ **Kids:** Aquatic activities in the Segre olympic park.

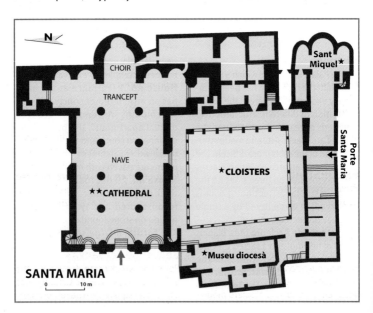

Inside, the nave rises on cruciform pillars, surrounded in French style by engaged columns. A most effective twin-arched gallery on the east transept wall reappears outside.

The **cloisters★** are 13C; the east gallery was rebuilt in 1603 and features granite capitals illustrating humans and animals carved by masons from Roussillon. The Santa Maria door (southeast corner) opens into the 11C **Església de Sant Miquel★**, the only remaining building of those constructed by St Ermangol.

Museu diocesà★

Housed in the cathedral, this museum showcases works of art dating from the 10–18C. The most precious of these is a beautifully illuminated 11C **Beatus★★**, one of the best-preserved copies of St John's Commentary on the Apocalypse, written in the 8C by the priest Beatus of Liébana. Other objects of note include an interesting **papyrus★** belonging to Pope Sylvester II. The crypt contains the 18C funerary urn of St Ermangol.

♣♣ Parc Olímpic del Segre

The artificial white water canal in this sports park was used for the canoeing competitions in the 1992 Olympics. It is still often employed for training but it is possible for anyone to practise a variety of water sports here. There are also facilities for mountain-biking (see "Activities" under "Addresses").

Parc del Valira

This park includes a modern cloister built by Luis Racionero. Its capitals depict distinguished people from recent history: Marx, Stalin, Franco, Marilyn Monroe, Picasso etc.

EXCURSION
Parc Natural del Cadí-Moixeró★

Information Centres in Bellver de Cerdanya, Casa del Bosc, ℘973 51 00 16; and Bagà (approx. 20km/12.5mi N of Berga), Centro del Parque, ℘93 824 41 51; www.parcsdecatalunya.net.
This 41,342ha/160sq mi park is located between the Cadí and Moixeró moun-

tain ranges, which form an imposing 30km/18.6mi-long barrier of altitudes varying between 900m/2,952ft and 2,647m/8,684ft.

Vertical cliffs enclose the deep valleys and canyons and the vegetation is exceptional; low temperatures and high humidity favour the proliferation of unusual Mediterranean flora.

More than 400km/248.5mi of hiking trails wind through the park, catering for all levels of ability.

➤ DRIVING TOUR

LA CERDANYA★★

145km/90mi from La Seu d'Urgell to La Molina. Allow about 5hr.
The fertile Cerdanya Basin, watered by the River Segre, was formed by subsidence. The northern section, La Cerdagne, was ceded to France under the Treaty of the Pyrénées in 1659.

The **Túnel del Cadí**, opened in 1984, facilitates access from Manresa.

From Ribes de Freser to Puigcerdà, the road cut into the cliff face up to the Collado de Toses commands impressive **views★** of the Segre and its slopes.

◗ Leave La Seu d'Urgell on the N 260 going east (towards Barcelona and Puigcerdà). Just before reaching the village of Martinet, fork left on the LV 4036 towards Lles de Cerdanya. La Pera lakes are 25km/15mi up this winding forest road.

La Pera lakes

Estanys de la Pera.
This group of lakes, situated in the upper valley of the Arànser, at an altitude of 2,330/7,645ft, is an authentic paradise for trout-fishers. The lakes are sheltered by the mountains of Monturull (2,761m/9,059 ft) and Perafita (2,752m/9,029ft).

◗ Return to the N 260 and continue E.

Bellver de Cerdanya★

Poised on a rocky crag dominating the Vall del Segre, Bellver de Cerdanya has a fine main square with beautiful balconied stone houses and wooden porches. This is one of the points of access to the **Parc naturel de Cadí-Moixeró**.

▷ Continue on the N 260 towards Puigcerdà. The road crosses the green plain of the Cerdanya.

Puigcerdà

It is very difficult to park in the town centre. Use the municipal carparks, generally close to the centre, in which the first hour is free.
The capital of Cerdanya, which developed on a terrace overlooking the River Segre, is one of the most popular holiday resorts of the Pyrénées, with old-fashioned shops, ancient streets and balconied buildings.

▷ Leaving Puigcerdà, follow the signs to "France - Bourg-Madame - Llívia". Just before the former frontier guardpost fork slightly to the left towards Llívia.

Llívia

6km/4mi from Puigcerdà, this Spanish enclave of 12sqkm/4.6sqmi, is entirely surrounded by French territory and owes its very existence to a question of vocabulary. The Treaty of the Pyrénées stipulated that the 33 villages of the Cerdanya (Cerdagne in French) would be ceded to France but Llívia had the status of town and thus remained Spanish. It consists of some picturesque little streets, the remains of a medieval chateau overlooking the town and ancient towers.
The **fortified church**, its door ornamented with typical Catalan ironwork, has a beautiful altarpiece from 1750.
Museu Municipal *Forns 10.* ☏*972 896 313.* ☞*Closed for redevelopment.* The town's museum contains, among other interesting exhibits, the well-known **Farmàcia de Llívia★**, one of the oldest pharmacies in Europe. The ceramic jars and all the apothecary's equipment (flasks, vessels and scales from the 17C et 18C) are worth seeing.

▷ Return to Puigcerdà and take the N 152 left for La Molina. As you climb, you have a panoramic view of the immense plain of the Cerdanya.

La Molina

www.lamolina.com.
This is one of Catalonia's most important ski resorts. The village of Alp is popular in winter and in summer.

VALL DEL SEGRE★

▷ *From La Seu d'Urgell to Tremp – 114km/71mi around 3hr.*
A great basin framed by mountains spreads around the confluence of the Valira and the Segre. To the north, the peaks of Salòria and Monturull, and their foothills, form part of the central axis of the Pyrénées. The mountains to the south present the characteristic scenery of the inner ranges of the pre-Pyrénées. Numerous lateral valleys, each different from the others, traverse the mountains from east to west.

▷ Take the N 260, which soon becomes the C 14, in the direction of Organyà.

Congost de Tresponts★★

The Segre winds through dark rocks (puzolana) and pastures. Downstream, the limestone of Ares and Montsec de Tost offers a typically Pyrénéan landscape dropping to a cultivated basin, where the river disappears.

Organyà

This picturesque village has a small medieval centre, with the old streets lined with arcades, porches and Gothic mansions. Organyà is renowned for the *Homilies*, the oldest known text written in Catalan, dating from the late 12C.

Pantà d'Oliana★

The dam is surrounded by grey rocks with lively waterfalls in spring. From the road the sight is quite spectacular.

▷ Turn right on the L 511 towards Isona to reach the Coll de Nargó.

Coll de Nargó

http://collnargo.ddl.net.

This hamlet has one of the most splendid Romanesque churches in Catalonia, dating back to the 11C: **Sant Climent★** has a single nave and a pretty apse adorned with Lombard bands. Its sober **bell tower★** is pre-Romanesque.

◐ Continue on the L 511 in the direction of Tremp.

Collado de Bòixols Road★★

Between the Coll de Nargó and Tremp, the L 511 follows canyons on slopes clad in pine and holm oak, or barren hillsides. Further on, the road proceeds up the slope, under yellow and pink crests, offering lovely **landscapes**, especially from the Collado de Bòixols.

Then the road enters a wide U-shaped valley, where terraced cultivation extends to the foot of the glacial ridge of Bòixols, to which cling the church and nearby houses. The road descends the valley until it eventually merges into Conca de Tremp.

◐ Continue on the L 511, then fork right towards Abella de la Conca.

Abella de la Conca

This tiny, don't-blink-or you'll-miss-it village is tucked behind the rocky Sarsús summit. Do not miss the Romanesque church of Sant Esteve (11C).

◐ Head back to the L 511 and continue to Isona.

Isona

This ancient Roman city was founded around 100 BC. Isona hosts an interesting **museum**, mainly devoted to Roman times and palaeontological sites in the area where the remains of dinosaurs have been found (it also organises tours). Its parish church was restored after the civil war of 1936.

◐ Head out of Isona via the C1412 in the direction of Lleida and turn right for Covet.

Covet

Covet's **Esglesia de Santa Maria** boasts a beautiful interior. The vaulted nave is reinforced by supporting arches and columns topped with carved capitals yet the **doorway★★** is the most remarkable feature. It has a beautiful carved tympanum and skilfully sculptured arch-based columns. Notice the figurines of angels, musicians, beasts, the characters of the Holy Family and scenes from the book of Genesis.

◐ Continue on the C 1412 towards Tremp.

Figuerola d'Orcau

This small medieval town has interesting streets lined with arcaded houses.

ADDRESSES

🛏 STAY

IN LA SEU D'URGELL

🛌 **Casa La Vall de Cadí** – *Ctra Cerc-Tuixent, 1km/half a mile from La Seu ner the Parc Olímpi. 𝒫973 350 390. www. valldelcadi.com. 7 rms. 45/55€. ⌑7.50€.* An old building containing beautiful, rustic rooms, which have been renovated, making the best of a combination of wood, cast-iron and exposed stone.

🛌🍽🍽 **Parador de La Seu d'Urgell** – *Sant Domènec 6. 𝒫973 352 000. www. parador.es. 🅿. 78 rms. 132/168€. ⌑16€. Restaurant 32€.* Arranged around a Renaissance cloister, this hotel is mainly modern in style and minimalist by design. Bathrooms are in marble. The vast Alt Urgell restaurant serves a traditional regional cuisine of great quality.

TOUR OF THE CERDANYA

🛌🍽🍽 **Hotel Fonda Biayna** – *Sant Roc 11, Bellver de Cerdanya. 𝒫973 510 475. www.fondabiayna.com. Closed 25 Dec. 17 rms. 65€. ⌑. Half-board 85€.* Handsome aristocratic building in a small village in which there are many stone buildings. The rooms are simple but comfortable and still have their original furniture. In spite of the small size of the bathrooms this is a charming place to stay.

Hotel del Lago – *Av. Dr Piguillem 7, Puigcerdà. ☎972 881 000. www.hotellago. com.* 🅿. *23 rms. 120/140€.* ☕*10€.* Small, family-run hotel close to the lake and surrounded by extensive grounds, which contain a swimming pool. The rooms are classic in style, and functional, with well-equipped bathrooms. The suites are particularly comfortable.

TOUR OF THE VALL DEL SEGRE

😊😊🛏 **Hotel Can Boix** – *Peramola (edge of the village), 17km/10mi southwest of Coll de Nargó. ☎973 470 281. www. canboix.cat. Closed mid-Jan–mid-Feb, 2 weeks in Nov.* 🅿. *41 rms. 106.50/148.50€.* ☕*12.20€. Restaurant 24/28€.* Nestled in a setting of exceptional natural beauty, this hotel is full of tasteful details. Rooms combine the warmth of wood and soft tones with modern facilities, notably in the bathrooms. High quality personalised cuisine.

🍴/EAT

IN LA SEU D'URGELL

😊😊 **Miscela** – *Av. Pau Claris 24. ☎973 350 104. 15/25€.* Pizzas, salads, pastas and a set menu at 12€ in a décor composed of tones of orange and violet.

😊😊 **Cal Teo** – *Av. Pau Claris 38. ☎973 353 393. Closed Sun evening, Mon. Around 30€.* Little restaurant in the middle of La Seu, which offers a warm welcome. Rustic decoration. Grilled meats are a speciality. A good place to take a break after visiting the cathedral.

TOUR OF THE CERDANYA

🍽 The typical dishes of **Puigcerdà** are *tiró amb naps* (duck with turnips) and rabbits, accompanied by the celebrated local pears.

😊😊 **Dolcet** – *Zulueta 1, Alàs i Cerc (7km/ 4.5mi east of La Seu d'Urgell). ☎973 352 016. Closed Fri, Nov–Dec, 2 weeks in Jun–Jul. 25/30€.* This family-run restaurant in the centre of the village serves a traditional Catalan cuisine made with ingredients from the market. Its strategic location on the road to the Parc Natural de Cadí-Moixero means that it is often busy, but it still manages to offer a warm welcome.

😊😊 **Grau de l'Ós** – *Jaume II de Mallorca 5, Bellver de Cerdanya. ☎973 510 046. Closed Mon, Tue. Set menu lunch 12€, à la carte around 30€.* Restaurant in an old peasant house, which has retained its authentic rustic style despite renovations. The cuisine is traditional in inspiration and includes some interesting dishes, such as chicken with mushrooms and cheese salad flavoured with apple cider vinegar.

😊😊 **Can Borrell** – *Retorn 3, Meranges (9km/6mi east of Bellver de Cerdanya). ☎972 880 033. Closed Mon eve, Tue. Set menu 24€. 27/39€.* Welcoming restaurant in a beautiful and peaceful little village in the mountains. Rustic style decoration with stone walls and wooden beams overhead. Comfortable rooms *(around 105€)* with a view of the valley.

😊😊🛏 **La Taverna dels Noguers** – *El Pont de Bar (15km/9mi east of La Seu d'Urgell on the N 260). ☎973 384 020. www.tavernadelsnoguers.com. Closed Thu, evenings except Sat. Around 32€.* Friendly restaurant in a regional style, with a fire-place, wooden ceilings and checkered tablecloths. Good value for home cooking. Also a hotel.

TAKING A BREAK

Caféteria Forn de Pa Serafí – *Major, 3. ☎973 350 502.* In front of the cathedral is this pleasant tea rooms suitable for a short stop. A piece of sweet *coca* goes well with a cup of tea.

ACTIVITIES

👥 **Parc Olímpic del Segre** – *At the southern end of the old quarter of La Seu. ☎973 360 092. www.parcolimpic. cat.* Sports complex with facilities for mountain bike riding and numerous white water sports: canoeing, rafting and riverboarding.

La Molina ski resort – *www.lamolina.com.*

SHOPPING

Market in La Seu – Every Tuesday and Saturday, La Seu holds one of the best markets in the region. The streets of the historic centre are filled with a colourful variety of fruits and vegetables from the surrounding valleys.

Market in Puigcerdà – Sunday in the plaça Cabrinety: fruit and vegetables.

Ripoll★

Nestled in a valley deep in the Pyrénéan foothills, this small industrial and commercial city is considered the "cradle of Catalonia". It derives its fame from the great Benedictine monastery of Santa Maria, founded in the 9C by Count Wilfred the Hairy, which, until the 12C, served as a necropolis for the Counts of Barcelona, Besalú and Cerdanya. The capital of the Ripollès comarca has a small historic core to explore and a few Art Nouveau houses to discover (Can Codina, Can Dou and Casa Bonada).

SIGHTS
Monasterio de Santa Maria★

Pl. de l'Abat Oliba. ⏱*10am–1pm, 3–6 (Apr–Sep 7pm).* ⌖*€3.* ✆*972 70 23 51.*
All that remains of the original monastery are the church portal and the cloisters. In 1032, Abbot Oliba consecrated an enlarged **church★**, a jewel of early Romanesque art that was damaged over the years. It was rebuilt at the end of the 19C to the original plan.

The **portada★★★**, or portal design, is composed of a series of horizontal registers illustrating the glory of God victorious over His enemies (Passage of the Red Sea). The **Claustro★** (cloisters) abutting the church dates to the 12C; others were added in the 14C.

Museu Etnografic

Opposite the monastery, ⚿*closed for renovations; temporary exhibitions in the town hall.*
The Ethnographic Museum traces the history of the area. Inaugurated in 1920, it contains more than 5 000 pieces: from clothing and ceramics and rooms devoted to the iron industry, showing ancient forges and firearms 16–19C.

EXCURSIONS
Monasterio de Sant Joan de les Abadesses★★

⏱*Open Mar–Apr and Oct 10am–2pm, 4–6pm; May–June and Sep 10am–2pm, 4–7pm; Jul–Aug 10am–7pm; Nov–Feb*

⚙ **Michelin Map:** 574 F 36.

▯ **Info:** Office de tourisme – Pl. Abat Oliba, 1. ✆972 702 351. www.ripoll.cat/turisme. 9.30am–1.30pm, 4–7pm, Sun 10am–2pm; Aug 10am–2pm, 4–8pm. Good leaflets on the town and its surroundings are available.

◖ **Location:** Ripoll stands at the confluence of the rivers Ter and the Freser, in a valley where it is sheltered by mountains, The town is 55km/34mi southwest of Prats-de-Mollo (in the Pyrénées-Orientales department of France), 110km/68mi north of Barcelona and 40km/24mi north of Vic by the C 17. It is connected to Barcelona by train (around 1hr 50min) via Vic (about 35min). There are daily bus services to Camprodon, Olot, Vic, Girona and Barcelona.

▣ **Parking:** There are pay carparks near the old centre, on the bank of the river Freser.

◉ **Don't Miss:** The monastery of Santa Maria de Ripoll; the monastery of Sant Joan de les Abadesses; an excursion to the Vall de Núria.

TRANSPORT

Cremallera (rack railway) – *www.valldenuria.cat.* From Ribes de Freser to Núria via Queralbs. 6 to 10 trains per day each way, according to the season. No service in November. From Ribes the journey takes 40mn and costs 22.30€ return (children 13.35€). From Queralbs the journey time is 20mn and the fare 20.10€ return (children 12.10€); less out of season.

Detail of the cloisters of Monasterio de Santa Maria

© L. Castaneda / Tips / Photononstop

Mon–Sat 10am–2pm, Sun and holidays 10am–2pm 4–6pm. €3. 972 72 23 53. *www.santjoandelesabadesses.cat.*
The monastery was founded in the 9C under the rule of a Benedictine abbess, though it soon shut out women.

With its arches and columns with carved capitals the church recalls those of southwest France.

A magnificent 1251 **Descent from the Cross★★** in polychrome wood is in the central apse. In 1426 an unbroken host was discovered on the Christ figure's head; it is venerated to this day.

Cloister★ – The present cloister is Gothic Catalan in style having replaced an old Romanesque cloister in the 15C. It was built according to the model adopted by mendicant orders with a wooden ceiling and tall graceful arches held up by fine colonnettes.

Monastery museum – *Access via the reception hall.* Interesting fragments of altarpieces, religious ornaments, sculptures and ancient crosses are on display here. Worth noting is the collection of **embroidered textiles** (extremely well-worked stoles and sumptuous Arab silks), as well as a drawing by Antoni Tàpies, undertaken for the 11th centenary celebration of the monastery.

Bishop's Palace (Palau de l'Abadia)
On the small square in front of the church, this building from the 14C houses the tourist information office. It has an inner courtyard with sculpted capitals and ample arcades. There are contemporary art exhibitions and displays on the myth of count Arnau, a legendary villainous nobleman from Ripoll and the subject of a popular Catalan ballad.

Church of Sant Pol
This church has an extraordinary sculpted tympanum representing Christ, the apostles Peter and Paul, and two angels.

DRIVING TOUR

VALL DE RIBES★
22km/13.6mi from Ripoll to Vall de Núria. Allow a couple of hours.
▷ *Take the N 152 north.*

The Vall de Ribes is popular with Barceloneses as an easily-reached skiing and hiking spot, particularly the Vall de Núria.

Ribes de Freser

www.vallderibes.cat.
This famous spa stands at the confluence of three rivers and is known for its waters' healing properties. A rack railway runs from here to Vall de Núria.

▶ Leave Ribes on the G IV-5217 heading north.

Queralbs

Up the river Freser, which runs peacefully between wooded mountains and endless fields, is the typical mountain village of Queralbs. From the plaça de la Vila, a **viewpoint** over the valley, it is possible to trace the line of the rack railway, which stops at Queralbs before climbing up to the Vall de Núria.

Vall de Núria★

The valley is effectively a rocky amphitheatre stretching from Puigmal to the Sierra de Torreneules. The Virgin of Núria, the patron saint of Pyrénéan shepherds, is venerated in a **sanctuary** located in the upper part of the valley.

ADDRESSES

☺ STAY

IN RIPOLL

☺ **Hostal del Ripollès** – *Pl. Nova 11. ☎972 700 215. www.hostaldelripolles.com. 8rms. 50€. Restaurant 12/30€.* Immaculate rooms and agreeable restaurant on the ground floor, with an outside terrace. Pizzas, Italian and Catalan cuisine.

IN THE VALL DE RIBES

☺☺ **Mas la Casanova** – *Ctra de Ribes de Freser, 3km/2mi from Queralbs. ☎972 198 077. www.maslacasanova.com. 6 rms. 57/67€. ☐6.50€. Dinner 15€.* Beautiful little rooms in an old farmhouse at the heart of the Vall de Ribes. Table d'hôte dinner on demand (excellent and generous regional cuisine). Warm welcome.

☺☺ **Catalunya Park Hotel** – *Pg Mauri 9, Ribes de Freser. ☎972 727 198. www.catalunyaparkhotels.com. Open Easter Week and Jun–Sept. 55rms. 68/78€. ☐Restaurant 15€.* Comfortable mountain hotel in which

the swimming pool is the big attraction. A good base for excursions to see nearby sights.

☺☺☺ **Hotel Vall de Núria** *Vall de Núria ski resort. ☎972 732 030. www.valldenuria. cat. Closed Nov. 75 rms 184/207€ (2 nights half-board) and 12 apartments (133/191€/2 nights).* A hotel standing in an exceptional natural setting. Attentive service and good restaurant serving local dishes.

⊞/EAT

NEAR RIPOLL

☺☺ **Can Dachs** *–C26 from Ripoll to Berga, km 181.8, Les Llosses (7.5km/4.5mi southwest of Ripoll). ☎972 714 425. Thu–Sun lunchtime, Fri–Sat dinner, daily in Aug. From18€.* Excellent cuisine based on regional ingredients. Specialities include charcuterie and meat grilled on a wood fire. There is also an "agro-shop" selling local produce.

☺☺☺ **La Fonda Xesc** – *Pl. Roser 1, Gombrèn (12.5km northwest of Ripoll on the N 152 (in the direction of Puigcerdà) then left on the GI 401. ☎972 730 404. www. fondaxesc.com. Closed Mon and Sun, Tue and Wed evenings, 2 weeks in Jan, 10 days in Jul. 46/66€.* A restaurant equipped with a spacious, vaulted dining room where a creative Catalan cuisine made with high-quality ingredients is served. Comfortable bedrooms (75/79€; ☐).

EVENTS

Festa de la LLana i el Casament a Pagès – *Ripoll. Sun following the day of the town's patron saint, St Eudald (11 May).* Folk festival in which sheep are sheared and an old-fashioned marriage is conducted.

Ripoll International Music Festival– *Jul–Aug.* In the monastery, including the cloister.

Ripoll Medieval Market– *11–12 Aug.* Assembly of local producers in the town centre. The inhabitants and the stall holders are in medieval costume.

Ball dels Pabordes – *Sant Joan de les Abadesses. 2nd Sun in Sep.* A folk dance that takes place during the town's annual Festa Major.

INDEX

INDEX

INDEX

INDEX

INDEX

🛏 STAY

🍷 EAT

MAPS AND PLANS

MAP LEGEND

	Sight	Seaside resort	Winter sports resort	Spa
Highly recommended ★★★		≗≗≗	✳✳✳	‡‡‡
Recommended ★★		≗≗	✳✳	‡‡
Interesting ★		≗	✳	‡

Additional symbols

🚇	Tourist information
═ ═	Motorway or other primary route
❶ ❶	Junction: complete, limited
⊏══⊐ ═	Pedestrian street
�⟩	Unsuitable for traffic, street subject to restrictions
⊞⊞⊞⊞ ‑ ‑ ‑	Steps – Footpath
🚆 🚆	Train station – Auto-train station
🚌 🚌 SNCF	Coach (bus) station
⊷	Tram
ⓜ	Metro, underground
🅿	Park-and-Ride
♿	Access for the disabled
✉	Post office
☏	Telephone
✉	Covered market
✵✕✵	Barracks
△	Drawbridge
℧	Quarry
✕	Mine
Ⓑ Ⓕ	Car ferry (river or lake)
🚤	Ferry service: cars and passengers
⛴	Foot passengers only
③	Access route number common to Michelin maps and town plans
Bert (R.)...	Main shopping street
AZ B	Map co-ordinates

Selected monuments and sights

◉ ═▭▷	Tour - Departure point
🏛 ✝	Catholic church
🏛 ✝	Protestant church, other temple
✡ ▣ 🕌	Synagogue - Mosque
▰	Building
■	Statue, small building
✝	Calvary, wayside cross
◎	Fountain
●━■▪	Rampart - Tower - Gate
✕	Château, castle, historic house
∴	Ruins
◡	Dam
✿	Factory, power plant
☆	Fort
⋂	Cave
▣	Troglodyte dwelling
�	Prehistoric site
▼	Viewing table
✕	Viewpoint
▲	Other place of interest

Special symbol

⊞⊞	Fortified town (bastide): in southwest France, a new town built in the 13-14C and typified by a geometrical layout.

Map Legend continued overleaf

Abbreviations

A — Agricultural office
(Chambre d'agriculture)

C — Chamber of Commerce
(Chambre de commerce)

H — Town hall (Hôtel de ville)

J — Law courts (Palais de justice)

M — Museum (Musée)

P — Local authority offices
(Préfecture, sous-préfecture)

POL. — Police station (Police)

⛨ — Police station (Gendarmerie)

T — Theatre (Théâtre)

U — University (Université)

Sports and recreation

Racecourse

Skating rink

Outdoor, indoor swimming pool

Multiplex Cinema

Marina, sailing centre

Trail refuge hut

Cable cars, gondolas

Funicular, rack railway

Tourist train

Recreation area, park

Theme, amusement park

Wildlife park, zoo

Gardens, park, arboretum

Bird sanctuary, aviary

Walking tour, footpath

Of special interest
to children

COMPANION PUBLICATIONS

MICHELIN MAPS

Motorists who plan ahead will always have the appropriate maps at hand. Michelin products are complementary: for each of the sights listed in The Green Guide, map references are indicated which help you find your location on our maps.

To travel the roads in this region, you may use any of the following:

♦ The series of local maps at a scale of 1:150 000 include useful symbols for identifying tourist attractions, town plans and an index. Get **Local map no 344**. The diagram below indicates which maps you need to travel in Pyrenees Roussillon.

♦ The **Regional maps 525 and 526** cover the main roads and secondary roads and show castles, churches and other religious edifices, scenic view points, megalithic monuments,

swimming beaches on lakes and rivers, swimming pools, golf courses, race tracks, air fields, and more.

And remember to travel with the latest edition of the **map of France 721**, which gives an overall view of the region, and the main access roads that connect it to the rest of France. Also available in atlas and mini-atlas formats.

INTERNET

Michelin is pleased to offer a route-planning service on the Internet: **www.viamichelin.com** **www.travel.viamichelin.com**. Choose the shortest route, a route without tolls, or the Michelin recommended route to your destination; you can also access information about hotels and restaurants from The Michelin Guide, and tourist sites from The Green Guide.

The Michelin Adventure

It all started with rubber balls! This was the product made by a small company based in Clermont-Ferrand that André and Edouard Michelin inherited, back in 1880. The brothers quickly saw the potential for a new means of transport and their first success was the invention of detachable pneumatic tires for bicycles. However, the automobile was to provide the greatest scope for their creative talents. Throughout the 20th century, Michelin never ceased developing and creating ever more reliable and high-performance tires, not only for vehicles ranging from trucks to F1 but also for underground transit systems and airplanes.

From early on, Michelin provided its customers with tools and services to facilitate mobility and make traveling a more pleasurable and more frequent experience. As early as 1900, the Michelin Guide supplied motorists with a host of useful information related to vehicle maintenance, accommodation and restaurants, and was to become a benchmark for good food. At the same time, the Travel Information Bureau offered travelers personalised tips and itineraries.

The publication of the first collection of roadmaps, in 1910, was an instant hit! In 1926, the first regional guide to France was published, devoted to the principal sites of Brittany, and before long each region of France had its own Green Guide. The collection was later extended to more far-flung destinations, including New York in 1968 and Taiwan in 2011.

In the 21st century, with the growth of digital technology, the challenge for Michelin maps and guides is to continue to develop alongside the company's tire activities. Now, as before, Michelin is committed to improving the mobility of travelers.

MICHELIN TODAY

WORLD NUMBER ONE TIRE MANUFACTURER
- 70 production sites in 18 countries
- 111,000 employees from all cultures and on every continent
- 6,000 people employed in research and development

Moving
for a world

Moving forward means developing tires with better road grip and shorter braking distances, whatever the state of the road.

CORRECT TIRE PRESSURE

RIGHT PRESSURE

- Safety
- Longevity
- Optimum fuel consumption

-0,5 bar

- Durability reduced by 20% (- 8,000 km)

-1 bar

- Risk of blowouts
- Increased fuel consumption
- Longer braking distances on wet surfaces

forward together
where mobility is safer

It also involves helping motorists take care of their safety and their tires. To do so, Michelin organises "Fill Up With Air" campaigns all over the world to remind us that correct tire pressure is vital.

WEAR

DETECTING TIRE WEAR

The legal minimum depth of tire tread is 1.6mm. Tire manufacturers equip their tires with tread wear indicators, which are small blocks of rubber moulded into the base of the main grooves at a depth of 1.6mm.

Tires are the only point of contact between the vehicle and road.

The photo below shows the actual contact zone.

NEW TIRE

WORN TIRE
(1,6 mm tread)

If the tread depth is less than 1.6mm, tires are considered to be worn and dangerous on wet surfaces.

Moving forward
means sustainable mobility

By 2050, Michelin aims to cut the quantity of raw materials used in its tire manufacturing process by half and to have developed renewable energy in its facilities. The design of MICHELIN tires has already saved billions of litres of fuel and, by extension, billions of tons of CO_2.

Similarly, Michelin prints its maps and guides on paper produced from sustainably managed forests and is diversifying its publishing media by offering digital solutions to make traveling easier, more fuel efficient and more enjoyable!

The group's whole-hearted commitment to eco-design on a daily basis is demonstrated by ISO 14001 certification.

Like you, Michelin is committed to preserving our planet.

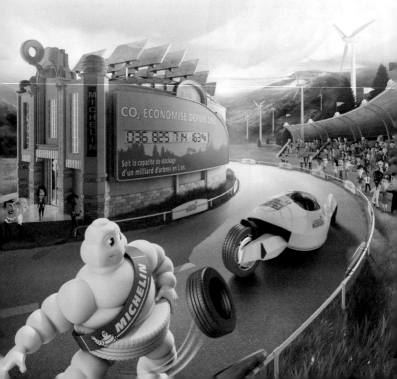

Chat with Bibendum

Go to
www.michelin.com/corporate/en
Find out more about
Michelin's history and the
latest news.

QUIZ

Michelin develops tires for all types of vehicles.
See if you can match the right tire with the right vehicle…

Solution : A-6 / B-4 / C-2 / D-1 / E-3 / F-7 / G-5

NOTES

NOTES

Pyrenees
Roussillon

MICHELIN

Michelin Travel Partner

Société par actions simplifiées au capital de 11 629 590 EUR
27 cours de l'Ile Seguin - 92100 Boulogne Billancourt (France)
R.C.S. Nanterre 433 677 721

No part of this publication may be reproduced in any form
without the prior permission of the publisher.

© Michelin Travel Partner
ISBN 978-2-067188-16-7
Printed: June 2013
Printed and bound in France - N°201305.0394